# Media, Modernity and Technology

This set of interlinked essays aims to intervene in some of the key debates in the fields of media and cultural studies.

The book features reflections on issues of periodisation, history and geography which are often neglected in these Eurocentrically defined fields and investigates the disciplinary dilemmas now created by their emerging theoretical canons and methodological orthodoxies. It also surveys the potential contribution of art-based discourses to these fields and offers critical perspectives on the emerging 'new media' of our age – defined here, from an anthropological perspective, as the realm of the 'new, the shiny and the symbolic' in which old traditions and new technologies are intertwined.

Based on interdisciplinary work on the interface of media and cultural studies, cultural geography and anthropology, spanning the past decade, the book is structured into five thematic sections:

*   Disciplinary dilemmas: canons and orthodoxies
*   Methodological matters: interdisciplinary approaches
*   The geography of modernity and the orientation of the future
*   Domesticity, mediation and the technologies of 'newness'
*   Techno-anthropology: icons, totems and fetishes

In these essays David Morley discusses the status and future of media and cultural studies as disciplines, the significance of technology and new media and the place of the magical in the newly emerging forms of techno-modernity in which we live today.

**David Morley** is Professor of Media and Communications at Goldsmiths College, London. His previous publications include *Home Territories: Media, Mobility and Identity* (2000), *Spaces of Identity* (with Kevin Robins, 1995), *Television, Audiences and Cultural Studies* (1992) and *Family Television: Cultural Power and Domestic Leisure* (1986) amongst many others.

# Media, Modernity and Technology

The geography of the new

David Morley

Routledge
Taylor & Francis Group

LONDON AND NEW YORK

First published 2007
by Routledge
2 Park Square, Milton Park, Abingdon, Oxon OX14 4RN

Simultaneously published in the USA and Canada
by Routledge
270 Madison Ave, New York, NY 10016

*Routledge is an imprint of the Taylor & Francis Group, an informa business*

© 2007 David Morley

Typeset in Perpetua by
Keystroke, 28 High Street, Tettenhall, Wolverhampton
Printed and bound in Great Britain by
Antony Rowe Ltd, Chippenham, Wiltshire

*British Library Cataloguing in Publication Data*
A catalogue record for this book is available from the British Library

*Library of Congress Cataloging in Publication Data*
Morley, David, 1949–
    Media, modernity and technology : the geography of the new / David Morley.
        p. cm.
    Includes bibliographical references and index.
    1. Mass media and culture.  2. Mass media and technology.
    3. Mass media–Technological innovations.  I. Title.
    P94.6.M673 2006
    302.23–dc22                                                    2006000660

ISBN10: 0–415–33341–5 (hbk)
ISBN10: 0–415–33342–3 (pbk)
ISBN10: 0–203–41305–9 (ebk)

ISBN13: 978–0–415–33341–2 (hbk)
ISBN13: 978–0–415–33342–9 (pbk)
ISBN13: 978–0–203–41305–0 (ebk)

# Contents

**PART IV**

**Domesticity, mediation and the technologies of 'newness'** 197

**PART V**

**Techno-anthropology: icons, totems and fetishes** 273

**PART VI**

**Coda** 311

# Illustrations

# Acknowledgements

First, my thanks to the UK's Arts and Humanities Research Council for the grant awarded to me under their Research Leave Scheme which enabled me to take time away from teaching to do this work, to Goldsmiths College for a term's sabbatical leave, and to all my colleagues in the Department of Media and Communications Studies at Goldsmiths who generously added to their own burdens by covering for me while I was away. My personal thanks are due, as ever, to CB, especially for the talking-while-walking which germinated the idea for this book.

My thanks are also due to all those who invited me to do the talks at which these ideas were tried out, and to those who gave me valuable feedback on earlier versions of this work, both in the UK, at the Universities of Birmingham, Lancaster, Manchester, Southampton and Surrey, at the Institutes of Germanic and Romance Studies and of American Studies at London University and, elsewhere, at the Annenberg Institute (University of Southern California) and at the Universities of Bergen, Burgos, Copenhagen, Cork, Evora, Helsinki (University of Art and Design), El Instituto Tecnologico de Estudios Superiores de Monterey, Klagenfurt University, Krakow University, Museo Elder de la Ciencia y la Tecnologia (Las Palmas de Gran Canaria), Northwestern University (Chicago), New York University, Ruhr-Universiteit (Bochum), the Universities of Tampere, Trondheim and Tuebingen and the University of Southern California (Santa Barbara).

## Permissions

Some of the chapters in the book have appeared elsewhere in earlier forms and I am grateful to their original publishers (listed below) for allowing permission to reprint them here.

Chapter 1: 'So-called Cultural Studies', first published in *Cultural Studies*, 12 (4): 476–498, 1998.

Chapter 2: 'Cultural Studies and Media Studies', first published (in German) as 'Radikale Verpflichtung zu Interdiziplinaritat', *Montage A/V* 6 (1): 36–66, 1998.

Chapter 5:  An earlier version of this chapter was published as 'EurAm, Modernity, Reason and Alterity: or, Postmodernism, the Highest Stage of Cultural Imperialism', in D. Morley and K. H. Chen (eds) *Stuart Hall: Critical Dialogues in Cultural Studies*, London, Routledge, 1996, pp. 326–60.

Chapter 7:  An earlier, and rather differently focused version of this chapter was published as 'What's Home Got to Do with It?', *European Journal of Cultural Studies*, 6 (4), 2003.

Chapter 9:  An earlier version of this chapter, but without the extended consideration of Nam June Paik's work included here, was published as 'Television: Not So Much a Visual Medium . . .', in C. Jenks (ed.) *Visual Culture*, London, Routledge, 1995, pp. 170–90.

# Introduction

This book brings together contributions to a set of theoretical, method-ological and substantive debates in media and cultural studies. The issues addressed range from the status (and future) of cultural and media studies as disciplines, within the institutional framework of the academy, to the significance of the new technologies of our day, the relation of those technological issues to our very definition of modernity and the problems raised by the insights of post-colonial theory for prevailing Western models of modernity.

The book also engages with debates about the current tendency towards the narrowing of both theoretical and methodological orthodoxies in these fields. In relation to media studies, my concerns are with how the object of study of the field might best be constituted, so as to deal with the dynamics of current technological developments. To my mind, one key theoretical issue here is how to develop a non-mediacentric analytical framework which will pay sufficient attention to the particularities of the media, without reifying their status and thus isolating them from the dynamics of the economic, social and political contexts in which they operate. These issues are of much more than theoretical interest. They also have very material consequences, in terms of funding and educational policy and have been loudly articulated in the popular imagination – not least in the recurring debates (or perhaps, 'pedagogic panics') in the UK, as to whether either media or cultural studies can ever possibly constitute 'proper' disciplines.

In pursuing these questions, my own work has drawn on an increasingly wider set of different disciplines: from cultural geography, anthropology and ethnology, design studies, literary theory and art history, to post-colonial theory and area studies. These latter disciplines have provided particularly important resources in trying, as I have, to move beyond a Euro-American perspective on these issues. Thus, the book's further ambition is to contribute to the development of a thoroughly 'de-Westernised' form of media and cultural studies.

One of the book's ambitions is to attempt to integrate theoretical modes of enquiry with the fruits of detailed empirical work in a variety of related fields. This commitment defines both the characteristic mode of enquiry and the style of presentation which runs throughout the different chapters. The book thus aims to offer a set of grounded and contextualised accounts of key cultural processes, where micromodes of analysis are set in a broad and interdisciplinary theoretical framework. The issues addressed here span from macro-questions such as how best to map the geography of modernity, to micro-questions such as how we are to understand the role of the mobile phone in transforming both the relations of the public and private spheres and the experiential texture of our everyday relationships.

The work presented here has been in gestation over some years and Chapters 1, 5, 7 and 9 have all appeared in English before, in earlier versions. However, with the exception of Chapter 1, which I felt was best left to stand in its original form, all the others in this category have now been very substantially reworked to reflect the subsequent development of my thinking on these issues. Many of the other chapters in the book can also be read as further developments of these original essays, but now moving into new areas and extending the perspectives with which I began this work in relation to different kinds of material. If the book has (as I hope, and as the reader must judge for themselves) a coherent narrative, it is, nonetheless, one which at various points circles back on itself before proceeding. I can only hope that my attempt to make the overall story cohere does not involve any unwelcome sense of repetition, as I explore my central concerns from different angles.

## Fundamentals and premises

My project here is founded on two, interlinked contentions (or premises), one spatial, one temporal. The first concerns the way in which our conventional sense of history is in fact founded on an uninterrogated conception of geography – which, in spatialised form, reads from right to left, on the standard map of the world. Thus, the narrative of historical development is assumed to run from its past in the Orient to its future in the Occident. The consequent equation of the West with all that is dynamic in history is one which we must interrogate closely, if we are ever to break out of the insidious grip of this one-way conceptual street. These matters are the particular concern of Part III of the book.[1]

My second premise is that media studies, in particular, as presently constituted, suffers from a drastically foreshortened historical perspective, the absence of which is all the more critical now, as we enter the word of the digital media. Thus, I argue that media studies needs to place contemporary developments, such as the constitution of cyberspace – with which much contemporary work is concerned – in a much longer historical perspective. As we now enter an era of digitalisation, technical convergence, individualised and interactive media systems, all these issues become all the more urgent. One of the key problems here is that so much work on the new media (whether in utopian or dystopian modes) falls back into technologically determinist forms of explanation, a tendency which the argument here tries to avoid. As Lynn Spigel has put it, the more we speak of futurology, the more we need to take a longer historical view of these issues. Moreover I argue, following Hermann Bausinger, that we need to explore the extent to which folk culture is alive and well in the world of modern technology.[2] This is to take seriously the 'marvellous' dimension of new technology. The symbolic dimension of technology has thus far been woefully neglected – a neglect that demands the theoretical resources of anthropology.

The link between these two propositions concerns the inadequate (and overdrawn) binary divisions frequently made, not only between the worlds of the old analogue media and the new media of the digital age but, more fundamentally, between the worlds of, on the one hand, tradition, culture, ritual, and irrationality and, on the other, the world of modernity, economics, functionality and rationality – which is often seen as being inscribed in these technologies. This is the fundamental issue referred to by the phrase in my subtitle: 'the geography of the new'. Thus, the chapters in Part III focus on the conventions by which the future is usually understood as Western in orientation (*sic*), while those in Parts IV and V focus on how the future is so often symbolised in and through new technologies. The same conceptual issue is at stake in both cases – whether the question is posed in geographical terms, as that of the analytic constitution of modern centres and backward peripheries, areas or regions (the concern of Chapters 5 and 6) or in temporal or historical terms, as a question of periodisation, in relation to the magical dreams of the era of technomodernity to have instituted a Great Divide which makes a clean break between itself and the traditional past, so as to move into a truly New Age (the concerns of Chapters 7–10). In either case, my argument is that claims that 'we' (in the West?) have now arrived (alone?) at the End of History, whether as a result of an inescapable historical destiny, based on the intrinsic superiority of liberal free-market capitalism to all other forms of social life, or as a result of the *deus ex machina* of the new digital technologies, are all badly misguided. My argument, throughout these sections of the book, is directed against these falsely binarised polarities, and the book's Coda, in Chapter 11, attempts to bring these various theoretical threads together, so as to offer a new way of conceptualising these issues which is more attuned to the many overlaps and continuities between the Occident and the Orient, the traditional (irrational) past and the logics of the modern, and between the realm of magic and that of technology.[3]

## Part I: Disciplinary dilemmas: canons and orthodoxies

The chapters in this section are concerned with different aspects of the question of disciplinarity, in relation to cultural and media studies. They deal with a set of contentious questions that have been both the site and stake of much theoretical debate in recent years, as the backlash against these new disciplines from those with more conventional positions to defend has gathered force. In Chapter 1, the claims of older established disciplines, such as sociology and anthropology, to be the privileged guardians of insight in the sphere of culture are scrutinised and challenged from an interdisciplinary perspective. In this context, I am concerned not only to defend cultural studies against the backlash of intemperate criticism which it has attracted in some parts of the UK academy in recent years, from the guardians of tried and trusted disciplinary wisdoms, but also to articulate my own particular vision of cultural studies' potential future.

The interview in Chapter 2 was originally conducted as part of a project to introduce both British cultural studies and media studies to a European readership. In this context, the interview addresses the necessity to 'de-familiarise' the specificities of that British tradition, as well as its differences from the more recent forms of American cultural studies. It also explores the ways in which these Anglo-American traditions of cultural studies have both, in effect, often functioned as forms of cultural imperialism, exporting ready-made forms of 'one-size-fits-all' abstract cultural theory (what has come to be just called 'Theory', in some quarters) to the rest of the world, via the conduit of the international market for English-language publishing. These theoretical questions are here addressed in the material context of the role of powerful institutions such as publishing houses, governmental agencies and academic institutions.[4] The question of how we should approach the constitution of a truly transnational field of study, in relation to questions of culture, media and communication, is among the key issues addressed here, in the context of the variety of different approaches to media and cultural studies now developing in Asia, Latin America and elsewhere.

## Part II: Methodological matters: interdisciplinary approaches

The chapters in this section address the methodological dilemmas faced by those wishing to develop new work in these areas from an interdisciplinary perspective.

The interview in Chapter 3 offers the opportunity for an informal and vernacular exploration of these theoretical and methodological issues. In the course of the interview, which focused on the concerns of new graduate students coming into these fields, I attempt to open up the 'black box' of research as a practice and argue for an understanding of research as a material form of intellectual labour, with the emphasis on the second of those two terms.

Here the theoretical questions at stake are exemplified by reference both to the way scholars in the field actually do their research and to the material factors governing their research practices (as opposed to their post-hoc rationalisations of their methodology, and of how and why it was chosen). I argue for a radical pragmatism in matters of methodology, based on the need to recognise the limitations (and 'opportunity costs') of *all* methods. Thus, the interview also focuses on the problems created by the sanctification of certain methodological procedures (for example, self-reflexive forms of ethnography) as if they could somehow function as the guarantors of Truth in contemporary intellectual discourse. The now taken-for-granted wisdoms of cultural studies, in relation to questions of epistemology and methodology, are closely interrogated here, as the interview revisits the debates that have developed as self-reflexive ethnography has been imported from anthropology to become to be the hegemonic method of choice within much of cultural studies. The difficulties attendant on this position are here subjected to serious critique, and consideration is also given to alternative positions in the field – such as the development, in some quarters, of new uses of previously scorned quantitative methods.[5]

It is not only academics, but also visual artists who have turned to ethnographic approaches in recent years.[6] In this context, Chapter 4 interrogates the theoretical significance of a variety of artistic and literary practices through which topics of concern to media and cultural studies have been approached. Thus, I address the work of conceptual artists such as Susan Hiller who have mobilised the techniques of the ethnographic museum in subversive ways, and of Krzysztof Wodiczko whose installations function as interrogative devices for the production of knowledge about power relations. I also consider the work of novelists and literary theorists such as Georges Perec and Italo Calvino, particularly in relation to the possibilities of what Perec calls an 'endotic anthropology of the infra-ordinary' and to Calvino's concerns with exactitude in matters of description and enumeration. The work of Sophie Calle and Christian Boltanski, which subverts conventional practices of ethnographic observation and questions the veracity of photography as a form of documentary evidence is also reviewed. The final section of the chapter compares the work of Ilya Kabakov, as an ethnographer of the 'lost world' of Soviet everyday life with that of the ethnographic filmmaker Jean Rouch, whose work documented the civilisations of West Africa. Rouch's work is given a particularly detailed consideration in the light of his enormous influence not only in the world of documentary film-making but also as a crucial (if little acknowledged) influence on the subsequent development of European 'New Wave' cinema, especially through his 'ethno-fictions'.

## Part III: The geography of modernity and the orientation of the future

The essays in this section explore debates about conventional models of Western modernity and address the urgent need to better theorise non-Western forms of modernity (and indeed, of cultural and media studies). These chapters explicate some of the fundamental conceptual difficulties in defining modernity (or postmodernity) adequately, by addressing some of the implicit (and deeply problematic) forms of historical periodisation which underlie much work in this field. One key issue concerns the need to avoid the kind of naively Eurocentric mode of analysis for which Cornel West has rightly criticised much French (or perhaps, more precisely, Parisian) work on postmodernity. If we are not to end up in Fukuyama's blind alley of imagining that 'We' (whoever that is) stand at the 'End of History', then we must avoid reducing history itself to the particular story of the West and avoid equating rationality with its familiar, Westernised forms. As David Forgacs has noted in his commentary on a previous version of Chapter 5, the argument there 'executes a precarious manouvre, rejecting the ethno-centrism involved in identifications of modernity with the West, while upholding Enlightenment notions of philosophical reason, rational debate, justice and tolerance, against radical forms of scepticism and epistemological relativism.'[7]

In Chapter 6, this argument is extended in the further context of my own frustrations with the limits of the various forms of global abstraction which have come to dominate the field in recent years, as one Big Theory of the inevitable fate of globalisation (be it the West's final victory, or its decline) has superseded another on the bookshop shelves with monotonous regularity, but with little grounding in (or intellectual purchase on) what is actually (and variously) happening in different parts of the globe.[8] In this context, I argue for a return to 'regional' theories and review the prospects for reinventing the long neglected discipline of area studies as a better basis for understanding the new global dynamics of our age.

Clearly such a reinvention would not be without its difficulties – some of which derive from the long inscription of area studies with matters of state power and global surveillance. There are also fundamental conceptual difficulties here, which have their origin in the continuing influence of Hegelian conceptions of the West as the origin of rationality and, thus, the

Archimedean point from which Western man (*sic*) produces knowledge about all those others who are still condemned to ethnicity. In this context I address the theoretical significance of current economic, cultural, political and technological developments in Asia. These developments have given rise to a variety of forms of non-Western (and often religious) modernities, which I analyse in the context of a reconsideration of the question of 'Occidentalism' and of dialogic forms of intercultural communication. My argument here also addresses the significance of the current development of a variety of regional forms of cultural imperialism, in different parts of the world. The questions that arise here involve the newly mediated forms in which Others see (or indeed, bypass or ignore) us, as much as how 'we' stereotype or Orientalise 'them'.

## Part IV: Domesticity, mediation and the technologies of 'newness'

The concerns of this section are both geographical and historical. In relation to the first of these issues, we must note that one of the key claims made on behalf of the new technologies of our age concerns their capacity to transcend geography – as a result of which geography itself has recently been pronounced dead. My argument disputes these contentions by means of a close analysis of the material geographies of new computer-based industries such as call centres and an examination of the continuing geographical concentration of hub web sites and of the dot.com industry itself. In temporal terms, the perspective here, as indicated above, also rests on the premise that media studies needs to place contemporary developments, such as the constitution of cyberspace, with which much contemporary work is concerned, in a much longer historical perspective.[9]

Such historical work as has been done in media studies has focused largely on institutional structures and modes of production, or on narratives of technical invention and has largely neglected the 'intimate histories' of how we live with technologies. Chapter 7 attempts to redress this imbalance by focusing on the history of the micro-processes through which a range of communications technologies have now been accommodated (*sic*) in the home. I situate the 'domestication' of television in the broader context of the entry of a range of other technologies to the home, such as the telephone, the radio and more recently, the computer. However, the story of the domestication of the media is here complemented by a consideration of a new narrative – that of their 'dis-location'.[10] Just as television now escapes from the home to colonise public space, individualised media, such as the mobile phone, now contribute to the radical dislocation of domesticity.[11] In Bill Gates's vision of the 'smart house', the contemporary home itself (in its digitalised or 'fully wired' form) is increasingly seen as the 'last vehicle' of mobility, rather than as a static space of retreat. As electronic forms of communication increasingly come to constitute the infrastructure of our newly mobile lives, the 'trellis' of domestic memory, of which Bachelard speaks, may itself now take an electronic, as much as an architectural, form.[12]

The further issue addressed here concerns the role of individualised mobile media delivery systems such as the Walkman, the iPod and the mobile phone in transforming the relations between the private and the public spheres, by giving people the capacity to conduct a virtual form of withdrawal from public space into a solipsistic aural cocoon or privatised sound bubble. This process has given rise not only to a new set of practical debates about the etiquette of pubic behaviour, but also, at a theoretical level, to debates about the political significance of this process, which has been described as one in which the space of the public sphere is filled now with the 'chatter' of mobile domesticity. In this context, John Tomlinson has argued that these technologies might best be understood not so much as 'tools for the extending of cultural horizons' but 'imperfect instruments by which people try to maintain some sense of security, within a culture of flow and deterritorialisation'.[13]

Chapter 8 contextualises the current 'rhetorics of the technological sublime' by placing them in the context of the long history of dreams of liberation-through-technology which have accompanied the rise of a variety of (once-new) technologies – from those of the steam and machine ages to those of electricity and digitalisation. The claims made on behalf of the new technologies of our own age – not least that they will usher in a world of better understanding and more inclusive citizenship – are questioned by reference to evidence about the extent to which, rather than overcoming social and cultural divisions, these technologies in fact, often replicate and reinscribe them in new technical forms. The simplistic binary which is taken to divide the words of old and new media is also questioned here and the argument explores many of the overlaps and continuities between these supposedly different technical 'ages' and offers a critical perspective on contemporary debates about media convergence.

Returning to my earlier comments on the problems of born-again technological determinism in the field of new media studies, this chapter also critically addresses current tendencies towards the resanctification of McLuhan as the true prophet of the age, whose prognostications are now, we are told, finally coming true, in the era of digital techno-convergence. Here McLuhan's own 'futurology' is critically examined and contrasted with what we may gain from a reconsideration of Raymond Williams's more historically nuanced approach to the relationship between technologies and the cultural (and institutional) forms in which they are materialised in any given period.

The chapter also offers a critical assessment of both the work of influential writers on these technologies, and of the now widely taken-for-granted assumption that Deleuze and Guattari have provided us with a theoretical framework that fits naturally with the non-linear forms of technology of the 'control society'.[14]

In search of alternatives to these ways of understanding technology, its determinations, effects and uses, the chapter then turns to the potential contribution to be made by design studies. One important issue here concerns the paradoxes of a technical rationality at a time when many consumers are effectively disabled by the growing range of functions of the increasingly complex technologies on offer to them. In this context I draw on work in design studies on 'unuseless' objects and, in architecture, on deliberately designed forms of inefficiency that defamiliarise taken for granted 'solutions' to technological problems.[15] This work embodies a critique of what Castoriadis has called the technological 'fantasy of total control' enshrined in the Taylorist dream of rational efficiency in all areas of social life.[16] One of the key issues explored here concerns the way in which technical 'solutions' to perceived problems often themselves create new problems for other people. This autocritical design work thus produces a valuable 'inventory of suspicion' of the taken-for-granted technological solutions with which we routinely live.

Drawing on the work of Forty, Hartley and Ross and on a long tradition of feminist scholarship on the uses, functions and symbolic significance of domestic technologies,[17] I take as my foci here the cultural meanings of not only the television set but also of other, neglected domestic technologies such as the washing machine and the fridge (now figured as the 24/7 command centre for the latest generation of 'smart homes') and, most recently, the 'kitchen computer'. One key question here concerns the gendered symbolism of the worlds of these white and black goods; another concerns the process through which particular technologies are made inconspicuous and the invisibility of domestic labour is now enshrined in the design of the contemporary home. Ultimately, my concern is to explicate the ways in which we might better understand the processes through which the 'inconspicuous omnipresence' of a variety of forms of the 'technical' is now constituted in our everyday lives.[18]

## Part V: Techno-anthropology: icons, totems and fetishes

This section focuses on the potential benefits to technology studies of taking an anthropological perspective on the symbolic dimension of a range of different technologies.

Chapter 9 turns its focus to television – for long the central concern of media studies. However, the symbolic centrality of television in post-war consumer culture has only been, thus far, explored in fragmentary ways.[19] In this chapter, television is addressed neither as an abstract set of programme discourses, nor simply as an institutionalised mode of production, but also as a material, and meaningful object of considerable symbolic significance. I thus attempt to integrate anthropological work on the symbolic dimensions of material culture and consumption with internationally comparative ethnographic work on the television set as the symbolic focus of domestic ritual practices. Like Chapter 4, this chapter also attends to how these matters have been explored outside the world of academia, in contemporary art practices which problematise and highlight the rich symbolic status of the television set as a sacred object, by also treating it as a form of sculpture, and use imaginative means to explore the 'enchantments' of technology.[20]

In the concluding section of the chapter, I focus on the path-breaking and prescient work of the video-installation artist and sculptor, Nam June Paik. In Paik's techno-sculptures, the authority of television as a medium is broken up by his deconstruction of the television set as an icon, as he reconstructs it in new ways and strips it of its conventional meanings, by displaying it in unfamiliar settings and using it as a 'container' for a range of both banal and exotic objects and a source of either (deliberately) incomprehensible data or (literal) interference. Paik's work clearly disputes the claim that it is only 'theory' which can dislodge television from its cosy nest of familiarity and highlights the potential contribution to media research of imaginative and artistic practices.

In developing the issues raised above about the symbolic dimensions of the television set, Chapter 10 takes up and further explores the anthropological perspective on the symbolic meanings of a range of new and shiny contemporary communications technologies from the television (and its associated aerials and satellite dishes which have, at different historical stages, functioned as signifiers of the modernity of the households to which they are attached) to the computer and the mobile phone. The chapter also explores the ways in which many of the latest technologies of our day are readily conscripted by existing traditions and folk cultures for recognisably traditional purposes and examines the role of ritual behaviour in the operation of new technologies. In conclusion, I focus on the symbolic significance of the mobile phone in particular, as the prime show-and-tell signifier of status, power and 'connexity' in contemporary life – the latest 'icon of the new' which seems to function, for many of its users, as a magical technology with the capacity to make everything alright.

## Part VI: Coda

Here I return, from a different perspective, to some of the issues raised in Part III, in relation to our conception of modernity, but now attempt to integrate the temporal and spatial issues at stake. The essays in that section focus on questions of space and geography, arguing against posing a clear divide between the West and the Rest, with the former peremptorily then seen as the true bearer of modernity. Here, the principal issues addressed are temporal, and the chapter argues against any simplistic binary division between the supposedly static world of tradition, with all its irrationalities and rituals, and the fluid and dynamic world of modernity (and with its hyper-functional logics). The chapter critically reviews the claims of contemporary 'rational-choice' economic theory to universal, rational status by exploring both the continued presence of the 'gift economy' in the modern world and the extent to which economic theory, as we know it, is itself derived from the nineteenth-century cult of positivism. Building on current anthropological theory, and drawing on Latour's attempt to 'demythologise' the modern world, the essay explores the logics of the changing forms of tradition, ritual and symbolism which are very much alive within the contemporary technological world of the 'new and the shiny' and explores the 'enchantment' of technology itself and its continuing connections with the realm of the magical.[21]

## Notes

1 This is not to simply reverse the conventional dominance of history over geography, but involves a different way of dealing with temporality – an attempt to deal with history as a spatio-temporal configuration. On this see Ed Soja *Postmodern Geographies*, London, Verso, 1989 and for a more recent, conceptually sophisticated approach to these issues see also Doreen Massey's *For Space*, London, Sage, 2005.

2 See the work of Lynn Spigel and Hermann Bausinger discussed in Chapter 7.

3 On this, see also, Vincent Mosco's recent book (2004) *The Digital Sublime: Myth, Power and Cyberspace*, Cambridge, Mass., MIT Press.

4 The very titling of this book provides a good example of these material determinations. In its original form, my title was 'The Geography of the New: Media, Modernity and Technology'. However, marketing considerations, premised on the fact that many book orders are now generated by computer 'keyword' searches, determined that this was unacceptable, as the computers might not recognise the book as relevant to the field of media studies, unless the word 'media' came first. Hence the title under which it now appears – clearly, a particular irony in a book which argues against technological determinism!

5 For a good example of an imaginative use of quantitative methods in cultural studies see Sujeong Kim (2004) 'Re-Reading David Morley's *The Nationwide Audience*' in *Cultural Studies* 18 (1). Re-analysing my data by using computerised

statistical techniques unavailable to me at the time of writing the original book, the author demonstrates that, contrary to the received wisdom of critical commentary, the patterns of decoding reported there were, if anything, more rather than less determined by social factors than I had claimed.

6  The work of the winner of the 2005 Turner Prize for British Contemporary Art, Simon Starling, was widely described as 'research-based art', thus further blurring the categories of art and social analysis.

7  See Cornell West, discussed in Chapter 5, and David Forgacs (1997) 'Introduction', *Paragraph* 20 (1).

8  See the work of Francis Fukuyama and Samuel Huntingdon, discussed in Chapters 5 and 6.

9  See the work of James Carey, Carolyn Marvin, and Siegfried Zielinski on 'technological histories' discussed in Chapter 8.

10  See the studies by Hugh Mackay and Darren Ivey, Shuan Moores and Roger Silverstone and Eric Hirsch, all discussed further in Chapters 7 and 8.

11  See Anna McCarthy's work on 'ambient television' discussed in Chapter 7.

12  See Paul Virilio and Gaston Bachelard referred to in Chapter 7.

13  See John Tomlinson on this point in Chapter 7.

14  For my discussion of the work of Marshall McLuhan, Raymond Williams, Friedrich Kittler, Lev Manovich, Gilles Deleuze and Félix Guattari see Chapter 8.

15  On the work of Kenji Kawakami, Elizabeth Diller and Ricardo Scofidio, Andrew Bauvelt and Aaron Betsky, see Chapter 8.

16  See Cornelius Castoriadis and Frederick William Taylor, discussed in Chapter 8.

17  See, for example, the work of Christine Hardyment and Ruth Schwartz Cowan discussed in Chapter 8.

18  Hermann Bausinger discussed in Chapter 7.

19  See the work of Tim O'Sullivan and Charlotte Brunsdon in the UK, Lynn Spigel and William Boddy in the USA, and Shunya Yoshimi in Japan – all discussed in Chapter 9.

20  See the work of Arjun Appadurai, Daniel Miller, Ondina Leal and Elizabeth Long, reviewed in Chapter 9.

21  On these issues, see my discussion of the work of John Gray, Bruno Latour and Alfred Gell in Chapter 11.

# Part I

# Disciplinary dilemmas

## Canons and orthodoxies

Nasruddin was walking along an alleyway when a man fell from a roof and landed on his neck. The man was unhurt; the Mulla was taken to hospital.

Some disciples went to visit him. 'What wisdom do you see in this happening Mulla?' they asked.

'Avoid any belief in the inevitability of cause and effect. Shun reliance upon theoretical questions such as: "If a man falls off a roof, will his neck be broken?"'

*The Pleasantries of the Incredible Mulla Nasruddin*, Idries Shah

# 1 So-called cultural studies
## Dead ends and reinvented wheels

I take as my starting point a review of a book which I co-edited on Stuart Hall's work (Rogers, 1996, reviewing Morley and Chen, 1996) in which the reviewer observed that cultural studies seemed to him to be no more than a series of truisms – such as that: 'our . . . post-industrial societies are driven by conflicts based on sex, race, religion and region, as well as class – and that people's sense of identity is shaped not just by economic but by cultural factors' (so that politics has to work) 'by appealing not only to people's economic interests but to their sense of who they are'. The reviewer's problem, he explained, was that, in his view: 'this seems so obviously a move in the direction of common sense that it hardly deserves all this attention.' Against this, I'd like to pose a quote from Stuart Hall's essay 'Culture, the Media and the Ideological Effect' (1977a). There Hall argues that 'what passes for common sense feels as if it has always been there, the sedimented, bedrock wisdom of "the race". A form of "natural" wisdom, whose context has changed hardly at all with time. However, common sense *does* have a context *and* a history'. Hall goes onto argue that

> it is precisely its 'spontaneous' quality, its transparency, its 'naturalness', its refusal to be made to examine the premises on which it is founded, its resistance to change or to correction, its effect of insistent recognition which makes common sense . . . spontaneous, ideological and unconscious. You cannot learn, through common sense, how things are: you can only discover where they fit into the existing scheme of things. . . . Its very taken-for-grantedness establishes it as a medium in which its own premises and presuppositions are . . . rendered invisible by its apparent transparency.
>
> (Hall, 1977a: 325–6)

My point is simply that if the things to which this reviewer refers are now 'common sense', this is because work in cultural studies has made them so.

Given the logical priority of the unsaid over the said, the study of the construction of common sense and of the changing nature of 'what goes without saying' or can be taken for granted is, by definition, about as important a cultural issue as you could hope to find – not least because it traces the changing limits of what can be thought, within the terms of common sense.

The argument from common sense has, of course, also been a notable feature of the recent attacks on media studies in the UK. Here the argument runs that, given the banality of its object of study, it's clearly a senseless activity: who needs to study what is obvious to everyone? Evidently, the appropriate response is to point to the importance of the analysis of *how* particular things come to seem 'obvious' to particular groups of people, and to the media's role in the construction of the classificatory categories within which 'common sense' is formed. That is why, if cultural studies sometimes seems to 'tell us things we already know in a language we can't understand' – none the less, the redescription of the every-day world of culture in the language of systematic analysis is the necessary form of the 'defamilariza-tion' of the everyday which is essential to cultural studies work. From this perspective, studying the media's role in the shaping of contemporary common sense, through the analysis of the popular cultural forms which the media produce, is a far from trivial activity – it involves the analysis of how the limits of our common knowledge are continually constructed, patrolled and redrawn.

Another review of the *Critical Dialogues* book (Morley and Chen, 1996) by Stefan Collini (1996) picks up the difficult question of how to square the circle between the demands of theoretical rigour and the demands of accessibility. In this connection, Collini points to the sense in which a lot of the public (and especially journalistic) resistance to cultural studies amounts to little more than a 'lazy resistance to new ways of thinking' (Collini, 1996). As Collini argues, traditionally, a certain level of technicality of academic language has always been recognized as the price of disciplinary rigour. However, in the context of critiques of media/cultural studies, accusations that cultural studies analyses are unreadable or jargon-ridden are, as Collini puts it, 'just the small arms fire of the border-guards of journalism, pointing at academics suspected of colonising the ancestral lands of the common reader' (ibid.).

The attacks on media studies in the British press have been tediously repetitive. But the attacks also come from other sources. They come from within the media industries themselves – the left-wing television drama producer, Ken Loach, at a conference on television drama in Britain, called for the closing down of all media-studies courses, on the grounds that their graduates were, in his view, illiterate. The attacks have also come from government – and not only the last (Conservative) government. Just as ex-government MP Chris Patten, in his comments on the 'decline' of higher education in Britain, jibed that media and cultural studies represented no more than 'Disneyland for the weaker minded', neither does the present Labour government in the UK seem too well disposed towards our field of study.

All of this, of course, has its echoes *within* the world of higher education itself, especially in relation to questions of funding. As the external attacks mount, so does the internal pressure to retreat from the interdisciplinary experiments of the past thirty years, towards a retrenchment into the more conventional, and now perhaps more 'respectable' disciplines which are more readily rewarded by educational funding institutions, such as the Higher Education Funding Council in the UK. Certainly, within the field, one can hear voices calling for a return to the (apparently) sounder and better established claims of the sociology of mass communications, or perhaps of sociology (or even anthropology) as the appropriate master (or mistress) disciplines of the terrain we study. It is precisely against these claims, which I take to be ill founded, that I feel the need to defend the centrality of interdisciplinarity to the project of cultural studies. In this respect, I am entirely in sympathy with Graham Murdock's reminder that the 'original project of cultural studies was precisely to disregard formal divisions between disciplines . . . [in] a celebration of trespass and border violations in the interests of constructing a more complete analysis of culture' (Murdock, 1995: 91). In this context, I would argue, to ditch the supposedly 'wilder' shores of cultural studies' interdisciplinary project for the safe havens of more [nowadays] 'respectable' disciplines such as sociology and anthropology and their 'tried and trusted' analyses of culture will get us nowhere at all.

## Cultural studies and the social sciences

One of the most crucial balancing acts in matters of interdisciplinarity is, of course, that between the 'textualizing' tendencies of literary versions of cultural studies and the deterministic or essentialist tendencies of the more social-science-based alternatives. Here I would point to one key and con-tinuous thread in Stuart Hall's comments on these matters – a thread that stretches at least as far as between his essay on 'The Hinterland of Science' (1977b) and his (closing) contribution to the new Open University course, 'Culture, Media and Identities', where he addresses the recent 'Cultural Turn' in social science (Hall, 1997). The central issue here concerns the troubled question of cultural studies' relation to sociology.

In his 1977 essay, Hall observes that: 'when Lévi-Strauss succeeded to the Chair of Social Anthropology at the Collège de France, and delivered the inaugural lecture which declared that the centrepiece of Social Anthropology should be the study of "the life of signs at the heart of social life," he was able to defend this enterprise as nothing more nor less than the resumption of the forgotten part of the Durkheim–Mauss programme' (Hall, 1977b: 23). In the 1997 version of this argument, Hall explains that 'the programme . . . inaugurated by Durkheim and Mauss . . . was defined for many years as "too idealist" for mainstream sociology . . . Durkheim's more positivistic work being preferred. . . [However] the much heralded "cultural turn" in the social sciences can more properly be read as representing a "return" to certain neglected classical and traditional themes' (Hall, 1997: 223). In this argument, cultural studies stands not against sociology per se, but rather against one particular, long dominant positivist tradition within it – and as the rescuer of a 'lost' tradition, the recovery of which has done much to reinvigorate contemporary sociology.

Hall himself has always argued that a crucial part of what was going on in Birmingham in the 1970s was the 'posing of sociological questions against sociology' (Hall, 1980: 21) as it then stood. In this connection, Greg McLennan has argued that 'if sociology is attractive today as . . . an increasingly eclectic forum, that is not least due to the impact of radical cultural studies and other avowedly interdisciplinary currents' (McLennan, 1994: 128). However, as he also notes, it does now seem to some commentators – who identify cultural studies exclusively with its relativist, postmodern variant – that if, once upon a time, cultural studies posed as the radical alternative to a moribund sociology, nowadays, sociology is perhaps in a position to wreak its revenge on cultural studies, taking the theoretical and moral high ground, on account of its apparently greater seriousness of moral (and critical) purpose (Tester, 1994). Thus, in a subsequent article, McLennan notes that

> once the critic of surface empiricism, cultural studies [in its post-modern, relativist/textualized mode] appears to have become its slave, content only to impressionistically describe contemporary culture, rather than explaining it; observing the plurality of cultural styles but avoiding considered moral evaluation of them; addressing a contemporary cultural scene, but refusing to anchor analysis in any serious theoretical or political stance, for fear of disciplinary totalisation, its 'theory' merely simulating late capitalist consumer images.
>
> (McLennan, 1998: 14)

It seems at things have reached the point where, according to some of its sociological critics, such as Keith Tester, cultural studies is a 'discourse that is morally cretinous, because it is the bastard child of the media it claims to expose. . . . Once a critical force, it has become facile and useless . . . about nothing other than cultural studies itself' (Tester, 1994: 3, 10). According to Tester, McLennan notes, sociology by contrast is informed by 'a seriousness of moral and cultural purpose . . . moral commitment and moral outrage' (Tester, 1994: 4, quoted in McLennan, ibid.).

The problem here, as McLennan adroitly observes, is that all this is as dependent on a caricature of what cultural studies is, as cultural studies' own earlier critique of sociology sometimes was. Certainly, neither McLennan nor I would have a great deal of patience with the attempts of some within the field of cultural studies to 'write off' sociology – on the grounds that its supposedly totalizing, generalizing predilictions were somehow *ipso facto* reactionary. While it has long been a minority position (and certainly so within the heavily textualized American version of cultural studies) there has always been one thread of cultural studies work which has maintained a commitment to sociological questions. To be sure, that work has always insisted on making a selective and critical appropriation of sociological theory, but it has always been there, as McLennan notes. This is a perspective which is concerned to critique the inadequacies of particular sociological positions, rather than to entirely dismiss sociology as a discipline.

Equally clearly, there is much in cultural studies, in both its postmodern and post-structuralist variants, which does push the argument against sociological theories of determination much further than I, for one, would want to go. It is relatively easy to find cultural studies work which ends up seeming to be so committed to questions of conjuncturalism and particularity that it (implicitly or explicitly) forsakes the ability to use even limited forms of categorization or generalization. However, these kinds of problems also pertain to the postmodern variants of the sociology of culture which is now proposed by some as the proper 'inheritor' of the cultural studies tradition – as McLennan notes, 'there is considerable confluence between social constructionist/post-modern variants of both sociology and cultural studies' (1998: 16).

The question is not whether cultural studies or sociology has the answer to all our problems: manifestly, there are all kinds of problems with work in both these fields. McLennan concludes by arguing that 'no solution to the crisis of sociology is to be found in cultural studies, unless it is the solution to cultural studies' own crisis'. The solution to that 'crisis' – if such there be – is for McLennan, as for me, to ensure that, in the face of the recent period of 'textualization' of cultural studies (what McLennan calls 'the comeback of English as the first parent of cultural studies' [1998: 12]), the genuinely multidisciplinary character of cultural studies is retained: including the best of the sociological perspectives on offer. However, both in the UK and the USA, there are a growing number of those who would claim that a reinvigorated sociology of culture (see, for example, Alexander, 1988; Alexander and Smith, 1993, and Smith, 1998), with sound and proper sociological protocols, is now in a position to move in on this field (which is, of course, recruiting students rather strongly) and 'clear up' a number of the unfortunate confusions created by cultural studies' various inadequacies. For some of us, and here I speak as one who has always defended sociological approaches in cultural studies, the price of that process of 'clarification by Social Theory' might well be rather too high. It all depends on how much store you put by 'Theory' with a capital T.

## Anthropological anxieties

However, it is plain that it is not only sociologists who are exercised about cultural studies. In 1996, the 'Group for Debates in Anthropological Theory' in the UK organised a debate at the Department of Anthropology at Manchester University on the notion 'Cultural Studies Will Be the Death of Anthropology'. The debate was originally motivated by the desire to explore the seeming convergence between the two disciplines, insofar as both 'are centrally concerned with meaning, experience and culture' (Wade, 1996: 2). However, some anthropological participants in the debate were very much more concerned with what Pnina Werbner characterized as

> a very real problem that anthropology faces vis-à-vis cultural studies. Cultural studies is attractive, fascinating and interesting. It sells, it is a commodity that has big sales markets; it's about issues and themes that speak to young people, to undergraduates, about gender and sexuality; it's familiar to them. Whereas good anthropology, serious anthropology, is a little bit dull; it's a bit slow; it talks about issues on the other side of the world that [students] may not be that interested in.
>
> (Werbner, in Wade, 1996: 52–3)

Werbner's point is plain: the problem is cultural studies' *superficial* attractiveness, notwithstanding anthropology's greater 'seriousness'; lest we misunderstand her, she glosses her point by explaining that this is one of those situations where, regrettably, 'bad money pushes out good money' (ibid.: 52; cf. Ferguson and Golding [1997: xx] who mobilize the same image of cultural studies as 'superficially glamorous').

Some participants in the debate also took the view that cultural studies is fundamentally parasitic on anthropology – insofar as, according to Aggers, 'a good deal of the momentum of cultural studies is provided by the cultural turn in anthropology' (Aggers, in Wade, 1996: 3). Some also took the view that, given that anthropology is (for some) by definition, queen of the sciences of meaning, because of its long tradition of expertise in matters of culture, it is also, by the same definition, the 'mistress' of cultural studies.

Certainly, in recent years there has been considerable cross trade between anthropology and cultural studies, perhaps most notably manifested in the 'turn to ethnography' as the prime method of empirical enquiry within cultural studies. Of course, this is complex territory, as this ethnographic turn within cultural studies occurred just when, within anthropology itself, the very possibility of ethnographic work had come under close scrutiny, in the wake of the interventions of James Clifford and George Marcus (cf. Clifford and Marcus, 1986). However, there are many within anthropology who take the view that cultural studies' attempt to import (or misappropriate) ethnography is seriously flawed, and who would question whether what passes for ethnography in cultural studies is anything like acceptable in terms of anthropological standards of depth and intensity of fieldwork. Indeed, there are also those within cultural studies, notably Paul Willis, who have argued exactly this case. Willis has argued that, for example, most of the work on media which describes itself as 'ethnographic' is in no sense ethnography proper:

> the media tradition of ethnography has truncated ethnography, whilst claiming its authority and power . . . audience studies [my own presumably, included – DM] do not actually produce, but more exactly fraudulently trade on, an assumed hinterland of ethnography and apparent anthropological knowledge of the communities, the groups, the cultures that are taking in the media messages under study.
>
> (Willis, in Wade, 1996: 39)

Indeed, for Willis, it is 'the lack of a really genuine (anthropological or) ethnographic root in cultural studies' which is the main problem with cultural studies itself, insofar as 'this engagement was, even in its heyday, not sufficiently empirical, nor sufficiently ethnographic. It lacked a firm basis in extensive fieldwork. . . . I don't think any cultural studies text has ever had a long-term field presence . . . [cultural studies] hasn't really had a genuine ethnographic tradition' (Willis, in Wade, 1996: 37–8)

My anthropological colleague at Goldsmiths College, Steve Nugent, in his introduction to an edited volume *Anthropology and Cultural Studies* (1997), similarly argues that the two disciplines' usages of the term 'ethnography' are quite incompatible. He quotes Marshall Sahlins to the effect that 'some cultural studies types seem to think that anthropology is nothing but ethnography. Better the other way round: ethnography is anthropology or it is nothing' (Sahlins, quoted in Nugent, 1997: 4). Nugent helpfully paraphrases Sahlins' argument thus: cultural studies is either redundant (anthropologists already do it) or it is out of the loop: 'Cultural studies practitioners are mistaken in thinking that what they do would be recognised by anthropologists as ethnography' (ibid.: 4). Nugent goes on to pose the question that 'if it is the case – as Sahlins declares – that "ethnography is anthropology" where does this leave those in cultural studies . . . who would seek to ally themselves with such an ethnographic tradition?' (ibid.: 6).

Happily, from my own point of view, there are, however, also those such as Mark Hobart who, in the Manchester debate referred to above, took a less embattled position. In line with George Marcus's view that as the conventional anthropological project exhausts itself, anthropology will be subsumed within an internationalized cultural studies, Hobart declared himself unworried by the fact that in his view 'anthropology has run out of episteme. It has had its day' (Hobart, in Wade, 1996: 12). For Hobart, if anthropology and cultural studies are not already 'the same', he is quite happy to see anthropology turning into comparative cultural studies. As he notes, 'in the real world, that flagship department of anthropology, Chicago, has (already) become the Centre for Transnational Cultural Studies' (ibid.: 14). For him, cultural studies will broaden and reinvigorate anthropology, and 'the transnational will effectively toll the death of the old anthropology and the emergence of new kinds of intellectual practice . . . (in the form of) comparative cultural studies' (ibid.: 18). This interdisciplinary perspective is also echoed in Paul Willis's closing remarks, in his contribution to the debate. Having earlier averred that he could easily see reasons for voting either way on the motion under debate (as to whether cultural studies would 'be the death' of anthropology), he concludes, notwithstanding his earlier critical comments on the deficiencies of the ethnographic tradition in cultural studies, with the rallying cry 'Anthropology is dead. Long live "TIES": theoretically informed ethnographic study' (Willis, in Wade, 1996: 41).

## The backlash: beyond cultural studies?

In a recent essay on this topic, James Carey declared that he had 'no interest in once again waking up the past in order to sing it back to sleep' (Carey, 1995: 87). I am sorry to say that I do feel compelled here to wake up some of the recent past, in the (perhaps forlorn) hope that we can then perhaps get it to sleep better. As indicated earlier, there has recently been a series of very strongly worded critiques of the overall project of cultural studies by scholars associated with a more conventional form of the sociology of culture and mass communications, which I feel stand in some need of reply. The critiques variously argue that cultural studies has led us into a political 'dead end' (particularly because of its emphasis on the study of cultural consumption); that it has abandoned 'politics' altogether (at least, in one definition of that term); that it has done little more than reinvent (in ignorance) the old (and indeed outmoded) theoretical wheels of an earlier sociological tradition, and/or that, in general, the 'flighty' excesses (see below) of its project have only confirmed the worst fears of those who were opposed to it in the first place.

In these critiques it is argued that it is (somehow) both time to move 'beyond' cultural studies altogether and time to return to the more secure disciplinary foundations and rigorous methodological procedures of sociology (and/or political economy). My answer is that, notwithstanding the very real problems and divisions within cultural studies itself, its advances over the past twenty years have now so transformed our field of study that this proposed return to 'The Good Old Ways' (and their eternal veities) is simply no longer possible, even if it were desirable.

As I have argued elsewhere (cf. Morley, 1997), there are important questions to be asked about the tendencies towards the over-'textualization' of some work in cultural studies, and about the creeping adoption of particular methodological and epistemological 'orthodoxies' within the field. However, as Greg McLennan (1998) has argued, these are questions about substantive positions within and across fields of study – *not* questions about whether cultural studies might be (just) a 'bad idea' altogether.

Let us take just a few samples of the backlash against (in the words of one critic) 'so-called British Cultural Studies (the Birmingham School)' (Frith, 1990: 233) just to get a flavour of it – so that we might then be able to read this discourse itself, symptomatically. In perhaps the most vitriolic of these critiques (Ferguson and Golding, 1997), we are told that the biography of cultural studies is a story of 'patron saints, superstars, hot gospellers and true believers' (p. xiv), characterized by an 'inward looking narcissism' (p. xv), an obsession with 'publicly re-examining its own entrails' (p. xvii) and a 'growing fascination with its own life story'. Ferguson and Golding remark scathingly that cultural studies scholars seem to be caught in a *folie de grandeur* which has 'all the appeal and significance of the premature memoirs of an adolescent prodigy' (p. xxiv) or, in Barker and Beezer's words, of an egocentric 'football star at 25 . . . busy writing [his] own autobiography' (Barker and Beezer, quoted in Ferguson and Golding, 1997: xxiv). All this 'picking over the ground of 1960's Birmingham', to Ferguson and Golding's stern gaze, is quite unseemly. To them, it seems that cultural studies scholars have made the unforgivably egocentric error of mistaking the work of the Birmingham Centre for Contemporary Cultural Studies for something equivalent to the 'mysteries of daily life in Plato's academy' (p. xxiv). If the tone of Ferguson and Golding's introduction to their edited volume is striking, it reads all the more oddly to one (such as myself) who was invited to contribute to what I had understood to be a debate about the future of cultural studies, but finds his contribution (Morley, 1997) framed by an introductory essay which reads to me more as a straightforward attack on cultural studies altogether, notwithstanding the editors' tactical use of others' critical quotes to carry the cumulative weight of their own implicit argument.

As if all this was not enough, we are further told that this narcissism has (apparently) led those working in cultural studies to be 'ignorant of significant developments elsewhere in academia', and to thus end up, in their ignorance, 'reinventing the conceptual wheel of cultural analysis' (Ferguson and Golding, 1997: xix). Even worse, this egocentricism is apparently com-pounded by obscurantism, so cultural studies is further charged with the use of a pointlessly obscure and convoluted style and with producing a 'literature of growing opalescence and distinguishing clarity' (p. xxi). At the same time, cultural studies has also been characterized as 'a sort of intellectual equivalent of rap' (Eagleton, 1996) and has been accused of suffering a 'narrowing of vision . . . exemplified by a drift into an uncritical populist mode of interpretation' (McGuigan, 1992: 244); or, in another critic's words, drifting into 'a near celebration of the ephemeral and superficial' (McQuail, 1997: 40).

In a similar vein, Frith and Savage, in their combatively titled article 'Pearls and Swine' (1993) argue that cultural studies, through its supposed mis-taken identification of consumption with resistance (cf. also Frith, 1990), can effectively be reduced to the forms of populism to which, they claim, it has regretfully (but it seems, inevitably) led. In this respect, they argue 'The great failing of our age is the idea . . . that to be popular you have to be populist, which means an uncritical acceptance of an agenda set by market forces'. They go on to claim that the language of cultural studies

> is irrelevant to pop culture producers . . . to consumers, and to those of us who would like to see a new language of pop culture: one derived from anthropology, archetypal psychology, (and) musicology. . . . It is time to reclaim pop from the populists: they have said much of nothing, but their chit-chat still poisons the air.
>
> (Frith and Savage, 1993: 116)

For these authors, this kind of 'cultural populism is more a journalistic than an academic project' (ibid.: 110). Neatly substituting 'studies' for 'populism' they can thus conclude that this 'helps explain the uneasy symbiosis between cultural studies and the *Modern Review*' (ibid.). Frith and Savage's attempt to lay the blame for Julie Burchill et al.'s later rantings in the *Modern Review* on cultural studies is succinctly echoed in the very title: 'Burchill's Daddies' of Ben Rogers' (1996) review referred to earlier, of mine and Kuan-Hsing Chen's edited volume on Stuart Hall's work. I will return below to the question of who, in these matters, can reasonably be held to blame for whose subsequent tears and disappointments.

## Dead ends?

In their denunciation of cultural studies, 'Cultural Compliance: Dead Ends of Media/Cultural Studies and Social Science', Greg Philo and David Miller (1997) begin by pointing a truly bleak and depressing picture of the transformation of the UK during the period of Conservative rule – a picture which seems to me to be entirely accurate. The problem is that they somehow seem to imagine that cultural studies is to blame for all this unhappiness. Minimally, their charge is that because scholars in cultural studies have not stuck to the narrow confines of the 'public knowledge' project (cf. Corner, 1991) and to the detailed study of 'bias' in television news and political reporting, they are culpable in failing to resist Thatcherism (notwithstanding Hall's own path-breaking work on the analysis of Thatcherism itself) as strongly as they might have done (and as strongly as the members of the Glasgow Media Group presumably did do).

Philo and Miller's paper is characterized by a rather odd combination of despair, blame and virulent denunciation of cultural studies for all these wrongs, alongside a seemingly intransigent conviction that they were right all along, and that all would have been well, if cultural studies had not 'seduced' media-studies scholars into the study of popular culture. Their perspective on the supreme (and exclusive) 'reality claims' of the traditional public sphere and of the unquestioned superiority of the traditional social-scientific approaches to the study of phenomena in that sphere is strikingly monocular. Indeed, they seem to be incapable of accepting that anything else is worth studying at all or that phenomena exist in more than one dimension. Thus, they are highly critical of Gillespie's (1995) study of young 'Punjabi Londoners' for concentrating on issues such as the symbolic function of commercial spaces, such as McDonald's, as places to escape parental supervision. Gillespie's failing, in their eyes, is that she does not address either McDonald's low-wage policies, or their relation to questions of animal welfare. Certainly, these are important issues, but they were not what Gillespie's study was about. For Philo and Miller, it clearly should have been, and they seem to be unable to grasp that any questions other than narrowly economic or conventionally 'political' ones are of significance.

Philo and Miller's central target is, in fact, a certain variety of postmodern relativism. However, first, they equate this particular perspective with cultural studies as a whole and fail to recognize currents of cultural studies work which are sceptical of the claims of both postmodernism and relativism. Second, in a classic 'post hoc ergo propter hoc' argument, they assume that cultural studies is to blame for the emergence of the various associated 'evils' with which they are primarily concerned. They quite fail to recognize that there are no necessary correspondences between being 'in' cultural studies and operating with a relativist epistomology and a commitment to post-modernism (cf. Morley, 1997). The fact that, conjunctually, this has been the predominant position within (especially North American) cultural studies over a certain period does not mean that it is a 'given', nor that other positions are not possible. Nor, indeed, do Philo and Miller address the problem that scholars outside the field of cultural studies also hold relativist/ postmodern views – which would seem to indicate that holding them is not necessarily the result of being 'in' cultural studies.

Among the 'dead ends' of media research within which Philo and Miller are concerned is research such as my own (and implicitly that of other scholars, such as James Lull and Roger Silverstone) which pays attention to the material, domestic context of media reception. They complain of scholars such as these, who have 'examined the "social texture of media consumption" – which could *come down to* asking people if they listened to the radio while they doing the ironing' (Philo and Miller, 1997: 13, my italics). This, according to Philo and Miller, is the sad and mistaken result of the long journey from the (apparently now halcyon) days of the 'encoding/decoding' model of the media to the sad days of 'television as toaster' (p. 13). As I have argued elsewhere (see Morley, 1986 and 1992), the whole point of my own research into the domestic context of reception was not to 'abandon' questions of media power, textuality (or indeed ideology) but rather to complement that perspective on the 'vertical' dimension of media power, with a simultaneous address to its 'horizontal'/ritual dimension. As to the implied obviousness of the idea that toasters are not worth analysing, it would seem that Philo and Miller are simply unfamiliar with the extensive anthropological literature (cf. for one starting point Appadurai, 1986) on the importance of the symbolic dimension of domestic objects (cf. also my own analysis of the television set as a 'visible object', rather than a 'visual medium': Morley, 1995; see also Chapter 9 below).

Philo and Miller quote Gitlin approvingly, when he claims that the problem with cultural studies theorists is that, for them, 'the unstated assumption is that popular culture is already politics' (p. 33). Quite right. It is. The question of whether it necessarily follows (*pace* Frith, 1990) that popular culture is only of interest for its moments of 'resistance', or whether an improperly celebratory account of certain forms of consumption as 'symbolic insur-gency' is necessarily entailed, is quite another question. Certainly, to imagine that popular culture is *not* 'already politics' is, it would seem to me, politically disastrous. As for the authors' further assumption, that cultural studies' attention to questions of consumption necessarily represents either a misguided attempt to celebrate the abilities of ordinary people, or a 'search for a replacement for the lost proletariat' (Philo and Miller, 1997: 34) that seems, at least to me, a moot and largely unproven point.

## Guilty as charged?

The charge of cultural studies' supposed narcissism runs alongside, as I have noted, the charge that it offers not only a 'complacent relativism', but also (in the words of my colleague at Goldsmiths College, James Curran) in its approach to media consumption, an ignorant form of 'new revisionism' in which 'old pluralist dishes' are rehearsed and presented as *nouvelle cuisine*, saying only things that good sociologists have 'long known' (cf. Curran, 1990). Here, it seems, we are back again, if in a more theoretical vein, with the question with which I began, concerning the construction of common sense and its changing historical limits – only this time, within the field of academic media studies. Thus, a number of scholars principally associated with the mass-communications perspective (cf. Garnham, 1995) have lately been heard to say that, of course, they have always recognized that there was more to life than questions of class and economic determination; that questions of culture and meaning have always been important to them; that, of course, questions of race, gender and sexuality have always been prominent among their concerns; that, naturally, the analysis of low-status forms of fictional media production is important; and that, certainly, they have never thought of audiences as passive dupes or zombies. Tell it to the marines, say I. A look back at some early debates between these scholars and those working in cultural studies (see Murdock and Golding, 1977; Connell, 1978, 1983; Garnham, 1983) shows quite a different story, in which all these things that now, it seems, mass-communications scholars have 'long recognized' have, in fact, had to be fought for, inch by inch, and forced on to the research agenda by those primarily within the cultural studies tradition, against the background of much wailing and gnashing of teeth on the part of the political economists.

One interesting issue here is that of the teleological structure of the arguments of many of cultural studies' critics. Greg McLennan has observed that, for some (e.g. Harris, 1992) it seems that 'once Gramscianism took off in cultural studies, postmodernism was (the) logical consequence' (McLennan, 1994: 28). In a similar vein, Simon Frith rhetorically poses the question of 'whether a populist approach is the logical conclusion of sub-culturalism' in cultural studies, and avers that he 'fears that the answer is, yes' (Frith, 1991: 104). Certainly, in my own field of research, critics of the supposedly 'pointless populism' of 'active audience theory' have tended towards a similarly post-hoc structure of argument, in which, having identified some particular case in which subcultural/consumer/audience 'activity' is uncritically celebrated by an author with cultural studies allegiances, they then retrospectively declare that this is the kind of (bad) thing to which cultural studies, in general, was bound to lead and that therefore (conveniently reversing the terms of the argument) we can now see that the whole cultural-studies enterprise was, from the start, misconceived, as it has (in fact) led to whatever example of bad practice they have identified. Which, of course, leaves cultural studies' critics in the happy (or perhaps smug?) position of saying that they always knew it would end in tears.

So much for teleology. The other issue, as I have argued in my response (Morley, 1996) to my colleague James Curran's criticism of the 'new revisionism' in audience research, concerns the historiographical problem of the wisdom of hindsight. My argument is that while the history which Curran offers of the sociological precursors of cultural studies work on audiences is a very illuminating one, it is one which could not have been written, by Curran or anyone else, before the impact of the 'new revisionism' (of which Curran is so critical) transformed our understanding of the field of audience research, and thus transformed our understanding of who and what was important in its history. My own view is that it is precisely this transformation which has allowed a historian such as Curran to go back and re-read the history of communications research, in such a way as to give prominence to those whose work can now, with hindsight, be seen to have prefigured the work of the 'new revisionists'. The point is that it is only now, after the impact of 'revisionist' analyses, that the significance of this earlier work can be seen. Previously, much of it was perceived as marginal to the central trajectory of mainstream communications research. The further problem, as Kim Schroder (1987) has argued is that, if sociologists already knew these things, why has it required cultural studies scholars to excavate this 'lost' sociological tradition? The answer that Schroder offers, and with which I, for one, incline to agree, is that in spite of the tributes now paid by Curran et al. to those who can, retrospectively, be identified as the forgotten 'pioneers' of qualitative media-audience research, 'the fact remains that, until the 1980's, their qualitative work [was] the victim of a spiral of silence, because they attempted to study what mainstream sociology regarded as unresearchable – i.e. cultural meanings and interpretations' (Schroder, 1987: 14).

## The gender of the real

Among some of those who call for a return to the eternal verities of political economy and the sociology of mass communications, it has now become fashionable to denounce the supposed depoliticization of cultural studies work as irresponsible, for redirecting attention away from the 'real' world of parliamentary politics, hard facts, economic truths (and their ideological misrepresentation by the media), towards the (by contrast) 'unimportant' realms of the domestic functioning of the media and of the consumption of fictional pleasures. In one version of this critique, it is argued that media power as a political issue has simply been allowed to slip off cultural studies' research agenda, as it has descended into 'a form of sociological quietism . . . in which increasing emphasis on the micro-processes of viewing relations displaces an engagement with the macro structures of media and society' (Corner, 1991: 4). This formulation seems to me to mal-pose the relation between the macro and the micro, both reifying the macro and unproblematically equating it with the real. In this connection we might also note the implicitly masculinist imagery of the complaint that cultural-studies work suffers from a 'loss of critical energy' – a complaint which calls to mind Richard Hoggart's deathless phrase about how popular culture is responsible for 'unbending the springs of action of the working class'. Shades of Viagra, perhaps.

Moreover, the critique of cultural studies work in this field quite fails to address the articulation of the divisions macro/micro, real/trivial and public/private with those of masculine and feminine. Ann Gray (1998) has perhaps captured the gendered spirit of this critique most sharply in her comments on Dennis McQuail's use of the words (which I referred to earlier) 'flighty and opinionated' (McQuail, 1997: 55, quoted in Gray) – to characterize cultural studies work. As Gray notes, the supposed 'loss of critical energy' involved in attending to the role of the media in the articulation of the public and private spheres, and in investigating the deep and complex inscription of the media in a variety of forms of (necessarily gendered) domesticities, could only ever be understood as an 'abandonment' of politics within a quite unreflexive and unhelpfully narrow definition of what 'politics' is (see also Brunsdon's comments on the problematic status, for some scholars, of television studies as a 'connotationally feminised field', Brunsdon, 1998: 108).

As Gray (1998) rightly observes, in her critique of Corner, his perspective simply presumes the greater 'reality' and superiority of the 'public knowledge' project (as he terms it) of media studies. I would entirely support Gray when she argues that the definition of 'politics' and the valuation of 'public knowledge' uncritically enshrined in the very premises of this critique must be understood to be heavily gendered (and 'race'-ed – see Husband (1994), Modood (1992), Pines (1992) on the largely unexamined issue of the 'whiteness' of the 'public sphere'). As Gray argues, within this perspective, the importance of current-affairs programming and of the 'public knowledge' project is simply taken for granted as is the implicit (and largely naturalized) hierarchization of the power relations therein, which this representation of the field demonstrates. Perhaps Liesbet van Zoonen puts it most starkly when she notes that the central problem here, which badly needs addressing, is the way 'the public knowledge project tends to become a new male preserve, concerned with ostensibly gender-neutral issues such as citizenship, but actually neglecting the problematic relation of non-white, non-male citizens to the public sphere' (Van Zoonen, 1994: 125, quoted in Gray, 1998). And, one might add, thus far at least, the 'public knowledge' project has largely tended to ignore the cultural dimensions of the economic institutions, market mechanisms and legal processes which are, in fact, integral (and indeed crucial) to the effective functioning of this sphere (see below).

It would be a great mistake to concede too much to those who call for a return to the 'eternal verities' of sociology, as a way out of the supposed 'dead ends' (see Philo and Miller, 1997) into which cultural studies work has supposedly led us. To do so would be to accept a quite truncated (and unreflexive) definition of what constitutes the 'real' and/or the 'political', built on unexamined premises in relation to the construction of gender, race and ethnic identities. The study of the media's role in the construction (for some people) of a relationship between the private and the public is logically prior to the study of the media's coverage of and contribution to the internal dynamics of that public, 'political' world itself. The sphere of political communication has as its necessary foundation the series of inclusions and exclusions, on the basis of which only the private, domestic experiences of some categories of people are connected or 'mediated' to the sphere of citizenship (cf. Morley, 1990). If traditional public-service-broadcasting news and current-affairs programming can be characterized by a serious, official and impersonal mode of address aimed at producing understanding and belief, then we must also note that the 'believing subject' which it aims to interpellate is by no means always available for conscription. In societies such as ours, where increasing numbers of people are quite alienated from the processes of formal politics on which 'serious television' focuses, it would be politically suicidal to fail to take seriously the field of popular culture in which people do find their attachments and identities (unless, that is, we prefer on account of their inadequacies to 'dissolve the audience and elect another' – to steal a phrase of Brecht's). Neither will it do to scorn the work of those who take seriously the investigation of these supposedly 'trivial' or 'apolitical' matters (cf. Morley, 1998).

## Consumption, culture and the economy

I want also to return briefly, in this connection, to the contentious issue of the analytical status and priority to be given to concepts of production and consumption. As Gray (1998) has argued, the critical literature on cultural studies is characterized by a repetitive figuration of 'active audience theory' as the source of all evil, in so far as it has supposedly led cultural studies into a trajectory of work which is banal, naively celebratory and politically irresponsible. Much of the responsibility for this regrettable state of affairs is routinely laid out at the door of John Fiske's popularization of certain aspects of de Certeau's work, but as Gray points out, this generalized scapegoat figure often comes to stand in for any serious or detailed consideration of the work in question. I have elsewhere (Morley, 1992) outlined my own differences with Fiske's occasional position, but it has to be said that the alternative offered by the political economists' dismal perspective on questions of consumption has certainly, up until now, left more to be desired than Fiske's work ever did, notwithstanding his lapses into romanticism. To still dismiss, as many of cultural studies' critics seem to want to do, the insights of recent work on consumption on the grounds of the deficiencies of some early examples of it, seems to me no more than wilful blindness.

In response to the continuing critique of work on consumption in cultural studies, it is worth noting that the origin of the model of the 'circuit of culture' and of the articulation of production and consumption outlined so elegantly in the Open University's course on 'Culture, Media and Identities' (Open University Course D318) can be found, in essence in Hall's (1973) 'Reading of Marx's 1857 "Introduction" to the Grundrisse' (Hall, 1973: 20–1). As that paper explains, for Marx, consumption was no secondary or dependent part of a linear narrative in which 'in the beginning was production'. In Hall's exposition of Marx, he notes that 'consumption produces production in two ways. First, because the production's object (the product) is only finally "realised" when it is consumed. . . . But secondly, consumption produces production – by creating the need for new production' (p. 21). As Hall notes, for Marx, neither production nor consumption can 'exist or complete its passage and achieve its result without the other. Each is the other's completion' (p. 20). So much for the political economists' claim that there is any warrant in Marx's account for treating consumption as a 'secondary' or inconsequential matter. As the introduction to the Open University course has it, 'rather than privileging one single phenomenon – such as the process of production – in its explanatory structure, this model involves a "circuit of culture" – so that it does not much matter where (on the circuit) you start, as you have to go the whole way round before your study is complete' (Du Gay *et al.*, 1996: 4).

However, the critique of cultural studies' research on consumption continues unabated. Thus Garnham (originally 1995, republished in a new version 1997) simply restates the now well-worked accusations that 'in focusing on consumption and reception and on the moment of interpretation, cultural studies has exaggerated the freedoms of consumption and daily life' (1995: 14), and that 'the tendency of cultural studies – in its desire to avoid being tarred with the elitist brush – to validate all and every popular cultural practice as resistance, is profoundly damaging to its political project' (p. 24). For Garnham, the solution is clear: 'to fulfil the promises of its original project, cultural studies now needs to rebuild the bridges with political economy that it burnt in its headlong rush towards the pleasures and differences of postmodernism' (p. 2). Thus, Garnham is quite happy to explain 'where . . . cultural studies has gone wrong and why political economy can help to put it right' (p. 3).

The problem with Garnham's argument, as Grossberg (1995) has noted, is that 'cultural studies did not reject political economy, it simply rejected certain versions of political economy as inadequate' because of their 'reduction of economics to the technological and institutional contexts of capitalist manufacturing . . . their reduction of the market to the site of commodified and alienated exchange and (their) ahistorical and consequently oversimplified notions of capitalism' (Grossberg, 1995: 80). The difficulty is that there can be no solution to the problems we face in returning to the version of political economy which Garnham advocates because, in Garnham's model, as Grossberg notes, production is too 'narrowly understood as the practices of manufacturing' and too 'abstractly understood as the mode of production', which is itself 'too easily assumed to be the real bottom line' (Grossberg, 1995: 74). Even classical political economy recognized that it too involved cultural premises (e.g. the utilitarian philosophy underpinning economic models of consumer choice). As Grossberg argues, if cultural studies must take economics seriously, none the less 'the way in which it takes economics seriously must be radically different from the assumptions and methods of political economy' (p. 78) if it is not to fall back into economic reductionism and reflectionism. This, after all, was a major part of the point of cultural studies' analysis of Thatcherism in the UK – as a political and economic project, which was dependent for its success on a set of cultural transformations, not only of economic organizations, but also of conceptions of the self and of subjectivity (cf. Du Gay 1997), involving the construction of both an 'enterprise culture' and of a widespread acceptance of forms of personal life founded on the notion of the 'entrepreneurial self'. This, then, is to address the cultural dimensions of the forms of economic life itself and to recognize that beneath the 'bottom line' of economic transactions there must always lie some cultural framework within which the economy itself is constituted. To fail to recognize this, as Carey (1995) observes, is to lock ourselves back into the perspective of 'an increasingly abstract economistic Marxism that eludicates laws that [apply] to everyone and no-one . . . in its rigid inability to adapt to local circumstances [or] understand local knowledge [or cultural forms] whether of a religious, familial, aesthetic or political sort' (Carey, 1995: 85). As Carey observes, without this kind of attention to the cultural specificities of particular forms of economic life, 'political economy usually seems dedicated to the solemn reproduction of the indubitable – which is to say that it is highly predictable and redundant, and rarely surprising' (p. 87). As Paul Willis observed long ago in this connection, the possibility of 'being surprised, of reaching knowledge not prefigured in one's stating paradigm' is crucial to the project of cultural studies (Willis, 1981: 90).

## The slippery slope of intellectual progress

There are endless dangers facing any attempt to develop a schematic overview of work in our field which attempts to establish too clear and one-directional a story-line of intellectual progress, characterized by a series of clear epistemological and/or methodological breaks. We have been down that road too often before. The problem, of course, is what happens to the ideas and theories which are critiqued and displaced: are they to be entirely discarded or rejected? If so, we are likely to enjoy a succession of exclusive orthodoxies, each themselves enjoying a brief, if absolute intellectual reign, prior to their being dethroned by the next intellectually fashionable paradigm and removed to the dungeons reserved for the intellectually *passé*. Clearly, rather than thinking in terms of a linear succession of truths, paradigms or models, each displacing the previous one in some triumphal progress, we are better served by a multidimensional model which builds new insights on to the old, in a process of dialogue transformation which, if necessarily at points selective, is none the less syneretic and inclusive by inclination. The point may seem simplistic, but the pressures of a competitive academic marketplace militate against this approach and encourage us all to make our way not, as Clifford Geertz once put it, by 'vexing each other more precisely' in a process of genuinely productive debate, but simply by putting others down, in order to raise ourselves up.

It is always necessary to appreciate the value of previous analytical work in the context in which it was produced. One very good example of this can be found in Hall's own subsequent self-reflexive comments on the 'encoding/ decoding' model, now so much reified in the field. When interviewed about the model, a few years ago, by Justin Lewis and his colleagues at the University of Massachusetts, Hall was at pains to stress the extent to which it had been developed, for quite specific polemical purposes, in the context of a particular debate with the dominant mass-communications models of the time. Moreover, he insisted that if the model still has any remaining purchase, that's 'because it suggests . . . an approach; it opens up new questions. But it's a model which has to be worked with . . . developed and changed' (Hall, 1994: 255). I would like to say something about the kinds of 'changes' involved here – about how and why such change is necessary and what it implies about previous work. To put the matter in autobiographical terms, when my own research shifted in emphasis, from the focus on the interpretation of a particular programme in the *Nationwide* work to the study of practices of media consumption, in *Family Television*, this was not because I no longer believed that the interpretation of programmes mattered. Rather, I was attempting to recontextualize the original analysis of programme interpretations by placing them in the broader frame of the domestic context in which television viewing, as a practice, is routinely conducted. This was not to argue for the supercession of the one concern by the other, but rather to attempt to move towards a model of media consumption capable of dealing simultaneously with the transmission of programmes/contents/ideologies *and* with their inscription in the everyday practices through which media content is incorporated into daily life.

At a more general level, in the abstract of a paper prepared for the International Association of Mass Communications Researchers' Conference in Glasgow in July 1998, Richard Johnson explains that his paper, 'Cultural Studies: The Revival of Polemic' argues that, in the face of recent criticisms of cultural studies work on 'the popular', the key point is that, in the formative period in which that work began 'there was a tangible political need to broaden our conceptions of power and politics . . . [so] the focus on culture, even at the expense of other forms of power, was a rational priority of those decades'. However, as Johnson then goes on to say, of course 'the priorities for today are different: to . . . re-embed cultural analysis in further accounts of the social'. But – and this for me is the key point –

> This will not succeed . . . unless we take advances in cultural studies seriously. This means taking on board implications for other approaches: the failure of communications studies . . . to grasp the characteristic pressures of cultural forms; and the challenge to political economy to see the cultural-in-the-economic, especially the cultural values and forms of social identity that sustain 'economical systems and lend them their inevitability'.

Now that does sound (provisionally, of course) like a good way forward to me. These are themes to which I will return in my concluding chapter.

## Note

This chapter is dedicated to the memory of Ian Connell, who would probably have disagreed roundly with some of it, but who always enjoyed a lively polemic.

## References

Alexander, J. (ed.) (1988) *Durkheimian Sociology: Cultural Studies*, New York: Cambridge University Press.

Alexander, J. and Smith, P. (1993) 'The Discourse of American Civil Society: A New Proposal for Cultural Studies', *Theory and Society*, 22.

Appadurai, A. (ed.) (1986) *The Social Life of Things*, Cambridge: Cambridge University Press.

Barker, M. and Beezer, A. (eds) (1992) *Reading into Cultural Studies*, London: Routledge.

Brunsdon, C. (1998) 'What is the "Television" of "Television Studies?"'. In C. Geraghty and D. Lusted (eds) *The Television Studies Book*, London: Arnold.

Carey, J. (1995) 'Abolishing the Old Spirit World', *Critical Studies in Mass Communications*, 12.

Clifford, J. and Marcus, G. (eds) (1986) *Writing Culture*, Berkeley, Calif.: University of California Press.

Collini, S. (1996) 'The Globalist Next Door' (Review of Morley and Chen [eds] 1996), *The Guardian*, 15 March.

Connell, I. (1978) 'Monopoly Capitalism and the Media'. In S. Hibbin (ed.) *Politics, Ideology and the State*, London: Lawrence & Wishart.

Connell, I. (1983) 'Commercial Broadcasting and the British Left', *Screen*, 24 (6).

Corner, J. (1991) 'Meaning, Genre and Context: The Problematics of "Public Knowledge" in the New Audience Studies'. In J. Curran and M. Gurevitch (eds) *Mass Media and Society*, London: Arnold.

Curran, J. (1990) 'The "New Revisionism" in Mass Communications Research', *European Journal of Communications*, 5 (2, 3).

Du Gay, P. (ed.) (1997) *Production of Culture/Cultures of Production*, London: Sage.

Du Gay, P., Hall, S., Jones, L., MacKay, H. and Negus, K. (1996) *Doing Cultural Studies*, London: Sage.

Eagleton, T. (1996) 'The Hippest', *London Review of Books*, 7 March.

Ferguson, M. and Golding, P. (1997) 'Cultural Studies and Changing Times', Introduction to their co-edited volume *Cultural Studies in Question*, London: Sage.

Frith, S. (1990) Review article, *Screen*, 31:2.

Frith, S. (1991) 'The Good, the Bad and the Indifferent: Defending Popular Culture from the Populists', *Diacritics*, 21:4.

Frith, S. and Savage, J. (1993) 'Pearls and Swine: The Intellectuals and Mass Media', *New Left Review*, 198.

Garnham, N. (1983) 'Public Service versus the Market', *Screen*, 24:1.

Garnham, N. (1995) 'Political Economy and Cultural Studies: Reconciliation or Divorce?', University of Westminster; reprinted (1997) as 'Political Economy and the Practice of Cultural Studies', in Ferguson and Golding (eds) 1997.

Gillespie, M. (1995) *Television, Ethnicity and Cultural Change*, London: Routledge.

Gray, A. (1998) 'Audience and Reception Research in Retrospect: The Trouble with Audiences'. In P. Alasuutari (ed.) *The Inscribed Audience*, London: Sage.

Grossberg, L. (1995) 'Cultural Studies versus Political Economy', *Critical Studies in Mass Communications*, 12.

Hall, S. (1973) 'A Reading of Marx's 1857 "Introduction" to the Grundrisse', *Centre for Contemporary Cultural Studies*, University of Birmingham.

Hall, S. (1977a) Culture, the Media and the Ideological Effect'. In J. Curran, M. Gurevitch and J. Woollacot (eds) *Mass Communications and Society*, London: Arnold.

Hall, S. (1977b) 'The Hinterland of Science', *Working Papers in Cultural Studies*, 10.

Hall, S. (1980) 'Cultural Studies and the Centre'. In S. Hall, D. Hobson and A. Lowe (eds) *Culture, Media, Language*, London: Hutchinson.

Hall, S. (1994) 'Reflections upon the Encoding/Decoding Model'. In J. Cruz and J. Lewis (eds) *Viewing, Reading, Listening*, Boulder, Col.: Westview Press.

Hall, S. (1997) 'The Centrality of Culture'. In K. Thompson (ed.) *Media and Cultural Regulation*, London: Sage.

Harris, D. (1992) *From Class Struggle to the Politics of Pleasure: The Effects of Gramscianism on Cultural Studies*, London: Routledge.

Husband, C. (1994) 'The Multi-Ethnic Public Sphere', paper to European Film and Television Studies Conference, London, July.

Johnson, R. (1998) 'Cultural Studies: The Revival of Polemic', paper to International Association of Mass Communications Researchers Conference, Glasgow, July.

McGuigan, J. (1992) *Cultural Populism*, London: Routledge.

McLennan, G. (1994) 'Margins, Centres', *Sites*, 28.

McLennan, G. (1998) 'Sociology and Cultural Studies: The Rhetoric of Disciplinary Identity', Department of Sociology, Massey University, New Zealand.

McQuail, D. (1997) 'Policy Help Wanted: Willing and Able Media Culturalists Please Apply', in M. Ferguson and P. Golding (eds) 1997.

Modood, T. (1992) 'Not Easy Being British: Colour, Culture and Citizenship', London: Runnymede Trust.

Morley, D. (1986) *Family Television*, London: Comedia.

Morley, D. (1990) 'The Construction of Everyday Life'. In D. Nimmo and D. Swanson (eds) *New Directions in Political Communications*, London: Sage.

Morley, D. (1992) *Television, Audiences, and Cultural Studies*, London: Routledge.

Morley, D. (1995) 'Not So Much a Visual Medium, More a Visible Object', in C. Jenks (ed.) *Visual Culture*, London: Routledge.

Morley, D. (1996) 'Populism, Revisionism and the "New" Audience Research', in J. Curran, D. Morley and V. Walkerdine (eds) *Cultural Studies and Communication*, London: Arnold.

Morley, D. (1997) 'Theoretical Orthodoxies'. In Ferguson and Golding (eds) 1997.

Morley, D. (1998) 'Finding Out about the World from Television News: Some Difficulties'. In J. Gripsrud (ed.) *Television and Common Knowledge*, London: Routledge.

Morley, D. and Chen, K. H. (eds) (1996) *Stuart Hall: Critical Dialogues in Cultural Studies*, London: Routledge.

Murdock, G. (1995) 'Across the Great Divide', *Critical Studies in Mass Communications*, 12.

Murdock, G. and Golding, P. (1977) 'Capitalism, Communications and Class Relations'. In J. Curran, M. Gurevitch and J. Woollacot (eds) *Mass Communications and Society*, London: Arnold.

Nugent, S. (1997) 'Brother, Can you Spare a Paradigm?'. In S. Nugent and C. Shore (eds) *Anthropology and Cultural Studies*, London: Pluto Press.

Philo, G. and Miller, D. (1997) 'Cultural Compliance: Dead Ends of Media/Cultural Studies and Social Science', Glasgow Media Group, University of Glasgow.

Pines, J. (ed.) (1992) *Black and White in Colour*, London: British Film Institute.

Rogers, B. (1996) 'Burchill's Daddies' (Review of Morley and Chen [eds] 1996), *Independent on Sunday*, 18 February.

Schroder, K. (1987) 'Convergence of Antagonistic Traditions?', *European Journal Of Communications*, 1:2.

Smith, P. (1998) *The New American Cultural Sociology*, Cambridge: Cambridge University Press.

Tester, K. (1994) *Media, Culture and Morality*, London: Routledge.

Van Zoonen, L. (1994) *Feminist Media Studies*, London: Sage.

Wade, P. (ed.) (1996) *Cultural Studies Will Be the Death of Anthropology*, Group for Debates in Anthropology, University of Manchester.

Willis, P. (1981) 'Notes on Method'. In S. Hall et al. (eds) *Culture, Media, Language*, London: Hutchinson.

# 2 Cultural studies and media studies

## Contexts, boundaries and politics

Interview by Johannes von Moltke for *Montage* magazine, Berlin (1997)

### Paths into cultural studies

Johannes von Moltke:   *David Morley, as a sociologist by training, you've come to situate your work today within the field of cultural studies. Could you retrace the path that led you into cultural studies?*

David Morley:  Having begun by studying economics, in the end, I studied sociology as an undergraduate at the London School of Economics (LSE) and, when I was there, the thing I was most interested in was a social philosophy course taught by Robin Blackburn, about 'beliefs in society'. I also had a tutor called Henry Bernstein who taught Third World development studies and who insisted that I read Barrington Moore Jr. as a materialist alternative to that kind of philosophical approach. Putting these two approaches together, I got the idea that I might want to do something about peoples' sense of identity.

   This was around 1970 and at that moment there were a set of debates starting up in Britain about the media and their role in society. There was an intense period of political activity in 1972 and 1974 with huge strikes by the miners' unions which practically closed down the country. There was a period when the Conservative Government, under Ted Heath, had to declare a 'three-day week': there was only enough electricity to keep the country running for three days a week! It was really a time of major political crisis, and there was an intense set of debates about the role of the media in all this. I developed the notion that it'd be interesting to do a Ph.D. on media representations of industrial conflict, given that industrial conflict seemed to be the crisis point of the system at that stage. So I asked around at LSE, but there was no one who would supervise a Ph.D. on this subject. I was slightly at a loss, because I was committed to living in London for various domestic reasons, so it was a question of where I could do a Ph.D. within a short radius of London. At that time, I was very involved in community politics in Hackney, the area of east London where I lived, running a community newspaper and involved in a sort of book-café project called 'Centreprise'. There I'd heard about someone called Krishan Kumar, who was involved in a liberal funding agency that gave money to alternative media projects of the kind I was involved in. He was at the University of Kent and I thought about about going there, though I also applied to come to Goldsmith's to do a Ph.D. in the sociology department here. However, this was the heyday of ethnomethodology in Goldsmith's sociology – Garfinkel's detailed studies of conversational practice: making close analyses of the premises of statements like 'The baby cried, the mummy picked it up' and so on. As I wasn't particularly interested in ethnomethodology, they weren't interested in me, and the sociology department at Goldsmith's wouldn't have me as a Ph.D. student.

So I decided to go to Kent to do this Ph.D. with Krishan Kumar. But then, just before I arrived, he was offered the opportunity to spend a year working in the BBC, as a producer in the current-affairs department, working on an observation study that he subsequently published under the title 'Holding the Middle Ground' – about the internal politics of the BBC – an article which I think is still one of the best things there is on that topic. Since he wasn't there when I got to Kent, I was allocated to a rather traditional Marxist called Frank Parkin as my tutor. When I explained to him that I was going to do a project on television coverage of industrial conflict, he said two things. First, he said that he didn't actually know anything about the mass media and that he couldn't imagine why he'd been assigned to me as a supervisor. Second, he couldn't see what the point would be of studying how television represents industrial conflict if you couldn't say something about what it meant to its audience. I was very annoyed with him for getting in my way in this fashion, suggesting that I revamp the project entirely and I fumed about this – though evidently, it was an influential conversation, as I spent much of the next twenty years trying to solve the problem he'd set. But before dismissing me, Parkin also suggested that I call up a professor at Birmingham called Stuart Hall who, he said, might know something about my topic. This was 1972, and the university system was so different then: if a student today did what I did at the time, it would just be laughable. I just rang Stuart Hall out of the blue and said 'I've heard you know something about this and there is this thing called the Cultural Studies Centre you've got there, I wonder if you could help me out?' He just said on the phone that they did have this thing called the 'Media Group' that met on a Wednesday mornings, and that I should just come up and see if we could usefully work together. So, towards the end of 1972, I started going to this meeting of the various people in Birmingham who were doing work on the media, who used to meet on a Wednesday morning. I never went and lived in Birmingham, while I was involved with the Centre for Contemporary Cultural Studies (CCCS), as I'd been brought up there and had been desperate to get away from the place! But I travelled up and down on the train on a Wednesday for some years afterwards. So I was brought back to the city by a completely incidental set of things – though, when I got there, I discovered a whole set of connections between what they were trying to do and what I was up to – not least because Stuart had just been reading Frank Parkin, as a source for what later became his 'Encoding/Decoding' piece . . .

There was also another kind of 'parallel track' between my interests and those developing at CCCS which came, again, out of my involvement in community politics. At that time, the cultural debate in Britain was very much at its sharpest around the questions of education, and in particular, questions of education, language and class. Harold Rosen, who was then at the Institute of Education, ran a study group called the 'Language and Class' workshop, a project in radical socio-linguistics which was intended as a critique of Basil Bernstein's work. They were involved in debates about race, class, language and schooling. That group had been meeting for a while, and I'd been involved in it, and one of the people who'd come and spoken there was Charles Woolfson, who was the first person I heard talk about the work of Voloshinov, which was subsequently so influential at Birmingham and in British cultural studies more widely. Anyway, before I went there, I'd already come across Voloshinov's work in the context of the 'Language and Class' group, and it was on the basis of that set of interests and accidents that I took the train to Birmingham.

JVM: *Could you describe the functioning of the CCCS at Birmingham University at that time?*

DM: The centre did have a formal attachment to the English Department, though by then it also had its independent existence – but it only had two members of staff: Stuart Hall and Michael Green. It was tiny, but it had been going for a few years then. And because there weren't enough staff to supervise the students, Stuart and Michael had invented a system where the students basically supervised each other. All the students who were working around media formed one subgroup; all the students who were working around subcultures formed another, etc. And either Stuart or Michael would go to the groups, carving them up between them. So it was a rather autonomous form of student self-help and self-organisation.

It had people who were registered formally, for MAs or Ph.D.s, who'd been formally interviewed and accepted there, and then it had this kind of floating population, people like me, who arrived from other connections.

JVM: *So at what point would you say retrospectively that your interests cohered around this concept of cultural studies? Was it when you started going to Birmingham? When did you label your work 'cultural studies'?*

DM: Well it was called cultural studies only in the sense that there was a thing called the Centre for Contemporary Cultural Studies, and that's where I was going to. But at that time, the work I was doing, I think, was still more understood as media studies I would say, and it was directly addressing questions about the media. At that time, I don't think there was really a strong sense of a thing called 'cultural studies'. There was a specific cultural studies perspective on and intervention in these various debates: into the media group, into the subcultures or sociology group, into the beginnings of debates in history as well; but it was like a set of different fields, into which interventions were being made from this place, which happened to be the CCCS.

## Theory and methodology

JVM: *Does the field of cultural studies contain a theory of media?*

DM: The problem with that question is that there is no discourse on the philosophy of communications or of the media in Britain in the way in which I think there is in Germany. There just isn't an equivalent I can think of.[1] Media work in Britain came out of two different things. On the one hand it came out of sociology and political science, to do with the institutions of the media, the political effects of the media, etc. Some of it came out of English and literary (and then film) theory – a kind of textual analysis. And then you got something called cultural studies, which was drawing on bits of those and various other things. But in terms of a theory of the media, in a kind of philosophical sense, I'm not sure what I would point you to, or in what institutional place it would have been legitimate to address the question of theories of the media. It's a caricature, but there is some truth in all that old stuff about how British academic culture was always empiricist, and pretty suspicious of theory. Though you could say that there's now been a backlash against that via the affair which the cultural left has been having with European theory over the past twenty years (though interestingly, until very recently, it has been almost exclusively French, with a bit of Italian, rather than German, theory which has been translated and taken up here.

Indeed, I'll go further: I think it's because of that absence of a theory of the media that for some people in Britain, belated as it is, there's recently been a sort of Habermas 'boom'. There's now this notion that Habermas might provide a kind of philosophical ground to the inquiry into the media – minimally around notions such as democratic communications, or the idea that you can have an ethics of communication and so on. Which Habermas produced originally twenty or thirty years back, and which was indeed translated, in one version, at that time, but for whatever reason, made little impact here until recently. So there's quite a gap between the context in which Habermas's belatedly influential works were written and the context of today – and little attention is paid to the problems about the applicability now of that early work, which are posed by the existence of that long gap in time.

Of course, nowadays things are quite different and media theory – or perhaps one should say 'medium theory' is now all over the place in the UK, just as it is elsewhere, in the wake of the resanctification of McLuhan and the rise of born-again technological determinism, especially in studies of the 'new media'. Indeed, people who do that kind of abstracted theoretical work are often now quite snobbish about the kind of empirically grounded conjunctural analyses produced by people working on the media from a cultural studies perpective. I think they'd regard what people like I do as 'middle-brow' theory, at best! But I return the compliment – to me, that kind of abstracted, speculative work about the so-called 'essences' and supposedly inevitable consequences or effects of different media is the theretical road to nowhere. So, it all depends on what value you put on what kinds of 'theory', and I'm certainly in the business of challenging the presumption that the more abstract the theory, the better it is! The point is that, yes, abstraction is a very powerful theoretical tool. But like all power tools, it needs to be used with great care, or else it rebounds against you – if you use it carelessly, you don't attend to the intellectual price of abstraction – i.e., how much contextual detail you're losing, by using a particular abstraction to analyse a specific phenomenon and I think it's always necessary to calculate those gains and losses very carefully.

JVM: *If in this sense, British cultural studies can't be said to offer a theory of the media, can one speak at least of an implicit methodology for the study of media? Or not even that?*

DM: Well, I'm actually very suspicious of that way of posing the methodological issue. In so far as cultural studies has come to imply a particular type of qualitative, reflexive, ethnographic methodology, I think there's no proper ground for that equation. What cultural studies has always signified to me, and what's always been most useful about it, has quite simply been a radical commitment to interdisciplinarity. As far as I'm concerned, that's what cultural studies means. It entails the idea that no one discipline has a monopoly on the truth. Personally, I'm very glad that I had the sociological training that I have had, but I came to realise that sociology did not have all the answers to everything, and that I'd be better off taking some things from sociology, some from sociolinguistics, some from anthropology, some from English and building my kitbox of coneptual tools from the best that a number of disciplines had to offer. The beauty of the Birmingham CCCS was precisely that it operated entirely in that mode. And on a very basic level, it was largely enabled by the simple fact of how hard Stuart Hall was prepared to work, how widely he was prepared to read texts in other disciplines, in order to introduce them to students and allow people to be informed by this wide range of perspectives. That's what cultural studies means to me, above all: the commitment to interdisciplinarity.

JVM: *How do you apply the tools from your cultural studies kitbox in practice? Specifically, regarding the status of 'the text' in cultural studies, how do you integrate actual textual analyses with the question of audience research, for instance, or with the more specifically sociological questions? I ask this because you have cautioned in your writing against the overwhelming textualisation of cultural studies, against reifying the reading metaphor and against the idea of analysing any one text in isolation. On the other hand, however, you point to 'the risk that contextual issues will overwhelm and overdetermine texts and their specificity'. In terms of your own methodology, then, how do you approach an individual text?*

DM: Well, I do think that it still makes sense to analyse texts. I say some of the things you quote precisely because – and I suppose this always happens in people's work – I've been rather frustrated to find my own work recruited to defend or legitimise positions that I don't myself hold. I've found a lot of people in the USA using my work to defend a position which would claim that texts don't really matter, because everybody reads them in such active ways all the time, in such marvelously creative different fashions, and they claim that context is obviously so constitutive of the meaning that it would seem we no longer need to analyse texts. However, as Charlotte Brunsdon says somewhere, the need to specify context and mode of viewing in any textual discussion, and even the awareness that these factors may sometimes be more determining of the experience of the text than any textual feature, does not necessarily eliminate the text as a meaningful category. I think she's got that completely right. I certainly see myself as having been in the business of *complicating* textual inquiry, saying textual inquiry isn't enough, and that you must take the context into account, since it's terribly important in specifiable ways. But I do, nonetheless want to say, with Brunsdon, that there *are* such things as texts, though not in a simple sense – and they still need to be analysed!

When I arrived at Birmingham to do my own work on news coverage of industrial conflict, it was just at the moment where things such as Olivier Burgelin's critique of content analysis (Burgelin 1972) were making an impact. Those were the beginnings of the notion of structural criticism, which demonstrated that frequency is not the same as significance, or that the most significant textual item might only take up three milliseconds of the whole thing, but would nonetheless be the fulcrum on which the narrative hangs. This was very much the kind of lead that I followed in making my own analyses of television news broadcasts. However, this raises a new problem: Burgelin's critique of the tradition of content analysis is based on the fact that the latter fails to treat texts as structured wholes, viewing them instead as disaggregated bits of information. The whole structuralist premise, by contrast, is that they are in fact wholes. Now, in the case of film studies that may well be the case. We characteristically go and see a film, walk in at the beginning, sit down and watch it through to the end. Consequently, it makes sense to analyse the single film as a text. But actually, that's *not* how people watch television a lot of the time. They switch it on, they flip channels, they often wander in and out and do something else at the same time. Regarding television, what is the structured text which you would analyse? As Raymond Wiliams puts it, it would need to be an evening's viewing perhaps, rather than a given programme – which brings you back to notions from content analysis, regarding repetitive propositions which crop up in different kinds of texts, which have an impact through sheer dint of repetition; indeed, maybe quantification does also have to come back into our analyses, if we are to deal with this.

So much for the pragmatic aspect. As for your question about the status of the text, let me refer you to Derrida, who is so often used these days to legitimate a notion that 'anything goes' in textual analysis and inter-pretation. However, the passage that I always quote to my students is from his debate with John Searle, where he says, 'you know actually you have misread me . . . Your reading is a *bad* reading! That's right, "bad" not "good". You must re-read me.' So here you have Derrida, of all people, specifying that Searle has *mis*-read him and has made an inadequate analysis, and thus clearly specifying, minimally, not the truth of a reading, but criteria by which we could define some readings as more adequate than others. And that kind of attention to text remains necessary. It's only at the moment in which you can pay the most detailed attention to the text *and* be sensitive to the context in which it's being consumed, *and* be aware of the broader political discourse and economic structures that have framed and produced this – and when you can keep all these things in play in the analysis simultaneously, that you get the payoff![2]

JVM: *Is the notion of polysemy that runs through a lot of cultural-studies texts important to you any more? For it seems like you've almost subsumed it in your description of contextuality on the one hand and a limited variety of possible readings on the other.*

DM: I think the slipshod way in which people use the concept of polysemy is awful. The way in which it is mobilised a lot of the time is as a kind of theoretical 'get out', an excuse. However, I do think that the concept of polysemy remains important: both in Stuart Hall's encoding/decoding piece for instance, and in the work that Charlotte Brunsdon and I later did on *Nationwide*, where we began to try and specify the textual mechanisms that function as directive closures, with the function of closing down the range of meanings: for me, that kind of work is what remains useful.

Indeed, I'd go even further: one of the most useful responses I ever got to the *Nationwide* stuff came from Tony Trew, then at the University of East Anglia, who argued to me – and I think he was right – that the concept of polysemy, as I was using it, needed to be amended to take account of the fact that polysemy is not only closed down by metadiscursive features, but that it also functions within the structure of the word (or sentence) itself. As soon as we go from one letter ('c') to the sequence of letters that makes up a word ('c-a-t'), we've begun to close down the possible interpretations of any single unit or element within it. In other words, the mere syntagmatic procedure of combination itself functions to begin to close down the potential meaning of any one element in the syntagm. That's a level of analysis that we actually didn't fully attend to in that initial work. For me, then, the function of the word 'polysemy' is to describe a problem, a tension between the attempts to fix meaning, which are always there, in many different ways, and the ways in which meaning still, in this process, often becomes unfixed. I do think this is an issue which still requires attention. I find it very distressing that what you get in so much cultural studies, and especially in American cultural studies, is a rather lax sort of 'resolution' of the problem, which doesn't go beyond simply asserting that meaning is fluid. And where does that get you? The question is exactly *how* fluid is it, in *which* instances?

## National varieties of cultural studies

JVM:  *In suggesting that the Americans are the prime misreaders of your work, where do you draw the line between British and American cultural studies?*

DM:  My flip answer would be that I think it's the difference between Foucault read through Gramsci, and Gramsci read through Foucault. In part, this simply has to do with publishing economics and the differential impacts of material from different nations in other places, over time. In Britain, for many of my generation, at least, Gramsci made a crucial impact before they came to Foucault. So people in cultural studies in Britain, at that time, generally encountered Foucault through the prism of Gramsci's work, which gave rise to questions concerning what Foucault could add to Gramsci, or whether and how Foucault might problematise or even undermine Gramsci. In America, on the other hand, because of the different period in which cultural studies came in, it was actually Foucault who made the first impact, for a lot of people. And so they then read Gramsci through Foucault. I think that's a very different constellation, and that would be one way of answering your question.

   Another way would be to look at what people in cultural studies in each place were responding to, or reacting against. It seems to me that in America one of the crucial issues was just how derelict the tradition of the sociology of mass communications had become, and the extent to which anyone who understood themselves as any sort of radical or a progressive had to define themselves *against* the sociology of mass communications. That produced a kind of 'leap' into cultural studies, and as I was saying before, into a kind of deification of qualitative work, again by contra-distinction to the bad 'parent discipline'. In Britain, while people to some extent were also wanting to differentiate themselves from the tradition of the sociology of mass communications, they weren't trying to do so in such a decisive way, because there was a tradition of radical political economy here, within the sociology of mass communication, which was actually very productive and was putting out important work.

   In a piece that I wrote together with Kevin Robins, we quote the Japanese scholar Naoki Sakai on the meaning of the term 'the West'. Sakai argues that this term does not merely reference a geographical category, but that 'it is, evidently, a name always associating itself with those regions, communities and peoples that appear politically or economically superior to other regions, coummunities and peoples' (quoted in Morley and

Robins, 1995: 159): 'the West' in other words, associates itself with a position of superiority, of advancement. I think you could almost say the same about the term 'cultural studies'. It's often not so much a positive thing in itself, it's more a way of describing a particular kind of advancement of position (in Britain, in America, or wherever) and of course that takes a different shape, depending on what the antagonist is, and depending on what it is exactly that one is wanting to advance from, or advance against.

JVM: *What about other contexts besides Britain and America? Do you see anything within cultural studies that makes them particularly exportable or that makes them travel poorly?*

DM: I think I see something that accounts for the exportability of cultural theory. Forgive the banality of the explanation, but these are the remnants of my initial training as a sociologist and my remaining commitments to a Marxism of a sort. I think it's best explained by the simple economics of the publishing industry. The thing that 'travels' best in publishing is theory. Because the more abstract the product, the less nationally specific it is, the bigger the market to which it can be exported. I think that's an abominable tendency, which leads to the fact that it's very often the worst, and least useful, most over-abstracted work which gets exported the most widely and is the most read. I had that experience myself when for some years in the 1980s I was involved in running a publishing project (Comedia Books, before it was taken over by Routledge) which was precisely committed to producing concrete analyses – in which we encouraged the use of theoretical models to analyse developments in a particular national society at a particular time (in this case, Britain in the 1980s). Economically, this project was, of course, disastrous in the end, because it only had a tiny, national market and you can't make enough money out of that to survive – unless the national market is as big as that of the USA! So I do think that, before we get to the question of which aspects of cultural studies one might want to 'export', we first need to explain what has happened in the field so far; and this, in my own view, is best explained by the economics of the publishing industry. Theory travels best.

Now, if you ask me what I think is good work, then as I said earlier, I think that kind of abstracted theory is the worst possible work.[3] To me, the idea that you can just produce some kind of 'one-size-fits-all' cultural Theory is outrageous. I was astounded when I first encountered such an idea from American graduate students – that there was this stuff just called Theory, which had a transcendent existence and application all over the world. I think that's just another form of cultural imperialism. If you're not very careful, a lot of cultural studies work, exported from an Anglo-American heartland to the rest of the world, in fact becomes a form of Western academic hegemony. To me, what's important is how concepts which might have been produced somewhere else can be refined and applied to different kinds of national circumstances. And the presumption has to be that they will need to be adapted, because the template for cultural politics produced in one country may well need to be entirely different in another. If you take the argument about Hoggart and Williams as the 'founding fathers' of cultural studies, that's produced out of an adult working-class white men's experience in Britain in the post-war period, through the 1950s and 1960s. How applicable is that to somebody in contemporary Korea or wherever else? The very idea that there just is this Theory, which can be exported wholesale in that way, is dreadful.

JVM: *What about the roots of British cultural studies themselves, though? You've mentioned Foucault and Gramsci, but one might also point to the debates in* Screen *around film theory in the early 1980s. Hasn't cultural studies imported its own range of 'theory' to conduct its studies and make its case? Isn't that a precondition of theory in both the bad and the good sense?*

DM: I'm most preoccupied at present with the bad sense, and I think that what I'm saying is rather like what Cornel West says when he attacks Lyotard for imagining that conditions on the Left Bank of Paris are the conditions of the world. Such a ludicrous, presumptuous thing can only happen in certain places. Maybe it can happen in Paris, maybe it can happen in London at a certain moment, maybe there are other metropolitan major cities where such a perspective can be generated. But the point is that these are moments in which something gets produced and its conditions of production get forgotten as it begins to be exported and mobilised in other places. The kind of outrage that someone such as Meaghan Morris often expresses in Australia about the importation there of Anglo-American cultural studies and this worldwide mythologisation of Birmingham and of the British 'founding fathers' of cultural studies is very understandable. That process can be deeply insulting to people elsewhere, and I sympathise with her entirely.

Let me give you an example of what I mean. In 1996, Stuart Hall, Angela McRobbie, Charlotte Brunsdon, Ali Ratansi, Colin Sparks and I went on a British Council-funded trip to Japan, to a conference in Tokyo dedicated to the topic of cultural studies in Japan. It was a very stimulating trip, but it was also full of tensions, not least about the extent to which cultural studies could – or indeed, should – be imported wholesale into Japan. I think it's that sort of encounter in which one learns the most.

British cultural studies *can* become an export, and that's why the British Council funded us all to go there. The British Council, originally an old imperialist organisation, had begun to realise that it was better off subsidising British cultural studies as an export industry, rather than English literature and travelling productions of Shakespeare, simply because there was more of a demand for cultural studies. Of course, you could see that as a rather cynical operation. But from their point of view, they're funded to do an export job, and in doing that, in this case, in a new and imaginative way, they successfully opened up a valuable space for new types of British academic work to be discussed in Japan with those who were interested in these things.

What's interesting is, of course, that, as we found in Tokyo, all this can go badly wrong if, when you get to Japan you're not sensitive to the fact that there is an indigenous tradition of what you could call cultural studies, from which we have as much to learn as the Japanese might learn from us.[4] The presumption that there is an Anglo-American thing called cultural studies, which has its truths, which can be exported even if they might be only partially applicable in other places, isn't good enough. There's also a question of what can be learned from traditions in other places. And the monoglot nature of the English education system, the fact that so few cultural-studies scholars, myself included, read any other languages, the fact that English has become the most powerful language in the world (we conduct this interview in English; I speak no German) reinforces a one-way system of communication, which is deeply damaging to the international intellectual development of the field.

JVM: *If cultural studies is, like the idea of 'the West', a way of claiming an 'advanced' position, would it be fair to describe the praxis of cultural studies as always some local form of studying nationally specific circumstances in a way that gets one away from a given parent discipline?*

DM: Absolutely. Take the question of nationalism. At present in Anglo-American cultural studies, cosmopolitanism and anti-nationalism are the keywords and bywords of discourse. But there are other places in the world where the discourse of nationalism can still be a very progressive, important and necessary orienting device. Cultural studies has got to be flexible enough to work with that. There's a great bit in Michael Ignatieff's (1994) book on nationalism where he reverses a well-known aphorism of Samuel Johnson's, who speaks of patriotism as the 'last refuge of a scoundrel'. Ignatieff turns that around, to say that anti-nationalism (and scorn for the nationalist aspirations of others) is the last refuge of those who can take a secure nation-state for granted. The key distinction, for me, is that between voluntary and involuntary cosmopolitanism. To give one example, as I undertsand it, the 'Trajectories' conference which Kuan-Hsing Chen organised in Taiwan in 1991 blew up around this question, because in Taiwan, at that time, the discourse of nationalism was still really very important. And many of the cultural-studies scholars from the West at that conference seemed to their Taiwanese hosts not to be able to grasp that very well.

## The politics of cultural studies

JVM: *Do you think that cultural studies is too wrapped up in being 'politically correct'?*

DM: Yes, increasingly so. Standpoints in cultural studies are becoming like a question of manners, a set of credos and of pre-given commitments – such as, for instance, the idea that you can only do qualitative work if you are to be among the 'elect'. But again, I think you've got to pay attention to different phases of development in that respect and to the different requirements of different moments of the formation of the discipline. To take the Birmingham case, which I know best, there's a very illuminating piece in the collection that Kuan-Hsing Chen and I did about Stuart Hall's work, where Charlotte Brunsdon recounts the early struggles around the eruption of feminism within the Birmingham centre. She makes clear how deeply contentious this issue was at the time, and how it was argued in terms of an emergent identity politics which produced disputing factions, and indeed, at some moments, the sound of the angry slamming of doors, rather than dialogue. The same was the case for the beginnings of the study of race at Birmingham. Then, at a later stage, as these 'new' issues reshaped the whole agenda, people were able to ease up and be less 'p.c.' in their requirements of each other and more open to difference and debate. But there are these formative moments, in which certain symbolic barriers do have to be put up and defended. In my own view, these forms of identity politics are an absolute necessity, at certain moments of development and in certain kinds of struggle, but it's ultimately regrettable if one can't, later on, get beyond them. I would hate to see cultural studies, as a practice, 'policed' any more than it already is – not least because if you'll only deal with those who already also bow down to the same idols as you do, you close doors to critical dialogues of various kinds.

Cultural studies needs to be better prepared to deal with a whole variety of others. It needs to do, theoretically, what Kobena Mercer talks about when he discusses the sheer difficulty of 'living with difference' in relation to debates about race and ethnicity. I think that cultural studies still has a lot of difficulty in living with its others. It's very understandable, because it's so often been an object of scorn from other more traditional disciplines, and we have often had to draw up the defensive barricades to defend the often small and vulnerable academic spaces which we've created.[5] But in my own view, it's very important to take those barricades down as soon as one can and get on with productive argument with others in other fields, in other disciplines, working in other ways, finding what one can learn from them, rather than imagining that we've already got all the answers within cultural studies, and that it's simply our job to export them to the ignorant. That approach turns cultural studies into a vanguard party – it then becomes a rather Leninist project, run by an elite cadre whose job is to bring the revealed truth to the masses.

JVM:  *So then how strongly would you draw the lines between fields such as cultural studies and adjoining or even integrated fields such as gender studies, queer studies, post-colonial studies? I'm asking the question both on an institutional level and on a discursive level. Do you think it makes sense to set up departments for all these things? And how important is it that these inquiries remain identifiably distinct before they can come to communicate with each other?*

DM:  That's an enormously complicated question. I'm in difficulty with it, because my own entry to the field was through having thoroughly learnt a discipline, in my case sociology, and then having the delight of breaking out of it, gradually opening myself up to debates in other disciplines. Conversely, I do find that with undergraduate students who move straight into cultural studies, there is a real difficulty in their learning to be interdisciplinary before they have much idea of what a discipline is. At that point, there is a very real temptation to (too rapidly) construct a discipline of cultural studies which just then teaches its own truths and becomes a closed set of perspectives. I find that very problematic.[6]

Of course, there are often very good institutional reasons for insisting on a large degree of institutional autonomy for cultural studies at a certain moment. Thus, I can see why institutionally, it's often necessary to make the space for a certain kind of work, to have a department of gender studies or queer studies or post-colonial studies. But what one needs to do in terms of the institutional politics of a particular educational system at a particular moment, and what would be most productive intellectually in the longer term, are very often in tension with each other. And one can easily get locked into intellectually unproductive and closed discourses, which you've entered into for entirely other, strategic and political reasons, without seeing what their longer-term intellectual consequences might be.

# Cultural histories

JVM:  *When you teach cultural studies, how do you design your syllabus?*

DM:  When I do it, I start with a little diagram about culture and industry, and how they're largely understood to be antithetical terms. I then make a set of parallels, suggesting that culture is to industry as the individual is to the masses, or as the past is to the future, or as Europe is to America, etc. – a set of tropes that illuminate some long-running historical debates. Then I go back to Matthew Arnold and debates about culture in Britain in the nineteenth century and the democraticisation and industrialisation of culture, and I introduce the debates between those who would still speak of culture simply in an aesthetic sense as the 'best that has been thought and said in the world' and those who take an anthropological perspective on (lived) culture. Then I introduce Williams and Hoggart; I address the issue of the culture industry; and I then begin to discuss consumption and subcultures, ending up with contemporary debates about cultural imperialism. This is of course only one way – and a self-consciously British way – of doing it.

But what is important to me throughout, though, is to make such an introduction concrete. But this can become a very real difficulty. Given my strong reservations about abstract theory and my desire to always do my theorising in relation to a concrete instance, I'm forever trying to give concrete examples of what I mean; but the problem is that my examples are, of course, relentlessly British, as that's the only cultural history I know well! And every time I try to make things more concrete, in fact, if I'm not careful, I make them more obscure to the overseas students (of whom we now have many at Goldsmiths), for whom the references that I make, far from functioning as helpful examples, only make them feel more shut out of this mysterious British culture in which they find themselves studying. And that is a very real difficulty to which I don't think I (or anyone else here) has a satisfactory solution. But it is the difficulty one faces if one maintains this commitment to grounded theorising, to try to make one's theories applicable in a concrete sense. Unless you have an encyclopaedic knowledge of world history and of other cultures, it's difficult to do that other than ethnocentrically at certain moments. This is one of the reasons why Kevin Robins and I decided to accept an invitation by Oxford University Press, who've belatedly picked up on the notion of cultural studies, to edit a volume called *British Cultural Studies*. We thought this was quite an interesting opportunity and plan to use it to deconstruct the notion of Britishness and of what the 'Britishness' of British cultural studies might consist in (Morley and Robins 2001).

JVM: *One of the titles in the burgeoning literature in the cultural-studies sections now is* Cultural Studies and the Study of Popular Culture *(Storey 1996). Is that a tautology, or what is the relationship between cultural studies and the study of popular culture?*

DM: It shouldn't be a tautology, because I think it's actually very important that the field of cultural studies also pays proper and full attention to what is understood as high culture. Cultural studies scholars should work on the audience for opera or for other high-art forms, as much as for television. They should study the production system of subsidised theatre and look attentively at contemporary productions of Shakespeare. It's a very dangerous development if it's understood that cultural studies can only – and should only – speak to the object 'popular culture', whatever that is. But, again, this is a development that arises largely out of historical necessity. In the beginning, in Britain as elsewhere, the kinds of low-status objects – comic books, popular music and so on – that one was arguing were important to study, were not even deemed worthy of study, except for folkloric interest. The positive revaluation of the importance of popular culture was an absolutely necessary strategic job that cultural studies, certainly in Britain, had to do at a particular moment. That was crucial, but it's equally important that one doesn't stay stuck in that moment, and that one doesn't imagine that only popular culture is important.

JVM: *You suggest that cultural studies should expand from the study of contemporary popular culture in a 'vertical' direction, so to speak, to address issues of high art; can it also construct it objects along the 'horizontal' lines of history? It seems that few studies on the history of culture would be labelled cultural studies, as though by introducing an historical dimension, cultural studies becomes something else, whether it's New Historicism or simply 'cultural history' of a more traditional sort.*

DM: Well, for one thing, the question of whether cultural studies might turn into something else called 'New Historicism' is not, for me, something that makes me very anxious. I don't think it's important to police that border. Second, to go back to the institutional history I know best: the first gap that was recognised and the first omission that was rectified at the Birmingham Centre for *Contemporary* Cultural Studies, to give it its precise title, was History. Thus, the first appointment that was made, after the initial stage, was that of Richard Johnson, a historian. That addition of a historical perspective was crucial to the development of cultural studies in Birmingham and in Britain. At a later moment, this led to the extremely interesting work in cultural history by people such as

Patrick Wright, who produced a book called *On Living in an Old Country* (1985). He'd been away in Canada for some years, and then returned to Britain, and partly because of that transcultural experience, was able to look at the country he'd come from with new eyes. So he began to write about the way in which a particular myth of British history was being produced contemporaneously: Mrs Thatcher's whole thing about the return to Victorian values, 'Britain being great' again, and so on. Here were the beginnings of an analysis that came from cultural studies and spoke of the production of history in the contemporary moment as a matter of politics. In other words, I think that a historical dimension is vital to good cultural studies work, because without it, I think one of the risks, always, is that of falling into an ahistorical perspective – in the order of Fukuyama's claims about the 'end of history' – where history is what other people used to live in, whereas 'we' have somehow now transcended it. As any good historian will tell you, that's simply what every age thinks about itself. And it's crucial that within cultural studies such an assumption is resolutely deconstructed. To do that, though, you need a historical perspective.

## Television and cinema

JVM: *Why have you chosen to concentrate on television in your own work? Is it just the biographical coincidence you mapped out earlier, or is there more at stake for you?*

DM:  No, I don't think there is much more at stake than that, in the end. I think it is partly a matter of which technological generation one is born into. I was born in 1949 and my parents got a television set in about 1954. I was five then, and television became the technology that was the most experientially transformative technology in my own biography. I was still a school student, in the 1960s, when McLuhan was first published in England. I don't think that for this generation now, television has anything like that kind of importance – for my own kids it was something they could just take for granted. At the same time, within the British media-studies world, it's ridiculous that there has been so little work on radio and so much work on television, considering the relative importance of the two media in people's lives. Television has always been treated as the most glamorous medium. It's the one that's attracted attention and status, though there's no particularly good reason for it. Certainly radio, as a medium, remains woefully under-researched to this day.

Consequently, in the work I did with Roger Silverstone and Eric Hirsch at Brunel on the household uses of information and communication technology (ICT), we actually defined the project as one in which television was only one of a set of information and communication technologies to be considered. We were interested as much in the telephone as the television, and the radio or whatever else. That is the theoretical position I'd still choose to take. The fact that the empirical cases I have taken, in my early work certainly, happen to have been about television isn't based on a principled argument that says this is the most important medium. It was much more to do with biographical, circumstantial and historical reasons that television happened to be the focus that my own early work took.

In relation to television, there's an old Walter Lippmann quote that I like very much, about how trying to find out what's going on in the world by watching television news is like trying to find out what time it is by watching the second hand on the clock – which, on the whole, is what I believe. I don't watch very much television – certainly not in order to find things out.[7] I watch football on television, and I watch comedy shows sometimes, but I never have watched a lot of television, except as a social activity, in order to be doing something pleasant at home with my family which we can all do together and talk about and so on. I don't find British television's products, on the whole, very engaging, apart from televised sports. And I may even stop watching that at home, because I've now discovered that my local pub has satellite transmission, and I've started to go to the pub to watch the football – since I actually find that much more enjoyable in the sociable atmosphere of a group of fellow sports fans watching the game.

That's precisely what I was interested in in the work that I did on family television and in the Brunel ICT study. What we were developing there was a comparative analysis of contexts of consumption, based on the perceived need to move away from the absurd idea that *all* television is is its texts. I remember years ago, when I was doing my Ph.D. in the early 1970s, I came across this piece of work by a Finnish scholar, Karl Nordenstreng who'd done this work in Finland in which he'd established that, according to a large proportion of the Finnish population, the news was one of their favourite programmes. He'd then gone round and interviewed lots of people, the day after they'd watched a particular news broadcast, asking them to recall the names and contents of the previous evening's news. He found out that, on the whole, they'd retained very little information from the news broadcasts, from which he concluded that watching television is merely a ritual activity that people engage in at certain times of the day, that it just functions to tell them when it's time to put the kids to bed – because the news has come on, etc. His conclusion was, then, that television's content is irrelevant. At the time, because I was busy with the question of ideology and power, I thought Nordenstreng was advocating an outrageous and irresponsible perspective; but, as time has gone on, I've come to see that one has to have both perspectives – on questions of ideology and power, and on questions of ritual. Because, whatever else it is, television viewing is indeed a ritual practice, which involves people coming home and switching it on, much as they put the light on. That doesn't at all mean necessarily that they're going watch it: watching the screen attentively is just one possible mode of television-viewing that some people display some of the time, in relation to some types of programme. But if we're looking for a theorisation of the practice of television-watching, there are many other modalities, and you've got to allow for all of them. Nowadays, of course, you've also got to allow for the fact that one can no longer ordinarily assume that television will only be watched in a domestic setting. Increasingly, you've got to theorise the non-domestic viewing of television: television in airport lounges, in shopping precincts, in cafés, in bars (see McCarthy 2001).

JVM: *Earlier you made the point about film and television being different for the fact that film might still have a discrete text and television doesn't. What initially they don't seem to be different in is that they both have people watch-ing it. And yet it seems surprising that in their attention to spectatorship and audiences, film and television studies have developed along such parallel but distinct lines, with barely any common ground. Where film picked up on psychoanalysis to study 'the spectator', television studies, at least the way you've been practising it, seems to have picked up on on cultural studies, focusing on 'the audience'. Do you consider this distinction to make sense, or do you see areas where the different forms of inquiry into watching audiovisual media might, or should, be made to connect?*

DM: I think the comparative study of television and film audiences is extremely interesting territory, and I'm continually bemused that so little has been done comparatively, across these media, especially since this is in an area where everything is now cross-penetrated so much. In cinema studies there is still only a tiny amount of work on the cinema audience in anything other than the abstracted psychoanalytic mode – which isn't really about the actual audience, but rather, about the implied audience that can be deduced from the text; so I regard that as a variety of textual study. There's some work that people such as Jeffery Richards and Philip Corrigan have done on the history of the cinema audience, and of the 'picture palace', and of cinema-going as a social activity. Also, Jackie Stacey and Annette Kuhn have recently done some work in relation to gender and the history of women cinema-goers that is extremely interesting. But it still puzzles me as to why so little empirical work has been done on cinema audiences. I don't understand why it's not done, except for really banal institutional reasons, which is that film studies has always legitimated itself by reference to English, to a mode of expertise, that is, which develops through the study of the text. It's only in the very recent period that you've had any attention to the reader within English studies, but again it's not really focused on the actual reader on most occasions, apart from in exceptional cases such as Janice Radway's work. On the whole, until very recently, it's been studies of the implied reader who might be deduced from the text.

Just as I've been arguing that television studies needs to take into account the various possible contexts of consumption, I think it makes a difference whether you see a given film in an art-house theatre or in a multiplex. Indeed, the whole issue of multiplex cinemas is fascinating. At a time when the cinema audience in Britain was heading rapidly downwards, the multiplexes were part of what turned that situation round, in the late 1980s, by constructing a different and more attractive kind of social experience for going to the cinema. I'm bemused that we've got a discipline of film studies in this country, and while a major development such as the development of multiplexes takes place, not one study that I'm aware of addresses the very salient question of what going to a multiplex is about. The only exception is the work that's being done in commerical market research, where you can certainly find extremely interesting studies but they, unfortunately, are very expensive to get at! So I think the 'multiplex' question is one of the most glaring absences in film/cinema studies and I really cannot understand why there isn't comparative audience work going on across the fields of film/cinema and television studies.[8]

## Discourse, ideology and the shades of Marxism

JVM: *Occasionally in cultural studies texts, one gets the impression that the term 'ideology' has been displaced by the term 'discourse'. What is your opinion on this development?*

DM: I think you're right to say that the two terms have been substituted. I'm personally never quite sure what it means when people say 'discourse'. At a certain moment, what they meant was 'Foucault rather than Althusser'. They meant practices as well as ideas, and that was, it seemed to me, a potentially useful shift. But if you asked me when did I last hear anybody use the word 'ideology', we're looking quite a long way back. And yet, I don't remember an articulate rationale for why we should stop using it. The word 'discourse' simply became the 'in' term and was substituted for it.

Of course, one doesn't use words necessarily because of what one thinks they mean oneself. One has to think about what they will mean to other people. Thus, if you think that using the word 'ideology' will inevitably bring up unwanted connotations about 'false consciousness' or something for your readers/listeners, then maybe that's a good reason to stop using it. But I don't see that there's been some big theoretical shift which has solved all the philosophical problems that go along with the concept of ideology. Instead, I see a lot of people nowadays talking about discourse analysis in Britain as though it was invented last Tuesday. That I find particularly troubling, since there are many previous forms of discourse analysis. There was a form developed by two scholars in the English department at Birmingham called Sinclair and Coulthard, which was based on classroom discourse, which was very influential in the mid-1970s. Then there was Michel Pêcheux's notion of discourse analysis, which I found very helpful, at another moment. Nowadays there are people such as Michael Billig, who work with an interesting social-psychological notion of discourse. As I understand it, the motivation for your question is the issue of how people have, in effect, attempted to construct a termi-nological solution to a theoretical problem. It's as though, if we just substituted the word 'discourse' for the word 'ideology' we could some-how solve the intellectual, theoretical and philosophical problems that pertain to the word 'ideology'. And I don't think that we have!

JVM: *The question was also meant to address the legacies of Marxism in cultural studies? How do you see cultural studies dealing with Marxism today?*

DM: Well, certainly in Britain there's still a pretty heavily entrenched political economy of the media with a Marxist inflection, as represented by people such as Nicholas Garnham or Graham Murdock. Such people form a significant presence in the field and, interestingly, they no longer situate themselves so far outside of cultural studies as they used to. Then there are a lot of people within cultural studies who have got, as you say, a Marxist past, or a Marxist unconscious. For my part, I think it's very important to defend those forms or elements of a Marxist perspective which are still pertinent. To take just one example: if you take debates about race or about gender around the question of essentialism, which has so often been a big issue in cultural studies in recent years, it seems to me a terrible mistake if you conduct those debates in ignorance of Lukács. Again and again, I encounter positions in debates about gender or race which are in fact very much in parallel with Lukács' position on the proletariat as the privileged vantage point of truth, compared to perspectives of other collectivities or other dimensions of analysis. As a result, people often seem not to realise that, even if they are talking about gender or race, as opposed to class, they're taking a philosophical position which is equivalent to earlier forms of essentialist Marxism, which in turn have very severe problems attached to them, about who is best placed to see the truth of a situation and what kind of epistemological 'guarantees' can or cannot be given to which collectivities.

To address the historical issue another way, let me tell you a little story. The first time I went to Berlin, it was just after the wall came down in 1989, and I was taken from the airport directly to a demonstration in East Berlin, where a group of people were defending the statues of the Great Marxists which were being taken down. The argument of the protestors was, of course, that one doesn't deal with history by just obliterating it. I think the same thing applies to Marxism within cultural studies. Just knocking all the monuments down and putting them in the 'park of dead statues' won't help . . . they're going to still be around and it'd be better to leave them standing there and deal with them properly, or else they'll return to haunt us in a whole other way. That goes for supposedly 'dead' theories, such as Marxism, just as much as it does for 'dead statues' – that's why Derrida's point about what he calls 'hauntology' is so important.

## Transitional spaces

JVM: *Let's turn to your text 'Notes from the Sitting Room' (1990). What is the status of the sitting room in your text? It seems like it's analysed mainly in its relational function to the global and less as an actual topographical and social site with internal distinctions.*

DM: That text, and the attention paid there to 'the sitting room' is very much a turning point in the trajectory of my work over a long period. In the 1970s I started off with a set of very abstract questions about politics, power and their coverage in prestigious or 'serious' media, such as news programmes. Then I went on to work on *Nationwide*, where we started looking at lower grade, more popular and less prestigious texts. From there, I moved on to the study of the consumption of *Nationwide* by different kinds of groups. But I was still dealing with fairly artificial contexts of consumption. And then, to make that deficiency good, I began to look at the consumption of television in the home; later on, that perspective was broadened, to look at the whole field of the household uses of ICT, rather than focusing on television alone.

This was the point where anthropology came into the picture for me, particularly regarding the question of rituals. Arjun Appadurai's work on *The Social Life of Things* became tremendously important to me. He traces the trajectories of 'sacred' objects, as they move in and out of a commodity mode, asking who can buy them and who can have access to them. Of course, traditionally in anthropology, this all refers only to the question of 'primitive' societies a long way away. But in the introduction, he beautifully demonstrates how you can transpose such questions back into our own context. In the Brunel study, we were dealing with a family where there was a teenage boy who referred to his Walkman as his 'life-support system', insisting that he couldn't leave the house without it. Now, as I recall, he had a slight speech impediment, whereby the letters 'w' and 'r' become muddled up when he talked; as a result, it had become a family joke to say that the boy had gone in his 'womb' rather than his room. The boy was in his 'womb' with his 'life-support system'. And the boy himself used this joke! In analysing such instances, the anthropological perspectives that I was introduced to around that time became indispensable in understanding the symbolic dimensions of different communications technologies.[9]

Do you know Ondina Leal's work on the television set in Brazil? There's a wonderful piece, where she talks about what people have on the top of their television set, arguing that this tends to be the place for the sacred emblems of the family: the sacred momento that was brought back from the honeymoon, the photographs of the family members at the classic anthropological moments of birth, marriage, graduation, etc. From her perspective, you can then begin to think about the extent to which the television set as an object functions in this symbolic way. In an art discourse, it's like the sort of stuff that Nam Jun Paik has been doing for years, deconstructing television sets and making us look at them in new ways.[10] I don't think that I would ever have got to see any of that, if I hadn't come across this very vibrant anthropological discourse which had nothing to do with cultural studies per se, but which actually gave us a whole other way of thinking about technologies.

As a result, I began to become very concerned with this notion of the media as having a double function – on the one hand, connecting the public to the private, and by the same token, transgressing the sacred boundary around the home. I've been working on a book called *Home Territories* (Morley 2000), which tries to bring these things together: notions of home and homeland, both at the micro and macro level; questions about the 'foreign' – inquiring into what is foreign and to whom, where the foreign is, where it starts, what it means. This, too, is very much informed by anthropological perspectives on the sacredness of different kinds of spaces, and it works with these questions about boundary and the role of different kinds of communications technologies in connecting different spaces, and by the same token transgressing, problematically, various different kinds of boundaries.

In this double trajectory of my work on the domestic media and their uses and on the boundaries that are created (and ruptured) by such practices, the 'sitting room' became a place which you could begin to think of both as the micro-destiny of that trajectory and as a way 'back up' into the broader trajectory of the macro-work that I've done with Kevin Robins, where we talk about the boundaries around the nation, the boundaries around Europe and about diasporic communities. In this context, the analysis of the sitting room became a site which I was very much committed to defending. Although it seems absurd now, when I began to work on family television, I had people denounce me for 'abandoning politics' in favour of the allegedly unpolitical domestic sphere – as if one could understand these macro questions about the construction of the nation as an imagined community, other than through an analysis of how all that works out in the domestic micro-space. For me, the sitting room is a way of articulating that moment of connection between the micro and the macro, the family, the household, the nation, the community, and the role of the different mediated networks passing through it.

## The question of 'experience'

JVM: *Can you say something about the way you deal with the category of experience? In the kinds of televisual environments that you analyse, does it still make sense to distinguish between unmediated forms of experience and some kind of more mediated experience – mediated, that is, through media and communications technologies on a global scale?*

DM: Yes, absolutely. Just consider the difference between watching football on television, and actually going to a football ground, or between speaking to me on the telephone and conducting the interview here in this room. Those are very different experiences. We discussed the possibility that technologically, we *could* have done this interview without you coming here: by you sending me a tape with your questions on it and me dictating my answers onto the tape. Well, you took the decision to come and do it this way for very good reasons, because you're well aware that it's a very different experience to meet and interact in person. The idea that somehow there isn't any longer a distinction between mediated and non-mediated experience is absurd, to my mind

JVM: *In your article, you certainly come close to blurring the boundaries between the two when you suggest that 'experience becomes unified beyond localities and fragmented within them', or that it's easier to get in touch with people beyond one's locality than by knocking on your neighbour's door.*

DM: OK, but again it's a strategic and polemical question. It seemed very important in 1990, when that 'sitting room' piece was written, to establish those new ways of thinking about our senses of diasporic community or whatever. That no longer seems to me to need establishing, in most of the contexts in which I operate. What I'm busy doing now, I suppose, in a different intellectual context, is to insist on the very material dimensions of geographical analysis. In Michael Ondaatje's the book *The English Patient*, the main character, who is obsessed with the original anthropologist-geographer Herodotus, has a line about 'the sadness of geography'. Kevin Robins and I have been arguing for some time now that geography does indeed matter – often as a 'sadly' limiting factor. I've been very much influenced by work in cultural geography over the past few years: if, in the late 1980s, I learnt most from the discipline of anthropology, in the 1990s it was from cultural geography.

Sure, technologies are making enormous differences. In 'Notes from the Sitting Room', I wanted to argue very hard for how much difference they made in the production of identity and of different senses of connectedness, of community, of interaction, all of which transcend the physically contiguous. Now, having done that, I want to deal with what's happened since, where people have gone rushing into that debate, as if now that we're on e-mail, we're all equally connected to each other. But as Chomsky (rightly) never tires of saying, most people haven't even made a telephone call yet in their lives, let alone become citizens of cyberspace! Such simple statistics become particularly important in a context in which you've got a whole raft of politicians celebrating this wildly optimistic discourse about cyberspace and how new technologies will mean that we're going to transcend everything. An Internet feed in every school, and the problem's solved! I don't think so.

The differential geography of postmodernity surely still plays an important role, everywhere – just as it did in your experience as an interviewer today, having come from a city in another country to be here this morning, when you'll be back there this evening. We've communicated by e-mail, and we're both symbolically and physically very mobile – which is a key asset in the type of work that we do. My question, these days, is increasingly to do with who has got what forms of access both to these modes of symbolic and to actual forms of physical mobility and transport? This goes back to very material questions about things such as the question of who's got cars? Who's got access to both the Internet and physical transport? Who feels safe about walking along which streets at night? It may be that it's a different moment in the debate, but I suppose if I was rewriting 'Notes from the Sitting Room' now, I'd be pushing a little harder at maintaining a perspective on certain aspects of the 'sadness of geography' which I do think, in the end, are neither transcendable nor remediable by technology.

JVM: *Thank you very much for talking with us.*

## Notes

1. On the subsequent development of 'New Media/Medium Theory' in the UK and elsewhere, see Chapter 8.
2. On Derrida, see Morley 1997.
3. Hence, the Mulla Nasruddin quote at the beginning of this section.
4. See Chapter 6 for more details of the issues surrounding the Tokyo cultural studies conference.
5. See Chapter 1 for my discussion of recent attacks on cultural studies in the UK.
6. In the context of these issues about 'learning to be interdisciplinary', in her Isaiah Berlin Lecture at the British Academy in December 2005 on the question of 'Useful Knowledge', the anthropologist Marilyn Strathearn raised some serious issues in her critique of contemporary tendencies towards the 'idolisation' of interdisciplinarity as always and necessarily a 'tick-box' Good Thing. As she observed, the creation of a universal intellectual context of interdisciplinarity would risk the dangers of an arid monoculture with no resort to the resource of 'serious intellectual difference' provided by separate intellectual disciplines (not least, in the variable constitution of their objects of study).
7. For my extended discussion of television news viewing, see Morley 1998.
8. Since the date of this interview, the situation in this respect has changed considerably and important work by Jancovich et al., Stokes (ed.) and Stokes and Maltby (eds) has now appeared – see bibliography below.
9. See Chapter 10 on symblism and technology.
10. For a further discussion of Leal's work, see Chapter 10; for more on Nam June Paik, see Chapter 9.

## Bibliography

Brunsdon, Charlotte (1989) 'Text and Audience'. In E. Seiter, H. Borchers, G. Kreutzner and E.-M. Warth (eds) *Remote Control*, London: Routledge.
—— (1996) 'A Thief in the Night: Stories of Feminism in the 1970's at CCCS'. In David Morley and Kuan-Hsing Chen (eds) *Stuart Hall: Critical Dialogues in Cultural Studies*, London and New York: Routledge.
Burgelin, Olivier (1972) 'Structural Analysis of Communications'. In D. McQuail (ed.) *Sociology of Mass Communications*, Harmondsworth: Penguin.

Ignatieff, Michael (1994) *Blood and Belonging: Journeys into the New Nationalism*, London: Vintage Books.

Jancovich, Mark et al (2003) *The Place of the Audience: Cultural Geographies of Film Consumption*, London, British Film Institute.

Kumar, Krishan (1979) 'Hoding the Middle Ground'. In J. Curran et al. (eds) *Mass Communication and Society*, London: Arnold.

Leal, Ondina (1990) 'Popular Taste and Erudite Repertoire: The Place and Space of Television in Brazil', *Cultural Studies* 4 (1).

McCarthy, Anna ( 2001) *Ambient Television*, Durham, NC: Duke University Press.

Massey, Doreen (1994) *Space, Place and Gender*, Cambridge: Polity Press.

Morgan, Michael (1989) 'Television and Democracy'. In I. Angus and S. Jhally (eds) *Cultural Politics in Contemporary America*, London: Routledge.

Morley, David (1997) 'Theoretical Orthodoxies'. In M. Ferguson and P. Golding (eds) *Cultural Studies in Question*, London: Sage.

—— (1998) 'Finding Out about the World from Television News'. In J Griprud (ed.) *Television and Common Knowledge*, London: Routledge.

—— (2000) *Home Territories*, London: Routledge.

Morley, David and Chen, Kuan-Hsing (eds) (1996) *Stuart Hall: Critical Dialogues in Cultural Studies*, London: Routledge.

Morley, David and Robins, Kevin (1995) *Spaces of Identity*, London: Routledge.

—— (eds) (2001) *British Cultural Studies*, Oxford: Oxford University Press.

Nordenstreng, Karl (1972) 'Policy for News Transmission'. In D. McQuail (ed.) *Sociology of Mass Communication*, Harmondsworth: Penguin.

Robins, Kevin (1997) 'The New Communications Geography and the Politics of Optimism', *Soundings*, 5: 191–202.

Seiter, Ellen et al. (eds) (1989) *Remote Control*, London: Routledge.

Stokes, Melvyn (ed.) (2000) *Hollywood Spectatorship*, London: British Film Institute.

Stokes, Melvyn and Maltby, Richard (eds) (1999) *Identifying Hollywoood's Audience*, London: British Film Institute.

Storey, John (1996) *Cultural Studies and the Study of Popular Culture: Theories and Methods*, Athens, Ga.: University of Georgia Press.

Wright, Patrick (1985) *On Living in an Old Country*, London: Verso Books.

# Part II

# Methodological matters

Interdisciplinary approaches

*Figure 1* Susan Hiller, *From the Freud Museum*. © Susan Hiller. Reproduced by courtesy of Timothy Taylor Gallery, London.

# 3 Methodological problems and research practices

## Opening up the 'black box'

Interview by Claudio Flores, Universidad Autonoma de Barcelona, October, 2000

Claudio Flores: *What are your main interests in the field of methodology, in media and cultural studies?*

David Morley: Well, the problem with that question is that actually, I'm not very interested in questions of methodology as such – I regard them pretty much as pragmatic questions, and I always have. For me, research is always a question of what you can do, in the circumstances you face, with the resources available, which is most likely to get you something like the kind of data that you want. You're never going to get exactly what you want. There's never going to be some scientific (or perhaps, better 'magical') methodology that we will invent one day, through which we will know the world perfectly . . . You just do things that you think might work and you try things out. I don't think that discussions about methodology conducted in terms like 'this method is good/this method is bad' are of much interest.

I do retain little bits of undersanding of economics, from my initial schooling in that discipline, and one of the most interesting concepts in economics is that of 'opportunity cost' – that which you must forgo when you make any particular choice. It's both a very simple matter and a very consequential one. To put it in colloquial terms, by coming here today and talking to me this morning, you forgo the opportunity to read in the library, and I can't get on with my teaching preparation for later today – or whatever. Methodological choices also have opportunity costs. Take the methodology of construction work. In work of that type, a hammer is good for some things and a screwdriver is good for others, but to imagine that only hammers are good, in themselves, is going to get you in a lot of trouble if you're trying to fix something to a wall, because there are occasions when you'd be better off with a screwdriver and some rawl-plugs, depending on what kind of a wall it is.

Although my academic work, as published in cultural studies, has principally been qualitative interviews and ethnography, I've actually done a lot of other types of work, and I know that for some things, statistics are better than anything else. In this respect, I entirely support the arguments made by people such as Justin Lewis and Darnell Hunt in favour of the use of quantitative methods, where appropriate, in cultural studies.[1] I spent a large part of the 1980s doing market research, so I've done quite a lot of statistical surveys, as well as a lot of qualitative focus groups, for social and political projects, as well as for commercial companies. There's an English phrase that says you should choose 'horses for courses': if you're betting on horse racing, it's important to know if the ground is muddy or dry, because some horses go better in the mud, some when it's dry, etc. In the same sense, depending on the problem, a certain kind of methodology will be more appropriate. Which, I can see, is a pretty uninteresting answer, from a theoretical point of view, but that is what I think.

CF:   *So does that mean that you agree with the postmodern / post-structuralist position which is very fashionable in cultural studies these days, which says that every methodological choice is OK, because it's just a personal decision — so, even a strategy of doing random interviews, as you wander through the city is fine, if that's what you want to do?*

DM: No — I wouldn't position myself in that camp at all! My view is that while I think that all methodologies are OK for some circumstances, I don't think that all methodologies are as good as each other for addressing a particular problem. For some purposes, wandering through the city and talking to people at random is fine as a technique (see situationist strategies of *détournement* which have been 'revamped' contemporaneously by writers such as Ian Sinclair in his book *London Orbital*, for example). For other purposes, that's a useless approach, and you'd be much better off with a standard statistical package and a perfectly straightforward sociological procedure.

I don't buy into the kind of relativism that says that you can equally well do just anything. What I'm saying is that in any situation, you're going to have to make a choice. There will be various different methods you could adopt, and there is probably one which is better than others for the kind of job you are trying to do. You'll never get it perfect, but there are better and worse choices that you might make. If I had tried to do the work that I did in *Family Television* by using statistical surveys, I would have got nowhere – because I was examining micro-practices that are too subtly differentiated to be readily grasped by statistics. The point, of course, also applies the other way round: there are certain kinds of things that you can only do with statistics. So my relativism is only a relativism of principle, which recognises that all methodologies have their virtues. It's not a relativism that says that in any particular circumstance you can do what you like. Some choices you might make, in any situation, could be very stupid.

## The perfect tense of methodological choice

CF: *When you read academic accounts of the methodologies that people chose for their research projects, it aways seems so very clear – at least to someone relatively new to the field – they always seem to say that there was some kind of inevitability about their choices, as if there was only ever one rational way that they could ever have chosen to do their research: the accounts of methodological choices always seem very 'definitive'.*

DM: Oh yes, but there's also often a very strong – and important – 'post-hoc', or retrospective dimension to those accounts. When you talk to people who've done research, they often feel forced into positions in which, in retrospect, they have to be able to give you a very confident account of what they were doing, whereas, if you'd been there at the time, they were probably rather less sure of themselves and were making quite a lot of incidental choices that only retrospectively acquire the gloss of being derived from clear methodological principles.

Apart from anything else, one of the things that's often disavowed is the fact that there's often a considerable quantity of the unforeseen – of surprises – in any research project.[2] Moreover, some anxieties that you might have about your research can turn out to be completely unfounded. Take the example of the Brunel project on the 'Household Uses of Information and Communication Technologies'. One of our big anxieties there was an ethical one, about the fact that we were going to be invading the privacy of the households we were investigating. In doing so, we knew we were also likely to be discovering all kinds of intimate things about their lives which, as it turned out, many people were (frighteningly!) happy to talk to us about. We were initially very worried about whether they'd end up feeling that we'd exploited them in some way (see below, for the particular point at which the issue of privacy and power did come up in the project). However, at the end, what came up again and again was that these people were actually very grateful for us having been there, because we'd taken their lives seriously and they'd had someone to talk to in a way they'd never had before, about how they lived, and about how they took decisions as a family and why they do things in certain ways. They'd actually found that very interesting and very useful to them. Now maybe that was just a question of egotism – that they were flattered to have so much attention paid to them. But it seemed to us that they also got something important out of it themselves – which wasn't something we'd anticipated. We'd had a whole set of plans about how we could 'bribe' them (which we did) in exchange for giving us their time, with gift vouchers and so on. But in fact, it actually it turned out to be much more of a two-way trade than we'd ever imagined it would be.

## Ethics, choices and justifications

CF:  *What about the relationship of methodology and ethics in research, more generally?*

DM:  Well, questions of methodology and of ethics are often intertwined, perhaps particularly so in the case of qualitative research. Now, in so far as qualitative methodology – and especially ethnography – involves the researcher's presence as a person, I'm not actually that sure 'methodology' is the right word at all. I think 'behaviour' might be the more important word. I think it's much more important how you behave as a person, at a human level, when you go into someone's house, than what fancy methodology you've got in your briefcase. The most important thing is the way you treat them and their space, what attitude you take towards them, whether you're patronising, whether you're straightforward, whether they feel you're honest with them, or that you're trying to exploit them, whether you're prepared to expose something of your own life to them, as much as you're getting them to expose their lives to you. Fundamentally, the question is whether your respondents feel that you are acting in good faith and that you are engaging in a reciprocal, rather than an exploitative, or 'extractive' relationship with them – and you don't need a Ph.D. in order to be able to tell when someone is trying to rip you off.[3] I actually think that how you behave and what attitude you take towards your respondents, and whether they think you are a decent person, make more difference than any methodological theory that you might espouse. You could have the best theoretical methodology in the world, but if you walk into someone's house and behave like a prat, you're going to get nowhere.

CF:  *But surely, there's still the important issue of what theories you use to take – and justify – methodological choices in your research?*

DM:  Well, yes, of course, but the problem here is that if I look back on my own research practice – and that of other people in the field whose work I know well – I don't think that the point at which you consciously think 'I am taking a methodological choice' is necessarily the most important moment. In my experience that's often, in fact, a relatively trivial element in a more complex mix of factors in play in the research situation. I think the important influences on research design are often much vaguer than that and probably not very much in the conscious mind.

Let me give you one example from the *Nationwide* project. There's an important moment there where I was showing this *Nationwide* video to a group of predominantly young, black working-class students in inner-city London. The programme had been banging on about what 'ordinary people' think and do and about how the programme's viewpoint represented the 'ordinary people' of Britain. But, in fact, what the programme was showing was very much a white, middle-class lifestyle – where people have houses with gardens, etc. For these young black students, who lived mainly in flats in tower blocks, the idea of an 'ordinary home' simply did not have the meaning which it was being given in the programme. An 'ordinary home' for them was a small, cramped place in a tower block. The last thing it's got is a garden. And so they actually just disengaged from the programme completely and they rejected the notion that what was being shown on the screen had any connection to their sense of what 'ordinary' life was.

Now the moment in the group discussion that revealed all that occurred in a seemingly inconsequential verbal 'aside' that one of them made to another. It wasn't a clearly articulated statement that was made explicitly. If I hadn't been familiar with Voloshinov's notion of the 'multiaccentuality of the sign', through my engagement with socio-linguistics, I couldn't have possibly have been sensitive to what happened in that moment and I couldn't have made the analysis I did about the contextual meaning of the way the word 'ordinary' was used in the programme. So, in that case, what seems like a methodological choice, to do with a particular analytical procedure, involving focusing on the words that people use in the interview, rather than simply the content of what they say, in fact had an extremely long and complex theoretical derivation. It wasn't really a methodological choice, it was more like a theoretically driven sensitivity. To that extent, I'm not sure how helpful it is to separate out questions of methodology.

CF:  *To go back to what you were saying earlier, about the 'post-hoc' construction of methodological rationales, to what extent do you think that their main function is a kind of defensive one, rather than a genuinely explanatory one?*

DM:  Exactly – especially if you think about it in Foucauldian terms, as a field in which there is a continual struggle for the authentication of knowledge. Of course, in that context, it's very dangerous if you don't have a big methodological stick to hand with which to beat off critics. You need to have it in case someone attacks you, but it's not necessarily true that the theory, or methodology, in the abstract, really played such a big part in the actual construction of your work – rather than what I'd call a theoretically informed, practical sensibility.

To me it's the concrete things – the material things – that interest me most of all. Let me give you one example of what I mean by this. The most useful discussion I've ever had with a colleague about methodology was to do with how you analyse interview transcripts. As it turned out, the key to this person's method of data analysis was that, in the room where he worked, he had these architect's drawing boards – the ones that stand at an angle to the wall, at chest height. He had a bank of these drawing boards all the way along the wall of his room, so if he had a thirty-page transcript, he could lay it all out, end to end and he could walk up and down alongside it with his coloured pens, marking it up and coding it. That's always been my way of working on transcripts as well – using a set of child's coloured pens to 'code' them – but I've never had a set of those drawing boards, I've always had to do it on the floor. Of course, that way, after a while, you get a sore back, whereas with the drawing boards, you can make yourself more comfortable when you're doing it, so you can go on doing it for much longer and thus be more thorough and systematic.

Do you know what Matisse says about painting? He says 'the first thing you need to understand a painting is a chair'. And it's like that with the data: the first thing you need to understand your data is a comfortable position from which to examine it, whether that's from a chair or spread out where you can best see it all, on the floor, or walking along a room where you've got your data laid out conveniently on drawing boards at eye level. Now that's what I mean by a good approach to data analysis. I don't mean some highly articulated set of theories, I mean an intelligent decision about how to get yourself into a position where you can, literally, see all of your data – the whole interview – and you can work on it in comfort for as long as it takes, until you see the important patterns within it – which bits fit together in which ways – and that can take a very long time. That choice, to install those drawing boards so as to lay your transcripts out in full visibility, is what I'd call an intelligent methodology of data analysis, not some kind of abstract theory. I'm very interested in *that* dimension of methodology – literally, treating it as an embodied form of labour.

CF:　*What about computerised forms of data analysis?*

DM:　I'm still not entirely convinced that with qualitative data, a computer can do what I want better than I can do it myself. In fact, given the choice, if was going to do another empirical project and I had a choice between a fancy piece of software or a separate room in which I could store my data and lay it out on a bank of those drawing boards, I'd definitely take the second option.

## Research as a form of labour

CF:　*So your redefinition of data analysis focuses on it as a form of labour in 'real time' and gives emphasis to how very long that kind of work takes.*

DM:　Well, for me, the whole point with the kind of qualitative data that I mainly work with is that you just need to read it again and again and again. That's also the point with transcription. If I'm teaching a course on methodology, one of the things I teach students is always be sure to transcribe the *whole* interview, including all the bits that you think, at first, are really boring and pointless, because it often turns out that those are where the key stuff is buried. I can remember, at the beginning of doing this kind of work, sometimes taking a 'shortcut' by listening to the tape, making a note of the 'good' bits and only transcribing them. And then I'd find that I'd missed crucial stuff. In a similar vein, Ann Gray, in relation to her research on the domestic uses of the early video recorders, talks about worrying that her respondents were going 'off the point' in their contextualising stories, and then later realising that, of course, those bits were crucial to making sense of what they said about the research topic in hand.[4]

You could say, in a sense, that it's a bit like the protocol in statistical procedure that you must analyse the *whole* corpus of data and not leave any out – because any system of coding that ends up with a large percentage of stuff in the 'left-over' box isn't working well.[5] I am talking about something comparable here; it's not a matter of transcribing all the data just for the sake of completion, but because the data that at first sight looks uninteresting is often, in the end, the most revealing – as that is where the most deeply embedded forms of common-sensical discourse and procedure are often revealed. Because I'm interested in questions of hegemony and cultural power, I'm particularly interested in the ever-changing forms of common sense (and its limits) which is, of course, precisely that which, on the whole, doesn't need to be explicitly said. I still believe, with Pêcheux, that 'the unsaid is always more important than the said'. And so, to go back to your earlier question about computerised analysis, I don't know what kind of computer can deal with that kind of issue – about the unsaid, or about significant silences or absences.

CF:   *When it comes to data analysis, what kids of conceptual tools do you use? How do you construct the categories you're going to use in the analysis? In* Nationwide *and* Family Television, *how did you construct your coding categories – and to what extent did you do that in advance?*

DM:   Well, the thing is, as I said before, what you plan for, in advance, going into a project, doesn't always work out quite as you'd expected. For example, when I set up the 'Family Television' project, I thought I was going to be doing a project principally about class differences in television-viewing practices. I wasn't originally intending to focus on gender, and the reason that the analysis in that book ended up focusing on that issue was because that is what emerged from the data. I don't mean to sound like some kind of simple-minded empiricist, but if I'm honest, what I did was that I sat there, looking at the transcripts, again and again, thinking about what categories would be most useful. I tried not to look at it with a predetermined set of categories. I simply read through the transcripts over and over again, with my system of coloured pens, trying to link things together and see what fitted with what, and then, when I had, for instance, a lot of orange marks, I would read all the bits on the transcripts marked in orange and think 'Well, what's that all about?'. I'd obviously thought the material was the 'same' in some way, which is why I'd coded it with the same colour, but the question then is 'What constitutes its "sameness"?' Of what are these things an instance? Obviously, the colours are incidental – they're just a heuristic device – like a metaphor perhaps – for differentiating one 'type' of thing from another, before I can name the typology. And then I'd start trying to name the categories. Very often, the first time you try to name a category, it doesn't work, so you rename it, or you realise that you need to merge two categories into one or split them in a different way. It's quite a banal procedure. But, in the end, the categories that I use are the ones that seem to me to produce the most efficient and meaningful way of dividing up the data (on the philosophical principle of 'Occam's Razor': never using a more complex system than is justified by the data and always choosing the simplest possible cate-gorisation unless there is a good reason to the contrary). I'm quite aware that those are ultimately subjective judgements that I have to make on the basis of my professional competence (though I could point to their 'justification' in my data). They are, inevitably, to twist Geertz's phrase, the categoriser's categories, for which I have to take responsibility.

CF: *So it seems a very complex, or complicated thing, this question of categorisation?*

DM: It's complex in one way and at another level, it's very simple. It's mainly just hard work. One of the things that's struck me as I've followed the work of people in this field, over the years, is that what distinguishes many of the most eminent researchers is not just that they're very clever but that they also have a capacity for sheer hard graft. You just have to be prepared to go on doing this kind of work on a project, examining the data for a long time and thinking very hard about it.

Many people would happily agree that doing research is a form of 'intellectual labour', but they tend to put the emphasis on the first word, '*intellectual* labour', whereas I would put the emphasis on the second word, 'intellectual *labour*', and I understand research, in the first place, as an embodied, material labour process. That is much more what it is actually about. I don't think there are any short cuts. You just do it for as long as it takes to do it, and having a set of fancy methodological ideas, frankly, isn't necessarily going to help you very much, because, as I said before, often one of their main functions, at least as people present them in their research reports or publications, is actually retrospective – as a way of legitimating the data they've produced. I'm evidently, but not only, speaking autobiographically here, about my own experience of doing and publishing research. To my certain knowledge, people often give accounts of the methodologies of their projects which sound far more certain than they actually were when they were doing the research!

The actual labour process of research practice is a bit like a 'black box' that very rarely gets opened up – as if everyone is scared to admit how very uncertain the process of research actually is and how much improvisation is always involved in it. I think that the professional pressures on researchers to present their methodology in a very sanitised and clinical way – so as to guarantee its 'scientificity' – does new scholars coming into the field no favours. It actually mystifies the research process and makes it seem even more daunting than it need be if people are given the impression that all the researchers of the past knew exactly what they were doing before they started – because it's not true, they didn't! And if they did, then they probably produced rather uninteresting work, in which they succeeded only in reconfirming the prejudices they already had when they began their projects.

To come at the point about who can best understand, or reveal things – and why – from an oblique angle, the ethnographic filmmaker Jean Rouch says of the May 1968 riots in Paris that the only good book about them is that by the Chief of the Paris Police who, precisely because he was so thoroughly surprised – and confused – by them, offers in Rouch's view the most useful account of what happened. Besides, as I said, pure chance also plays a role in research – a fact that is not often recognised. I very much like Rouch's approach to these issues, especially when he says at one point that 'in respect of method, I love the fact of not knowing where we are heading'. So he talks somewhere about those 'unpredictable moments in the field – in which everything is decided, in which all can fall apart – or all can succeed – and which often depends on a single look, a single gesture, a single word'. In referring to the famous story of how Rouch invented the method of hand-held camera use when he broke, lost or abandoned his tripod while filming in West Africa (depending on which story you believe), Paul Stoller describes Rouch's improvisational way of working as the '*Pourquoi-pas?*' method (that being also the name of the ship on which Rouch's father had explored Antartica).[6]

## Ethical responsibilities

CF:　*I see that, but for the moment, let's go back to what you said before: what about the ethical responsibility that the researcher has towards the subjects of their research. That seems to me a very complex issue – how do you resolve that?*

DM:　I think that's an important ethical dimension of the work. It is very difficult, and it's particularly revealing when you work with respondents with different degrees of power. For instance, in the Brunel Household Uses of Information and Communication Technologies project, we had all the usual conventions of reassuring everyone we studied that their names would be changed and that they wouldn't be individually recognisable in the published form of the work, as they'd be given pseudonyms . Nobody complained about that, until we began to interview people of a higher social class. Then we came to interview one family where the couple were both senior civil servants; one of them was disabled and, as far as I recall, they had three daughters. Obviously the whole point about ethnographic work is that you're trying to present the data in its natural context, so you want to give the reader as much of a sense of the background of these people's lives, so the reader can understand where what they say is coming from. Anyway, at a certain stage in the project, the man in this couple said to us 'You must be joking! Yes, you might change my name, but there are only three other civil servants at my level who are disabled, and none of the others live in this particular area of north-west London, and they certainly don't all have three daughters. The fact that you are offering not to put our actual names in is irrelevant. Some people will still be able to work out that it's us you're talking about!' And at that point, the family declined to take any further part in the study. Now, nobody else from the lower-class groups, all of whom could have legitimately made the same argument, had actually thought of themselves as the kind of person who had the *right* to confront us, as researchers, in that way. It was very interesting that it was only at that level of the social scale, where we were dealing with people who had a considerable degree of cultural power and self-confidence, that our respondents actually raised that issue.[7]

It is a very difficult issue, because if you decontextualise and anonymise the data too much, in order to preserve your respondents' privacy, the better it is for your respondents, but the worse for your reader. Conversely, the more you fill in the context, the better for your reader and the worse for your respondents' privacy, because they have opposite interests – so the best you can do is to try to steer a course between those opposite dangers. At that point, there is a very delicate balance, because you are trying to do things that are fundamentally in contradiction with each other. And the question is 'How you are going to deal with that balance?' You're never going to be able to resolve it perfectly, because it is a fundamental contradiction. The reader of your work and the respondents in your study do have fundamentally different and opposed interests, and you've got to be honest in facing up to that. Hiding behind excuses like 'Oh well, don't worry, there won't be many copies of the book, so not many people will ever see it' is not an adequate answer.

## Pragmatic choices

CF: *If I understand you, one of the themes among the things you're saying is that the key thing is a kind of balance between creativity and economy in the research process, where you're always having to make choices within the parameters set by institutional frameworks and material issues such as the availability of resources – is that right?*

DM: One always has to be pragmatic about resources, because they're scarce by definition – that's another premise that I still take from my training in economics. I'm also very influenced by Bertolt Brecht's saying that 'we're not trying to build the perfect wall, we're trying to build the best wall that can be built in the circumstances and with the resources available'. I do get suspicious about debates concerning methodology which seem to have an almost religious dimension to them, where it's presented as a matter of how, if you follow certain rules, then you will be among those who are 'saved', and if you go any other way, you risk damnation. I'm not very sympathetic to those kind of absolutist notions: you just have to do the best you can in the circumstances you face, with the time and resources you've got.

I'm not sure about 'creativity' either; it might be something more to do with 'sensitivity'. Certainly, in qualitative research, it's rather as if you've got to be a 360-degree calculating machine, on several different dimensions. You have to be thinking simultaneously about a whole variety of questions, such as 'What kind of room am I in?', 'How am I getting along with this person?', 'What kind of tone of voice am I getting back from them?', 'How does that fit with the ideas I came with?' In that context, you've got to transform yourself into a sensitive data-gathering instrument. You've also got to use your peripheral vision – and then you still come out and afterwards and think 'Damn! What was that picture on the wall above my interviewee's head?' You perhaps never quite took it in, but you realise afterwards that there was something interesting about it and you have to try and reconstruct it from memory . . . That might seem like only 'background' to what you're trying to find out about, but again and again, in my experience, that 'contextual' data turns out to be incredibly significant, in thinking about how you understand what someone has said to you.

## Particularity, abstraction and power

CF:   *What's your position on recent debates about whether ethnography is somehow 'better' than all other approaches, on political grounds, because it allows the voices of the people to be heard more directly than in research done by statistical methods?*

DM:   Well, take the case of reflexive ethnographies in which the analyst 'shares' his or her account with their respondents. It's not clear to me that's always necessarily a good thing . It's like Trinh T. Minh-ha says: whether reflexivity or 'multivocality' contribute anything valuable to ethnography depends on how they're practised in a given instance. Multivocality isn't necessarily a 'solution' to the problem of hierarchical forms of knowledge production because sometimes it just serves to hide or 'mask' the analyst's own voice as they 'ventriloquise' what their respondents say.[8]

It all depends on what your objective is; it depends what kind of thing you want to find out. Take the case of Bourdieu's classic study of the museum-going population of France. In order to reveal the very interesting things he did about the way in which, on the whole, only middle-class people with certain types of cultural capital seem to have the confidence to go to certain kinds of institutions, you have to use statistics. You couldn't actually reveal that pattern by any other method. For some purposes, you do need statistics, which are always based on a system of categories for coding the data. Of course, any categorisation, or indeed any generalisation, is of its nature, reductive. The question is always whether *this* particular form of abstraction or 'reduction' is worth the price. You have to ask yourself whether the benefit that you are getting, in so far as it contributes to your ability to make some ordered analysis of cultural patterns, is sufficient to outweigh the fact that, in making that abstraction, you are losing some part of the particularity of your data.

The anthropologist James Carrier makes a very nice observation in this respect. He says that the issue is the usefulness of *particular* abstractions or 'essentialisations'. As he says, we can't make any sense of things at all without using categorisations of some type – which, in their nature, are always essentialising. The simple act of calling what I'm sitting on a 'chair' involves just such a moment of categorisation, which loses sight of the particularities of *this* chair – but it's nonetheless, a helpful way of organising our perception of the objects in the room. So the issue is not whether or not people should 'reduce' things to essences or 'reduce' people to their status as mere members of a category – we have to do that anyway, to make sense of the world. The question is whether those 'reductions' become so naturalised that we can't also stand back from them and distinguish between when they are helping and when they are hindering us.[9]

But it's not as if data and its particularity is inherently 'good' and abstraction is inherently 'bad'. The difficulty with that approach is that, beyond a certain point, and especially in context-sensitive qualitative work where you can easily amass a mountain of material from the field, the key task is to dump the inessential data, once you've worked out which part that is (which of course, isn't easy) and to get rid of as much of that as possible, in order to better highlight the good stuff that you've got.[10]

Let me give you another example of the difficulty here. I'm examining a Ph.D. at the moment and I'm having a great deal of trouble with it, because the person who did it seems very much caught up in this notion that you must always just quote people extensively and represent their own particular voices and not make any generalisations. I'm most of the way through reading it and I'm thinking 'Well, yeah, OK, but what have I learnt?'. I've heard all these different voices, but I can't see a pattern here, I can't see an effective analysis – because the researcher has been so concerned with this kind of semi-ethical consideration that they shouldn't make abstractions or generalisations at all. I think that, in the end, that approach is just disempowering for the analyst, in a pointless and rather regressive way.[11]

CF: *How do we resolve the tensions between the need to gain scientific validity and credibility for this kind of research and the need to avoid just getting caught up in a completely personalised and ultimately subjective representatation of the world, where 'anything goes'?*

DM: Here, again, I'm very influenced by Clifford Geertz, especially when he says that while 'all we can do is tell stories about the stories that people choose to tell us'. This doesn't mean to say that one story is just as good as another. One does have a responsibility to try to be insightful about the social world, not just to tell a series of micro-narratives, however fascinating they may be in themselves. As Lévi-Strauss says somewhere, the ethnographer does have the responsibility, as he puts it, of 'enlarging' a specific experience to the dimensions of a more general one.[12]

One of the things that concerns me about the emphasis on self-reflexive methodologies that's been very prominent in cultural studies in the past few years is that, although it has many things to recommend it, there is also a great danger that it can become a kind of solipsistic theory. First of all, you get the kind of substantive 'political' criticism: 'What is a white person doing, researching people of another ethnicity?' That's certainly a very real and genuine problem, which has to be addressed carefully, but the difficulty is that what that very easily spins into is a notion that, for instance, because of this problem, only people of Asian origin, for example, can do research on other Asian people. But of course, 'Asian people' is still a pretty big category, so then you'd have to argue that only Asian people from south-east London could do research on Asian people in south-east London and so on; logically, it's a potentially infinite regress. That was a tendency that did trouble me a great deal in cultural studies at one stage, though I think its high point is perhaps over now. The difficulty is that, in order to escape this dilemma and to avoid that kind of 'politicised' criticism, people can then end up, effectively, only doing research on themselves – autobiographical work. That can certainly be interesting, in its way, but autobiography is not necessarily the same thing as social and cultural research. There did seem to be a point in cultural studies at which, because of this terrible anxiety about power relations of researcher and research people began to feel that the only research that they could do – the only object of research left to them – was themselves.[13]

## Multiple perspectives and triangulation

CF: *So what are you saying about the relative advantages of different methodologcal procedures and how one should choose the best one for a particular research project?*

DM: One thing that reinforced my own pragmatic willingness to use *any* methodological procedure, if it seemed like it would be useful, was a very fruitful experience in the Brunel research which I talked about earlier, where we actually used a very wide range of different procedures: we were interviewing people; we had them completing diaries; we had people hanging about in the house with them; and then, on top of everything else, we came up with the notion of using 'mental mapping'.

So one of the things we did with the people in the households we were studying was to ask all the people in the household to draw a map of the technologies in their house. Again, this was in itself a very simple procedure, but it proved very powerful because, of course, different people count different things as a 'technology'. All the women certainly counted their washing machine as a technology – but for the men, it wasn't usually even in their drawing. It was as if either it was just 'invisible' to them because they didn't use it themselves, or else they thought 'it's not a technology, it's only a washing machine'.[14] We also found that some technologies were drawn at different sizes by different people. For many teenage girls, telephones tended to be really big in their drawings, whereas for other people, the telephone was often quite a little thing.[15] It was an extraordinarily simple procedure, but it turned out that if you asked four different members of a family to do this one elementary thing – 'Could you just do us a drawing of the technologies in all the rooms?' – that 'exploded' many of the key differences between different household members in how they perceived the technological environment in which they lived their domestic lives. And, of course, it was all the more revealing precisely because we could then put the results of that exercise next to what people had said to us, and next to what we'd seen people do, and that notion – of the 'triangulation' of data – perceived, recorded and acquired through different methodological routes – seems to me a terribly good one.

My main point, in telling that story, is that very often methodological discussions are conducted on the premise that what you're trying to decide is what is *the* methodology which is appropriate for a particular purpose. And I just think it's worth hesitating and saying 'What about the premise of the question?' Why should one ever assume that there will only be one particular methodology which is appropriate to a particular research problem? Isn't it more likely that, in most cases, there are probably several different ways you could find out about whatever the topic is, and that to know something about that topic from various different angles is probably going to be more useful than just to know about it from one angle? I know that's a banal, elementary thing to suggest, but actually that's not how most methodological discussions are conducted. It's still often as if people think they've got to find the Holy Grail, this one methodological approach that will somehow – 'magically' – reveal the whole truth. Multiperspectival, multidimensional ways of trying to understand the situation always seem to me better than ones that just stick to one methodology, however good that may be in itself.

CF:　*What about the problems of team research? To use all these different methods often requires a team of researchers rather than just one individual – but doesn't team research also always give rise to difficulties, such as the variations between how different team members might observe or record or interpret the same material or data?*

DM:　I think that in team research, you can get somewhere with those kinds of problems through pilot studies, in which you try things out to reveal those kind of differences and then discuss them – so you can then ask, 'Okay, so how are we going to try and work to some kind of more common format, at a subsequent stage?' But in the end, you're right, it's still an issue. Certainly, the research I am always most confident in, so far as its validity goes, is the research in which I was myself the person who was there, doing the interviews and making the observations. By contrast, the Brunel project that I've spoken about was very much a 'team business', which at some points had four or five people working on it. So in many cases, given my particular role in the team, I never went to the house of a particular 'panel' member among the respondents. Much as I have confidence in the colleagues with whom I worked on the project, in the end, when I hadn't been there myself, to a particular household, I couldn't possibly be as confident in the analysis, as I can when I can say, 'I know first-hand what I saw; I know what the person was like; I know what their tone of voice was'.

There is an 'immersionist' sense in which I think that, if you're treating the researcher as the research instrument, who is taking things in through many different senses and on many different dimensions, you do need your own 'on the spot' version of the 'triangulation' of the data, so that you can have some confidence in your analysis. Of course, sometimes you may still be wrong and sometimes misguided, but you can at least then have a certain confidence in your own perceptions, whereas, as soon as you're relying on someone else's perception, someone else's description, it's always a problem. So again, it comes down to a 'trade off', which you have to make in a particular situation. The question is, 'For *this* particular problem, will the undoubted benefits of team work outweigh the inevitable difficulties to which it also gives rise?'

CF:　*That's like an even more complicated version of what Geertz says about 'telling stories about the stories that your respondents tell you'. With team research, maybe there are sometimes just too many intermediate stories — because then you're analysing the stories your colleagues have told you about the stories which the respondents told them.*

DM: It's not necessarily a question of there being 'too many' mediations. Team research just produces a different kind of knowledge from that generated by an individual ethnographer. I think all you can do, at any point, with any of these issues is just to be honest about the limitations of the knowledge you've got, and of the procedures you used to get it, and to be open about the things that you don't know about or about the extent to which you can only be provisional about saying things because it is a second-, or third-hand story that you're telling.

One last comment. Years ago, I think when I must have been an undergraduate, I came across a very simple-seeming, common-sensical thing that the sociologist Howard Becker says about all these questions of methodology, and I still think it covers most of the main issues pretty well. Let me find it for you  . . . Here we are: he says 'What do we do? We take sides as our personal and political commitments dictate, use our theoretical and technical resources to avoid the distortions that might introduce themselves into our work, limit our conclusions carefully, recognise the hierarchy of credibility for what it is, and field, as best we can, the accusations and doubts that will surely be our fate'. I think that about covers it, so far as I'm concerned.[16]

CF: *Well, thank you. I don't think we've solved any of these methodological problems in our discussion, in any final sense, but I think we have explored some interesting difficulties!*

## Notes

1. See Darnell Hunt, (1997) *Screening the LA Riots* (especially Appendix A), Cambridge: Cambridge University Press; Justin Lewis (1997) 'What counts in Cultural Studies', *Media, Culture and Society*, 19.
2. See Georges Perec on the positive role of 'chance' in research, discussed in Chapter 4 and Jean Rouch's comments on these issues quoted later in this chapter.
3. See Jean Rouch on this in Chapter 4.
4. Ann Gray (1992) *Videoplaytime*, London: Routledge.
5. See Perec's comments, quoted in Chapter 4, on the discipline of proper enumeration.
6. For a fuller discussion of Rouch's work, see the last section of Chapter 4.
7. See Rouch's comments (discussed in Chapter 4) on the difference in power relations, for a Western anthropologist, when interviewing in rural Africa, as opposed to in metropolitan Europe.

8. See Trinh T. Minh-ha, 'Speaking Nearby' quoted in L. Taylor (ed.) (1994) *Visualising Theory*, London: Routledge, pp 439–40.

9. James Carrier (1995) *Occidentalism*, Oxford: Oxford University Press, p. 8. See my earlier comments on theoretical abstraction in the interview in Chapter 2.

10. See David Silverman (2001) on this, in his *Interpreting Qualitative Data*, London: Sage.

11. See Ulf Hannerz on the need to produce patterns in our analyses, not just individual stories.

12. Claude Lévi-Strauss (1963) *Structural Anthropology*, New York: Basic Books, p. 16.

13. See Geertz's comments on 'epistemological vertigo' and 'moral hypochondria' in postmodern ethnography in his (1988) *Works and Lives*, Cambridge: Cambridge University Press. See Chapter 4 on more imaginative artistic strategies in auto-ethnography.

14. See Chapter 8 for more on the washing machine.

15. This was in the pre-mobile phone period. For how the mobile phone has changed things, see the discussion in Chapter 7.

16. Howard Becker (1970) *Sociological Work: Method and Substance*, Harmondsworth: Penguin, p. 134.

# 4    Visions of the real

## The ethnographic arts

The greatest works of the imagination begin with the premise that a universe is revealed in the luminous facts of ordinary life . . . [and] the ditziest Hollywood production bears a subversive documentary message for viewers in China or Chad: 'this is what ordinary people in the US have in their house . . . [or] . . . in their refrigerator.' Even the most fantastical films 'document' their culture.[1]

## Introduction

In a retrospective interview, after the publication of his book *Routes*, James Clifford is somewhat apologetic about the fact that his chapter in that book on the work of the artist Susan Hiller consists of a collage of descriptive observations, quotes, extracts from documentary sources and philosophical reflections, rather than taking the standard form of an academic essay. Thus, he explains, the piece turned into a kind of 'intersectional meander of a quite precarious kind'. More generally, he observes that the book as a whole (of which, I should make it clear, I am a great admirer) makes considerable demands on its readers, requiring them to shift gear repeatedly, as it changes voice, rhetoric and genre, from one chapter to another – about which some reviewers complained. However, in defence of his strategy in compiling the book, Clifford explains that he wanted to resist the usual academic conventions which artificially foreshorten the many different modalities of thought (analytic, poetic, descriptive, meditative) through which one actually engages with any topic, in favour of the production of the appearance of a 'consistent, conclusive voice or genre' in the finished text. For this reason, he says, he thought it 'worth risking some confusion' in order to 'aerate the academic text' by the infusion of topics and modes of expression of a less familiar kind.[2]

My own intentions in this chapter are more limited, but it is in the same spirit of 'aeration' that I offer here a consideration of a variety of artistic and literary practices which seem to me to be of value in addressing some of the methodological issues which have been of concern within academic media and cultural studies in recent years. One of the other informing sources of the chapter is Italo Calvino's complex orchestration, in his novel *Mr Palomar*, of different registers of expression (descriptive, narrative and meditative) as devices for the exploration of different aspects and dimensions of visual experience, anthropological or cultural phenomena, and 'cosmic' or philosophical issues. In my choice to present the material in this way, I am also influenced by Bill Nicholls's argument that we need, at least on some occasions, to reach beyond the conventional academic 'discourses of sobriety' that treat their own relation to the real as non-problematic. It may be that we should look far more attentively than is usual in academic circles to what literary and artistic practices can offer us as methodologies for understanding the social and cultural worlds in which we live. In this connection, we might also usefully recall Clifford Geertz's counter-intuitive comments on the important role of the imagination in science and of organisational principles in the arts, in relation to what he calls the 'extravagant' nature of quantum mechanics as opposed to the 'methodical' nature of Italian opera.[3]

I begin the chapter with a consideration of the work of two artists – Susan Hiller, mentioned above, and Krzysztof Wodiczko – who, in their different ways, both mobilise the devices of fiction and rhetoric as interrogative tools for the understanding of the institutional power structures of the contemporary world. The main narrative arc of the chapter then runs from literary methodologies for the scrutiny of the everyday (notably in the work of both Calvino and the novelist and literary theorist Georges Perec) through the work of three installation artists (Sophie Calle, Christian Boltanski and Ilya Kabakov) who all utilise and at the same time subvert the conventions of anthropology and ethnography in their imaginative address to the process of documentation of the different cultural life-worlds which are their own chosen objects. Finally, the chapter moves to an extended consideration of the work of the ethnographic film-maker Jean Rouch, which explores not only his exemplary approach to the power relations between the subject and object of the research process, and the problematic nature of the relationship between the fictional and the factual, but also his approach to the painstaking documentation of that which, to Western eyes is, strictly speaking, incredible in Others.

## Conceptual art as an interrogative practice: Susan Hiller and Krzysztof Wodiczko

Although Susan Hiller, having originally trained as an anthropologist, gave up that profession in the 1960s, in her subsequent art practice, she has continued to work by means of the techniques of anthropology: gathering, collecting and presenting her data in systematic ways that often mimic the curatorial practices and archiving techniques of the ethnographic museum. At the same time, she is also concerned to subvert these practices themselves, explaining that her work, 'although contesting the whole notion of the rational and the objective' is often given 'the look of the rational'.[4] By these methods, she gently mocks the hierarchical processes through which the history of culture is ordinarily created by powerful institutions. Thus, one of Hiller's earliest works *Enquiries* was a slide show of 'facts' culled from an encyclopaedia and presented so as to reveal the culturally partisan presumptions lurking beneath its guise of objectivity.[5] In various projects she plays with the very idea of 'witnessing' – such as her *Witness* (2000), which presents an array of audio reports of sightings of UFOs by people all over the world. Here her informants, in the manner of a judicial process, supply a variety of corroborative details to their experiences (their names, addresses, and the exact date, place and time of their 'sighting'), producing testimony of their presence at these marvellous, other-worldly events as if they were participants in a formal judicial process.[6]

She characteristically works by 'collecting objects, orchestrating rela-tionships and inverting fluid taxonomies' while, unlike a conventional anthropologist 'not leaving myself out of them'.[7] In this, her aim is to create a dynamic that defeats 'any certainty of the visible, developing an intentional disequilibrium of knowledge', thus creating a meta-discourse parallel to the languages of the scientific disciplines, where she manipulates suspicion and doubt to pass beyond established conventions.[8] In her exhibition *After the Freud Museum*, Hiller invented a 'fictional' museum, originally displayed in the London house in which Freud spent his last years. In doing so, as Clifford puts it, she was attempting to transform that shrine to European psychoanalysis into, in his terms, a 'contact zone' in which, by interspersing objects and texts from other cultures among Freud's own collection of classical Greek and Egyptian antiquities, the certainties of the European tradition would be questioned and dislodged. In this interpretation of Hiller's work, Clifford recruits her to his own utopian category of 'ethnographic surrealism'. For Clifford, in drawing from a range of other cultures and ideas of 'civilisation' (Australian Aboriginal art, matriarchal cults, Mayan ritual), the value of Hiller's work lies in its intellectually challenging provocations, in so far as she ' supplemented Freud's masculine, European world view in a way that firmly pried open that tradition' – by no means 'consigning Freud to the junk heap of history', but 'placing him in a complex intersection of [different] histories'. To this extent, Hiller's strategic deployment of an avowedly 'fictional' mode of presentation can be seen as being of considerable intellectual consequence in helping us to resituate Freud's work in a broader comparative perspective.[9]

*Figure 2* Freud's desk. Photo reproduced by courtesy of the Freud Museum, London.

Hiller claims that, given the enormous influence of Freud's work, in the West we already 'inhabit an historically-specific museum of culture which might as well be called the Freud museum',[10] and she explains that her project was driven by the need to question the status and place of Freud in the history of Western civilisation. As she puts it,

> Freud's impressive collection of art and artefacts can be seen as an archive of the version of civilisation's heritage he was claiming; my collection is more like an index . . . [using what for Freud were worthless materials – his discards, fragments and rubbish] to some of the sites of conflict and disruption that complicate any such notion of heritage . . . [to produce] . . . a provocative poetic accumulation of contexts.

The archive she constructed for the exhibition is an 'index of misunderstandings and ambivalences that have emotional resonance in the present'[11] constructed by 're-ordering' Freud's own collection and addressing the 'gaps' in it, by including the debris and other ephemera from his archives (such as his collection of 'magic lantern' slides) which Freud himself had left out or left uncategorised.[12]

In Hiller's case, we see a conceptual artist using imaginative means to dislodge some of the accumulated 'certainties' surrounding one of the central figures of European intellectual history. However, such strategies can equally well be deployed at a more quotidien level, as rhetorical devices for the interrogation of our taken-for-granted assumptions about the social problems of the contemporary world. Krzysztof Wodiczko's work sometimes operates 'above ground', by means of the projection of large-scale images onto public buildings (such as his projection of a swastika onto the frontage of the South African embassy in London during the Apartheid period, so as to visually 'contaminate' the physical site with new and often subversive significance). At other times, his work operates, literally, at street level – as in the case of his *Homeless Vehicle* (or *Poliscar*).

Here we confront a case where an art object has been designed to function as a 'machine' for the production of knowledge about the world. The (fully intended) irony is that the art object in question is itself, literally, a machine: the *Homeless Vehicle* which Wodiczko intended as an 'intervention' in, or stimulant to, debates about homelessness in the USA. I have written elsewhere about the substantive significance of Wodiczko's work for the understanding of ideas of 'home'. Here I wish to concentrate on the aesthetic strategies used by the artist in attempting to produce new forms of public knowledge about this issue.[13]

Wodiczko's *Homeless Vehicle* takes the form of an adapted, large-scale supermarket shopping trolley, which functions simultaneously as a mobile home for its user, with a sleeping space within it, as a 'container' for keeping their possessions safe, as a 'work tool' for those who make their living by collecting and selling recyclable materials, and, in some versions, also as a portable bathroom. The vehicle is, in Wodiczko's words 'a speech-act machine' for homeless self-representation and expression, designed to challenge a-priori notions of what homelessness is and to 'offer a position from which nomadic evicts could begin to talk back'. It is an interrogative device, intended to function as a 'conundrum' or 'impediment to closure . . . designed to lengthen the hiatus between what we think is probable and what we imagine might be possible'. It is, thus, simultaneously, a technical mechanism and a symbolic operation by which concepts are visualised as external realities and an interrogative tool for examining social relations. In particular, it is a machine for producing understanding of the processes through which what Marshall Berman has called 'urbicide' itself produces homelessness, in the form of urban nomads or 'evicts'.[14]

The vehicle is, for Hebdige, an *unheimlich* or uncanny phenomenon, which is best understood as a kind of moving metaphor, an interrogative device that functions to provoke its various potential audiences by aiding their 'sluggish imaginations' and which invites us to pause and look again at what homelessness is. It is 'an ironic rhetorical statement, conjugated in the future perfect tense' and 'implicit in [the vehicle's] impermanence is a demand that its

*Figure 3* Krzysztof Wodiczko, Swastika projected onto South Africa House, London, 1985. © Krzysztof Wodiczko. Courtesy Galerie Lelong, New York.

function become obsolete'. It demands that we acknowledge the existence of the crisis of homelessness, 'reflect upon its causes and respond to the question it provokes: if not *this*, then what do *you* suggest?'. Its makers report that many urban dwellers, on seeing one of the vehicles for the first time, approached them, asking 'What is this for?' As Wodiczko and Lurie note, 'These same people see evicted individuals every day on the street and they never ask questions. Now they are provoked to ask questions'. Thus, 'as they move around the city, the vehicles and the discussions they engender, work to shift the terms in which homelessness is . . . understood'. The vehicle's beauty finally consists, as Hebdige puts it, in the 'tact, precision, elegance and wit with which it highlights the hidden face of power'.[15]

*Figure 4* Krzysztof Wodiczko, *Poliscar in front of Evicts' Camp*, New York, 1990–1. Courtesy Krzysztof Wodiczko ©, New York.

## Literatures of exactitude and enumeration

In phrasing his appreciation of Wodiczko's work as he does, Hebdige also provides us with a 'pre-echo' of the significance of one of Italo Calvino's six principal 'literary virtues' – the often underrated, but nonethless crucial virtue, as he names it, of 'lightness'. It is to the work of Calvino, and also that of Georges Perec that we now turn. I begin with Perec's proposals for what he calls an 'endotic anthropology of the infra-ordinary',[16] designed as a corrective to the spurious forms of mediated 'general' knowledge which he felt had come to so much dominate the world.

### Georges Perec: towards an endotic anthropology of the infra-ordinary

In media studies, one of the key categories is that of news, the reporting of 'what is happening' in the world. The classic definition of newsworthiness is that it should concern unusual or dramatic and, ideally, unexpected events in unlikely places, performed by unusual people, which have profound consequences. Clearly, this category is constructed by contrast to our sense of the everyday, which is routinely constructed by ordinary people, performing habitual actions, in their expected places, with predictable consequences. Such activity, by definition, is *not* news and, thus, on the whole, not deemed worthy of media attention. One of the problems with this, as Raymond Williams argued long ago, is that for many people, the world of spectacular events presented to them by the news media, while exercising a certain 'fascination at a distance', is felt to have little or nothing to do with their everyday lives. Indeed, one could make an argument that the recent rise of television genres such as 'Reality television', 'lifestyle' and 'makeover' shows is perhaps understandable as a reaction to this problem, in so far as these genres offer representations of a more familiar world, which do have the basic attraction of relating to that in which most of us live.

Elsewhere, I have explored some of these issues in relation to their consequences for our understanding of the consumption of television news (and other genres), with particular reference to the significance of all this for contemporary debates about the mediated public sphere – and about its abandonment, by many viewers, in favour of the quotidien pleasures of low-status genres which do depict everyday life as it is lived by the majority of the media audience.[17] However, here I want to explore these issues from a different angle and am concerned with the methodological consequences for social and cultural enquiry of the invidious tendency to examine the world from a perspective that shares many of the presumptions enshrined in the media industry's conflation of the important with the spectacular, in the form of news.

The central problem is elegantly formulated by Perec when he notes that

> what speaks to us, seemingly, is always the big event, the untoward, the extra-ordinary: the front-page splash, the banner headlines. Railway trains only begin to exist [for us] when they are derailed and the more passengers are killed, the more the trains exist. [It is as if] aeroplanes only exist when they are hijacked.[18]

As he observes, from this perspective, it is 'as if life reveals itself only by way of the spectacular'. Most importantly of all, for Perec, the key thing is that 'the daily papers talk of everything except the daily' (Perec, ibid., p. 209). The daily, as we have seen, is presumed to be, by definition trivial and thus not worthy of attention.

For Perec, to fall in line with these conventional assumptions is the biggest intellectual mistake we could possibly make, if we wish to gain any serious understanding of the world around us. His own principal commitment is to the development of a sociological understanding of the everyday. His point is that we tend to live the habitual without questioning it 'as if it carried within it neither questions nor answers, as if it weren't the bearer of any information'.[19] To then replicate this habitual attitude in our analytical approach is a serious mistake, for precisely the same reason that, within the realm of discourse analysis, Pecheux argues that it is mistaken to concentrate only on that which is said explicitly in discourse.[20] The issue here is the way in which the 'unsaid' – the variable content of that which 'goes without saying' within a particular society or (sub)culture – always dominates the 'said', by providing the unspoken frame of assumptions within which particular statements or actions can be deemed to have significance.

The reconstruction of the taken-for-granted, unspoken assumptions that frame our everyday actions and statements is, thus, far from a trivial concern. From this point of view, their very 'un-newsworthiness' – their deeply embedded nature as the unconscious foundations of social life – is precisely what constitutes and guarantees their analytical importance. Perec's fascination with the banal finds a close parallel in the work of the painter Gerhard Richter (discussed below) who explains that he 'uses the so-called banal to show that the banal is the important and the human'.[21] Richter's interest is in 'banal' photographs that awake, at most, a moderate interest – that are neither touching nor astonishing, neither fascinating nor shocking. He further explains: 'I was trying to avoid everything that touched on well-known issues – or any issues at all, whether painterly, social or aesthetic. I tried to find nothing too explicit, hence all the banal subjects'. As Rochlitz notes, as a result, 'what is most fascinating about Richter's images is the insignificance of their pretext; in this way they draw attention to their generic characteristics'.[22]

This is the terrain of the sociology of the everyday – or, as Perec puts it elsewhere, the 'endotic anthropology' – which he aimed to develop. He argues that 'what's needed is . . . to found our own anthropology . . . one that will speak about us, will look in ourselves for what for so long we've been pillaging from others. Not the exotic any more, but the endotic'. The objective of such an anthropology would be to 'describe what happens every day and recurs every day: the banal, the quotidien, the obvious, the common, the ordinary, the infra-ordinary, the background noise, the habitual . . . to question the way we spend our time, our rhythms . . . to question that which seems to have ceased forever to astonish us'. The methodology he recommends for this work is that of careful and exhaustive *description* (of things such as the staircases we routinely use, without looking at them); *comparison* (how, exactly, the bus numbers change at the edge of the city; in what precise ways the two sides of a border differ); *enumeration* (as he says, contemporary writing has lost the art of enumeration, and while nothing seems easier than to draw up a list, in actual fact it's much more complicated than it appears, as one often misses something out, and is always tempted, at a certain point, to simply write 'etc.'); and *inventory* (listing the quotidien in the form of the objects carried in your bag or pocket, and their uses). If such questions ('How many movements does it take to dial a phone number? Why?') should seem trivial or futile, for Perec 'that's exactly what makes them just as essential, if not more so, as all the other questions by which we've tried in vain to lay hold on our truth'.[23]

The basic problem, he argues, is that precisely because the structure of the everyday is so deeply embedded in our unconscious, we tend only to notice 'the untoward, the peculiar, the wretched exceptions', whereas what we should be doing is the precise opposite. His methodological prescriptions for how we should conduct our observations in this respect are striking:

> Force yourself to see more flatly . . . Is there anything that strikes you? . . . Nothing strikes you. You don't know how to see . . . You must see it more slowly, almost stupidly. Force yourself to write down what is of no interest, what is most obvious, most common, most colourless . . . make an effort to exhaust the subject, even if that seems grotesque, or pointless . . . You still haven't looked at anything, you've merely picked out [again] what you've long ago picked out [already].[24]

The point of the exercise, for him, is not to discover the new, the grandiose, the striking, the exceptional or the unexpected, but rather to (re)discover, or perhaps see well for the first time, the realm of that which is already familiar and, thus, largely unseen. If, as John Sturrock points out, this 'pure topography' is 'plain to the point of obviousness', few of us give enough attention to what is truly daily in our daily lives, to the 'banal habits, settings and events of which those lives almost entirely consist'. In consequence, it is only this kind of 'willed objectivity', as a constitutive part of the analytical commitment to the 'infra-ordinary' that Perec recommends, which can reveal again that which usually goes, literally, without seeing or saying. Moreover, to speak of literary, rather than analytical matters, it is also worth noting that, besides his commitment to the careful description of the seemingly inconsequential, in the mobilisation of a certain sense of the ultimate comedy of our everyday affairs and habits, Perec's approach exemplifies the 'lightness' of which his friend Calvino spoke. It is to Calvino's own work that I now turn.[25]

## Lightness and exactitude: Italo Calvino's literary virtues

Calvino identifes the six cardinal literary virtues as being those of Lightness, Quickness, Exactitude, Visibility, Multiplicity and Consistency. Here, I shall concentrate on those of Lightness and Exactitude. Following Galileo's definition of good thinking as being characterised by 'quickness, agility in reasoning, economy in argument, but also the use of imaginative examples', he argues that just as there is a lightness of frivolity, there is also 'a lightness of thoughtfulness', a 'weightless gravity' which 'goes with precision and determination, not with vagueness and the haphazard'.[26]

### Persons, objects and magic

In line with Perec's lamentation of contemporary writers' failure to enumerate things properly, Calvino claims that, today, description is a very neglected art – a topic that he expores in his novel *Mr Palomar*. He is concerned that language is often used 'in a random, approximate, careless manner . . . [which] distresses me unbearably', and in his own search for exactitude, he focuses on the effort to 'present the tangible aspect of things as precisely as possible'. Here, his position comes close to Barthes's radical suggestion that perhaps there should be a new science for every object – a '*mathesis singularis*' – so as to capture its singularity and particularity or, in Ernesto Laclau's terms, to restore the 'dignity of the specific'. Calvino's hero in *Mr Palomar* begins by staring at everything but 'becomes concerned that only some things are to be looked at, others not, [so] he must . . . seek the right ones. To do this, he has to face, each time, problems of selection, exclusion, hierarchies of preference'. Rather than the cultivation of precise nomenclatures and schemes of classification, in the end, Mr Palomar prefers 'the constant pursuit of . . . precision'. He decides to 'confine himself to watching, to establishing down to the slightest detail what . . . he manage to see' and sets himself to 'describing every instant of his life . . . until he has described it all'.[27]

Sharpness of eye and exactitude in description are the key virtues here. Indeed, Calvino argues that this applies not only to scientific endeavour, but also to the realms of folklore and magic, for 'the very first characteristic of a folktale is economy of expression. In them, the most outlandish adventures are recounted with an eye fixed on the bare essentials'. Here Calvino is interested not simply in exactitude (the key characteristic of knowledge, in his view) but also in the confluence of its role in the realms of science, literature and magic. Thus, he argues,

> it would not be pushing things too far to connect the functions of shamanism and witchcraft documented in ethnology and folklore with the catalogue of images contained in literature. On the contrary, I think that the deepest rationality behind every literary operation has to be sought out in the anthropological needs to which it corresponds[28]

For Calvino, 'in a narrative, any object is always magical . . . the moment an object appears in a narrative, it is charged with a special force and becomes like the pole of a magnetic field' and 'around the magic object there forms a kind of force field that is in fact the territory of the story itself'. Because of this, we need to understand that there is a potential web of influence radiating out from every object. From this point of view, in narrative terms, 'a plot can always be described in terms of ownership of a certain number of objects, each one endowed with certain powers that determine the relationships between certain characters'.[29] Calvino's own example here concerns the narrative significance given by Defoe to all the objects that Robinson Crusoe saves from the shipwreck, but we might also think of more contemporary examples, such as the role of the bridge itself as a 'participant' in the Balkan conflicts described in Tito Andric's *Bridge over the River Drina*, or of the accordion which is, as it were, the central character in E. Annie Proulx's historical novel of immigrant life in America, *Accordion Crimes*.[30]

*The novel as an encyclopaedia of the world*

Calvino proposes that the contemporary novel is best understood as a form of encyclopaedia, as 'a method of knowledge . . . and above all, as a network of connections between the events, the people and the things of the world'. In this context, the key issue is that 'everything should be precisely named, described and located in space and time'. Thus, he speaks approvingly of

Humboldt's aim to write 'a description of the physical universe' in his *Kosmos* and praises Balzac's attempt, in his later work, to produce a minute description of the world.[32] For Calvino, the key case is that of Flaubert, who proclaimed on beginning his final work *Bouvard et Pecuchet*, that he was trying to write 'a book about nothing' and then spent the last ten years of his life writing possibly the most encyclopaedic novel ever written, in the research for which he consumed 1,500 books on topics as diverse as horticulture, economics and astronomy. In the end, his heroes resign themselves to the fact that their project to understand the world in all its dimensions is an impossible one, faced as they are by an escalating series of epistemological contradictions, as they move through the academic disciplines, one after another. In the end, they thus resolve that they would be best employed simply copying out existing books by hand, having deconstructed the entire edifice of the sciences of their time from common-sense principles. However, this not because Flaubert, their puppet-master, is himself anti-science – rather, he says, he is *for* science: to 'precisely the extent that it is sceptical, reserved, methodical, prudent and human'. His horror is of the invasion of knowledge by dogma and metaphysics, the extent of which he painstakingly demonstrates, in his heroes' journey through the established sciences of their day. Indeed, Flaubert's original intention had been to subtitle his novel 'On Lack of Method in the Sciences', and Lionel Trilling claims that it is Diderot's great enterprise of the *Encyclopédie* which is 'the heroic and optimistic model of which the researches of Bouvard and Pecuchet are the comic and pessimistic counterpart'.[32]

Precisely because each of us is 'a combinatoria of experiences, information, books we have read, things imagined' and each life 'an encyclopaedia, a library, an inventory of objects', Calvino is quite prepared to provide an apologia for the concept of a novel as a 'vast net' in which all these things can be captured. It is for this reason that he has a particular enthusiasm for Perec's writing . Negatively put, he claims that no one was more exempt than Perec from what he regards as 'the worst blight in modern writing . . . vagueness'. He thus admires Perec's 'collectionism', his passion for catalogues, for the enumeration of objects, each defined 'both in itself and by its belonging to an epoch, a style, a society', which could, of course, for Perec only be possessed by the deployment of the most precise terminological exactitude in their enumeration and description.[33]

## Ethnographies of the visible in contemporary art

Here I now turn from the literary to the ways in which contemporary visual artists have used ethnographic techniques traditionally associated with the discipline of anthropology to explore a variety of everyday life-worlds. In doing so, they also raise important questions about issues of identity and autobiography, the real and the fake, the factual and the fictional and the status of documentary evidence.

### Sophie Calle's **Double Games** *and the creative subversion of ethnographic practice*

Sophie Calle is a self-styled ethnographer of the everyday, who uses the techniques of ethnography to make art out of her own and others' lives. Her work is based on processes of hyper-detailed observation and data-gathering, using complex strategies of surveillance, reportage and documentation. Thus, in her piece *Double Games*, a project in which she lived out a fictional role written by her collaborator, the novelist Paul Auster, Calle based herself in a phone booth in New York, engaging with pedestrian life in the locality by smiling at passers-by and exchanging cigarettes with them – all the while listing obsessively the number of smiles and cigarettes given and returned and the time each conversation lasted. Her *Suite Venitienne* also begins in the Bronx, with Calle 'tailing' strangers who she sees in the street, in the manner of a private detective. However, the project detours when Calle follows one of these strangers, unbeknown to him, when he travels to Venice. She continues to track and photograph him, keeping hourly reports of her surveillance, but subverts conventional ethnographic practice by also introducing into her written report her own account of her excitements and fears as she finds and loses him again, rather as if she were stalking a lost lover. In his commentary on *Suite Venitienne*, Baudrillard talks of how the follower 'seduces' themselves into their quarry's destiny, by doubling their path – being a mirror for the other, who is unaware of being under scrutiny'.[34]

In *L'Homme au carnet*, Calle profiles a stranger whose address book she has found by chance, contacting everyone listed in it and asking them about the man. The same project also contains a series of photographs which she took while working 'undercover' as a hotel chambermaid – secretly photographing the possessions in the rooms of the hotel's occupants and the contents of their drawers, as if she were a private detective searching for clues or building up evidence about their lives for a divorce case. At other times, Calle turns the process of surveillance around – arranging to have herself followed (in *The Shadow*), and hiring a detective to photograph her clandestinely, 'to provide photographic evidence of my own existence'. In all of this, Calle subverts the traditional practices of ethnography in fascinating ways, by deploying them in new settings and for unfamiliar purposes. In the end, as Suzanne Kuchler notes in her commentary on Calle's work, the techniques of surveillance work to draw attention to the ever-changing viewpoints of both

*Figure 5* Sophie Calle, decorated phone booth, Brooklyn, New York City. © ADAGP, Paris and DACS, London, 2005. Courtesy of the Paula Cooper Gallery, New York.

the surveiller and the surveilled. Calle's supposedly 'documentary' photographs, thus, often 'obscure rather than reveal their object, betraying more about the follower than the followed', and all of her work challenges us to think in new ways about the nature of what we think of as 'documentary evidence'.[35]

The issues that Calle's work explores have an evident resonance with the work of the photographer Nikki S. Lee, who also addresses issues of documentary and ethnographic practice. Since 1997, Lee has been photographing herself (or being photographed by a friend) in a variety of subcultural guises, 'going native' by insinuating herself into the life of these groups for short periods and adopting their appearance, to the extent of being able to 'pass' for one of their members (and thus producing what might perhaps be understood as the reverse/negative images of Cindy Sherman's chameleon-like photographic self-portraits). In the critical reception of Lee's work, as Miwon Kwon notes in her commentary, 'much has been made of the snapshot-like quality of her images – the casualness of the poses, the subject's direct address to the camera, the date and time stamp on each shot and the lack of a slick "professional" finish'. To this extent, the studied informality of the photos and Lee's 'snapshot aesthetic' signify what is, in fact, a problematic form of intimacy with her subjects. The photos seem, at first sight, to index a quality of extended experiential engagement with these subcultures, which one might well assume to be based on some deep form of knowledge, rapport and trust. In this respect, the intimate style of the photos appears to function to 'guarantee' the authenticity of Lee's participation in and engagement with these groups. However, as Kwon argues, not only does Lee not actually have a relationship of this kind with her subjects, but their major appeal for their viewers might perhaps be better understood as speaking to the general 'longing for the referent' (in Hal Foster's phrase), and the 'desire for a proximate relation to the real' among the contemporary art market which both Lee and Calle address. Here, again, we are forced to reconsider our assumptions about the nature of visual evidence.[36]

### Christian Boltanski: autobiography, fiction, and identity

Christian Boltanski is famous for his installations of old photos, clothing and personal effects, which are presented as archives tracing and memorialising individual lives. Through his work, he has also created a fictitious 'autobiography' for himself, by means of the cumulative and obsessive use of 'found' photos, which mischievously play with the uncertainties of all identities. He often uses everyday objects and documents, such as passport photos, school portraits and family albums, to 'memorialise' the lives of

*Figure 6* Christian Boltanski, *The Dead Swiss* installation. Reproduced by courtesy of the Whitechapel Art Gallery, London.

ordinary people. The people in the photos might be victims of tragedy, such as unknown children killed in the Holocaust, the deceased citizens of a Swiss town (who, being Swiss, have in his own words 'no reason to die') or the now-redundant ex-employees of a factory. His work is not about the 'large memories' of recorded official history, but about the attempt to give dignity to and preserve the 'small memory' (of everyday events and things) which are, in fact, what make people unique and out of which they construct their individualities.[37] His is a popular art, which attempts to give an almost religious sense of grace to the lives and beliefs of *les gens de peu* (the 'little people') through the ritualistic evocation of the quotidien experiences of loss and memory and their 'resurrection' as icons of memory. The key terms in Boltanski's aesthetic strategy are those of memory/memorial, spectre and phantom.

Boltanski disarmingly 'confesses' (Catholicism being a key trope in his work) that while he has often 'pretended' to speak about his own childhood in his work, 'I have lied about it so often that I no longer have a real memory of this time'. Thus, speaking of himself in the third person, in his own ironic autobiographical notes, he avers that 'he told so many stories about his childhood, so many dubious anecdotes about his family that, as he often said, he no longer knew what was true and what wasn't [as] he no longer had any [actual] memories of his childhood'.[38] However, rather than seeing this as a problematic lack of verisimilitude, he argues that, in a sense, 'everything you do is a pretence' and that not only his own art practice, but all of life is, necessarily, about the ongoing construction of ever-fragile identities and about 'making stories', the exact factual truth of which is but one consideration among others. For him, the manipulation of truth and the mobilisation of uncertainty are simply the aesthetic strategies that he finds it necessary to use in his work, in order to illuminate our understanding of the problematic nature of identity itself.[39]

Much of Boltanski's work consists of a story about his life, developed through the ongoing 'reconstitution' of the elements out of which it has been made 'from beginning to end, like the life of a secular saint'. He creates a parodic museum of the self, in which the objects he displays come from his own mythology, all the time working towards the development of a fictional life which gradually becomes 'real'.[40] He says simply that 'my work tells a story and asks questions, in a process in which 'I hold a mirror to my face,so that those who look at me see themselves and therefore I disappear'. In obscuring himself, he creates not so much a false biography as an individual mythology, as his self-portraits are imprecise enough to be as communal as possible, 'composed not only of images of himself, but of French children, Austrian adolescents, Russian Jews and Swiss bourgeois', and his 'temples of imaginary victims' are constructed out of amateur snapshots of ordinary people.[41] Boltanski himself is the intercessor through whom the relics he displays assume a 'magical' value. As ever in his work, this is a teasingly ambiguous process. Just as we shall see later in the case of Jean Rouch, who might be considered as both Shaman and 'fairground barker', promoting his cinematic wares, Boltanski can perhaps be seen as the 'preaching vicar, half-serious, half-fraudulent'. By way of underlining the point, he frequently calls attention to the parallel between his own practice and the character of the 'evil preacher' famously played by Robert Mitchum in the film *The Night of the Hunter*.[42]

For Boltanski, the question of identity can only be understood in relation to its inevitable and ultimate annihilation – in the form of individual death. Thus, at one point, he ironically declares that a project dear to his heart is that of 'preserving oneself whole, keeping a trace of all the moments of our lives, all the objects that have surrounded us, everything that we've said and what's been said around us . . . The task is vast and my means are frail'. Still, he declares, the effort must be made, so that his life will finally be 'secured, carefully arranged and labelled in a safe place, secure against fire theft and nuclear war, from whence it will be possible to take it out and assemble it at any one point, and [thus] being assured of never dying, I may finally rest'.[43]

## Anthropology, relics and art

Boltanski's work has always been influenced by his early experiences of seeing the anthropological, tomb-like displays of 'dead cultures' in the Musée de l'Homme in Paris.[44] As he puts it:

> It was there that I saw big metal showcases containing fragile and insignificant little objects. In one corner of the showcase there would be a yellowed photo showing a 'savage' handing these objects. Each showcase presented a world that had disappeared: the person in the photo was probably dead, the objects were useless now, or at least no-one knew how to use them.

As he remarks, 'nobody really knows what all the different objects on display were actually used for'. In the same way, he explains, in his own work, 'what I was trying to do was take strange objects – [which] we know have been used for something, but we don't know exactly what, and show their strangeness'. Thus, he uses objects from his own life and those of his contemporaries to better articulate the 'strangenesses of our own taken for granted beliefs and cultures'.[45]

In his work, Boltanski often uses everyday objects such as biscuit tins as the containers for his 'relics' (to which he gives the patina of age by soaking them in urine or Coca-Cola) because these are recognisable to his audience and, thus, more 'affective' – and, more simply, because 'we have all kept our small treasures in biscuit tins'. He makes inventories of utilitarian objects with no particular aesthetic quality, which have now also lost their personal value, when they were 'separated from their owner . . . [and now] mark out [that] absence which makes them desperately useless'.[46] He works by bricollage, creating cumulative inventories that work to illuminate, in Weisenberger's phrase, the 'luminosity of everyday objects'. These bricollages feature the do-it-yourself art of ordinary people or, in some cases, consist of a display of the personal possessions of someone now dead. These pieces present domestic life itself as a form of 'identity embodied in labelled and arranged objects', such as Boltanski's *Inventory of Objects that Belonged to an Old Woman of Baden-Baden* (1973) and the *Inventory of Objects Belonging to a Young Woman of Charleston* (1992).[47]

*The photographic, the autobiographical and the fake*

One principle of inspiration for much of Boltanski's work concerns the 'melancholy' of how a scientific exactitude of documentation and description nonetheless often combines with a perennial uncertainty of interpretation. He explains that he uses photographs in his work because 'everyone can relate to them'. Although, as he remarks in his characteristically *faux-naïf* way, 'it's very difficult to separate true and false', nonetheless, when we look at a photo we tend to believe in its reality, even though its relationship with its subject is always, by definition, now lost, as photography is, in itself, 'bound to absence'. Thus, despite ourselves, we tend to 'really feel that the people were there'. It is, of course true that 'in principle, a photograph cannot lie, unless it is technically falsified – which is why it can count, in law, as a trace or "evidence" of an event – but there is nothing simpler than making a photo lie through its caption'. In his work, as Semin remarks, in some cases 'it may be that the captions to the photographs which he uses correspond to a historical reality; [but] just as often, the clues supplied are entirely . . . or partly false'. Thus, Boltanski continually exploits the plural, ambiguous and vague nature of the messages that photos give us.[48]

Despite the fact that much of his work is concerned with autobiography, the paradox is that Boltanski's private life rarely appears in his own work . He hardly ever uses photographs of his own family, but rather recycles 'found' ones, often using photos of the same faces repeatedly, in different pieces. Most strikingly, perhaps, in his photographic presentation of *The Dead Swiss*, what we confront are 'photos of unknown people emptied of the affection that other unknown people (so close to ourselves) had placed in them . . . in a nostalgic play of displacement'.[49] The 'rapporteur' of his fictional autobiography says of his notional conversations with the artist that he 'showed me a load of engagement calendars that he'd bought at the flea market and in personal property liquidations . . . he said he was using the calendars to imagine what the lives of these people might have been like' – a practice that might almost be understood as an imaginative form of necrophilia. The effect is

> as though the faces were fragments of existence that he has excavated from some ruin of time – a remote past, all the more intangible by reason of the blurred look of the photos, a sign of temporal erosion. They belong to collective memory . . . but the content of the memory is at once uncertain and matter-of-fact, obscure yet straightforward, indistinct yet unmistakeable . . . [his] photos are mnemonic traces, but it is not clear what the materialised memories mean . . . [they are] ambiguously meaningful, sybilline, oracular . . . unsettling.[50]

*The uncertainty of meaning*

Like Perec and Calvino, Boltanski is fascinated by the virtues of exhaustiveness, exactitude and inventory. Thus, a number of his pieces are constructed by means of the painstaking enumeration of evidences of 'actuality' and verifiable truth – such as his *Daily Report* (1994), a facsimile of the logbook of all the calls made to a Barcelona police station in one day, or his later piece *Les Abonnés de telephone*, in which he collated and exhibited all the telephone books of the world, listing their subscribers, country by country, in alphabetical order, from Afghanistan to Zimbabwe. Here we might also recall Perec's stipulation that enumerations should always be complete, and his attempt to literally 'exhaust' a particular Parisan sight in his description of it.[51] This, for an artist concerned with memory, must also, of course, include the documentation of that which is absent – as in Boltanski's *The Missing House* (1991) in which, in his concern to also document that which can no longer be seen, he photographs the vacant space in which houses bombed during the Second World War once stood.[52] In a similar manner, his photographic pieces often take the form of visual inventories (in, as it were, the past tense) of all the members of a particular group – often complete cohorts of children, such as the *Children of the Jewish School of Grosse Hamburgerstrasse in Berlin 1938* (1994) or the *Children of North Westminster Community School* (1992).

However, much as in the work of Calvino, we are often deliberately left puzzled by the exactitude of these mysterious fragments, not knowing what overall picture these pieces of the puzzle add up to. Perec himself avowed that his own memory contained an odd list of luminous 'exactitudes', the originary selective principle of which he had no way of accounting for:

> my uncle had a Citroen 2 CV, license plate number 7070 Rl2; that Art Tatum called one of his pieces 'Sweet Lorraine' because he had been in Lorraine during the war of 1914–18; that in [the children's game] 'Monopoly', *Avenue de Breteuil* is green, *Avenue Henri-Martin* red and *Avenue Mozart* orange; that Lord Mountbatten's real name was Battenburg.[53]

### Boltanski, Richter and Sebald

If Boltanski explores the complex nature of documentary and of 'memorialisation', he also embraces ambivalence, performing an elaborate balancing act between truth and deception . He is attracted to photos because they are perceived as truthful, as proof that the event they picture is real, but he deliberately uses them as traps to ensnare their viewers' emotional engagement, by manipulating the evidential role assigned to photography. In

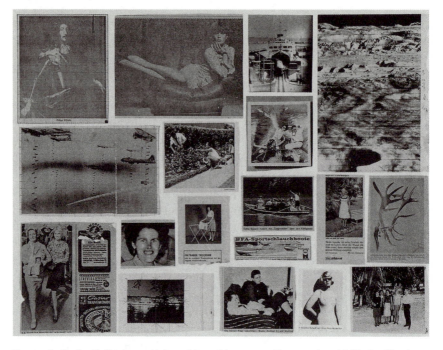

*Figure* 7 Gerhard Richter, *Atlas: 10 – Newspaper Photographs, 1962–8*. © photo
Städtische Galerie im Lenbachhaus München.

all of this his work can usefully be compared with that the painter Gerhard
Richter and the writer W.G. Sebald.

Richter's single most famous work is his *Atlas*, which takes its name from
the historical form of a book that compiles and organises geographical and
astronomical knowledge. However, Richter uses this form in an unsettling
way: his *Atlas* functions as a palimpsest, collecting together all the photos
(from newspapers, family albums, 'found' photos) which played (or could
have played) an important role in his work from 1964 onwards. In his *Atlas*,
the worlds of people, things and nature all appear under the sign of ephemer-
ality.[53] Although the project mimics the systematic forms of organisation
of knowledge associated with didactic and educational modes of presentation,
Richter archives his materials according to principles which are themselves
opaque to the viewer. But if the organisation of his imagery is deliberately
'mendacious', it is not for any frivolous reason, but has a strong theoretical
foundation. As a form of mnemotechnics, photography's capacity for recording makes it the foundation of both public and private archives.[55] However,
in his use of photographs, Richter is also deeply influenced by the 'media
pessimism' of Siegfried Kracauer, who believed that the increasingly universal
presence of the photographic image may inhibit or even destroy fundamental

cognitive and mnemonic processes. For Kracauer, the 'flood of photos sweeps away the dams of memory' in an age which, while being more 'informed' (by means of mediated images) than any other before, knows less and less about itself, and increasingly tends towards a condition of collective anomie.[56] If 'the photograph is the "credible" image par excellence, the "cult" image of our time',[57] the very wariness and inconclusiveness of Richter's style – manifest in the blurring and shadowiness of his portraiture, his cityscapes and still lives – can be read as an index of a terrible doubt and a fierce mistrustfulness of all images and what they purport to convey, and for him, this 'quality of doubt' necessarily also extends to the photographic image.

The work of the late W.G. Sebald also shares many characteristics with that of Boltanski, especially in the use of visual material in his written texts. His books have a documentary look and use uncaptioned black-and-white photos, along with other visual materials such pictures of train tickets or a torn-out leaf from a pocket diary, drawings, a calling-card, newspaper clippings, a detail from a painting – whose exact status is often unclear, in relation to the texts that they illustrate. The images anchor the author's writing in a documentary reality, seeming to provide evidence for the truth of what he is saying, but they are always impossible to vouch for – and the surrounding prose is all the time dissolving the very reality that the images

*Figure 8* W.G. Sebald, photograph (pp. 120–1) from *Austerlitz* by W. G. Sebald. © The Estate of W.G. Sebald, 2001.

purport to support. They remain as imperfectly focused snapshots, tantalisingly juxtaposed with the narrative they interrupt. We read these enigmatic images through the story that Sebald provides and then, later, come to the suspicion that they were something more (or less) than an illustration or documentation of the story. In the end, the very uncertainty/unreliability of the photos induces a meditation on the questions of visibility and of visual truth. Sebald's texts thus produce an 'effect of the real' by literary and visual means, characterised by a deep unease and a feeling of unsettled documentary – but then, all novelists combine fact and fiction, and are in some measure necessarily engaged in a form of forgery.

Sebald's writing continually transcends and transgresses the boundaries of existing genres – even his British publishers, Harvill, have hedged their bets by classifying his work, rather uncertainly, as 'fiction/travel/history'. A blurring of the boundaries between artifice and reality, memory and history is embedded in his very tone – so the reader is never sure what is fact and what is fiction. James Wood claims that Sebald is writing in a new genre that 'stretches the novel form beyond its frame, to harass realism into a state of self-examination', mixing 'established fact with unstable invention' so that the two categories copulate to produce a kind of fictional truth characterised by the 'scrupulous uncertainty' with which Sebald invests his texts.[58] In fact, Sebald can be seen as writing a new kind of history, as much as a new kind of fiction, by going at history from an oblique angle, because of the impossibility of confronting the dreadful facts of twentieth-century history (and, particularly, the history of his native Germany) head on. In so doing, he produces a fascinating meditation on both the tenacity and the fallibility of memory and on the status of visual evidence.[59] In all of these bodies of work, we are left with the glowing embers and fragments of memory, which are, in themselves, at the same time, both exact and mysterious, the significance and epistemological status of which we must puzzle out for ourselves.

### Ilya Kabakov: the anthropology of Soviet everyday life

The work of Ilya Kabakov, the Russian installation artist, can best be understood as that of someone pursuing Perec's strategy for an 'endotic anthropology' under very particular historical conditions. In her study of Kabakov's work, Amei Wallach suggests that he is the 'secret archeologist of the "lost civilisation" of Soviet life'. As Boris Groys observes, the particular point of interest of Kabakov's work, in this respect, is that 'Soviet civilisation is the first modern civilisation to have actually died before our eyes: all other dead civilisations were pre-modern'.[60] Kabakov's enterprise is to describe the Soviet system from the perspective of the life of the proverbial Russian 'Little Man'. In pursuance of this project, he has produced an imaginative analysis of the cosmos of *Homo Sovieticus*, through the documentation of everyday life as it was lived in the USSR, which captures, above all, the bizarre tone of Soviet life, in the grotesqueries of its everyday deprivations. Kabakov once declared that his intention was to 'build a Disneyland of the USSR', and the experience of his installations has been likened to that of 'walking into an image lifted from a story book and rendered into three dimensions'.[61] If the political climate of the 'Stalin time' in which Kabakov lived his early life was like a kind of immutable weather, a 'natural' fact about which no one felt they could do anything, his is a specifically Soviet surrealism, which explores the secrets of the mundane and hidden aspects of life under the Soviet regime, by providing us with what Wallach calls 'atmospheric models' of life in the former USSR.[62]

Like Calvino's Mr Palomar, Kabakov is primarily concerned with the look of things, how they work, the minutiae of living – of which he takes inventory as meticulously as the bookkeeper his mother once was. His self-effacing claim is that he is 'a typical Soviet character, but with only one difference: I observed this character well'. He is concerned, above all, with documenting the life of both the people and objects of Soviet life: his aim is to write a commentary to go with each object, detailing where it came from, why, and how it got there. In this project, his strategy is to compile lists and to make detailed records. Of course, if he is a 'bookkeeper' of this lost civilisation, it was itself, par excellence, one of documentation – replete with certificates, passes, lists, plans and schedules.[63]

*Living in a world of garbage*

Kabakov's work is an anti-art, constructed out of the litter of Soviet life – set in a milieu of unfinished projects, teeming apartments, substandard objects, unusable tools, garbage and junk. The appropriateness of this aesthetic strategy to his particular object of study is founded on the perception that the USSR was itself an enormous littered space of junk of various kinds – poorly made, shoddy and malfunctioning, where garbage was the basic material of life. His project is to try to make sense of the pathetic remnants of this world, in the form of its detritus. If he can be said to share the somewhat romantic fascination with the 'cast-off' of American artists such as Robert Rauschenberg and Joseph Cornell, his more specific – and more explicitly political – project is that of revealing the disavowed underside of the supposedly rational Soviet system, in his elevation of the 'garbage man' to the role of hero – most economically expressed in the name of the character from his installation *The Man Who Never Threw Anything Away*.[64] Kabakov's interest in garbage has strong philosophical lineage: in Plato's

*Figure 9* Ilya Kabakov, *The Man Who Never Threw Anything Away*. Reproduced by courtesy of Ilya Kabakov.

*Parmenides* the young Socrates is admonished that his lack of interest in garbage is a mere consequence of his immaturity but that 'when philosophy shall have a firmer grasp of you . . . you will not despise even the meanest things'.[65]

Bizarre as his installations can look to Western eyes, Kabakov's project is by no means as exclusively personal or idiosyncratic as it might seem. Following his approach, other Soviet artists have also explored similar themes, most notably Vladimir Arkipov, in his *Post-Folk Archive*. Arkipov's work is also inspired by the experience of the 'Soviet everyday' being routinely constructed through the recycling of detritus. He understands himself to be engaged in the documentation of a 'new folklore' of contemporary hand-made consumer items – a collection of improvised objects celebrating do-it-yourself creativity, such as a lawn-roller made out of a milk churn filled with concrete waste and attached to a piece of scrap metal for a handle. Both these artists' work can be understood as replaying, in an aesthetic context, a quotidien tradition of spontaneous invention as a reaction to the hardships of Soviet life and the lack of affordable 'ready-made' consumer durables – a mode of individual (and, thus, at times eccentric) imagination in the face of the collective experience of 'standardised deprivation'. The resulting 'inventions' – assembled objects, fused from the fragments of other things, recycled to meet individual needs – are best understood, contextually, as private projects in the public world of a failed and disintegrating utopia. The work is, however, not only resonant within the Soviet context; in the case of Arkipov's *Post-Folk Archive* as exhibited at the Ikon Gallery in Birmingham in 2002, the objects were made not in Soviet Russia but in poor districts of the West Midlands in the UK.

*Collective eccentricity*

Much of Kabakov's work and, in particular, his *Ten Characters* project (1989) is inspired by his own childhood experience of growing up in one of the communal apartment buildings – or *kommunalka* – which characterised Soviet urban life for many poor families. These came into being after the revolution, when poor people took over the grand houses of the tsarist elite in the big cities. The large houses were subdivided into large numbers of apartments for 'proleterian living', where each family had only one private room, while sharing a communal kitchen and bathroom with the rest of the house's inhabitants. Ludicrous as it may now seem, the Soviet planners of the time had high hopes that this arrangement would forge close positive bonds between the residents, and they regarded the innovation as an exciting experiment in socialist living.

For the USSR, with its worship of communalism, privacy (the literal home of all the eccentricities that Kabakov lovingly cherishes and documents) was an obscenity that the enforced collectivity of the *kommunalka* was designed to monitor and survey. To this extent, the communal apartment represented a radically intrusive environment, where the individual was constantly exposed to the surveillant gaze of others.[66] Nonetheless, within the small privacy of their rooms, many inhabitants of the collective apartments nourished their dreams. Recalling his childhood memories of the *kommunalka*, Kabakov explains that within them 'everybody's lives [were] closely examined by the others. Everyone lived in the communal apartment as if they were under a magnifying glass . . . and yet some of the inhabitants led a mysterious, even secretive existence . . . [so] . . . myths grew up around them'.[67] He is fascinated by the way in which these people, within the precarious privacy of their homes, 'devoted their energies to piecing together a fanciful world of their own' from the refuse of the so-called workers' paradise. In this context, his project is to reassemble the history of the very individualities and eccentricities that the Soviet system was designed to destroy.[68]

In his own mind, Kabakov's childhood was populated by a variety of strange and comic individuals, each of whom, it seemed to him, had an unusual idea, one absorbing passion belonging to them alone. To enumerate them in full, in the spirit of Perec, the 'characters' he exhibits are: The Man Who Flew into His Picture, The Man Who Collected the Opinions of Others, The Man Who Flew into Space from his Apartment, The Untalented Artist, The Short Man, The Composer Who Combined Music with Things and Images,

The Collector, The Man Who Never Threw Anything Away, The Man Who Saved Nikolai Viktorivich and, perhaps self-referentially, The Person Who Described His Life through Characters. Perhaps the most striking of all these 'characters' is 'The Man Who Flew into Space from his Apartment', who did this by constructing a giant catapult, by means of which, as the installation reveals, he succeeded in projecting himself into space through the apartment's broken roof. All this, we should recall, is set in the era when, despite its total failure to provide for the everyday needs of its own people, the USSR was proud of having been the first nation to put a man into space – the national hero of the times, Yuri Gagarin.

As Wallach observes, this installation, like much of his other work, if more vividly, embodies Kabakov's own feeling that Soviet life as a whole was characterised by a sense of 'caged rage and thwarted reach'. However, here the personal most definitely is also the political, as the distinguishing obsession of life, for many Soviet citizens of the period, was indeed 'escape' in some form or other – imaginative, if not actual, given the difficulties of getting an exit visa. To this extent, Kabakov's work is militantly committed to exploring and representing the fantasy worlds of the anonymous citizens of Soviet Russia, mental worlds in which ordinary people escaped their predicament by means of flights of the imagination. In this respect, Kabakov's characters belong to a long tradition of Russian literary heroes, such as Dostoyevsky's 'lonely little people living in very tight circumstances, but nonetheless obsessed by universal ideas' in their imaginations.[69]

To return to my earlier claims about the value of literary and artistic approaches to the understanding of the social worlds in which we live, I would argue that the tension between the ludicrously over-regulated and cramped space of Soviet communal life and the deep eccentricities of their various inhabitants are perhaps better expressed in Kabakov's imaginative installations than they have been in any academic analysis of life in this period. His mobilisation of forms of exaggeration, popular stereotyping and caricature provide us with an exemplary typology of the resurgent forms of eccentricity and individuality that continued to exist within the confines of the Soviet system of 'really existing Socialism'.

If Kabakov is to be understood as an anthropologist of the strange, lost world of Soviet civilisation, his concerns can usefully be compared to those of the ethnographic film-maker Jean Rouch, to whom I now turn – as an anthropologist of geographically distant civilisations of West Africa. Both are concerned with how to represent what are, to us, the inconceivable forms of strangeness of everyday worlds which were – and are – thoroughly familiar in the quotidien lives of these others.

*Figure 10* Ilya Kabakov, *The Man Who Flew into Space from his Apartment*. Reproduced by courtesy of Ilya Kabakov.

## Magical realism in the cinema of Jean Rouch

Thus far, we have dealt with novelists, literary theorists, visual and conceptual artists who have all, in their own ways, explored the issues of ethnography and documentation that have long been the province of the discipline of anthropology. Jean Rouch's own intellectual journey was made in the opposite direction, moving from ethnography through documentary film to the production of what he described as his cinematic 'ethno-fictions'. As the widely acknowledged master of his craft, who produced through his long career a vast and complex body of work addressing many of the issues of concern to those who I have discussed earlier, it seems appropriate that we consider Rouch's work in some detail as the culminating point of this chapter.

### Truth, trust and the incredible

As noted above, if Kabakov stages a now 'lost world' of Soviet civilisation, Rouch addresses an equally unfamiliar world for Westerners – that of the so-called 'primitive' societies of Africa. Rouch made his films to show 'African truths', but his purpose was to move beyond the mere surface description of events and things to that of 'revelation', by showing what otherwise might be thought incredible in other cultures and thus dislodging our own cultural presumptions.[70] His finest achievement in this respect is perhaps also his most controversial film *Les Maîtres fous*, which I shall discuss in detail later. In that film, which depicts a harrowing sequence of a possession ceremony among the Hauka sect in West Africa, Rouch simply – and dramatically – shows us things about 'post-colonial madness' which quite transcend what words alone could tell us. As he puts it: 'it was impossible to describe . . . all I needed was to register it in colour and sound . . . that was what brought me to cinema'.[71]

The crucial question here concerns the necessary foundations for this type of work. Rouch's is a cinema of contact, built on trust – and it took time for his respondents to feel sure of this 'strange, persistent white man, who asked tiresome questions'. For the ethnographer, the critical issue is patience, thus Rouch cautions, 'Never be in a hurry. You have to wait'.[72] As one way of demonstrating this virtue, when visiting the Songhay, he made a point of always going on horseback, rather than by car as most Westerners would do, which meant that they saw him as a 'traveller' rather than a 'tourist', a crucial distinction for them. Paul Stoller reports that, when asked why they trusted Rouch, the Songhay replied simply that it was because he 'knew how to sit with the elders'.[73] The key issue is evidently what an ethnographic film-maker has to do to win the trust of those who he/she films. Many of the Africans whom Rouch filmed do not, in general, like strangers. They are certainly suspicious of Europeans, but their suspicions extend much further than this for they mistrust all 'outsiders', and, initially, Rouch's African guide was also snubbed by them, because he too was, in their eyes, a stranger.[74]

Friendship is a key component in Rouch's notion of participatory ethnography, and it is only on the basis of friendship that 'the people who know him and trust him can reveal themselves openly, honestly and directly to us, through the medium of his camera'. In this respect, the crucial thing, for him, was 'the assurances I gave these men that nothing would be repeated or published without their agreement' which was 'a sign of my respect for them – for those who had welcomed me and treated me as a friend'.[75] From this point of view, a strategy such as using a hidden camera could only produce 'stolen images', whereas Rouch insists that the people filmed must always see and respond to the camera itself. Moreover, if the mediums in his films of possession rituals provide him with his material, Rouch then enters into dialogue about his portrait of them, so that 'knowledge is no longer a stolen secret . . . [only] later devoured in western temples'. For Rouch 'it's impossible to make a film with the people concerned if you stop contact with them when the film is finished'. One of the central purposes of his film-making is 'to show another just how I see him', thus using the camera to start a dialogue with his subjects, in which their own dignity is respected.[76]

For Rouch, film is not simply a device for collecting data but an arena of enquiry. His intention was to 'transform anthropology, the eldest daughter of colonialism, a discipline . . . [normally] reserved to those with power, interrogating people without it. I want to replace it with a shared . . . anthropogical dialogue between people belonging to different cultures'. By way of example, he suggests that if we asked a follower of a totemic religion 'Do you believe in God?', the only possible answer would be 'Do you?', because the interaction has to be to do with human beings posing questions to each other.[77] In this respect, Rouch's approach to his respondents can usefully be compared to that of the British documentarist, Charles Parker. For some people, it was a matter of bemusement that an evidently upper-class, public-school-educated Englishman, with a clearly 'posh' voice such as Parker (who also had something of the manner of a Second World War submarine commander) could get the working-class people who he interviewed in programmes such as his 'Radio Ballads' to respond to his questions as honestly and openly as they did. The crux of the matter is, perhaps, that for Parker, as for Rouch, there was no question of making some attempt to disguise his identity or of disavowing the very real and manifest differences between him and his respondents. Rather, the very honesty of his own self-presentation – in all its difference from them – was precisely what made his respondents feel that they could trust him.[78]

In relation to the question of the power relations between the film-maker and his subjects, the case of *Chronique d'un été* (1960), when Rouch returns to film his own 'tribe' the French, in the metropolis, is particularly instructive. Of this experience, he remarks that: 'In the Third World we came from a rich country, with lots of equipment . . . people there were perhaps a little overawed, so we could enter [their] lives more easily – here [in Paris] we can get only a short interview, we can't see into people's everyday lives'. In the early part of the film, we see instructive scenes, where his interviewers find it difficult to even get people to stop in the street and answer their simple question ('Are you happy?'). One replies 'Sorry, I'm late enough as it is'. Others simply walk past and ignore the interviewers. A small boy backs off in fright while the interviewers try vainly to reassure him that 'we're not going to hurt you'.[79]

### The participatory/mobile cameraman: radical empiricism and the provocation of truth

Rouch's radical empiricism, rather than drawing a clear boundary between observer and observed, focuses on their interaction and interplay – and he inserts himself as one of the participants in the scenes we witness through his camera.[80] To take one example, *Les Tambours d'avant* (1971) is perhaps best understood as a 'cinetrance' of one person filming the trance of another, in which we are invited not simply to observe others but to observe an observation of others. The crucial thing here concerns Rouch's use of the camera. Having lost (or abandoned) his tripod when filming, he was able to be mobile and move through the ceremonies – avoiding what he has described as the colonial gaze of the 'observation post' to which the tripod limits one. Thus, he 'identifies his own body with the camera. The perpetually moving camera is a testament to its embodied status: as a hand-held shot, it is an extension of his body; as an embodied person, he does not have (or allow the camera to have) an omniscient perpective'.[81] Similarly, in *Initiation a la danse des possédés* (1959), Rouch moves about freely while filming, and his own mobility means that 'the spectator, rather than remaining at a fixed vantage spot and surveying the scene with a detached "colonial" gaze, is placed amidst the possession rituals and is forced to participate, along with the camera'.[82]

Rather than hiding behind its recording function, for Rouch the camera must announce its responsibility for the events taking place before it. He said of *La Pyramide humaine* (1959) that, in making it 'the camera was not an obstacle to expression, rather it was an indispensable witness which made that expression possible'.[83] He observes that 'Very quickly, I discovered that the camera . . . was not a brake but an accelerator. You push people to confess themselves . . . The task is not to film life as it is, but as it is provoked'. The camera provokes subjects to reveal themselves, by making them aware of the fact that they are being filmed and by turning them into actors of themselves. He then films reality as it is created by his presence, a new reality that reveals a new kind of 'cinematic truth'.[84]

Perhaps the most striking case of this was Rouch's filming of *Tambours*, referred to above, when after three days of the ceremony, no possession had taken place – until the moment when he started filming. The question, evidently, is why his filming should have then precipitated the trance among others.[84] How could the presence of his camera have this effect on both mediums and spirits? Rouch suggests that perhaps the explanation was that he had become so absorbed in the technical aspects of filming that he had effectively entered a trance-like state himself. Thus, like the mediums, his self was displaced – and his feat of filming stimulated the spirits and deities to appear, as they recognised his actions as belonging to their realm.[86] Rouch claims that it was precisely because he participated with these people in their cultural rites as a 'spectator among other spectators' that 'the deities came to greet me as well as my neighbours, and spoke at length with me'.[87]

### Negative capability: dealing with the unthinkable

Above all, ethnography, as the science of the thought systems of others, is for Rouch 'a permanent crossing point from one conceptual universe to another [involving] acrobatic gymnastics, where losing one's footing is the least of the risks'.[88] He attempts to construct an anthropology that is capable of recognising and dealing productively with what appear to be 'blatant incongruities, confounding ambiguities and seemingly intolerable contradictions' in the cultures of others. In doing so, he follows John Dewey in drawing on what Keats called 'negative capability': the capacity to embrace, even relish, the ambiguities, uncertainties and imponderables of lived experience and the capacity for 'being in . . . mysteries, and doubts . . . without any irritable reaching after fact or reason'. Critically, this involves 'a deep respect for other worlds and other ideas, ideas often preposterous to our way of thinking'. From this point of view, other men are not the 'savages' of fable, and their social institutions are 'just as complicated, their religions just as worthy of respect, their behaviour just as logical'. This also involves the necessity to 'believe in the beliefs of the other: when someone says this person is possessed . . . then you respect that'.[89] Here Rouch's approach foreshadows that of Clifford, who once defined ethnography as 'the science of cultural jeopardy', which 'presupposes a constant willingness to be surprised . . . and to value – when it comes – the unclassified, unsought Other'.[90]

Rather than engaging in observational cinema, Rouch's films aim for a truth 'beyond representation'. As Stoller argues, they 'make no claim to representational truth, but the images in his works embody the truths of the worlds and peoples they portray'. This is a form of cinema which is 'a little like surrealist painting: using the "realest" possible products of reproduction . . . in the service of the unreal, putting them in the presence of irrational elements. A postcard in the service of the imaginary'.[91] Thus, in *Les Maîtres fous*, as Stoller observes, the images of the trance into which the participants pass during the ceremony document, in a truly unsettling way, the existence of the incredible and the scientifically unthinkable in the world in ways that challenge us to decolonise our own thinking. (How can fire not burn flesh? How can trance be simultaneously so violent, irreverent, brutal and funny?) And yet, 'all we need to do is watch the screen to observe . . . incontrovertible evidence of the Hauka's otherworldliness'. Rouch does not try to explain or reduce the inexplicable – rather, he films images that challenge the rationality of our own thought.[92]

Moreover, Rouch insists that these possession rituals are not simply to be treated as exotic, and, to this end, he places them squarely in the context of the quotidien. He understands possession not as something to be marvelled at, but as an accepted part of communal life in this context, which has a definite role to play in ensuring its continuity.[93] Thus, after the trance in *Les Maîtres fous*, the participants are shown the next day, back at work in their everyday lives, apparently quite at ease with their transition between these two worlds. Rouch observes simply that when you compare their relaxed manner, the next day, to their gruesome expressions during the trance 'you cannot help but ask whether these men know of some remedies which allow them not to be abnormal, but perfectly integrated into their surroundings'.[94]

### Fiction, truth and the imaginary: representing post-colonial madness

In *Moi, un noir* (1957) and *Jaguar* (1967), Rouch aims to provide a portrait of the joys and anxieties of the African urban generation of that period that can expose the conflicts produced in a situation where encroaching Western influences, interacting with traditional forms of indigenous culture, produced new dreams and hybrid new languages for the expression of desire. The subject of these films is the power-laden dialogue between African and European cultures and practices.

The relation of the factual and the fictional in Rouch's work is a complex one: *Jaguar*, for example, he describes as a 'cine-fiction'. But if it is a fictitious story, it is one based on years of fact-gathering ethnographic research. It is also a fiction derived from real elements, a 'made-up' story, but with real people playing the parts. Thus, if *Moi, un noir* or *Jaguar* are fictions, the people in them are telling the stories of their own lives as migrants from the countryside to the new cities of African modernity. They show what the everyday life of an African migrant in a city on the Gold Coast was like in that period, and the people themselves are the ones who construct and dramatise the stories. For Rouch, this kind of 'fiction' is the best way to penetrate reality – by comparison to which, he argues, the means of sociology remain 'exterior' ones. He explains that in *Moi, un noir*, he

> wanted to show the African city . . . I could have made a documentary full of facts and observations. That would have been deadly boring. So I told a story with characters, their adventures and their dreams. And I didn't hesitate to introduce the dimensions of the imaginary, the unreal . . . I can then use the film to tell what cannot be told otherwise.[95]

In these films, Rouch accepted that his subjects were actors and that, through the process of acting out the stories of their lives on screen, they could project and reveal a greater understanding of the situation in which they lived. Thus, *Moi, un noir* does not content itself with the mere documentation of its characters' external lives. It tries, instead, to find ways to represent their inner mental states, their hopes and dreams, which they live out through the personae of the fictional characters whose names they adopt. If the characters in the story call themselves – and each other – names born out of a desire to be someone else, the characters they play, in both their lives and the film, are as much a real part of them as anything else.[96] They are already living out a 'fictional' reality in the city of Treichville, far from their homes and their traditional lives in Niger. They have adopted the pseudonyms of famous movie stars as a way of coping with their new lives and, in effect, they are living their everyday lives through these 'dual personalities'. Rouch describes them as 'trying to reconstitute, every Saturday and Sunday, a sort of mythological Eldorado, based on boxing, the cinema, love and money'. Their nicknames in the film are based on how they acted in real life. Thus the stevedore was already called 'Edward G. Robinson' because his friends said he looked and behaved like the movie actor; the boxer was already called 'Tarzan' and his girlfriend 'Jane'; the prostitute called 'Dorothy Lamour'. Rouch explains that faced with the complexities and frustrations of life in this strange city they chose to believe in the 'idols' they found in the cinema. In this sense, as Mick Eaton notes, the concerns, if not the form, of the film are very close to those of *Les Maîtres fous*.[97] As one of the characters puts it,

> I dream of a day when, like all who are rich, I'll have a wife, a house and a car. I'll soon be married to Dorothy Lamour . . . I'll be an actor like Marlon Brando and she'll be in my house – she'll wait for me,

day and night . . . In my house I'll have Dorothy Lamour AND my radio
– and she'll talk love to me.

Rouch thus uses fictional situations to bring out the characters' hopes and
dreams, to reveal the landscape of their inner lives, not simply to document
the mere surface description of their existence, because 'the camera allows
us to reveal a fictional part of us all, but which for me is the most real part
of the individual'.[98] The actions of the characters in these 'ethno-fictions'
reflect the films they have seen, the comic books they have read, the stories
they have been told, which they then refashion into a new narrative.[99] The
films reveal not only their participants, but also, by implication, all of us, to
be creatures of imagination, fantasy and myth. If they act for the camera, they
play a role that is not, strictly speaking, who they are; but the fact that they
play those roles (or that people play fictional roles at all) tells us all something
about how we live our lives.[100] However, in all of this, we must remember
that fiction is not necessarily a matter of falsity – the Latin root simply signals
that something has been made, not that it is therefore 'made up' or untrue.[101]
In this connection, it is also worth noting that Rouch's own preferred term
for his style of cinema is not 'cinema verité' but 'cinema sincerité'.

*Figure 11* Jean Rouch, film still from *Les Maîtres fous*. Reproduced by courtesy of the
Ronald Grant Archive.

Let me now turn to address *Les Maîtres fous*, the most contentious, but also one of the most rewarding of Rouch's films. The film shows a ceremony in which members of the Hauka sect in Ghana, during the period of British colonial rule, enter into a state of collective possession. We might expect that they would be 'possessed' by ancestral spirits, but instead they are taken over by the 'spirits of power' personified by the English ruling class of Ghana at that time. The men writhe in frantic caricatures of their 'Mad Masters', mimicking the behaviour of the English Governor, the other officials, their wives and secretaries. The mimicry has its own logic and precision: when one of the possessed breaks the white of an egg over the head of their fake statue of the Governor, Rouch cuts to documentary footage, showing the white plume on his actual dress-parade helmet. Rouch's commentary notes that, by acting out and identifying with these aspects of European power, the Hauka are, in fact, being deeply rational, as this frenzied form of possession has a psychotherapeutic function that allows them to better deal with the contradictions of the colonial situation in which they are trapped. Most shockingly, during the ceremony, the Hauka eat a dog – which, as Muslims, is forbidden to them. Here we see the anxieties that accumulate when traditional forms of life are disrupted by colonialism, expressed in a hysterical act of self-abasement, which allows the Hauka a symbolic form of release, in dealing with the otherwise unbearable tensions of their situation.[102]

Rouch himself later explained that 'the title [of the film] is a pun – the British colonial masters are the ones who are mad'.[103] His commentary to the film thus works to shift the terms of emphasis away from a simple focus on the exotic sights that are shown, so that, in the end, it is the colonial administration that emerges as bizarre and irrational, rather than the Hauka's actions. As an African commentator interviewed in Manthia Diawara's film *Rouch Reversed*[104] observes:

> the title speaks for itself . . . it's a crazy story, but then again, all the governments in Africa then really were 'Mad Masters' . . . when you look at it, you see the roles the Africans assume, in the therapeutic environment that Rouch has filmed . . . and you find everything there . . . all the figures of the future – from the the crazy President to the Minister who annoys us by not working . . . it's like going through transference with your analyst.

Rather than see the film, as some of its critics have done, as 'insufferably cruel', I would agree with Stoller that it too, like some of the other work that I have considered in this chapter is, indeed, infused with 'the brilliance of lightness'.[105]

## 'Reversal' as an aesthetic strategy

Mathia Diawara's striking ethnographic film about Rouch's work begins with shots of him on the plane, en route to Paris to meet his 'subject'. He explains that his project is to move beyond Rouch's own notion of 'shared anthropology', to one of what he calls 'reverse anthropology'. In this case, Diawara, the African, now working as Professor of Cinema in New York, is to make an ethnographic film about the white man Rouch, set in his own 'natural habitat', in his working environment at the Musée de L'Homme in Paris. On the plane, en route to begin filming, Diawara explains that he feels rather like the character Damoure in Rouch's film *Petit à petit* (1969), who flew from Niger to Paris to explore French life and customs. His observation is certainly apposite, as strategies of reversal are, in fact, central to Rouch's whole aesthetic. We have already seen how, in *Les Maîtres fous*, the Hauka are shown reversing the conventional relations of colonial power, as they act out the behaviour of their 'mad masters' during their trance. *Chronique d'un été* was Rouch's own attempt to 'return' from the African periphery and to reverse his usual perspective, by filming the white natives of metropolitan Paris. Furthermore, the terms of reference of Diawara's own project are also, to some extent, foreshadowed by Rouch's own *Cine portrait de Margaret Mead* (1977) in which he films his 'totemic ancestor' (as he describes her) in her own 'habitat' in the Museum of Natural History in New York where she had then worked for fifty years. However, as Diawara observes, within Rouch's œuvre, it is perhaps *Petit à petit* which comes closest to his own project.

Rouch's specific concern in that film was to get away from the idea that only the powerful should be the subjects, rather than the objects of anthropological enquiry, by placing Africans in the position of those who are to make a 'journey of discovery' to enquire about the strange customs of others – in this case Parisians. The title of the film comes from the slogan of the company set up by the three heroes of Rouch's earlier *Jaguar* ('Little by little, the bird builds its nest'). In *Petit à petit*, our heroes, having now decided to build a luxury hotel in Niger to cater for European tourists, decide, like good anthropologists, to send one of their number to Paris to study these people in their natural habitat. The Africans' intention is to study Parisian lifestyles and consumer preferences, so as to design their hotel's interior decor in a way that will appeal to the tastes and preferences of their intended guests. They also plan to observe and measure them precisely, so as to build their hotel furniture to the correct dimensions for its guests. Thus, in one scene, which light-heartedly ironises centuries of 'racial' theory, we see Damoure in Paris, posing as a medical student earnestly measuring the exact physical dimensions of the French with anthropometric calipers.[106]

When they are preparing for their journey, one of the travellers remarks to his companions that, first of all, 'you'll have to learn Parisian geography – where is East, where is West. What they eat. How they have fun. Where they work. How they dress.'[107] These ethnographers certainly find some Parisian customs very strange. As they observe, here, 'When night falls you can still go shopping' and, even more curiously, 'At the weekends, they go to the country. It rains. The roads are bad. But they still go.' Nonetheless, they find some things relatively familiar: 'The Seine is like our Niger at home, except it's been strangled', 'French cows are like our hippopotamuses, or warthogs – very frightening – but God has given them very thick coats for the cold'. The difficulty they are most troubled by is that of communicating their bizarre findings to those back home; as one of them puts it, 'For them, Paris is just a postcard of the Eiffel Tower – that's all – they won't believe all this other stuff'.[108]

However, *Petit à petit* is not the first film in which Rouch features Africans as the explorers of strange lands, it is simply the first one in which the lands to be explored are in Europe, rather than in other parts of Africa. *Jaguar* is not just a narrative of discovery about three young men from Niger en route to the Gold Coast. It is also 'a story of others' Others'.[109] Of course, it is not only the case that Europeans are Others for Africans, just as Africans are for Europeans. If we are not to fall into the grossest form of Orientalism, we must recognise that other Africans are also Others, for Africans. As Stoller observes, what makes Rouch's commentary to the film particularly biting is that he chooses as his heroes for this quest men whom Western-educated urbanites would least expect to embark on a journey of cross-cultural discovery in a conceptually sophisticated manner.

Rouch's gambit in the film is to play on the fact that while we might well expect a Western anthropologist to travel to exotic places in search of enlightenment, we do not expect the same of these young men from Niger. As Stoller notes, what Rouch does in *Jaguar* is to force us to face up to our colonialist assumptions that in their backwardness all Africans are alike and that they lack the capacity to extract wisdom from the encounter with difference. All of these expectations are confounded in the film as our heroes from Ayoru confront their own Others – both those who they themselves regard as primitive and the African colonial elites who they cuttingly describe as *bien-nourris* (well-nourished). Thus, 'at all junctions in the film, difference is underscored [and] distinctions are made between Northerners and Southerners, Christians and Muslims, traditionalists and moderns' so that Africa is presented not as a continent of 'sameness', 'it is rather, a land of finite distinctions, a space for the politics of difference'.[110] Thus, when Rouch's travellers meet another tribe, the Semba, who are naked except for penis sheaths, one of them says to his companions that, nonetheless, they shouldn't treat them as savages, because 'The Semba are very nice. Don't laugh at them because they are naked. The good Lord obviously wants them that way, just as he wants us to wear clothes'.

Rouch observes that 'this is intended as a commentary on a primary African ethnography, founded on the respect one should have for a culture which is not one's own'.[110] This respect is not only the foundation of his own work, but a fundamental requirement for any serious ethnographic activity for the future, even if that project must now be conducted without the presence of Rouch's own guiding spirit.[112]

## Notes

1. Eliot Weisenberger (1994) 'The Camera People'. In L. Taylor (ed.) *Visualising Theory*, London: Routledge, p. 5.
2. James Clifford (1997) *Routes*, Cambridge, Mass.: Harvard University Press; James Clifford (2000) 'An Ethnographer in the Field'. In Alex Coles (ed.) *Site-Specificity: The Ethnographic Turn*, London: Black Dog Publishing, p. 71.
3. Italo Calvino (1994) *Mr Palomar*, London: Minerva; Bill Nicholls (1994) 'The Ethnographer's Tale'. In L. Tayor (ed.) *Visualising Theory*, ibid., p. 63; Clifford Geertz (1998) *Works and Lives*, Cambridge: Polity Press, p. 143.
4. Guy Brett (2004) 'Analysis and Ecstasy'. In James Lingwood (ed.) *Susan Hiller: Recall*, Gateshead: Baltic Gallery, p. 34.
5. Lingwood (2004) 'Introduction'. In Lingwood (ed.) ibid., p. 9.
6. Louise Milne (2004) 'On the Side of the Angels'. In Lingwood (ed.), ibid., p. 144.
7. Susan Hiller (1995) 'Afterword', *After The Freud Museum*, London: Bookworks np.
8. Stella Santacaterina (2004) 'Anamorphis of the Gaze'. In Lingwood (ed.) ibid., p. 120.
9. Clifford (2000), ibid., p. 70. For Clifford's original acount of Hiller's Freud exhibition, see the chapter 'Immigrant' in his *Routes* op. cit.
10. Hiller, quoted in Lingwood (ed.) ibid., p. 11.
11. Hiller (1995), ibid., Hiller, quoted in Rosemary Betterton (2004) 'Susan Hiller's Painted Works'. In Lingwood (ed.), ibid., p. 18.
12. Hiller, quoted in Denise Robinson (2004) 'Scarce Stains the Dust'. In Lingwood (ed.) ibid., p. 101.
13. See my (2000) *Home Territories*, London: Routledge, pp. for my earlier discussion of Wodiczko's work. In all that follows, I rely heavily on Dick Hebdige's commentary (1993) 'In the Tracks of Krzysztof Wodiczko's Homeless Vehicle Project', *Cultural Studies*, 7 (2).
14. Hebdige ibid.; Krzysztof Wodiczko (1991) *The Poliscar*, Restless Productions; Marshall Berman (1986) 'Take it to the Streets' (1986) *Dissent* (summer); David Lurie and Krzysztof Wodiczko (1988) 'Subject: Homeless Vehicle Project', *New Observations* 61.

15. Hebdige, ibid.; Rosalyne Deutsche (1990) 'Krzysztof Wodiczko's Homeless Projection and the site of Urban Revitalisation', *October* 36 (Fall). For an example of some innovative thinking about the the design of shelters for the homeless in the UK, see Jane Hughes (1998) 'Homeless Get Hi-Tech Shelters', *Independent on Sunday* 29 November.

16. Georges Perec (1999) 'Approaches to What?', in *Species of Spaces and Other Pieces*. Harmondsworth: Penguin, p. 210,

17. David Morley (1998) 'Finding Out about the World from television News: Some Difficulties'. In Jostein Gripsrud (ed.) *Television and Common Knowledge*, London and New York: Routledge.

18. Georges Perec (1999) 'Approaches to What', in his *Species of Spaces and Other Pieces*, Harmondsworth: Penguin 1999, p. 209.

19. Perec, ibid., p. 209.

20. Michel Pecheux (1982) *Language, Semantics and Ideology*, London: Macmillan.

21. Jean-Francois Chevrier (2000) 'Between the Fine Arts and the Media'. In B. H.D. Buchloh, J.F. Chevrier, A. Zweite and R. Rochlitz *Photography and Painting in the Work of Gerhard Richter*, Barcelona: Museu d'Art Contemporani de Barcelona, p. 36.

22. Armin Zweite (2000) 'Gerhard Richter's Album of Photographs, Collages and Sketches'. In Buchloh et al., ibid., pp. 93–4. Rainer Rochlitz (2000) 'Where We Have Got To'. In Buchloh et al., ibid., p. 113.

23. Perec, ibid., pp. 210–11.

24. Ibid., pp. 50–3.

25. John Sturrock (1999) 'Introduction' to Perec, ibid., pp. ix, xi, xiv.

26. Italo Calvino (1996) *Six Memos for the Millennium*, London: Vintage, pp. 43, 10, 19, 16.

27. Calvino, ibid., pp. 56, 74; Roland Barthes (1980) *La Chambre Claire* 21, Paris: Flammarion, quoted in Calvino ibid., p. 65; Roland Barthes (1984) *Camera Lucida*, Paris: Flammarion, p. 8; Laclau quoted in Hebdige, ibid., p. 53. See Hebdige's own dedication of his *Hiding in the Light* (London: Routledge, 1988) to William Blake's ambition of achieving Particular, rather than General, Knowedges – the latter being, in Blake's view, the 'knowledges of idiots'. See also Perec's passion for the unique – that is, the collection of objects of which only one specimen exists, Calvino, ibid., p. 122; Italo Calvino (1994) *Mr Palomar*, London: Minerva, pp. 101, 21, 56, 113.

28. Calvino (1996), pp. 37, 27.

29. Calvino (1996), pp. 32–3.

30. Tito Andric (1995) *The Bridge Over the Drina*, London: Harvill; E. Annie Proulx (1997) *Accordion Crimes*, London: Fourth Estate. Calvino's approach to the relation between persons and objects shares much both with that of Actor Network theory, and also with that of ethnographers such as Jean Rouch, who have attempted to explore the world of magic in its emphasis on the powers of objects. On 'Actor Network Theory', see Latour quoted in Chapter 11; on Rouch, see the last section of this chapter.

31. Calvino (1996), pp. 105; 107.

32. Calvino (1996), pp. 114–15. For an interesting parallel here, see also Jimmie Durham's comments on science, quoted in my concluding chapter. Lionel Trilling 'Introduction' to Gustave Flaubert (1954) *Bouvard and Pecuchet*, New York: New Direction Press.

33. Calvino (1996), pp. 122, 124.

34. Jean Baudrillard (2001) *Suite Venitienne* and *Please Follow Me*. In H. Rickett and P. Phelan (eds) *Art and Feminism* London: Phaidon. Calle's practice here has an important historical forebear – in the 'Mass Observation' project in the UK in the 1930s, the anthropologist Tom Harrison also used to encourage his volunteer observers to follow strangers in the street at random.

35. Susanne Kuchler (2000) 'The Art of Ethnography: The Case of Sophie Calle'. In A. Coles (ed.), ibid., pp. 95–8. For a subtle consideration of the nature of evidence, especially that collected from 'marginal' phenomena of various kinds, see Carlo Ginzburg's essay (1983) 'Clues: Morelli, Freud and Sherlock Holmes'. In Umberto Eco and Thomas A. Sebeok (eds) *The Sign of Three: Dupin, Holmes, Pierce*, Indianapopolis, Ind.: Indiana University Press.

36. Miwon Kwon (2000) 'Experience vs Interpretation: Traces of Ethnography in the Works of Lan Tuazon and Nikki S. Lee'. In Coles (ed.), ibid., pp. 74–94. See Hal Foster (1996) *The Return of The Real*, Cambridge, Mass.: MIT Press.

37. Tamar Garb (2001) 'In Conversation With Christian Boltanski'. In Didier Semin, Tamar Garb and Donald Kuspit, *Christian Boltanski*, London: Phaidon, p. 19.

38. Christian Boltanski (1990) 'What They Remember'. Reprinted in Semin et al., ibid., pp. 130–43.

39. Boltanski, ibid., 130; Garb, ibid., p. 8.

40. See my earlier discussion of Hiller's creation of a 'fictional' museum. See also Peter Greenaway's exhibition *Luper at Compton Verney* which curated the life of a fictitious character with uncanny verisimilitude (Compton Verney Arts Centre, Warwickshire, 2004).

41. Lynn Gumpert (1994) *Christian Boltanski*, Paris: Flammarion, p. 13.

42. Didier Semin (2001) 'From the Impossible Life to the Exemplary Life'. In Semin et al., ibid., pp. 46, 68; Garb, ibid., pp. 19, 16, 24.

43. Boltanski, ibid., p. 126. Here we see a clear parallel with Sophie Calle's practice of arranging to have photos of herself taken, to provide reassuring 'proof' of her own physical existence.

44. See my discussion later in this chapter of Manthia Diawara filming Jean Rouch in that same museum, as his workplace/natural habitat.

45. Semin, ibid., p. 55; Garb, ibid., p. 17. The clear parallel here is with literary debates about the aesthetics of '*Ostranie*'/making strange – and with the ethical responsibility for current Western anthropology to recognise, above all, the 'exoticness' of the West, rather than of 'primitive' cultures.

46. Garb, ibid., p. 24; Semin, ibid., p. 60.

47. Semin, ibid., pp. 47, 56; see below on the art of Ilya Kabakov – especially his *Ten Characters*, who are defined by their possessions and private obsessions.

48. Garb, ibid., pp. 25, 30; Semin, ibid., pp. 60, 65, 86, 87, 46. We should also

note here the epistemological complexities added to all this by the emergence, since the time of Boltanski's statements here, of digital photography.

49. Semin, ibid., p. 60.

50. Boltanski, ibid., p. 138; Donald Kuspit (2001) 'In the Cathedral Dungeon of Childhood'. In Semin et al., ibid., p. 98.

51. Georges Perec (1974) 'An Attempt at Exhausting a Parisian Site'. Reprinted in Semin et al., ibid., p. 120.

52. See the attempts made to document the vanished history of the Jews in Germany by Claude Lanzmann in his film *Shoah* (1984) and by Susan Hiller in her *J. Street Project* in which she photographed all 303 of the street signs still scattered across Germany that reference the absent Jewish communities who once lived there. See Susan Hiller (2005) *The J.Street Project*, Berlin: Compton Verney Arts Centre and Kunstlerprogramm.

53. Georges Perec (1978) 'I Remember'. Reprinted in Semin et al., ibid., pp. 118–19. I am aware that this positive account of Boltanski's autobiographical practice may seem at odds with my sceptical views of some recent forms of 'auto-ethnography' in cultural studies, expressed in the interview in Chapter 3. The simple difference is that, to my mind, artists such as Boltanski are not only more imaginative, but also much more rigorous, and therefore more insightful, in their exploration of these complex issues than cultural studies scholars have thus far been.

54. See Zweite, ibid., p. 98.

55. See Chevrier, ibid., p. 47.

56. Kracauer quoted in Buchloh et al. (2000) ibid., p. 22.

57. Rochlitz, ibid., p. 117.

58. James Wood (1998) Review of Sebald's *The Rings of Saturn*, *The Guardian*, 30 May.

59. W. G. Sebald (1996) *The Emigrants*, London: Harvill; (1998) *The Rings of Saturn*, London: Harvill; (2000) *Vertigo*, London: Harvill; (2004) *Austerlitz*, London: Harvill.

60. Boris Groys (1998) 'The Movable Cave'. In B. Groys, Chicago, Ill.: *Ilya Kabakov*, London: Phaidon.

61. Amei Wallach (1996) *Ilya Kabakov; The Man Who Never Threw Anything Away*, New York: Harry N. Abrams, pp. 45, 11, 13, 90, 8. In what follows I rely heavily on Wallach's exemplary account of Kabakov's oeuvre.

62. In a more literal but nonetheless revealing application of this 'atmospheric' point, Mick Taussig has rightly complained about how anthropologists very rarely even mention the immense cultural significance of the heat, which 'conditions' their work in their ethnographies of tropical countries, Mick Taussig, Lecture to Tate Modern *Fieldworks* conference, London, September 2003.

63. Wallach, ibid., pp. 22, 69, 93.

64. Wallach, ibid., pp. 39, 171, 68.

65. *Parmenides* quoted in Groys, ibid., p. 49.

66. Groys, ibid., p. 62.

67. Kabakov, quoted in 'Exhibition Guide' to his *Ten Characters* exhibition, Institute of Contemporary Arts, London, 1989.

68. Walach, ibid., pp. 8, 92.

69. Ilya Kabakov (1989) *Ten Characters Exhibition Catalogue*, London: Institute of Contemporary Arts; Wallach, ibid., p. 73; Groys, ibid., p. 44.

70. Paul Stoller (1992) *The Cinematic Griot: The Ethnography of Jean Rouch* (1992) University of Chicago Press, p. 99; Mick Eaton (1979) 'The Production of Cinematic Reality'. In M. Eaton (ed.) *Anthropology-Reality-Cinema*: The Films of Jean Rouch, London: British Film Institute, p. 51; Eaton, 'Introduction' in ibid, p. 6. But see also Appiah's critique of the idea that there could be such things as specifically 'African Truths', discussed in Chapter 5.

71. Jean Rouch (2000) interviewed in *Crossing Boundaries* video, Departamente de Antropologia, Universidade de São Paulo. In that video, Dominique Gallois argues that 'Rouch's contribution lies in showing that anthropologists can gain much by working more with expression, which comprises speech, body, image . . . complete cultural manifestations which are conveyed directly by a film, which has less "filters" than writing . . . which is much less accessible to the audience'.

72. Stoller (1992), ibid. pp. 159, 172, 43; Rouch in *Crossing Boundaries*, ibid.

73. Stoller (1992), ibid., pp. 40, 83. The film-maker Wim Wenders was reported to have walked from Munich to Paris to visit a dying friend 'so as to have time to think about it'.

74. Stoller (1992), ibid., p. 106; see my comments in David Morley and Kevin Robins (1996) *Spaces of Identity*, London and New York: Routledge, p. 211 on the variety of African forms of alterity. On this issue, see also, F. Kramer (1993) *The Red Fez: Art and Spirit Possession in Africa*, London: Verso.

75. Eaton, ibid., p. 51; Rouch in Stoller (1992), ibid., p. 84. See my comments in Chapter 3 on the importance in the research context of simply behaving decently towards one's respondents.

76. Rouch interviewed in Manthia Diawara's (1995) *Rouch in Reverse*, Formation Films London; Rouch quoted in Dan Morgan, Programme Notes to *Les Tambours d' Avant*, *Possessing Visions* Conference, Institute of Contemporary Arts, London 2000; Rouch quoted in Eaton, ibid., pp. 4, 61. When *Les Maîtres fous* was first shown in Paris it created a scandal because of its shocking subject matter, with Rouch being accused of filming Africans 'like an entomologist studying insects'. It has long been mired in debates about how its imagery of the possessed Africans might encourage racist responses from its audiences, whatever Rouch's own intentions in this respect were. For this reason, Rouch was subsequently always very careful to control the circumstances of the film's screenings, in order to try to guard against such unwanted reactions.

77. Stoller (1992), ibid.; Rouch, quoted in Eaton, ibid., p. 26; Rouch in *Crossing Boundaries*.

78. For recent commentaries on Charles Parker's long-neglected œuvre, see the work of Paul Long of the Department of Media and Communications, University of Central England, Birmingham: paul.long@uce.ac.uk.

79. See my comments in Chapter 3 on the middle-class respondents' greater confidence in defending their anonymity in the Brunel Home Uses of Information and Communication Technology study. In that case, it was a matter of class differences; here, it is a contrast between the attitudes and differential sense of empowerment in relation to the film-maker, on the part of colonial and metropolitan interviewees.

80. Eaton, ibid., p. 48.

81. Dan Morgan, Programme Notes to *Tambours*, ibid.

82. Dan Morgan, Programme Notes to *Initiation*, *Possessing Vision* Conference.

83. Dan Morgan, Programme Notes to *La Pyramide humaine*, *Possessing Vision* Conference. Of course, the camera potentially has other useful functions too. Thus Rouch notes that when filming *Moi, un noir* 'the camera was a kind of passport – we could go in all these dangerous places (bars, dives) . . . where people were drunk . . . the camera gave us a pretext' (Rouch interviewed in Diawara, ibid.).

84. Dan Morgan, Programme Notes to *Chronique*, *Possessing Vision* Conference. See my earlier comments on Wodickzo's *Homeless Vehicle* as 'machine' for revealing things that would otherwise remain hidden about the situation of the homeless. Rouch's theory involves an idea of 'cinema-provocation' in which the camera acts as a catalyst inducing greater spontaneity, expression and 'truth'. This is to conceive of cinema as the creation of a new reality: the truth of cinema itself. All of this is presided over by Rouch himself as shaman and master of ceremonies at this cinematic ritual, with his camera as his own magical instrument (Eaton, in Eaton (ed.), ibid., p. 51).

85. Stoller, ibid., p. 169.

86. Dan Morgan, Programme Notes to *Tambours*, *Possessing Visions* Conference.

87. Rouch quoted in Paul Stoller (1994) 'Artaud, Rouch and the Cinema of Cruelty'. In L. Taylor (ed.) *Visualising Theory*, London and New York: Routledge, pp. 83–4.

88. Rouch quoted in Stoller (1992), ibid., p. 218.

89. Dewey, quoted in Stoller (1992), ibid., pp. 212–13; Stoller (1992), ibid., p. 215; Rouch quoted in Eaton, ibid., p. 46; Rouch interviewed in Diawara, ibid.

90. James Clifford (1981) 'On Ethnographic Surrealism', *Comparative Studies in Society and History* 23 (4): 564.

91. Stoller (1992), ibid., pp. 201–6; Rouch quoted in Eaton ibid., 22.

92. Stoller (1992), ibid. pp. 158, 216. See my later discussion of magic in the context of technologically advanced societies in my concluding chapter.

93. Morgan, Programme Notes to *Tambours*.

94. Rouch in *Crossing Boundaries*.

95. Rouch quoted in Eaton, ibid., p. 8.

96. Dan Morgan Programme Notes to *Moi, un noir*, *Possessing Visions* Conference.

97. Eaton, ibid., p. 8.

98. Rouch quoted in Eaton 'The Production of Cinematic Reality', in Eaton (ed.), ibid., p. 51.

99. Lucien Goldmann (1979) 'Cinema and Society' in Eaton (ed.), ibid., p. 73.

100. Morgan, Programme Notes to *Moi, un noir*, *Possessing Visions* Conference.
101. See Clifford Geertz's comments on the root meaning of *fictio* in the original Latin as 'something made . . . [or] . . . fashioned . . . not that it is false' in the essay 'Thick Description' in his (1973) *The Interpretation of Cultures*, New York: Basic Books, p. 15.
102. Arthur Howes (2000) 'Into Africa', *The Guardian* 2 June.
103. Rouch, quoted in Ronald Bergan's obituary of him, *The Guardian*, 20 February 2004.
104. Diawara, ibid.
105. Stoller (1994), ibid.
106. Stoller (1994), ibid., p. 95. For another interesting 'reverse anthropology' see Tete Michel Kpomasie's ethnography of the Arctic (2001) *An African in Greenland*, New York: Review Books.
107. See Sakai in Chapter 6 on the essentially relative meaning of the terms 'East' and 'West'.
108. Quoted in Rouch *Petit à petit*.
109. Stoller (1992), ibid., p. 142.
110. Soller (1994), ibid., pp. 91–2.
111. Rouch, quoted in *Crossing Boundaries*.
112. Jean Rouch was killed in a car crash in Niger in February 2004.

# Part III

# The geography of modernity and the orientation of the future

*Figure 12* Sign for 'Global Forum' based in Tübingen, Germany, whose very name indicates the conventional equation of the Global with the West. Photo by author.

# 5 EurAm, modernity, reason and alterity[1]

## After the West?

## Decentring EurAm man?

Kevin Robins and I have argued elsewhere (Morley and Robins, 1992) that EuroAmerican panics about the 'economic threat' posed by Japan and the 'Four Tigers' of the South-East Asia economy (Taiwan, Hong Kong, South Korea and Singapore) have to be understood in the broader context of the destabilization posed by these developments to the established correlation between the concepts of West/East and modern/pre-modern. To that extent, the supposed centrality of the West as the (necessary) cultural and geographical focus for the project of modernity (or indeed postmodernity) is thus put into question. One effect of all this is then to highlight both the extent to which the Occident/Orient binary is itself a temporal (as much as a geographical) division and conversely, the extent to which the 'temporal' division between modernity and the realm of the pre-modern (or the 'traditional') has long had a crucial geographical sub-text. As Sakai notes 'the West is not simply . . . a geographic category . . . [but rather] a name which always associates itself with those regions . . . that appear economically superior . . . [thus] . . . the historical predicate is translated into a geographical one and vice versa' (Sakai, 1988: 476–7). If history is not only temporal or chronological, but also spatial and relational (and if, conversely, our understanding of geography itself is never historically innocent), then it follows that our analysis of ideas of postmodernity must consequently be informed by this kind of geo-historical perspective, if we are to avoid the worst excesses of EurAmerico-centrism.

Julien and Mercer note the irony that while there has been much talk in contemporary cultural theory of the 'end of representation', or even of the 'end of history', it is only much more recently that the 'political possibilities of the end of ethnocentrism' have begun to receive anything like a comparable degree of attention. They go on to argue that the crucial project for postmodern cultural theory, in relation to questions of 'race', ethnicity and ethnocentrism is not simply to now celebrate that which had previously been deemed 'marginal', but rather to attempt to deconstruct 'the structures that determine what is regarded as culturally marginal'. Their central point is clearly expressed in their very title: 'De Margin and De Centre' – as they argue, the crucial issue is 'to examine and undermine the force of the binary relation that *produces* the marginal as a consequence of the authority invested in the centre' (1988: 2–3; my emphasis).

Although 'postmodernism' is often presented as a description of some supposedly universal condition, its definition is almost always constructed within the terms of what is, in fact, an Anglo-European (or EurAmerican, to use the Japanese term) provincialism – indeed Huyssen speaks of what he calls the 'specifically American character of postmodernism' (1986: 190). Writing from a Latin American perspective, Beverley and Oviedo (1993: 2) note that Octavio Paz claims that postmodernism is simply another imported *grand récit* that does not fit Latin America, which, they argue 'needs to produce its own forms of cultural periodisation' (1993: 2). Their point is that the dominant conceptions of postmodernism (such as Jameson's influential [1985] version) are almost always quite ethnocentric, and tend to involve, as Ahmad argues, 'a suppression of the multiplicity of significant difference among and within both the advanced capitalist countries and the imperialized formations' (Ahmad, 1987: 3; quoted in Beverley and Oviedo, 1993: 4).

Of course, not only postmodernism, but modernism itself, properly understood, can take many forms: Appiah (1993: 249–50) has argued that, in certain African contexts, modernity has, in effect, been represented by Catholicism; Bruner (1993) argues that postmodernism itself is best understood as the specific form that modernity takes in Latin America. Thus Calderon (1993: 54) speaks of how, in Latin America, the very temporalities of the culture are incomplete, mixed and dependent 'because we live in incomplete and mixed times of premodernity, modernity and postmodernity' (cf. Braudel 1984 for a theoretical model for the analysis of simultaneous, differential temporalities), each of which is linked historically to corresponding cultures that are, or were, in turn, epicentres of power. Bruner further points to the differentiated modes of participation in modernity (and postmodernity), as between 'centre' and 'periphery'. As he puts it, 'modernity cannot be read in the fashion of Marshall Berman (1983), as a singular collective experience . . . nor as variations of that same experience that, in the long run, will tend to converge' (1993: 42). He argues that modernity is necessarily a differentiated experience in the capitalist world. Moreover, as he notes, this world still 'has a centre, which radiates a zone of marginal and dependent peripheries' which, despite the complex 'postmodern' dynamics of heterogeneity and displacement, 'continue to be tied to the hegemonic centre' (1993: 52). To this extent, Latin Americans are condemned to live in a world where all the images of modernity and modernism come to us from the outside and become obsolete before we are able to materialise them . . . In all fields of culture . . . the important modern cultural syntheses are first produced in the North and descend later to us . . . This is how it has happened . . . in the long run, with our very incorporation into modernity.

(Bruner, 1993: 52–3)

Beverley and Oviedo (1993) go beyond the 'billiard table' theory of cultural imperialism in which nations impact on each other while remaining, themselves untransformed, 'given' entities. Their point is that the United States itself, long the 'centre of centres' in the imperial world system, is itself being transformed by demographic and linguistic change: soon, the United States will be the third-largest of the world's Hispanic nations. By the advent of the tricentennial of the American revolution (2076), a majority of the United States' population will be of African, Native American, Asian or Latin descent: to this extent the 'centre' itself is not simply being invaded, but transformed by its own erstwhile margins.

However, Richard (1993) takes the matter further when she identifies the contradictory nature of postmodernism's 'heterological disposition' which, as she notes, 'would appear to benefit the resurgence of all those cultural peripheries until now censured by European-western dominance and its universalist foundation in a self-centred representation' (160). She observes that postmodernism loudly proclaims its own role in 'decreeing the end of Eurocentrism', claiming that its own critique of modernity has 'damaged the superiority of the European model, by weakening its fantasies of domination, through the relativisation of absolutes and the delegitimization of universals'. Thus, it seems, the erstwhile subcultures, margins and peripheries are to be invited to be prominent parts of a new 'antiauthoritarian modulation of postmodernity, finally respectful of diversity'. Richard, however, is sceptical about this new tendency to the 'revaluation' of the 'subaltern', in so far as, despite the apparent altruism of the 'postmodern' gesture, these subaltern categories of the margins are still 'spoken for by postmodernity, without obliging the cultural institution [of the centre] to loosen its discursive monopoly over the right to speak'. As Richard goes on to point out, 'celebrating difference as exotic festival . . . is not the same as giving the subject of this difference the right to negotiate its own conditions of discursive control . . . [and] the identity/difference conflict [thus] continues to be arbitrated by the discursivity of the First World'. The simple catch, as Richard observes, is that 'even when their current hypothesis is that of decentring', intellectuals of the most powerful imperial nations continue to be situated at the centre of the debate about decentring (Richard, 1993: 160–1).

As she puts it elsewhere (Richard, 1987), just as it appears that the very heterogeneity of the cultures of Latin America, created out of the discontinuous, multiple and hybrid parts of the continent, are deemed to have prefigured the model now approved and legitimized by the term 'postmodernism' and 'Latin America finds itself in a privileged position, in the vanguard of what is seen as novel', at the same moment, that 'privilege' is withdrawn. As she argues, 'just as it appears that, for once, the Latin American periphery might have achieved the distinction of being post-modernist *avant la lettre* . . . postmodernism abolishes any privilege which such a position might offer . . . dismantles the distinction between centre and periphery and, in so doing, nullifies its significance' (10).

## How Other is the Other?

Todorov (1984) is concerned with what he characterizes as the 'dangers of excessive relativism' in contemporary cultural theory. He concedes, readily, that 'excessive universalism' is a correlative danger, in so far as the 'so-called universality of many theoreticians of the past and present is nothing more nor less than unconscious ethnocentrism, the projection of their own characteristics on a grand scale', to the extent that what has thus been presented as 'universality' has, in fact, been a set of descriptions only appropriate to 'white males in a few European countries'. His central point, however, is that this failure should not lead us, by way of negative reaction, to simply abandon the 'very idea of shared humanity' between and across cultures, which he argues 'would be even more dangerous than ethnocentric universalism' (374). In this connection, Todorov notes Jan-Mohammed's comments on the dangers of 'Manichean allegory', in which 'a field of diverse yet interchangeable oppositions between white and black, good and evil, superiority and inferiority' (Jan-Mohammed, 1986: 82) are produced. In that kind of 'Manichean' writing, Todorov argues, 'racial others are either noble savages or filthy cows . . . [and] whether they are judged inferior (as by those who worship civilization) or superior (as by those who embrace primitivism) they are radically opposed to European whites' (Todorov 1984: 377; cf. Ahmad's account, 1994: 94–5, of his discomforting discovery, on reading Jameson [1986], that 'the man whom I had . . . from a physical distance, taken as a comrade was, in his own opinion, my civilization other').

Suleri, somewhat acidically, argues that if cultural criticism is to address the uses to which it puts the agency of alterity 'then it must . . . face the theoretical question that S.P. Mohanty (1989) succinctly formulates: "Just how other, we need to force ourselves to indicate, is the other?"' (Suleri, 1992: 9). Suleri's argument here is that, while the decentring of colonial discourses in recent social theory has been an essential step forward, there are limits beyond which an articulation of Otherness serves merely to 'ventriloquise the fact of cultural difference'. As she notes, a mere rehearsal of the proven manifestations of alterity finally leads to 'a theoretical repetitiveness that . . . entrenches rather than displaces the rigidity of the self/other binarism governing traditional discourse on colonialisation'. The problem, as she notes, is that the language of alterity can all too easily be read as 'a postmodern variant on the obsolescent idiom of romance: the very insistence on the centrality of difference as an unreadable entity can serve to obfuscate and indeed to sensationalise that which still remains to be read' (11). Her point is that the 'fallacy of the totality of otherness' is but the necessary complement to 'the fiction of complete empowerment both claimed by and accorded to colonial domination' (13). Similarly, she argues, while 'alteritism' begins as a strategy designed to destablize Eurocentric or Orientalist perspectives, 'its indiscriminate reliance on the centrality of otherness tends to replicate what, in the context of imperialist discourse, was the familiar category of the exotic' (12).

Chow (1993) argues that, strangely enough, the first cousin of the Orientalist is the Maoist (in his or her latter-day 'subaltern' form, within American cultural studies) who 'contrary to the Orientalist disdain for contemporary native cultures of the non-West' tends towards a Third Worldist fantasy which 'turns all people from non-western cultures into a generalised "subaltern" that is then used to flog an equally generalised "West"' (13). Chow's point is that this notion of 'subalternity', 'when construed strictly in terms of the *foreignness* of race, land and language, can blind us to political exploitation as easily as it can alert us to it' (9), not least because, most particularly, 'the representation of "the other" as such ignores . . . the class and intellectual hierarchies within these other cultures' (13).

In a similar vein, Ahmad (1994) criticizes much recent work on 'alterity', in so far as it displays a tendency to set the issue up as a matter of 'civilisational, primordial, difference'. As he notes, from this kind of perspective, the 'whole history of western textualities, from Homer to Olivia Manning' then tends to be treated as a 'history of orientalist ontology', against which is posed a simple category of 'Third World' literature as 'prima facie the site of liberationist practice' (64). Against this kind of Manichean approach, Ahmad is concerned to defend a concept of difference 'written with a lower-case "d", as something local and empirically verifiable, not . . . [as] any epistemological category or perennial ontological condition' (90). He is vehemently opposed to the tendency towards the representation of the colonized (or post-colonial) Other as an undifferentiated 'mass' (cf. Raymond Williams's oft-cited comment to the effect that 'there are no masses, only ways of seeing other people as masses').

Todorov's central argument (1984) is that what he regards as the over-relativistic tendency in contemporary postmodern cultural theory has too often led to the affirmation of the existence of incommunicability among cultures which, in his view, 'presupposes adherence to a racialist, apartheid-like set of beliefs, postulating as it does insurmountable discontinuity within the human species'. His own position is founded on the premise that the comprehension of Otherness possible, in principle, precisely because Otherness is never radical, in so far as if we are 'separated by cultural differences, we are also united by a common human identity' (374; see also West [1994] for a perspective that also goes 'Beyond Eurocentrism and Multi-Culturalism').

For the same reasons, Todorov is impatient with the radical critique of Orientalism, in so far as that critique often seems to suppose 'that there is no such thing as a Japanese culture or Near Eastern traditions – or that this culture and their traditions are impossible to describe . . . [or that] past attempts at describing them tell us about *nothing* except the observers' prejudices' (1984: 374; original emphasis). His particular scorn is reserved for that kind of relativistic cultural analysis which approaches, as he puts it 'texts which speak of tortures and lynchings . . . with a critical apparatus that precludes any interrogation concerning their truth and values, or which combats the very idea of seeking truth and values' (379). Clearly, Todorov would, in this respect, have concurred with the late Bob Scholte, when he concluded that 'while we may never know the whole truth, and may not have the literary means to tell all that we think we know of truth . . . shouldn't we nevertheless, keep trying to tell it?' (Scholte, 1987: 39). Todorov's argument continues with Appiah's salutary comment on W.E.B. Du Bois' work on racism, to the effect that Du Bois 'throughout his life . . . was concerned not just with the meaning of race but with the truth about it' (Appiah, 1986: 22). As Todorov wryly observes, it is only within a certain kind of sheltered academic institution that it is possible to flirt with the sceptical or relativistic suspension of all values and truth-claims. Getting away from the 'worshipping [of] dogmas as immutable truth' need not entail by any means, the abandonment of 'the idea of truth itself' (Todorov, 1984: 379).

## There are no 'African' truths

Appiah (1993), in his discussion of whether the 'post' in post-colonial is the same as that in postmodern, begins from the premise that the 'modernist characterisation of modernity must be challenged' (233). More specifically, he argues that Weber's characterization of modernity, as entailing the gradual but inevitable rationalization of the world, must be rejected, not least on empirical grounds. Thus, Appiah argues, what we see around us is hardly anything so grand as 'the triumph of Enlightenment Reason . . . but rather what Weber mistook for that . . . the incorporation of all areas of the world . . . and of formerly "private" life into the money economy' (234). Appiah's point is that, according to Weber's theory, modernist rationalization should be accompanied both by a systematic process of secularization and by the decline of charisma – neither of which have occurred. As he notes, twentieth-century politics has been dominated by a series of charismatic leaders (Stalin, Hitler, Mao, etc.) and religions (not to mention nationalisms) are growing all over the world (not least in the United States – see my comments in Chapter 6).

His claim is that Weber got modernity fundamentally wrong; that 'the beginning of postmodern wisdom' (234) is to recognize that Weberian 'rationalization' has not occurred. In large part this is, according to Appiah, because Weber sets up 'tradition' and 'modernity' too simplistically, as mutually opposed and necessarily mutually exclusive categories. For Appiah, this binary, apart from anything else, simply fails to fit the facts of his own Ghanaian childhood, in which, he recalls, if 'I grew up . . . believing in constitutional democracy . . . I also knew that we owed respect to the chiefs of the Asante'. For Appiah, the benefits of modernity were clear from an early age: 'by the time I was old enough to be *for* democracy, I knew we were also *for* development and modernisation; that this meant roads and hospitals and schools (as opposed to paths through the bush, and juju and ignorance)'. However, crucially, in terms of recent debates concerning identity and alterity, Appiah notes: 'None of [this – that is, the fruits of development] of course, did we take to rule out the proper pouring of libation to the ancestors. . . . In a slogan: I grew up believing in development *and* in preserving the best of our cultural heritage' (1993: 256–7).

At another point in his argument, Appiah simply advises that 'we must not overstate the distance from London to Lagos' (121). He is vehemently opposed both to 'what we might call "alteritism", the constitution and celebration of oneself as other' (251) and to being 'treated as an otherness-machine' (253; cf. Suleri, 1989) by a postmodernism/post-colonialism which 'seems to demand of its Africa . . . [something] all-too-close to what modernism . . . demanded of it' (Appiah, 1993: 253–4) – that is, a source of 'primitive authenticity'. Appiah's contention is, reasonably enough, that the 'role that Africa – like the rest of the Third World – plays for Euro-American postmodernism . . . must be distinguished from the role that postmodernism might play in the Third World' (254).

Appiah's concern is to get away from the 'postulation of a unitary Africa over against a monolithic West' – as an unproductive binarism of self and Other which, he suggests, is 'the last of the shibboleths of the modernisers that we must learn to live without' (251). Indeed, overcoming this binarism is, according to Appiah, crucial for all concerned, in so far as he suggests that 'the question what is to *be* modern is one that Africans and westerners may ask together. And . . . neither of us will understand what modernity is, until we understand each other' (172).

The complement to Appiah's critique of binarist theories of alterity is an equally fierce opposition to all forms of postmodern relativism, whether in matters of ethics or of epistemology. In his sympathetic reading of Yambo Ouologuem's 1968 novel *Bound to Violence* (published in English in 1971), Appiah notes approvingly that, rather than 'make common cause with a relativism that might allow the horrifying new-old Africa of exploitation to be understood – legitimated – in its own local terms', the basis for Ouologuem's 'project of delegitimation, is very much *not* the postmodernist one: rather, it is grounded in an appeal to an ethical universal . . . an appeal to a certain simple respect for human suffering' (Appiah, 1993: 246).

Similarly, in matters of epistemology, in his discussion of 'Ethnophilosophy and its critics', Appiah is sympathetic to Wiredu's (1979) critique of the apostles of *Négritude*, in his essay 'How Not to Compare African Thought with Western Thought'. In that essay, Wiredu, as a believer in the universality of reason (cf. Gellner, 1992), argues that ideas that there is something particularly 'African' about superstitions concerning spirits, etc. are quite misguided – in so far as this, Appiah notes, 'derives from a failure to notice that these beliefs are very like beliefs widely held in the European past' (Appiah 1993: 164). As he notes, 'what is distinctive in African traditional thought is that it is traditional; there is nothing especially African about it' (167; see also Ahmad's [1994: 289–90] critique of Jameson's theory of Third World literature as 'national allegory', for a similar argument concerning Jameson's failure to see the relevant parallels with the literature of medieval Europe). Appiah supports both Wiredu's analytic contention, that the 'traditional' mode of thought is not specifically African (or 'Third Worldist'), and his negative evaluation of its authoritarian dimensions, which, on Enlightenment grounds, Wiredu holds to be deleterious, in that they function to hold back 'development'. This process Wiredu defines as 'a continuing world-historical process in which all peoples, Western and non-Western alike, are engaged', which is to be 'measured by the degree to which rational methods have penetrated through habits'. For Appiah, as for Wiredu himself, 'there are no African truths [cf. Chow, 1993: 6, on this], only truths – some of them about Africa' (quoted in Appiah, 1993: 166).

## Postmodernism, anti-imperialism and the Enlightenment project

In his critique of much postmodern and post-colonial theory, Ahmad (1994) is particularly critical of metropolitan critics whose 'radicalism', in his view, can be equated with the rejection of rationalism (or the 'Enlightenment project') itself. For them, as he puts it, it seems that 'any attempt to *know* the world as a whole, or to hold that it is open to rational comprehension, let alone the desire to change it . . . [is] to be dismissed as a contemptible attempt to construct "grand narratives" and "totalising knowledges"'. Ahmad's epistemological position is rather hard-edged, as can be judged from his stringent assertions that 'the more recently fashionable postmodernisms offer false knowledges of real facts' and that 'postmodernism . . . is, in the most accurate sense of these words, repressive and bourgeois' (35–6). For Ahmad, it is the postmodernists' 'dismissal of class and reason as so many "essentialisms"' which is reprehensible – not least because, as he rightly notes, this leads logically (and inevitably) to a methodologically individualist standpoint (with the decentred individual as the only possible locus of mean-ing) while, he notes, 'the well known postmodernist scepticism about the possibility of rational knowledge impels that same "individual" to maintain only an ironic relation with the world and its intelligibility' (36).

In a parallel argument, in his review of Bhabha, Eagleton notes that, like many postmodernists, Bhabha is opposed on principle to fixed binary oppositions, such as that between colony and metropolis, or any version of 'us or them'. However, Eagleton argues that Bhabha's own analysis ultimately remains trapped in these same oppositions:

> On one side we have a set of unqualifiedly positive terms: the marginal, the ambivalent, the transitional and the indeterminate. Against these, line up a set of darkly demonised notions: unity, fixity, progress, consensus, stable selfhood. Like most postmodern writers, Bhabha romanticises the marginal and the transgressive, and can find almost nothing of value in unity, coherence or consensus.
>
> (Eagleton, 1994)

The point, as far as Eagleton is concerned, is that Bhabha's analysis remains stuck in the predictable and repetitive orthodoxies of 'the language of cultural difference' which displays an orthodoxy every bit as tenacious as the one it aims to critique. As Eagleton argues, 'post-colonial thought, too, has its rigorous exclusions, its canon, its compulsory key words', and within it one is 'allowed to talk about cultural differences, but not – or not much – about economic exploitation' (Eagleton, 1994).

Ahmad's own critique of Bhabha's postmodernist claims, in his earlier *Nation and Narration* (Bhabha, 1990) is, in part, founded on the simple but telling observation that Bhabha himself lives in just those 'material conditions of *post* modernity which preserve the benefits of modernity as the very ground from which judgements on the past – of this *post* – may be delivered.' In Ahmad's view, 'it takes a very modern, very affluent . . . kind of intellectual to debunk both the idea of "progress" . . . not to speak of "modernity" itself, as mere "rationalisations" of "authoritarian" tendencies within cultures' (1994: 68). His point is that by way of contrast, 'those who live . . . in places where a majority of the population has been denied access to . . . [the] . . . benefits of "modernity" . . . can hardly afford [literally] the terms of such thought' (68–9).

Ahmad is concerned with the 'sociology of knowledge' of post-colonial theory itself, which he provocatively characterizes as 'an upper-class émigré phenomenon, at odds with its own class origin and metropolitan location' (1994: 210), which in his view, tends to the overdramatization of the 'fate of exile', often misrepresenting 'personal preference as fate ordained by repression' (209). One of the dangers Ahmad focuses on concerns the extent to which, as he puts it, the 'East, reborn and greatly expanded now as a "Third World" . . . seems to have become, for many postmodern theorists again, a *career* – even for the "Oriental" this time, and within the "Occident" too' (94, original emphasis; on this see also Chow, 1993: 15). Even though these descendants of the Maoists [American 'subalternists' may be quick to point out the exploitativeness of Benjamin Disraeli's "The East is a Career", they remain blind to their own exploitativeness, as they make "The East" their career'.

However, beyond these contentious and perhaps unnecessarily personalized barbs, Ahmad has one very serious concern in mind. It is not the simple disingenuity of the upper-class émigré that Ahmad is troubled by, when such writers focus exclusively on their exile status and disavow their own personal class origins. The further issue concerns the effect of this disavowal, in distorting subsequent analytic work, from which the issue of class differences then tends, unsurprisingly, to be evacuated. Thus, Ahmad is acerbic about what he describes as 'the issue of post-modern, upper-class migrancy', where the

> migrant in question comes from a *nation* which is subordinated in the imperialist system of inter-state relationships but, simultaneously, from the *class* . . . which is the dominant [one] within that nation . . . [making] it possible for the migrant to arrive in the metropolitan country to join . . . the professional middle strata . . . [and] to forge a . . . rhetoric which submerges the class question and speaks of migrancy as an ontological condition.
>
> (1994: 12–13)

We are back, once more, with the question of reason, alterity and the Other – and with the crucial question as to whether difference is to be (implicitly or explicitly) written with a small or a large 'D' – because the suppression of internal class difference is, in Ahmad's view, the correlative of Manichean theories of alterity. Ahmad's point is that, too often in contemporary cultural theory, 'the whole of the "Third World", with all its classes singularised into an oppositionality' is idealized as 'the site, simultaneously, of alterity and authenticity' (33). Thus, he notes that ideas of 'cultural nationalism' frequently resonate with concepts of an autonomous/indigenous 'authentic' tradition, and that in many analyses of this sort, the tradition/modernity binary of the early 'modernization' theorists (cf. Lerner, 1964) is simply inverted, in an indigenist direction, so that tradition is then held to be superior to modernity, for the Third World, and the most obscurantist positions can then be defended in the name of cultural nationalism.

Ahmad is centrally concerned to deny that nationalism is 'some unitary thing, always progressive or always retrograde' (1994: 11). His criticisms are most pointedly aimed at what he describes as the patently postmodernist way of debunking *all* efforts to speak of origins, collectivities . . . [or] determinate historical projects'. This tendency he views as having the disabling consequence of making critics operating from such premises incapable of distinguishing 'between the progressive and retrograde forms of nationalism' so that 'what gets debunked, rather, is nationalism, as such' (38). This is an outcome which Ahmad abhors, precisely because of the fact that, as far as he is concerned, given that 'for human collectivities in the backward zones of capital . . . all relationships with imperialism pass through their own nation-states', the national struggle remains crucial, since 'there is simply no way of breaking out of that imperial dominance without struggling for . . . a revolutionary restructuring of one's own nation-state' (1994: 11). Ahmad is most concerned to avoid what he describes as 'monolithic attitudes towards the issue of nationalism' (1994: 41), whether those are attitudes of unconditional celebration or contemptuous dismissal: his own interest is in a conjunctural analysis of the differential functions of nationalism, in various historical circumstances (cf. Mattelart, 1979).

Brennan (1989) offers a parallel analysis to that of Ahmad in this respect, drawing on Gramsci's argument that colonization is not simply an international but always also a domestic matter. In this he supports Mattelart's argument that

> Imperialism can only act when it is an integral part of the movement of a country's own national social forces. In other words, external forces can only appear and exercise their deleterious activities in each nation

through mediation with internal forces . . . To pose the problem of imperialism therefore also means posing the problem of the classes which act as its relays in these different nations.

(Mattelart, 1979: 58–9)

It is for precisely this reason, as Brennan notes, that Gramsci argued that the 'international situation has to be considered in its national aspect' (quoted in Brennan, 1989: 13).

I shall return to the question of nationalism and of its resurgence as a troubling feature of our postmodern times in the final section of this chapter. In that section I shall argue that what we may see, in the future of EurAm, at least, resembles not so much the 'postmodern culture of fun' (Mestrovic, 1994), but something rather darker, associated with Europe's own 'Dark Ages'. However, before arguing that the future of EurAm may be going backwards, I want to return to some of the implications of cross-referencing the temporal and spatial perspectives which I outlined at the beginning of my argument. I noted earlier, in relation to the recent 'Japan panic' in the West, that modernity (or perhaps postmodernity) may perhaps in future, be located more in the Pacific than the Atlantic: a prospect that fundamentally undermines the long-established equation of the Occident with modernity, progress and the keys to the world's future. I now want to explore the extent to which, viewed in the *longue durée* of historical development, the West's association with (and dominance over the definition of) modernity (as constituted by reason, science and progress), amounts precisely to no more than a historical phenomenon (if one of relatively long duration) in so far as, up to about the fifteenth century, the Occident can be seen to have lagged far behind the Orient in many respects. Put more plainly, this is to argue that the association between the Occident and modernity has to be viewed as radically contingent, in historical terms. If there is no necessary relation between these terms, then it follows that to oppose either one of them it is not necessary to oppose the other.

## From techno-Orientalism to Oriental proto-modernism

Nowadays of course, a playful postmodernism is itself seen to transcend the dismal travails of modernity itself. The main burden of the work of historians such as Wolf (1982) and Wallerstein (1974) is to dislodge the narcissism of the traditional perspective, with its overemphasis on the internal, self-generating narrative of the West, and to resituate it within the broader context of world history (cf. also Amin, 1989). The general thrust of this argument is that we must get away, finally, both from this emphasis on

EuroAmerican 'exceptionalism' and from its shadow – 'ethnohistory' – which, as Wolf observes, perhaps 'has been so called to separate it from "real" history, the study of the supposedly civilized' (Wolf, 1982: 19). In fact, as Wolf notes, 'the more ethnohistory we know, the more clearly "their" history and "our" history emerge as part of the same story'. As he puts it, in a formulation parallel to that of Appiah (1993), 'there can be no "Black history" apart from "White history" – and of course, *vice versa*' (cf. also Davis, 1992).

In fact, within the now largely discredited field of 'Orientalism', a number of authors, such as Hourani (1992) and Hodgson (1993), offer insights similar to those of Wolf and Wallerstein. For example, it is to Hodgson (1974: xvii) that we owe the characterization of the traditional 'Mercator' projection of the map of the world, centred as it is on Europe (and thus systematically distorting our image of the southern hemisphere) as what he called the 'Jim Crow projection'. Hodgson's project, as Burke notes, in his 'Introduction' to Hodgson's *Rethinking World History* (1993), was precisely to 'resituate the history of the West in a global context, and in the process, unhook it from Eurocentric teleologies (or what we might call, post-Foucault, the European master discourse on itself)' (in Hodgson, 1993: xii). The issue is how to think of modernity, not so much as specifically or *necessarily* 'European' (*contra* Weber's analysis in *The Protestant Ethic and the Spirit of Capitalism*, 1958) but only contingently so. Hodgson is concerned to avoid, in Burke's phrase, the kind of 'Westernism' that gives us 'the history of the West as the story of freedom and rationality . . . [and] the history of the East (pick an East, any East) as the story of despotism and cultural stasis' (Burke, in Hodgson, 1993: xv). In Hodgson's analysis, Islam was, for long, the vastly richer and more successful Other against which the West defined itself, and it was not until around 1500 that western Europe reached the cultural level of the major Oriental civilizations. Thus, Burke notes (see also Wolf, 1982) that the conventional picture of modernity, as an 'ascending curve which runs from ancient Greece to the Renaissance, to modern times' is but an optical illusion (1993: xix). In fact, Hodgson argues that, for most of recorded history, Europe was actually an insignificant outpost of mainland Asia. Indeed, his argument is that if the history of 'civilization' is to have a 'centre', then, from a world historical point of view, that centre is Asia. Moreover, as Burke points out in relation to the question of modernity itself, for Hodgson

> the Renaissance did not inaugurate modernity. Instead, it brought Europe up to the cultural level of the other major civilisations of the Oikoumene ('the world of settled agriculture, cities and high culture', Hourani, 1992: 3). It did so . . . by assimilating the advances of other Asian

civilisations. The list of inventions which developed elsewhere and diffused subsequently to Europe is very long.

(Burke, in Hodgson, 1993: xix)

It is, indeed, a very long list, and one of some consequence, given both the centrality of ideas of technological advance to our conception of 'progress', 'civilization' and 'modernity', and the taken-for-granted assumption that technology is largely a (if not *the*) key sphere of western superiority (but see also the argument below on the significance of Japan's recent 'repositioning' as the key site of current technological advancement).

Claxton observes that the English philosopher Francis Bacon (1561–1626) selected three innovations – paper and printing, gunpowder and the magnetic compass – which had done more, he thought, than anything else to transform the world. Claxton notes that Bacon considered the origin of all these inventions to be 'obscure' and died without knowing that they were all, in fact, originally Chinese (Claxton, 1994: 27). The central point is, of course, that the European Renaissance, far from being self-generated, drew very heavily on Arab cultures, not least because the European rediscovery of classical Greek knowledge in the Renaissance was based on Arabic trans-lations, which had been, through Europe's 'Dark Ages', their principal repository (cf. Brown, 1991, on the role of the Byzantine empire in this respect). The recapture by Christian Spain of Toledo (in 1085) and of Cordoba (in 1236), two leading Muslim centres of learning, gave Christian Europe access to Muslim scientific knowledge and the Arabic system of numeration. Thus, Claxton argues, far from being something *inherently* Western, 'what we call science arose as a result of new methods of experi-ment, observation and measurement, which were introduced into Europe by the Arabs . . . [modern] science is the most momentous contribution of the Islamic civilizations' (Claxton, 1994: 18).

Indeed, Claxton quotes Singer's *History of Technology* to the effect that it was in fact 'largely by imitation, and, in the end by improvement of the techniques and models that had come from or through the Near East, that the products of the West ultimately rose to eminence' (quoted in Claxton, 1994: 18). For our purposes, one of the most interesting points is that, if this is seen to be so, then the relation of European to Muslim science and technology in the early modern period (in which western inferiority rose eventually to superiority, first through imitation and later through improve-ment on models copied) can be seen to be in close parallel with the relation of Japanese to EuroAmerican technologies in the late twentieth century, in which the originally inferior 'imitators' finally surpass their erstwhile 'masters' (see also Morita, 1986, for a detailed history of this 'trans-formation', in the case of Sony).

If the future is to be technological and the Orient is fast colonizing the realm of high technology (cf. Singapore as the first 'fully wired', postmodern city-state), then it must follow that the future will be Oriental too. What of the future for EurAm? As has been widely reported, the past few years have seen the United States fundamentally rethinking its traditional 'Atlantic' orientation. Recently we have seen the rise of a conflictual relationship between the United States and the European Community as a whole (*vide* the conflicts between the United States and France in the last round of GATT negotiations and the 'teeth-gritting' nature of the EuroAmerican alliance's contortions throughout the crisis in Bosnia). Now the United States shows increasing signs of seeing its own economic future as focused on Pacific rather than Atlantic trade agreements. Perhaps President Roosevelt's pronunciation of the dawn of the 'Pacific era', made originally in 1903, is finally coming to fruition: 'The Mediterranean era died with the discovery of America, the Atlantic era is now at the height of its development and must soon exhaust the resources at its command; the Pacific era, destined to be the greatest of all, is just at its dawn' (quoted in Knightley, 1991). If so, the Parisian origins of much postmodern theory notwithstanding, what are the prospects for Europe itself, in the era of postmodernity?

## Postmodernity in EurAm: the return of the Dark Ages?

The French historian, Alain Minc, argues that what the future of Europe offers is something rather similar to the experience of its own 'Middle Ages'. We are, in his view, going back, with the contemporary collapse of the nation-state, towards a situation of 'a lasting, semi-stabilised disorder, which feeds on itself' (Minc, 1994). This point is amplified by the British historian, Norman Stone, who similarly claims that we may well be heading towards a situation comparable to that of England during the 'Wars of the Roses' in the fifteenth century, where the dominant form of sociality was not so much nationalism as tribalism (Stone, 1994; see also Maffesoli, 1994). Stone further offers an analogy between the current status of the European Commission and that of the papacy in the fifteenth century – as a 'shadowy sovereign body which doesn't have much in the way of teeth; which is the ultimate law-making body, but where, in fact, there are huge areas simply without the law' (Stone, 1994), as the nation-state disintegrates, both from above and from below.

Minc makes much the same point, when he argues that we are now well beyond the Foucauldian nightmare of the 'all-seeing eye of the state' or the 'long arm of the law'. The emergence of 'grey zones', which are effectively 'no-go' areas for agencies of social control, places where legislative power no longer exists, again parallels the experience of the Middle Ages, in his view. As he puts it, perhaps rather melodramatically, 'when you go into a "difficult" suburb of Paris today (or of Birmingham for that matter) – there is no more enforcement of social order – no more policemen, social workers – the only form of social organisation comes from the drug economy. They are, of course, small areas, but they did not exist five years ago' (Minc, 1994). Many North American cities perhaps still run a little ahead of Europe in this respect.

The point is that if, for three centuries, in Europe, the state has been established to create order, today we are seeing areas developing without any kind of order or state power. Minc's view in this respect, is again reinforced by Stone:

> The writ of the central state, which had been growing [in Europe] since the time of Absolutism in the 16th century, has now ceased to run in parts of many countries . . . You can see tower block estates, for example, in many European cities, which are in fact run by drug barons. In those areas, you simply have to come to terms with the local robber baron . . . and in that sense, you are then back in something very like the experience of the Middle Ages.
>
> (Stone, 1994)

Both Enzensberger (1994) and Mestrovic (1994) have also offered analyses of the tendencies towards societal disintegration with which Minc and Stone are concerned. Enzensberger offers a cogent analysis of the ways in which the end of the Cold War has in fact resulted in a new era of large numbers of uncontrollable 'civil wars', large and small. Similarly, Ignatieff (1994) argues that, in the post-Cold War period, when large sections of the world no longer come within any clearly defined sphere of imperial, or great power influence, 'huge sections of the world's population have won the right of self-determination on the cruellest possible terms – they have been simply left to fend for themselves' (Ignatieff, 1994: 8).

Both Enzensberger and Ignatieff argue that we may be moving towards something unpleasantly similar to the Hobbesian 'war of all against all'. In this situation, conflicts tend to perpetually subdivide those who had previously been able to exist peaceably as neighbours (under a system of what Ignatieff calls 'civic nationalism') into enemies (with the terms of 'ethnic nationalism'). Writing in the mid-1990s Enzensberger offers the example of the civil war in Afghanistan, and argues that

> as long as the country was occupied by Soviet troups the situation invited interpretation along Cold War lines: Moscow was supporting its

surrogates, the West the Mujahedin. On the surface it was all about national liberation, resistance to the foreigners, the oppressors, the unbelievers. But no sooner had the occupiers been driven off then the real civil war broke out. Nothing remained of the ideological shell . . . the war of everyone against everyone else took its course . . . what remains is the armed mob.

(1994: 17)

Recent images of the conflicts in Somalia and in Rwanda would seem, unfortunately, to bear out many of Enzensberger's gloomy prognostications.

In precisely this vein, in his analysis of the conflicts in ex-Yugoslavia, Ignatieff argues that 'Ethnic nationalism [has] delivered the ordinary people of the Balkans straight back to the pre-political state of nature where, as Hobbes predicted, life is nasty, brutish and short' (1994: 30). Mestrovic (1994) offers, as his subtitle has it, a disturbing analysis of the 'confluence of postmodernism and postcommunism' in eastern Europe, as presaging the potential 'Balkanization of the West'. He defines 'Balkanization' as a process of 'the breaking up of a unit into increasingly smaller units that are hostile to each other' but adds immediately, lest his emphasis be misunderstood, that 'there is no good reason to understand Balkanization literally, as something that must apply only to the Balkans' (ix). Mestrovic notes that the term 'Balkanization' was, of course, invented 'to denote *those people* in the Balkans who seem likely to slaughter each other' as opposed to 'the civilised Americans, French and British' (viii, original emphasis). However, his own analysis leads him to conclude that this is no matter of there being some special tendency towards bloodlust and hatred, on the part of the people who happen to inhabit that particular geographical region (which would be, as Ignatieff observes [1994: 15], to 'make excuses for ourselves . . . [by dismissing] the Balkans as a sub-rational zone of intractable fanaticism'). Rather, in Mestrovic's view, the conflict in ex-Yugoslavia presages the beginning of a broader process of the unravelling or 'Balkanization' of both the former Soviet Union and, potentially, many parts of Europe. So much, as Mestrovic observes, for the 'postmodern culture of fun' as opposed to the 'grim realities of postcommunism' (1994: 1).

Ignatieff's (1994) account of life in ex-Yugoslavia conforms depressingly well to what might, at first sight, appear to be the rather over-pessimistic views of Minc and Stone (quoted earlier). Thus, for example, Ignatieff notes that, in the Balkans, what had been one of the most civilized parts of Europe (particularly in terms of multiculturalism: for a novelistic account see Andric, 1993) has now returned to the barbarism of the Middle Ages, where such law and order as there is, is administered by warlords. There is little gasoline, so the villages have returned to the era before the motor car. Everyone goes about on foot . . . Late 20th-century nationalism has delivered one part of Europe back to the time before the nation state, to the chaos of late feudal civil war.

(1994: 34)

Indeed, Ignatieff's own experience would seem to substantiate Minc and Stone's speculations concerning the return of medieval figures, roles and institutions. Thus, he noted that

Large portions of the former Yugoslavia are now ruled by figures that have not been seen in Europe since late medieval times: the warlords. They appear wherever the nation state disintegrates . . . in the Lebanon, Somalia, Northern India, Armenia, Georgia, Ossetia, Cambodia . . . With their carphones, faxes and exquisite personal weaponry, they look postmodern, but the reality is pure early medieval.

(1994: 28)

What is distinctive about Ignatieff's analysis is that, beyond these descriptive or generalized observations, he also offers an account of the causal dynamics which drive the processes of 'Balkanization' and ethnic hatred. He offers an account of this 'slide into hatred', as neither an expression of some innate human tendency to abhor or reject 'Otherness', nor as an irrational aberration. Rather, for Ignatieff, what we see here is the all-too-understandable response of frightened people to the collapse of the framework of social order which had previously been sustained, however partially, by the nation-state. The situation is perhaps not too dissimilar from that which has long confronted many young blacks in the ghettos of Los Angeles, for whom it is often not so much a matter of choosing to wear the colours of the Cripps because they hate the Bloods (or *vice versa*), but rather a matter of it being too dangerous to have no allies in a 'war-zone' and of therefore being forced into choosing sides. For any one individual, this is, of course, a fear-driven, defensive strategy. However, as Durkheim (1964) observed, social processes operate behind the backs of individuals, and the overall, if unintended, social effect of this formation of defensive allegiances is, of course, to reinforce the need for others to do the same. Thus the vicious cycle of fear becomes self-sustaining.

In the Balkan situation, Ignatieff argues that what we see now as 'ethnic hatred' is largely the result of 'the terror that arises when legitimate authority disintegrates' (1994: 16). In his account, what happened was that 'in the fear and panic which swept the ruins of the communist states, people began to ask: so who will protect me now?' (1994: 6). In his analysis, 'nationalism' and 'ethnic belonging' are seen to be persuasive precisely because they offer 'protection'. As Ignatieff puts it

> The warlord offers protection . . . a solution. He tells his people: if we cannot trust our neighbours, let us rid ourselves of them . . . The logic of ethnic cleansing is not just motivated by nationalist hatred. 'Cleansing' is the warlord's coldly rational solution to the war of all against all. Rid yourself of your neighbours, the warlord says, and you no longer have to fear them. Live among your own, and you can live in peace, with me and my boys to protect you.
>
> (1994: 30)

In this, perhaps, we see some of the features of the darker side of post-modernity, where alterity and heterogeneity are less cause for celebration than for fear. It is beyond dispute that the history of the 'Enlightenment project of Modernity' (cf. Habermas, 1987) is riddled with EurAmerico-centrism, and with class, gender and racial biases. If, however, as I have argued earlier, the relation of the project to its geohistorical and social origins is a contingent one, then the exposure of those origins, and the critique of these disabling biases, should perhaps lead us not to abandon the project, but rather to attempt to pursue it more tenaciously, elsewhere, even if its days are numbered in EurAm.

## Note

An earlier version of this chapter appeared in D. Morley and K.H. Chen (eds) (1996) *Stuart Hall: Critical Dialogues in Cultural Studies*, London and New York, Routledge. Written as this chapter was before the American invasions of Afghanistan and Iraq, some of this analysis is now, inevitably, dated. I would, however, still stand by the main thrust of the argument developed here. DM, August 2006.

## References

Ahmad, A. (1987) 'Jameson's Rhetoric on Otherness and the National Allegory', *Social Text* 17.
—— (1994) *In Theory: Classes, Nations, Literatures*, London: Verso.
Amin, S. (1989) *Eurocentrism*, London: Zed Books.
Andric, I. (1993) *The Bridge Over the Drina*, New York: Harvill.
Appiah, K.A. (1986) 'The Uncompleted Argument: Du Bois and the Illusion of Race', in H.L. Gates, Jr (ed.) *'Race', Writing and Difference*, Chicago, Ill.: University of Chicago Press, pp. 21–38.
—— (1993) *In My Father's House: What Does it Mean to Be an African Today?*, London: Methuen.

Berman, M. (1983) *All That Is Solid Melts into Air: The Experience of Modernity*, London: Verso.

Beverley, J. and Oviedo, J. (1993) 'Introduction', *Boundary* 2, 20 (3), *Special Issue* on 'The Postmodernism Debate in Latin America', Duke University Press, 1–18.

Bhabha, H. (ed.) (1990) *Nation and Narration*, London: Routledge.

—— (1994) *The Location of Culture*, London: Routledge.

Braudel, F. (1984) *The Perspective of the World* (*Civilization and Capitalism*, Vol. III), New York: Harper & Row.

Brennan, T. (1989) 'Cosmopolitans and Celebrities', *Race and Class* 31 (1): 1–19.

Brown, P. (1991) *The World of Late Antiquity*, London: Thames & Hudson.

Bruner, J. (1993) 'Notes on Modernity and Postmodernity in Latin American Culture', *Boundary* 2, 20, 34–55.

Calderon, F. (1993) 'Latin American Identity and Mixed Temporalities: or, How to Be Postmodern and Indian at the Same Time', *Boundary* 2, 20 (3), 55–65.

Chow, R. (1993) *Writing Diaspora*, Bloomington, Ind.: Indiana University Press.

Claxton, M. (1994) *Culture and Development: A Study*, Paris: Unesco.

Davis, J. (1992) 'History and the People without Europe', in K. Hastrup (ed.) *Other Histories*, London, Routledge.

Durkheim, E. (1964) *The Rules of Sociological Method*, New York: Free Press.

Eagleton, T. (1994) 'Goodbye to the Enlightenment', *The Guardian*, 5 May.

Enzensberger, H. (1994) *Civil War*, London: Granta Books.

Gellner, E. (1992) *Postmodernism, Reason and Religion*, London: Routledge.

Habermas, J. (1987) *The Philosophical Discourse of Modernity*, Cambridge: Polity Press.

Hodgson, M.G.S. (1974) 'In the Centre of the Map: Nations See Themselves as the Hub of History', reprinted as ch. 2 in Hodgson (1993), below.

—— (1993) *Rethinking World History: Essays on Europe, Islam and World History*, Cambridge: Cambridge University Press.

Hourani, A. (1992) *Islam in European Thought*, Cambridge: Cambridge University Press.

Huyssen, A. (1986) 'Mass Culture as Woman: Modernism's Other', in T. Modleski (ed.) *Studies in Entertainment*, Bloomington, Ind.: Indiana University Press, pp. 188–208.

Ignatieff, M. (1994) *Blood and Belonging: Journeys into the New Nationalism*, London: Vintage.

Jameson, F. (1985) 'Postmodernism and Consumer Society', in H. Foster (ed.) *Postmodern Culture*, London: Pluto Press, pp. 111–25.

—— (1986) 'Third World Literature in the Era of Multinational Capital', *Social Text* (fall).

Jan Mohamed, A. (1986) 'The Economy of Manichean Allegory: The Function of Racial Difference in Colonialist Literature', in H.L. Gates, Jr (ed.) *'Race', Writing and Difference*, Chicago, Ill.: University of Chicago Press, pp. 78–107.

Julien, I. and Mercer, K. (1988) 'De Margin and De Centre', *Screen* 30 (1): 1–10.

Knightley, P. (1991) 'Spider's Web across the Ocean', *Guardian Weekly*, (17 March).

Lerner, D. (1964) *The Passing of Traditional Society*, Glencoe, Ill.: Free Press.

Maffesoli, M. (1994) *The Time of the Tribes*, London: Sage.

Mattelart, A. (1979) 'For a Class Analysis of Communication', in A. Mattelart and S. Siegelaub (eds) *Communication and Class Struggle: Capitalism, Imperialism*, New York: International General, pp. 23–73.

Mestrovic, S. (1994) *The Balkanization of the West: The Confluence of Postmodernism and Postcommunism*, London: Routledge.

Minc, A. (1994) interviewed for *The New Middle Ages*, *The Late Show*, BBC2, London (28 November).

Mohanty, S.P. (1989) 'Us and Them', *Yale Journal of Criticism* 2 (2).

Morita, A. (1986) *Made in Japan*, New York: Dutton.

Morley, D. and Robins, K. (1992) 'Techno-Orientalism: Foreigners, Phobias and Futures', *New Formations* 16: 136–57.

Ouologuem, Y. (1971) *Bound to Violence*, London: Secker & Warburg.

Richard, N. (1987) 'Postmodernism and Periphery', *Third Text* 2 (winter 1987/8): 5–12.

—— (1993) 'Cultural Peripheries: Latin American and Postmodernist Decentring', *Boundary 2*, 20 (3): 156–62.

Sakai, N. (1988) 'Modernity and its Critique: The Problem of Universalism and Particularism', in M. Miyoshi and H. Harootunian (eds) *Postmodernism and Japan*, special issue of *South Atlantic Quarterly* 87 (3): 475–505.

Scholte, B. (1987) 'The Literary Turn in Contemporary Anthropology', *Critique of Anthropology* 7 (1): 33–47.

Stone, N. (1994) interviewed for *The New Middle Ages*, *The Late Show*, BBC2, London (28 November).

Suleri, S. (1992) *The Rhetoric of English India*, Chicago, Ill.: University of Chicago Press.

Todorov, T. (1984) *The Conquest of America: The Question of the Other*, New York: Harper Collins.

Wallerstein, I. (1974) *The Modern World System*, Vol. I, New York: Academic Press.

Weber, M. (1958) *The Protestant Ethic and the Spirit of Capitalism*, New York: Scribner.

West, C. (1994) 'Beyond Eurocentrism and Multiculturalism', *Public* (Toronto) 10.

Wiredu, J.E. (1979) 'How not to Compare African Thought with Western Thought', in R. Wright (ed.) *African Philosophy: An Introduction*, Washington, DC: University Press of America, pp. 166–84.

Wolf, E. (1982) *Europe and the People without History*, Berkeley, Calif.: University of California Press.

*Figure 13* Modern Indian shopping bag. Photo by Martin Durrant, Goldsmiths College.

# 6  Beyond global abstraction

Regional theory and the
spatialisation of history

## The modern and the Western: colonialism, time and contingency

> Their own coming . . . was not a tragedy, as we imagine, nor yet a blessing,
> as they imagine. It was a melodramatic act which, in the passage of time,
> will change into a . . . myth . . . Over there is like here, neither better nor
> worse – but I am from here, just as the dark palm standing in the courtyard
> of our house has grown in our house and not in anyone else's. The fact that
> they came to our land, I know not why, does that mean that we should poison
> our present and our future? Sooner or later they will leave our country, just
> as many people, throughout history, left many countries. The railways, ships,
> hospitals, factories and schools will be ours, and we'll speak their language
> without either a sense of guilt or a sense of gratitude. Once again we shall
> be as we were – ordinary people – and if we are lies, we shall be lies of our
> own making'.[1]

According to the conventional narrative, it is of course, the industrialisation
of western Europe (and in the first place, of England) which is heralded as
marking the beginning of modernity. In that history, all the key events which
are taken to symbolise modernity are then ascribed to an imagined
cartographic area called 'the West'.[2] This geopolitical equation of modernity
with the West certainly has profound consequences for our understanding
of what (and where) 'history' is. Recalling his own experience of being taught
history at school, the British-Asian musician Nitin Sawhney fumes at the
memory of how Eurocentric the basic perspective always was: 'Don't tell
me . . . [that's] 'history' . . . it's *some* history of some parts of the world that
you consider more important than others'. As he says, at best, 'if you're
taught African history, you learn about it in terms of slavery, or if you learn
about India, you'll learn about it in terms of colonialism'.[3]

The fundamental problem with the cartographic imaginary on which
modernisation theory is founded is that in it the West is conceived not simply

as one particular form of modernity, but as a universal template for mankind. Moreover, as Naoki Sakai observes, the schema that it prescribes is 'hierarchically organised into the West and the Rest, the modern and its Others, the white and the colonial'.[4] This cartography is, of course, not only spatial, but also temporal – and, specifically, historicist. Thus, the conventional notion of modernity is still based, as Dipesh Chakrabarty observes, in the same historicism that allowed Marx to claim that 'the country that is more developed industrially only shows to the others, to the less developed, the image of its own future'.[5] This historicist vision posits time itself ('First in Europe, then elsewhere') as a measure of the cultural distance assumed to exist between the West and the Rest. As Chakrabarty argues, the 'modern European idea of history . . . came to non-European peoples . . . as the European's . . . way of saying "not yet" to somebody else . . . a recommendation to the colonial to wait', in the face of 'anti-colonial democratic demands for self-rule (which) harped insistently on 'now' as the temporal horizon of action'. However, as we know, in actuality, and outside the 'waiting room of historicism', in Chakrabarty's phrase, 'The time of modernity is never unitary . . . [because] modernity always appears in multiple histories'.[6]

The further problem is that this schema, in reducing the category of the West to the status of a unitary geographical site, overlooks all the forms of heterogeneity that have always existed – and continue to exist – within the West. Moreover, it leaves no room for any idea that there might be a multiplicity of modernities, some of them of non-Western origin: that the Rest might be capable of generating their own forms of modernity. To recognise this latter possibility is also to grant that modernity has no necessary tie to any particular race, ethnicity, nationality or temporal location. Thus, Sakai argues, we must recognise that:

> What once appeared exclusively European no longer belongs to the Euro-American world, and there are an increasing number of instances in which non-Euro-American loci are more 'Western' than some aspects of North America and European life. This diversification of the West allows us to discover something fundamentally 'Asian' and 'African' in those people who fashion themselves as 'Westerners' [and *vice versa*] and to conceive of relations among people in many locations . . . in an order other than the racialised hierarchy of the Eurocentric world.[7]

I shall return to these issues later, but first it is necessary to address the further equation of modernity with secularisation.

# Modernity, faith and secularisation

## The de-secularisation of the West

In the conventional schema of things, it is assumed that religion will auto-matically decline as society becomes more reliant on science. The problem is that empirically things don't quite match up to this expectation. If, as a result of the formal defeat of religion in what Goran Therborn calls the 'European Civil War of Modernity', Europe remains the most secularised part of the world (with only around 20 per cent of its citizens describing themselves as 'religious'), nonetheless, elsewhere – from the USA to Japan and South Asia – religion is very much active, and is itself a living and vibrant part of modernity. Indeed, the revival of religion – *la revanche de Dieu* as Gilles Kapel puts it, or the 'unsecularisation of the world', for George Weigel – is one of the principal trends of contemporary social life, worldwide.[8]

This is partly a matter of the continuing pertinence of ancient histories. One could readily point to the many 'half-secularised' forms in which remnants of Christian traditions continue to appear in the public institutions and rituals of Western societies.[9] However, more recent histories are also instructive in this respect. If one of the defining events of the late twentieth century was the collapse of the USSR and its empire, we must note the crucial role played in that process by religion – and most particularly by Catholicism, as represented by the Polish Karol Wojtyla – Pope John Paul II . As Timothy Garton Ash has succinctly put it, 'without the Polish Pope, no Solidarity revolution in Poland in 1980; without Solidarity, no dramatic change in Soviet Policy towards Eastern Europe under Gorbachev; without that change, no "Velvet Revolutions" in 1989'.[10] In the light of such considerations, John Gray has argued that we must recognise that religious faith is thriving in the contemporary world, while the 'secular faiths' of the Enlightenment are in retreat, so that 'we live in a post-secular time. Religion is once again a pivotal factor in war and politics and the humanist dream of a godless world looks more fantastic by the day'.

There is also a serious philosophical question at stake in all this concerning the precise meaning of terms such as 'secularisation' and 'atheism'. As Gray goes on to argue, 'as we know it today, atheism is a by-product of Christianity. It is not a world-view in its own right, but rather, a negative version of Western monotheism and can have little interest for anyone whose horizons extend beyond that tradition'. Moreover, just as atheism is dependent on Christianity, modern ideologies of human emancipation, such as communism and neo-liberalism can be seen as the 'illegitimate offspring of the Christian promise of universal salvation'.[11] If atheism is a specifically post-Christian cultural form, then the question also arises as to whether this is also true of secularism. Thus Ziauddin Sardar argues that there might be alternative forms of Muslim secularism, which would be quite different from their European, post-Christian counterparts: possibly to the extent of not being anti (a specific) religion but rather, being equally respectful of all belief systems, whether secular or religious, as Iftikar Malik suggests. At the end of that philosophical road, as Sardar points out, lies the position of the (for Westerners) deeply challenging 'equal opportunities doubter', the Muslim Scholar Al Ghazali, who even-handedly entertains philosophical doubt not only in relation to any particular variety of religious faith but also in relation to instrumental reason itself.[12]

## Faith and politics: Indian peasants and American fundamentalists

The case of Indian politics is instructive here. It is on the basis of the conventional equation of modernity with the secularisation of society that, as Ranajit Guha has argued, many Western historians (such as Eric Hobsbawm) have dismissed peasant actions in India as 'pre-political', in so far as they did not display the requisite, secular characteristics of modern rationality. Rather, as Dipesh Chakrabarty notes in his commentary, they were often organised around a variety of particularistic axes (of kinship, religious and caste) and called upon 'gods, spirits and supernatural agents as actors alongside humans'.[13] However, Guha's argument is that these peasant actions, which mobilised gods and spirits within the domain of the political, should not be dismissed as some mere anachronistic remnant of tradition in the modern world. Rather, we must recognise that if their actions 'stretched the category of the political beyond the boundaries assigned to it in European political thought' and if they did not follow 'the logic of secular-rational calculations' designated appropriate within those terms, they nonetheless participated, very effectively, in the modern. If some of their beliefs could be traced back to pre-colonial times, they were 'by no means archaic in the sense of being antimodern'.[14] More ambitiously, Chakrabarty concludes, this instance also provides us with a general model for understanding how 'the non-secular supernatural exists in proximity to the secular and . . . both are to be found in the political'. Thus, he notes 'while the God of monotheism may have taken a few knocks – if not actually died', in the nineteenth-century European story of the 'disenchantment of the world', the gods and other agents inhabiting the practices of superstition have never died anywhere.[15]

However, the critical case here is that of America. If modernity is usually understood as secular by definition and as Western by implication, and if America is the most advanced country of the modern West then, for the syllogism to hold, America should evidently be secular. Clearly, the syllogism does not hold at all for, as John Gray rightly observes, it is in many senses still appropriate to follow de Tocqueville in noting the intense religiousity of American society. Indeed, not only does America have by far the most powerful fundamentalist religious movement of any advanced country, but that the USA now enjoys, in many respects, a less secular regime than does, for example, contemporary Turkey, the recent rise of Islamic politics in Turkey notwithstanding.[16]

As Luc Sante notes, in his essay, on America as 'God's Country', 'The full extent of American religious certitude has not always been visible to outside observers, and certainly not to those familiar only with the citadels of wickedness on the East and West coasts'. In this connection, Todd Gitlin has argued that, for present political purposes, the term 'America' is in fact a heavily regionalised concept, and in effect, means 'the Sunbelt – the Old Confederacy plus the mountain states and the prairies'. As he notes, when *that* America scorns the secularised (and to them 'corrupted') values of Europe, 'it also sneers at the American North East. To them 'Washington DC' is an insult and 'New York' is where Europe begins'.[17] In the Republican heartlands of Middle America – graphically represented by the areas of blue on the psephological maps of the USA produced after George W. Bush's re-election – 'the American nation . . . remains . . . a fortress of the righteous . . . 84 per cent of the population believes in miracles . . . and an equal number believe in life after death . . .' while 40 per cent describe themselves as 'born again'. This latter figure is an index of the extent to which fundamentalist religion, in particular, has come to dominate the centre ground of contemporary American life.[18] America has thus been described by Simon Schama as now divided in two – not just between Democrat and Republican, but between a 'worldy' America on the coastal peripheries, which faces outwards and 'freely engages commercially and culturally with Asia and Europe' and a 'Godly' landlocked America, 'its tap roots of obstinate self belief buried deep beneath the bluegrass and the high corn' which is at heart 'a church, a farm, and a barracks; places that are walled, fenced and consecrated'. The shock, for the 'Worldlies', as Schama describes them, is to discover that 'Godly America is its modernity; that so far from it withering before the advance of the blog and the zipdrive, it is actually empowered by them'.[19]

The new dimension to all this is that the Bush Administration has brought the fundamentalist religious discourses of Middle America (and especially the Midwest) not only to the centre of the domestic political scene – for instance, in the shape of federally funded initiatives in support of virginity, and against abortion – but also onto the world stage. Thus, America came to have not only an attorney general, John Ashcroft, who had himself anointed before taking office and who firmly believed that the very existence of the USA is proof of a divine purpose in human affairs, but also an evangelical Christian general, William Boykin, taking a leading role in the 'War against Terror'. Lieutenant General Boykin views himself as a Christian holy warrior and has described this war as a religious crusade between Judaeo-Christian values and Satan, fought by the 'army of God'. The General described his certainty of victory, in a previous military posting in Somalia, as fortified by the belief that 'I knew my God was bigger than theirs. I knew my God was a real God, and theirs was only an Idol'.[20] In a disturbingly similar spirit, George W. Bush himself was reported as presenting himself at his pre-election rallies as standing for 'the Right God' and as ultimately representing a majority that is perhaps more theocratic than Republican. The party certainly derives a great deal of its money from fundamentalist Christian groups, and ecclesiastical organisations have been described as playing a crucial electoral role as the 'sinew and muscle of the party'.[21] In this context, Gray claims that 'part of the drive to reshape the Middle East comes from the Christian Fundamentalist belief that a major confligaration will fulfill biblical prophecies of a catastrophic conflict in the region'. To this extent, he claims, 'American foreign policy is itself fundamentalist'.[22]

While, in the present context of international politics, religious fundamentalism is common-sensically assumed to be a 'foreign' (and predominantly Islamic) phenomenon, as Benjamin Barber notes, we can also readily identify an American version of jihad, represented by the 'moral majority' of the Christian Right, which reaches into the heartland of contemporary American culture through both prime-time television and radio talk shows.[23] The strength of this widespread religious feeling can perhaps be judged by the form of the insult shouted at *New York Times* journalist Chris Hedges, when students at Rockford College, Illinois objected to his 'Commencement' Address at their graduation ceremony, in May 2003, where Hedges had offered a critical commentary on current American foreign policy and was loudly denounced by hecklers as an 'Atheist Stranger'.[24]

It must be remembered that, if the Enlightenment in Europe represented an escape from the power of religion, for the Puritan settlers who left for America, their voyage represented, conversely, 'an escape into the religious freedom of the New World – an escape into faith, rather than away from it' as Salman Rushdie has observed. The continuities between the early Puritans and the politics of today are striking – not least in so far as the current US Government seems to share the Puritans' faith that the world exists in order to be conquered by Christians.[25] The contemporary resurgence of Protestant fundamentalism in the USA follows in a long line of such periodic outbursts of religious fervour, going back to the 'Great Awakening' of the 1730s. The current version once again calls for a return to 'traditional family values' based in the observances of church-going and school prayer, which would reinstate a 'Protestant Christian America'. Thus the president of the 'moral majority', Jerry Falwell, has called for his followers to 'fight against those radical minorities who are trying to remove God from our textbooks, Christ from our nation. We must never allow our children to forget this is a Christian nation'.[26] The irony of all this, as Ziauddin Sardar rightly claims, is that, in their religious fundamentalism, the Christian neo-conservatives who currently drive both American domestic and foreign policy share much with the Islamic 'terrorists' against who they have declared war. Just as Wahabbist Islam advocates 'a return to the purity and simple profundity . . . (of) the words of the Qu'ran' – which are to be taken literally, with no space left for 'interpretation' or adaptation, so in many American states, we now return to the point where, for instance, the teaching of evolutionary theory in schools is disallowed because it contradicts the 'literal truth' – or the 'innerancy' in Baptist terminology – of the Bible.[27]

Of course, if we are to avoid the trap of reifying and essentialising these forms of contemporary fundamentalism, we have to recognise, with John Gray, that they are themselves modern phenomena, rather than some kind of puzzling hangover from a previous era.[28] Rather, these cultural forms must be seen as themselves emerging in dialogic response to the pressures of both internal and external colonisation and the advance of modernity. As Roger Keesing and others have pointed out, movements designed to preserve traditional ways or *Kastom*, seen as under threat from modernisation, may well involve the idealised reformation of the tradition in question, but can only be understood in the context of the encounter of the traditional with the modern. Those who lived fully within established traditions did not think of themselves as 'traditionalists', because they were unaware of the alternatives – an epistemological position which is, of course, impossible to sustain in our contemporary, media-saturated world.[29]

Thus, Malise Ruthven distinguishes fundamentalism from the realm of the traditional, which is commonly unself-conscious, or unreflective. Fundamentalism, Ruthven argues, is 'tradition made self-aware and consequently defensive'; it is, precisely, a self-conscious response to the anxieties generated by the disruptive challenges of modernity. Thus, at broadest, fundamentalism may be defined as a 'religious way of being that manifests itself in a strategy by which beleaguered believers attempt to preserve their distinctive identity as a people or group in the face of modernity and secularisation'. To this extent, fundamentalism has to be understood as an essentially modern phenomenon even if it usually looks back to a Golden Age, whose certainties and values it aims to restore. This is not only true of the Taliban government in Afghanistan, who wished to restore the mythic era of Afghan tribal society, but also of contemporary Christian fundamentalists in the USA, who wish to restore a romanticised vision of the morally upright and socially stable America which they imagine to have existed between the end of the Second World War and the débâcle of Vietnam.[30]

However, there is yet a further twist to the tale, as there is a sense in which de Tocqueville's comments on the 'religiosity' of America transcend the question of formal religion and also involve questions of nationality. As Ian Jack argues, in this connection, 'The sheer fact of being American is, for many Americans, to be part of an evangelical, patriotic faith – to be one of the elect, to be one of the saved'. Here we confront the issue of 'the faith of the only country on earth that believes in itself in this way, the only country where citizenship itself is an act of faith'.[31] This faith in America and its 'mission' in the world belongs, of course, to the discourse of what is usually called 'American exceptionalism'. However, as John Gray points out, there is, in fact, nothing 'exceptional' in historical terms about such a belief, as the contemporary American conviction that their country has a 'mission' to be the agent of universal civilisation was also held by many previous imperial powers – by the nineteenth-century British, the eighteenth-century French, and the seventeenth-century Spanish and Portuguese.[32]

## Modernity and its moving centre: the constitution of peripheries

As we know, in its history, modernity has had no constant centre. Fernand Braudel observes that the various 'long durations' of history are marked precisely through the process of the continual 're-centring' of the world economy. Thus, as he notes:

> The splendor, the wealth, and happiness of life are [always] united in the centre of the world economy, in its very nucleus. That is where the sun of history gives brilliance to the most vivid colours; that is where are manifested high prices, high salaries, banking, profitable industries . . . that is where the point of departure and arrival of . . . foreign trade is situated . . . An advanced economic modernity is concentrated in the nucleus: the traveller recognises this when he contemplates Venice in the 15th Century, Amsterdam in the 17th Century, London in the 18th Century and New York in the present.[33]

It is in this same spirit that Bonaventura de Souza Santos notes 'each historical period or cultural tradition selects a fixed point which functions as the centre of its current maps, a physical symbolic space to which a privileged position is attributable and from which all other spaces are distributed in an organised manner'. The 'superiority' – and power – of such a 'centre', as Nelly Richard observes, depends on its 'being invested with sufficient authority to qualify it as a giver of meaning'.[34] Moreover, the relation between the 'centre' and the periphery which it constitutes for itself has to be understood as one of mutual implication. If modernity is, historically, a European phenomenon, it cannot be understood in isolation, but only within the terms of its relations to the 'non-modernity' which it correspondingly creates on its periphery. Thus, as Dussell argues, 'modernity appears when Europe affirms itself as the "centre" of a World History that it inaugurates: the "periphery" that surrounds this centre is consequently part of its self-definition'.[35]

The hegemonic relations of the centre to the periphery are not only constituted spatially, but also temporarily.[36] Thus, in this model, while the centre is the realm of 'eventfulness' from which the new derives, the periphery, in its 'backwardness', is constituted as itself outside the time of modernity. In the context of imperialism and colonialism, the centre, as the site and source of modernity, progress and metropolitan advance is thus set up as the power node of a binary opposition with the periphery – as the site of traditionalism, regionalism and provincial backwardness. In this binary, the centre acts as a model – or point of originary reference – while the periphery can only ever be a poor copy, 'a reflex extension condemned to the reproduction and imitation of a succession of original moments'. The periphery may be understood to have some active (if limited) powers, in 'translating' or 'adapting' for local consumption the cultural forms it ingests from the centre. However, it is still seen as involved in a process of mimesis that translates those discourses into an 'inferior, subordinated tongue' – and the peripheries are thus primarily defined as takers, rather than givers of meaning.[37] If a simple model of the 'world system', operating from a single imperial centre (even one which changes historically over time), is no longer appropriate to our times, still the position of the West – and that of other imperial centres – within that system remains a critical question.

## From Fukuyama to Huntingdon: the triumph, or decline of the West

It is, of course, the West which has long been understood to be the centre of world civilisation and which has defined all other regions of the world as peripheries of variable consequence. At the point in 1989 when the Berlin wall came down and the Soviet Union crumbled, it seemed to some that there was literally now only one centre to the world system, in the shape of America. This was the moment of Western triumphalism, exposed most vigorously by Francis Fukuyama.[38] For Fukuyama, liberal, free-market capitalism was more than contingently victorious on the world stage: his argument was that this was (and had been all along) a historical inevitability. Moreover, he claimed, the ongoing process of modernisation made for the further inevitability that all societies, worldwide, would come to be modelled on the template of the West. This was so, he argued, because the process of modernisation 'guarantees an increasing homogeneity of all . . . societies . . . All countries undergoing economic modernisation must increasingly resemble one another: they must unify nationally, on the basis of a centralised state, urbanise, replace traditional forms of social organisation like tribe, sect and family with economically rational ones, based on function and efficiency'.[39] For Fukuyama, of course, the 'economically rational' was equated with Friedmanite economics, the superiority of which, as a mode of both constructing and understanding human affairs, brooked no argument. However, as we know, things did not quite go according to Fukuyama's plan, over the past decade and a half, and we now live not so much amidst the global triumph of liberal capitalism, as among what might be described as a 'New World Disorder'.[40]

If Fukuyama's *The End of History and the Last Man* was a triumphalist reading of the West's seeming historical victory in the context of post-1989 euphoria, Samuel Huntingdon's work constitutes a more downbeat (and, indeed, paranoic) account of the West's decline. While Huntingdon's work is based on a number of deeply problematic assumptions and is ultimately driven by a radically conservative view of history and politics, it is nonetheless worthwhile attempting to disentangle some of his genuine – and useful – insights from their reactionary political motivations.[41] As Huntingdon rightly claims, from a long-term historical perspective, one can mount a perfectly cogent argument, contra Fukuyama, that the global power of the West peaked at the end of the First World War, in 1919, when the leaders of the USA, the UK and France, meeting in Paris, were able to determine what countries would exist and which would not, what new countries would be created, what their boundaries would be and who would rule them, and how the Middle East (in particular) and other parts of the world would be divided up among the victorious powers.[42] Indeed, in that very year, Paul Valéry expressed his anxieties about how the worldwide spread of science and technological power, indexed by the rise of nations such as Japan, might lead to a situation in which Europe would decline in significance to become again 'what it really is . . . a little promontory on the continent of Asia' and lose its historic position and role as 'the elect portion of the terrestrial globe, the pearl of the sphere, the brain of a vast body'.[43]

In fact, from that point onwards, the West's dominance has consistently declined, and seems likely to continue to do so. Thus, against many conventional assumptions, Huntingdon demonstrates that the number of people in the world speaking English, for example, has declined (from 9.8 per cent of world population in 1958 to 7.5 per cent as early as 1992), as compared with the growing numbers speaking Mandarin – though, against this overall numerical decline, it is important to note the continuing (and now insti- tutionalised) dominance of English in key technological areas, such as computing, scientific research and air travel. According to some predictions, by 2020, compared with the position at the end of the First World War, the West's proportion of global population will also have declined – from 50 per cent to 10 per cent; its control of global territory from 50 per cent to 25 per cent and of economic production from 70 per cent to 30 per cent – with corresponding increases, in all these domains, for China, India and the Muslim world. Indeed, if current growth rates were to persist in China and India, by 2050 the 'Chindia' region would account for roughly half of global production.

In all these fundamental respects, Huntingdon argues, 'the balance of power among civilisations is shifting: the West is declining in relative influ- ence'. Indeed, while bemoaning its consequences, Huntingdon approvingly quotes Michael Howard's assertion that 'the common Western assumption that cultural diversity is a historical curiosity, being rapidly eroded by the growth of a common, western-orientated Anglophone world culture, shaped by our basic values . . . is simply not true'.[44] At its simplest, Huntingdon argues that nowadays, 'for the first time in history, global politics is both multipolar and multicivilisational' and that 'modernisation is distinct from Westernisation' and 'is producing neither a universal civilisation . . . nor the Westernisation of non-Western societies'.[45] He is well aware that modernity will take a variety of forms in the future and is itself in no sense intrinsically 'Western'. As he points out, 'Japan, Singapore and Saudi Arabia are modern, prosperous societies, but they are clearly non-Western. The presumption . . . that other peoples who modernise must become "like us" is a bit of a Western arrogance'.[46]

Even if Huntingdon's own interest, in the end, is simply in bolstering the dominance of (a culturally purified version of) America in world affairs, he nonetheless grasps that the 'Western' phase of world history is over and he approvingly quotes Spengler's denunciation of the West's myopically 'Ptolomaic' view of history. Spengler argued, as far back as 1918, that it was necessary to take a Copernican view and to substitute for the 'empty fragment of one linear history the drama of a number of mighty cultures'. The central point, for Huntingdon, is that 'European colonisation is over; American hegemony is receding. The erosion of Western culture follows, as indigenous, historically rooted *mores*, languages, beliefs and institutions reassert themselves'.[47]

Evidently, one important limitation of Huntingdon's argument here is that he can only conceptualise such forces as historical 'hang-overs' from an earlier period, reasserting themselves as eternal verities, rather than seeing them as genuinely modern cultural elements arising in the present, as responses to, and co-eval with, Western forms of modernity.[48] Nonetheless, from this perspective, Western hegemony in world affairs cannot simply be assumed, and as Huntingdon puts its 'in fundamental ways, the world is becoming more modern and less Western'.[49] Interestingly, from the opposite end of the political spectrum, Immanuel Wallerstein takes a similar view to Huntingdon. For Wallerstein, it is equally clear that American world power is in decline, and he takes all protestations to the contrary to be little more than an index of real (and well-justified) anxieties about the fragility of Western claims on power. As he puts it 'We [Americans] have spent the last 30 years insisting very loudly that we are still hegemonic and that everyone needs to continue to acknowledge it. But if one is truly hegemonic, one does not need to make such a request'.[50] More recently, Wallerstein's position has also been supported by John Ralston Saul's argument that, having risen in the 1970s, globalisation saw its high point with the establishment of the World Trade Organisation (WTO) in 1995, and that its fortunes have since declined. Thus, Saul argues that globalisation has, in fact, now been in retreat ever since the Asian Financial Crisis of 1997–8 (after which countries such as Malaysia imposed capital export controls) and specifically since the breakdown of the talks on the Multilateral Agreement on Investment in 1999, in the face of coordinated resistance to those proposals from the developing world. To this extent, he claims, since 1999, the WTO has been largely paralysed and, as a result, the process of American-led globalisation has been in retreat.[51]

## Distinctions and differences: towards regional theories

Without falling into any postmodern dismissal of all Grand Narratives, one might reasonably complain that the problem which Fukuyama, Huntingdon and Saul's approaches share, opposite though their conclusions may be, is that they all deal in sweeping generalisations about the story of history, modernisation and globalisation. Rather than these generalist schemes, which try to reduce the whole of history to one Big Story – be it of the inevitability of Western hegemony or of Western decline – we may perhaps be better served by some differentiations between the stories and perspectives of a variety of regions, areas and periods. This is to insist on questions of particularity and of locality – the better to avoid the vacuum of abstracted global theory of an undifferentiated kind. However, this is not to argue that 'particularity' is all – but it may well be that we can only hope to transcend the contingent limitations and specificities of 'local' experiences by addressing them directly.

In his classic study *The Social Origins of Dictatorship and Democracy*, Barrington Moore Jr. offered a comparative historical analysis of the continuing political effects of the different routes (bourgeois-democratic, nationalist, communist) taken to industrialisation in various countries (England, France, America, China, Japan, India). In a similar vein, Goran Therborn offers an analysis of the continuing significance of the different routes taken to modernisation: in Europe, the route of 'civil war', as in the French Revolution; that of the colonies, where modernity came from the outside in the form of imperialism; that of countries such as Japan, which engaged in a form of 'reactive modernisation', deliberately importing it from abroad; and that of the New Worlds of European settlement such as the Americas, where the settlers were the internal force of modernity, in opposition both to local native populations and previous European colonial powers . Nonetheless, because the central position of western Europe in the emerging pattern of early globalisation was secured by its early success in industrialisation, which relegated the previously powerful cultures of South Asia and China to the periphery, that centrality, as Therborn observes, still throws a long shadow. As he notes, there is still no country colonised by Europe or by the USA, which has subsequently been successful in achieving industrialisation and modernisation.[52]

While mainstream discourse on globalisation contains a lot of unsubstantiated hype about a 'borderless world', where the juggernaut of globalisation simply flattens everything in its path, the empirical evidence at our disposal concerning current trends toward the regionalisation of global trade points in a quite different direction. For Therborn, what is needed is a historically informed regional approach, which focuses on 'different regional vistas on current globalisation and their outcomes'. In part, this is a historical matter, and he argues for the continuing significance of the regional differences between 'still enduring, large scale, usually inter-ethnic cultural areas . . . largely synonymous with the patterning of . . . world religions and their functional equivalents of cosmologies and ethical philosophies'.[53] Therborn's claims, in this respect, support those of Huntingdon, who also notes that economic regionalisation is an increasing force in Europe, North America and East Asia, where the proportion of trade that flows within each of these regions has been consistently increasing for some years now. The last part of the twentieth century certainly witnessed a strong tendency towards a greater regionalisation of world trade. In that period, intra-regional trade increased notably, both within Europe, within the North American continent, within Asia and within Latin America, as well as being more strongly institutionalised, in all of these regions, through organisations such as the EU, NAFTA, ASEAN and MERCATOR, respectively. The 'Greater China' economic area (linking mainland China, Hong Kong, Taiwan and the

South-East Asian Chinese diaspora) now looks set to become the fifth major (and particularly fast-growing) area of intra-regional trade in the twenty-first century. However, the key point is that if global flows are increasingly region-alised, even relatively recent and new directional flows still often follow the established paths of previous histories – such as the post-Second World War pattern of immigration into Europe from its ex-colonies and the prepon-derance of the overseas Chinese diaspora in contributing the vast majority of current 'foreign' investment in China.[54]

In the light of these considerations about the significance of 'regional' theories, let us look again, now from a different angle, at the issue of how the over-abstraction of most theorisations of modernisation and globalisation might be critically addressed.

## Problems of over-abstraction and universalism in modernisation theory, post-colonial theory and cultural studies: the view from area studies

Contemporary modernisation theory is, as Bruce Cummings rightly argues, dominated by a model of 'economic man' (*sic*) derived from Milton Freidman's 'rational choice theory'. This very limited and contingent model of the rational, interest-maximising individual, while rooted in the specific history and culture of Western ideas of the 'free market', not only 'collapses the diversity of . . . human experience into [this] one category', but has now come to colonise the study of modernisation worldwide.[55] This approach has a long pedigree in development studies, and is premised on a failure to recognise that the dynamics of the capitalist free market itself presumes the existence – below the 'bottom line' of economic calculation – of particular cultural frameworks and concepts of personhood which are, in fact, far from universal.[56] Alternatively, it could be argued that modernisation theory presumes the viability (and in some variants, the desirability) of instituting these cultural forms as hegemonic, worldwide and obliterating all vestiges of other cultures. These are issues to which I will return in my concluding chapter on modernity and tradition.

One problem here is that this kind of abstracted and improperly univer-salised model of the processes of modernisation and globalisation fails 'to recognise modernity as a specific cultural . . . form . . . which differs according to [the] . . . experience of place as much as [of] . . . time', and is based on a totalising vision of 'rational choice' economics. In the light of these manifest deficiencies, even so august a body as the North American Social Science Research Council (SSRC) has recognised that 'there is no making sense of the world by those ignorant of local, context-specific issues . . . [nor] by those indifferent to cross-regional forces'. The issue is not simply that globalisation has made all areas 'more porous, less bounded and less fixed'. The central difficulty lies with the nebulous global framework of much current research, which is not properly rooted in 'place-specific histories and cultures'.[57] In the light of all these difficulties with current theories of modernisation (not least their overly abstract character – of which more below) it is worth exploring the possibility that the now-neglected field of area studies, with its accumulated expertise in regional forms of under-standing, might be able, minimally, to supply a useful corrective to their inadequacies.

There are, of course, a number of objections to the practicality of any proposal to turn to area studies for solutions to these problems. For one thing, as Paul Bové acerbically notes, area studies cannot easily be reformed, precisely because it was invented to serve the foreign-policy interests of the state powers which have always been its main funder – and if it stops doing that job, it will lose its funding, as this would no longer be in the state's interest. Evidently, if we take the case of the USA, in the period since the World Trade Center attacks, the relations of state power to the American university system have been very clear – and teaching anything not deemed to be properly 'American' (whether in area/American studies or any other field) has become an increasingly contentious issue.

Morever, there is the fundamental conceptual problem that, in a world in which America is the last remaining superpower, the object of study of a 'new' area studies would have to be the world market, or the globe itself as the stage upon which America acts in its imperialist project. To this extent, as Bové notes, not only would it be hard to delimit the 'area' which was, and was not, of concern to such a project, but the supposedly progressive proposal could easily have the ironic result of simply reconstituting the remit of American studies as co-extensive with the study of the globe.[58] If, as Rey Chow observes, area studies has long been involved in the production of specialists whose principal role is to report back to their masters about other regions and ways of life, for Bové, the further issue is that the USA has positioned itself not only as the principal legitimate agent of knowledge about the rest of the world, but also as a uniquely placed 'subject-agent . . . for which the world [is] "naturally" the field of action'.[59]

Nonetheless, and despite these difficulties, the way forward may still perhaps be through a reformed version of area and/or American studies. In this proposal, American studies itself would be reconceptualised as part of area studies, and thus treat America simply as one area among others, rather than granting it the privileged status of any presumed universality. It has been further suggested that such an approach should take its cue, in matters of multicultural sensitivity, from post-colonial and cultural studies. However, as Chow observes, one key problem with the idea that area studies can be 'rehabilitated' through an increasing sensitivity to matters of multi-culturalism, is that this liberalist politics of 'recognition' is still 'largely a one way street . . . of white culture recognising non-white cultures'.[60] Moreover, for both Cummings and Harootunian there are yet further problems. In the first place, they both argue that such multiculturalism is merely complicit with the machinations of transnational corporations, as they 'versionise' their products, the better to adapt them for local markets. From this point of view, they see the SSRC's proposals as merely following the lead of multi-nationals such as Coca-Cola (which was the first such American company to transfer ultimate control of its affairs to its 'world' rather than its national office). Thus the 'neo-modern' celebration of multiculturalism is, for Harootunian, indistinguishable from the capitalist fetishisation of small differences expressed in slogans such as the 'United Colours of Benetton'. If some of these oversimplifications of the complexities of consumer culture can be seen as the kind of reductionism characteristic of scholars working from a classical political economy perspective, they must nonetheless give us pause for thought.[61]

More tellingly, these critics also tax post-colonial and cultural studies with themselves falling, in some respects, into forms of abstracted universalis-tic theorising which are every bit as inadequate, in their own ways, as those of the conservative theorists of modernisation. In the case of post-colonial studies, Anne McLintock argues that the singularity of its terminology, when it speaks of The colonial condition or of The post-colonial experience, 'effects a re-centring of global history . . . which signals a reluctance to surrender the privilege of seeing the world in terms of a singular and ahistorical abstraction'.[62] If the development of post-colonial studies has been dominated by the major figures of Edward Said and Homi K. Bhabha, both of them are argued by these critics to be prone to the same fault of abstracted 'singularisation'. Thus, in relation to Said, Harootunian argues that his work shows an 'astonishing indifference to the rest of colonial experiences and . . . regions . . . classified as Third World, which . . . had a prior colonising experience that ended in the nineteenth century – such as Latin America – or none at all, like Thailand or Japan'.[63] In Bhabha's case, Harootunian argues that his work is problematic not only because it is based on a universalised version of a psychoanalytic framework which is in fact culturally specific to Europe, but also because, although it is mainly based on the particular history of the English empire in India (or rather Bengal), it has served to typify the 'putative relationship between the English and their Bengali subjects as a muscular trope promising to stand in for the relationship between coloniser and colonised everywhere'.[64] While these criticisms may perhaps more properly apply to those who have inadvisedly universalised Said's model of Orientalism or Bhabha's model of post-colonialism, rather than to what either author themselves claimed for their work, they remain nonetheless important. For Harootunian, the central point is that

> the chronology of the coloniser is not always the same as for the colonised: [moreover] Bengal under British rule is differently temporarily and spatially from Korea under the Japanese, even though they are contemporary to each other; and the forms of colonial domination differ widely from Africa to Asia, demanding sensitivity to the specific political and economic histories [which] postcolonial theory rarely . . . manages to address.[65]

However, beyond this, Harootunian also argues that the way in which Said and Bhabha's work has been taken up so broadly – and exported worldwide – through the medium of 'English' studies, is worthy of attention in itself.[66] In this respect, he accuses English studies of 'seeming eagerly to ape both imperialism and colonialism itself'. In a similar spirit, James Fujii critiques the current worldwide academic imperialism of (originally British) cultural studies, when he notes that if it can now be (tritely) 'represented as the all-encompassing software for academic production in the humanities today, we are apt to miss seeing that the constituent "language" of that software is unmistakeably English'.[67]

Indeed, in this context, Stanley Aronowitz has argued that the recent world- wide academic dominance of what was originally understood as British cultural studies, but which has now been 'exnominated', and is known simply as cultural studies, represents for him another deeply problematic development. He argues that this, in effect, constitutes yet another, un-declared form of cultural imperialism, in which what is, in fact, a specifically British canon of work, largely (if critically) derived from English literary studies, has now been exported to and become hegemonic within areas characterised historically by quite different cultural concerns and canons. For these reasons, he argues that perhaps it would be more appropriate to think of cultural studies as itself no more than a particular, regional form of area studies, in this case, the area studies of the UK, which has come to be improperly generalised as a model for understanding cultural questions throughout the world. In the case of American studies – the discipline with which he is himself most closely associated – he argues that one motive for its rise was precisely the felt need on the part of North American academics, often working in low-status departments, to assert and validate a specifically American agenda of concerns about popular culture, in the face of the historical dominance of English studies. Here, it is perhaps important to distinguish carefully, as Stuart Hall himself did, when pressed on the issue by questioners at the 'Critical Dialogues in Cultural Studies' conference held in Tokyo in 1996 (an event organised by the British Council, about which Fujii is extremely critical) between 'British cultural studies' and 'cultural studies in Britain'. The latter formulation, in its very geographical simplicity, usefully disavows any notion of the particular 'belongingness' of any specific form of cultural studies to one specific location or of any proprietary relationship between those terms.[68]

## Theorising regionality

If we are to look to a revised form of area studies – whether informed by post-colonial/cultural studies or not – to supply a more concretely region-alised perspective on globalisation, there is yet a further difficulty to be faced, which concerns the definition of the units of analysis to be used in such an enterprise. As Arjun Appadurai has pointed out, the problem with most forms of regional analysis, and specifically with the established paradigm of area studies, is that they mistake 'a particular configuration of apparent stabilities for permanent associations between space, territory and cultural organisation'. These approaches rely on a conceptualisation of areas as relatively fixed or immobile aggregates of cultural traits with 'more or less durable historical boundaries and . . . enduring properties' (a tendency of which Huntingdon is perhaps the extreme case). However, we should recognise that they are, in fact, no more than 'heuristic devices for the study of geographic and cultural processes', rather than themselves being 'permanent geographical facts based on any bedrock of natural, civilisational or cultural coherence'.[69]

This, ultimately, is the force of Appadurai's argument about the significance of the disjunctures and contradictions between the global flows of objects, people, images and discourses across the surface of the globe – which often function to destabilise the boundaries of any given area or region. As he notes, the paths (or vectors) of the various global flows are not at all necessarily 'coeval, convergent . . . or consistent', but have different 'speeds, axes, points of origin . . . [and] termination, which often are in contradiction with each other'.[70] Thus, when the consumer advertising generated by the transnational mediascape functions so as to write the scripts of the migratory imagination worldwide, for many, who lack the visa required to physically enter the realms of their dreams, it is indeed hard for geographical diversities, cultural differences and national boundaries to remain isomorphic. To this extent, we might be better off, rather than taking geographical areas as the units of our cartography (and presuming that, within each one, we will find only one set of exclusive or dominant properties), if we take the various properties themselves (cultural, political and economic forms, for example) as the basic units, and then look to see where they are to be found, without assuming that they are naturally bound to geography. From this perspective, not only might we argue that the world now consists of a number of (various) powerful centres, each of which constitutes its own periphery, but also, following Immanuel Wallerstein, that cores and peripheries are better seen, not so much as linked locations, but as linked processes, which are only tendentially and provisionally inscribed in particular geographical places.[71]

Having now mapped out the terrain of our difficulties in understanding the regional geographies of globalisation, we must now turn to some fundamental philosophical difficulties concerning the relations of Western power and knowledge. These are problems which have a particular pertinence for area studies.

## The philosophy of history: the consequences of Hegel

Although it represents a critical step forward in our understanding of globalisation, it has now become something of a commonplace to observe that there has been a historically contingent conflation of the West with modernity. However, Pheng Cheah goes much further than this when he argues that the presumed 'isomorphism between the universal structures of reason and the social structures of the West' on which this conflation rests, is something more than historically contingent.[72] His position is that it is, in fact, the inevitable result of the (lamentably) continuing influence of a Hegelian view of history in the Western social sciences. While few scholars, these days might continue to consciously take Hegel's views on this matter very seriously (apart from Fukuyama and his disciples), Cheah argues that nonetheless Hegel's influence, in this respect, remains both profound and widespread, if largely unacknowledged.

Cheah's central claim is that Hegel's 'Lectures on the Philosophy of World History' continue to supply the underlying philosophical and conceptual matrix for much of the Western social sciences, particularly those concerned with development and modernisation, and specifically for the discipline of area studies. Hegel's argument was that, fundamentally, history is to be understood as a gradual process of the realisation of freedom, which is to be achieved through self-knowledge. He claimed that this process is carried, at each stage of world history, by that nation whose 'spirit' best captures and expresses this quest for freedom and self-knowledge. In his own time, Hegel argued, it was the German *Volksgeist* that best expressed the 'modern world spirit', by transcending its own particularity and attaining a state of 'universal' consciousness of the nature and destiny of mankind: today that mission (or 'burden') would seem to be claimed by the USA.[73]

Thus, Hegel granted the European nations – and their forms of knowledge, both of themselves and others – a transcendent status, while other nations and areas of the world (such as the Orient, which Hegel likened to the realm of mankind's childhood) were consigned to the role of the 'living dead', existing on the periphery of world history, without the capacity to transcend their own particularity or ever achieve universal forms of knowledge. In Hegel's scheme, not only could they never 'know' themselves, but they were simply objects of knowledge, which could only ever be properly understood by (Western) others. Thus, as Cheah argues, Hegel's conceptual matrix 'predetermines that non-Western areas are *a priori* distinct from a self-conscious subject of Universal Knowledge', a subject which, of course, from this point of view, can only be Western.[74] Given this premise, it follows that all that the non-Western Others of the rest of the world can offer are empirical fieldwork opportunities for the application of the universal forms of theoretical knowledge produced about them by and in the West. This distinction between the self-conscious universalism of Western theory and the unreflexive particularism of all other local forms of culture is, for Cheah, among other things, the conceptual foundations on which area studies rests.

In line with Cheah's comments on how, following Hegel's view of the Orient as the childhood of mankind, the rest of the world is designated simply as a space of empirical investigation for Western theory, Miyoshi and Harootunian observe that the ethnographic project of area studies has always been similarly conceptualised, as a study of the 'primitives' and 'natives' designated as belonging to a realm of childhood similar to that of Freud's 'uncanny'.[75] The fundamental issue here concerns what Harootunian elsewhere calls the 'directional tyranny' that names – as 'East' or 'South' – the place where one goes to do fieldwork. Reminiscing about his own experiences as a graduate student in area studies, Harootunian recalls that other places – be they Japan, Asia or Africa – were understood simply as where you had to go and do first-hand observation in order to 'penetrate and thus grasp the concealed secrets of native knowledge and sensibility'.[76] As he notes, the differentiation between the 'field' to be studied and the consciousness of the Western observer was also a temporal one in so far as, while both evidently inhabited the time of the present, everything proceeded as if, in traversing the physical distance to their field of study, the observer was actually travelling back in time, into the realm of the pre-modern, to study those who (somehow) still lived in the past.[77]

These points go far beyond the conventional (if still important) criticism that area studies has long been implicated in the production of what we might call 'dirty knowledge', in the service of the interests of powerful nations who simply recognised the need to 'know their enemies' (and competitors) better, in order to control or defeat them. Certainly, as Appadurai notes, in the USA, the particular 'Cold War-based geography of fear and competition' installed in the institutional epistemology of area studies cannot be understood separately from the security agenda of the US Government, which for fifty years now has funded so much of area studies' work. However, as we have also seen, this cartography has also been premised on the assumption that theory (and proper research methodology) are somehow, naturally or intrinsically, both Western and modern, so that the rest of the world was only seen in the 'idiom of cases, events, examples and test sites' for the application of Western theory.[78]

To argue this is simply to recognise the constitutive significance of the political and institutional apparatuses through which areas are produced – given that they are 'not facts, but artefacts of our interests and our fantasies, as well as of our needs to know, to remember and to forget'. If we might say, quite neutrally, that an area is generally understood to refer to a 'cartographically delimited region . . . isomorphic with a distinctive anthropological culture', then the one place that cannot be designated as one area among others, is the West itself – because that area defines itself as the site of universal knowledge. Within this conceptual framework, it is only from the vantage point of the West that other places can be designated *as* 'areas'. Indeed, for Cheah, an area is always regarded as 'having the two fundamental characteristics of being non-Western and being bounded . . . [thus] non-Western is inevitably a cognate, even a synonym of "area" and vice versa'. Given these fundamental limitations, if area studies is to help us produce the kind of multiperspectival, regionally differentiated unders-tanding of globalisation that we need, it will, as Cheah notes, certainly have to 'attempt to ask more of itself than it traditionally has'.[79]

## Relocating the West

One of the peculiarities of the terms 'Western' and 'non-Western' is that while they propose themselves as cartographical, they are evidently rather more than that. From a North American point of view, the non-West is clearly not just everything which lies outside that geographical region, for it was long used to include some, if not all, parts of Europe. Indeed, it has been fascinating, in recent years, to watch how Europe itself has been differentiated in this respect. To take one example, not so long ago, Poland, as part of the 'Eastern Bloc', was not conventionally seen as part of the West. However, in the context of the second Gulf War, it was designated as part of a 'New Europe' which was then seen as more a part of the West than the 'Old Europe' of France and Germany – and in geopolitical terms, Warsaw then seemed to be 'West' of Paris. Thus, as Cheah puts it, 'the principle for inclusion in the Western world . . . seems to be the existence of a relationship of "familiarity and consanguinity" to the USA, qua centre'.[80]

The identity of that elusive entity 'the West' is also the topic of an intriguing essay by Naoki Sakai, who argues that, crudely put, we might functionally define the West as 'the group of countries whose governments [at any one moment] have declared . . . their military and political affiliation with the USA'. Sakai goes on to query the propriety of the application of the definite article to the term 'the West', as if it were the name of a singular place of region. As he observes, in geographical or cartographical terms, 'west' is an essentially relative concept, simply designating the direction from which, from any particular vantage point, the sun sets. In these terms, every place has its own west, and everywhere is a west far somewhere else. There is thus no reason, in geography itself, given the spherical nature of the Earth's surface, why any one particular place should be designated as 'the' west.[81]

Following Gramsci, Sakai argues that the solution to this mystery lies in the fact that the 'geographical indices incorporate the particular vantage point of those who view the world from their position as the centre'.[82] Thus, the geographical location of the West cannot be understood without reference to the historical question of how Europe (and then America) came to dominate and thus define the cartography of the world. To speak of Iraq as being in the Middle East and Japan as being in the Far East is only intelligible from a Euro-American vantage point, whose 'middle' and 'far' easts they are, respectively. However, the potential lability of all this can readily be seen if we note that that, if it was, from a Japanese point of view, the European cities of Paris and Berlin that symbolised Western modernity in one period, at another point, it was Tokyo itself which performed the same symbolic function for modernising cities in Taiwan. Similarly, for the Taiwanese, at that point, it was the ability to speak Japanese, rather than a European language that characterised the highest form of desirable cultural capital, by being associated with scientific, rational thought.[83]

Sakai's central point is that there is no single quality – neither religion, a particular form of economic life, democratic politics, nor 'race', nor indeed any specific combinations of them – which could be adequate to define the substantive identity of the West. If we take the specific criterion, deriving from the historical identification of Europe with Christendom, of the Judaeo-Christian religious traditions as definitive of the West, then we would have to include places outside the geographical west, such as Ethiopia, Peru, Israel and the Philippines as part of the West, while excluding from it both particular countries (such as Bosnia or Albania) or regions (parts of South Yorkshire, Lancashire and the Midlands in the UK) where Christianity is no longer the dominant religion. If, alternatively, we take economic development and its cognate forms, such as architecture, as indices of 'Westernness', its definition is particularly problematic and confusing. In the present day, these forms of modernity are by no means any longer confined to Euro-America, and many geographical locations outside that territory are – and look – notably more modern, in various respects, than some places within it.

## Is Greece in the West?

If we consider the question of what areas do and do not belong to the West, Greece functions as a particularly revealing 'limit case'. Thus, it has been argued by some that studies of classical Greece cannot properly be part of area studies, on the grounds that it is about the very beginnings of the West – which as we have seen, finds it difficult to view itself simply as one area among others. As Simon Goldhill puts it, ancient Greece cannot be treated as just 'an other' because it is one of the privileged sources from which modern Western culture derives its values.[84] However, at the same time, it is sometimes argued that studies of modern Greece *are* properly defined as part of area studies because modern Greece is now not Western but 'part of the Balkans region and is therefore properly included among the countries making up Eastern Europe'.[85] Furthermore, as Michael Herzfeld argues, the 'peculiar cultural historiography' of Greece has often been understood as being 'caught between Levantine tawdriness and degenerated Hellenism'. Thus, in modern Greece, the situation is further complicated by the fact that, as a result of the long period of Ottoman rule, it is only through a 'practical Hellenism' expressed by means of the disavowal of these 'Oriental' influences and by the re-excavation of the long-buried (if not defunct) remnants of what are, in fact, a much older set of Hellenic traditions that Greece now struggles to redefine itself as a Western, and thus modern, nation.[86]

However, if we are to understand the special place of classical Greece in the European imagination, we have to go back to the nineteenth century and, specifically, to the place of ideas about classical civilisation in the construction of German national identity. Here we find a complex and ambivalent story about 'European' history and identity which, in one version, can be argued to run 'from Athens to Auschwitz'.[87] If the turn to classical antiquity was a pan-European phenomenon in the late nineteenth century, nowhere was that more true than in Germany, and only there was the 'rediscovery' of antiquity wrapped up in the project of the invention of national identity. This process led to a form of what has been described as 'Graecomania', whereby it was felt that Germany could invent a new identity for itself, in the trauma following its defeat by Napoleon and could even rise to equal the status of the ancients, precisely by cultivating a *Volksgeist* modelled on that of the Greeks.[88] In this manic vision, Europe's 'special path' had begun in Athens, and the Greeks had been the 'eye of the needle through which the whole of world history had to pass before it could arrive at the modern stage'. If the baton of world history had been passed from the Greeks to the Romans, and then to Catholic Europe, it was now to be passed to the modern, rational, bureaucratic state of Germany.[89] Thus, Ancient Greece became, for cultured nineteenth-century Germans, a thoroughgoing source of inspiration and aspiration and 'to long for Greece, to find in Greece a true home, was seen as the sign of the great German soul'. For Hegel, Greece was 'the focus of light in history . . . with the Greeks we feel ourselves completely at home'; Nietzsche longed for 'the only place in which one can be at home . . . the Greek world'; Schiller encouraged Goethe to 'find a Greek homeland inside himself'; Wagner felt himself to be 'more truly at home in ancient Athens than in any condition the modern world has to offer'. The study of Greek was held to be essential to the formation of the new German national character and the whole education system was reorganised on the basis of this rampant Philhellenism. For Humboldt, in 'knowledge of the Greeks . . . we find the ideal of that which we ourselves would like to be', and the new Germany was thus modelled on the ideals of Greece.[90]

These were not simply intellectual matters, for this whole cultural movement gave as much importance to the body as to the mind. In his commentary on Leni Reifenstahl's infamous documentary about the Berlin Olympics of 1936, *Olympia*, Goldhill observes not only how throughout the film we are shown many images of Greek sculpture alongside the athletes' bodies, but also that in its final image, the classical sculpture by Myron *The Discus Thrower* begins to rotate and then fades into that of a modern athlete, who is thus represented as the new 'embodiment of the ancient sculpted ideal'. Tellingly, he further points to how the cult of the body fed into German nationalism and its aggressive promotion of the trained, Aryan physique. As he notes, Nietzsche provides a clear link between the romantic nineteenth-century cultural Philhellenism and the cult of the body in Nazi ideology, when he claims to have 'joined anew the bond with the Greeks, the hitherto highest form of man'. As Goldhill observes, we see here the ideologically charged claim that both intellectually and physically, the German race descends from the Greeks and that, as they were the highest form of man, so the Germans now aspired to that pinnacle.[91]

One key problem with this cultural trajectory – or projection (*sic*) – according to Goldhill's cogent argument, begins with Freud, whose theories represented a deep provocation to the new German/Hellenic sense of identity. Not only was Freud writing at the pinnacle of the German world's love affair with Greece, and at the time of a growing German nationalist fervour, but he uncovered 'the dirty secret of desire and violence in the family history of the race'. His mobilisation of Greek mythology in a psychoanalytic discourse exposed 'scandalous truths which threatened Germany's national myth of a pure, white origin in Greece' – for if Freud offers a story of 'where we come from', it is hardly the story of a glorious ancestry. Here we meet the darker side of European identity. For Meier, the tombstone of Greece's tyranny over Germany was Max Horkheimer and Theodor Adorno's *The Dialectic of Enlightenment*, which traces the collapse of bourgeois civilisation in the Nazi period precisely to these Philhellenic infatuations with rationality and perfection.[92] In the new era of Fortress Europe we see, from longer historical perspective, a rerun of the dreams of those earlier great pan-Europeanists, Napoleon Bonaparte and Adolf Hitler, in which we are once again encouraged to reimagine European culture as somehow beginning from and continuous with the world of classical Greek mythology. However, as Stuart Hall reminds us, this has always been a retrospective process in which Greek culture has been artificially detached from its Asian and Egyptian roots, the better to provide Europe with a pure Aryan genealogy.[93]

## Provincialising Europe: the question of reciprocity

As the case the Greece demonstrates, it is not so easy, in fact, to distinguish what properly belongs to the West and what to the East. Conversely, it is certainly hard, as Dipesh Chakrabarty notes, to think about the question of political modernity anywhere in the world without invoking concepts that originally derived from Europe. As he observes, historically, many members of the Indian middle classes 'warmly embraced the themes of rationalisation, science, equality and human rights promulgated by the European Enlightenment', and without them, modern critiques of the Indian caste system, for instance, would have been, literally, unthinkable. By the same token, while his project is one of 'provincialising' Europe, Chakrabarty insists that this is by no means a matter of discarding what was originally 'European' thought. He argues that if European thought is 'both indispensable and yet inadequate' in thinking through the experience of modernity outside the West, 'provincialising Europe becomes the task of exploring how this thought – which is now everybody's heritage, and which affects us all . . . can be renewed . . . for and from the margins of the very globe which that thought has historically helped to create'.[94]

In making these arguments, Chakrabarty perhaps also provides us with a possible solution to the problem that Rey Chow poses when she rightly bemoans the way in which, from some quarters, the whole of theory is now dismissed on 'political' grounds. As she puts it, nowadays, in an age 'of the general criticism of Western imperialism', the empirical study of non-Western cultures itself somehow 'assumes a kind of moral superiority' and the most conservative practitioners of area studies can thus 'now safely endow their own retrograde positions with the glorious multiculturalist aura of defending non-Western traditions'. In this backlash, a simplistic anti-theoreticism is validated, on the argument that we should not 'use Western theory to understand other areas of the world'.[95] This is clearly a regressive move, which depends on the unargued assumption that theory is necessarily 'Western' and belongs only to the West – a position which is readily countered by Chakrabarty's recognition that new forms of what was originally Euro-American thought may now find their best expression in quite other territories.

Ultimately, we must recognise that the 'capability to imagine regions and worlds is now itself a globalised phenomenon'; that all areas produce their own 'areal perspectives'; and that what are commonly treated merely as subsidiary 'regions' themselves produce their own cartographies of the world.[96] The question then is how others see not only us, but each other, and how these 'other territories' conceptualise themselves, whatever the historical or geographical origin of the theoretical frameworks they mobilise in doing so. These are complex matters of comparative cultural typology. If we take the case of the Zulu experience of Westerners in southern Africa in the late nineteenth century, there was, as Robert Thornton notes, no simple 'West' in the Zulu field of vision, but rather 'a confusing array of actors of uncertain power . . . For the Zulu, the encroaching West was highly differentiated. It included English, Dutch, Portuguese and a range of other European nationalities' – all of whom not only behaved differently from the Zulus, but were also often in conflict with each other. In this situation the Zulus were not simply responding to some overwhelming and undifferentiated Western invasion – not least because it was not clear to them which of the different European groups posed the greatest danger.[97] If we turn to the contemporary USA, among the Zuni Pueblo Indians we find that they have a four-part typology of the tourists who routinely visit them, which differentiates between (1) New Yorkers (2) Texas types, who wear cowboy boots and drive Cadillacs (3) Hippie types, who wear tie-dye T-shirts, join uninvited into Indian dances and insistently ask questions about peyote and (4) Save-the-Whale types – all of which figures are now themselves ironically incorporated into the Indians' dance routines.[98] In contemporary Japan, we find categorisations of the West, some of which do not differentiate at all between Europe and America ('EuRam'), some of which (*oh-bei*) principally use the USA alone as a symbol of contemporary modernity, while others (*sei-yo*) refer principally to Europe – and specifically to France, as the site of modernity's high-status European cultural heritage.[99]

The issue is then how the 'others' whom the West allocates to specific, designated forms of regionality themselves perceive the world. As Appadurai notes, from a Western perspective, the concept of the 'Pacific Rim' may now produce a more useful and coherent sense of regionality than one which

divides the Pacific down the middle, as was historically done by the international date line. However, the question still remains as to whether people
within what the West designates as that region necessarily think within these
terms at all, and what divisions are produced within their own topology and
cartography of the world. More fundamentally, it may now be that, rather
than continue to presume the centrality of the West and its visions of others,
it is now time, as Francesco Bonami suggests, not only to see how the world
looks from other vantage points than that of the West, but to let the other
search for us, influence and maybe (even) dismiss us. '[For] Soon we will be
[just] another culture'.[100]

## The fictive ethnicity of the West

In recent years, cultural-studies scholars such as Richard Dyer and Stuart Hall
have argued that 'whiteness', rather than being itself marked as a specific form
of 'race' or ethnicity, functions as the (invisible) 'norm', against which all
others are marked.[101] Similarly, Naoki Sakai argues that the West still presents
itself as the universal norm of humankind, rather than simply as one anthropological form of life among others. In this respect, Sakai's argument functions
in parallel with that of Cheah, in focusing on the Hegelian sleight of hand
through which the West presents itself as the only proper source of universal,
theoretical knowledge and as the vantage point from which all other forms
of human life are to be known and defined. In this conceptual operation, as
he notes, Western humanity arrogates to itself the transcendent status of
'Man' (*sic*), while the rest of the world is anthropologised and thus 'demoted
to ethnicity'.[102] In this context, Trinh T. Minh-ha remarks poignantly,

> when people inquire matter-of-factly about my 'next film in Vietnam' I
> cannot but ask 'Why Vietnam? Why do I have to focus on Vietnam?'
> Marginalised peoples are herded to mind their own business. So the area
> . . . in which they are allowed to work remains heavily marked, whereas
> the areas in which Euro-Americans' acitivites are deployed go unmarked.
> One is confined to one's own culture, ethnicity, sexuality or gender.[103]

For Sakai, the West ultimately 'owes its putative unity to various statements
about itself and its differences from the Rest', as it distinguishes between
itself – as the possessor of scientific rationality – and all others, who are
deemed to still dwell in the superstitious realms of premodernity, and thus
be incapable of transcendent knowledge. For Sakai, as for Bruno Latour, it
is precisely this foundational division which is most problematic. If the West
is a form of 'fictive ethnicity', it is in the topography of the colonial
unconscious, rather than in the material geography of the world that 'the
proper understanding of the distinctions between the West and the Rest must

be sought'. This is no search for any mysterious unicorn; rather, for Sakai, it involves the simple recognition that the 'Rest' are now scattered throughout the geographical heartland of Western civilisation, just as the traces of the West itself are now dispersed throughout the world. From this point of view, we can then recognise both 'the transformative dissemination and living-on of Euro-American ideas in non-Euro-American sites' as well as the legacies of non-Euro-American cultural forms in Western locations. It is only this, as Sakai rightly argues, that will 'allow us to see the traces of the West, as well as of the non-West in all of us'.[104]

## Starting from another place: modernity in East Asia

Most discussions of globalisation, Westernisation or cultural imperialism are still condensed around a binary division between those who argue the 'strong case' that the cultural products of the West continue to have significant effects in other places and, on the other hand, those who argue that these 'effects' are deflected, to some extent, by the active processes of cultural consumption, through which 'others' reinterpret the Western material they consume. However, both sides in this argument share the presumption that the West remains the starting point and the key polarity around which these cultural flows are organised. Thus, we still tend to think of global-local interactions in terms of how the Rest respond to the West (via imitation, appropriation or resistance) whereas the dynamics of interaction between countries outside the West remains badly under-explored.[105] While I have argued elsewhere that we should not underestimate the continuing importance and consequences of American cultural imperialism in empirical terms, it is also true at a conceptual level that, as James Carrier reminds us, the West, real or imagined, need not necessarily, nor always, be the pole against which the Rest define themselves.[106] The current cultural dynamics of South and East Asia are particularly instructive in this respect, as we find there a number of instances where it is no longer America but, in different circumstances, Japan, Taiwan or Hong Kong, which are seen by people in that region to offer more persuasive models of what it is to be modern.

These matters can be explored concretely if we consider the work of Koichi Iwabuchi and Mandy Thomas on how questions of cultural similarity and distance are perceived by consumers in East Asia, in relation to the import of cultural goods from different neighbouring countries in the region. If we take the case of Vietnam, it is clear that it is now the symbols and products of popular culture from other East Asian cultures – Taiwanese soap operas, Hong Kong videos, Cantopop and Japanese computer games and 'Manga' – rather than those of America, which symbolise the desirable forms of urban cosmopolitanism and 'cool' for many young Vietnamese people. As one

Vietnamese puts it 'Japan, Taiwan, South Korea – they are our models. We'll be like them in a few years. They make much better things than Americans'. Of course, as Thomas notes, in Vietnam, as much as elsewhere, the 'foreign' is inevitably an ambiguous category, representing both a reaction of desire and opportunity and, at the same time, a focus of fearfulness and anxiety.[107]

However, the key issue, for the purposes of my argument, is that as a particular form of foreignness, East Asian culture, if not entirely familiar to Vietnamese people, nonetheless feels significantly *less* foreign to them than does the modernity represented by America or the West. Here we encounter an instance of what Iwabuchi has called the ambivalent dynamics of 'familiar difference' and 'bizarre sameness' in contemporary global culture. According to the evidence of his study, in Taiwan, it is specifically Japanese rather than American television programmes which provide for many people 'a concrete model of what it is to be modern in East Asia', for the simple reason that they find it easier, for reasons of 'cultural proximity', to identify with cultural materials imported from Japan, rather than those from America. Thus, his Taiwanese respondents variously note that '*Tokyo Love Story* . . . is not a story about somebody else. It is a story about our generation, about us, about myself . . . I can easily identify'; another says that 'the West is so far away from us, so I cannot relate to American dramas'; yet another declares that 'Japanese dramas better reflect our reality . . . *Beverley Hills 90210* . . . is not our reality or our dream'; another simply observes that 'I can relate easily to Japanese [dramas]. They are more similar to our feeling'.[108]

All of this must certainly alert us to the fact that models of the desirable forms of modernity may appear in different guises, in particular parts of the world – and are not always, nowadays, necessarily derived from the West. However, Iwabuchi's argument goes further than this. In his recourse to notions of 'cultural proximity' he might be seen to replicate Huntingdon's invocation of 'civilisational' differences as explanatory of the potential of (and limits to) cultural flows.[109] However, while Huntingdon treats these 'civilisational' patterns as if they were reified, natural or eternal truths, Iwabuchi is concerned to explicate how such cultural preferences and resonances are produced historically, within particular conjunctures. This is to argue that cultural proximity, as an influence, for instance, on viewing preferences, is not a given fact or static essence, but is rather a function of a cultural dynamic which must be understood in its specific historical context.

From this point of view, the emerging Taiwanese identification with Japanese cultural products as symbols of modernity can only be understood within the context of the historical legacy of Japanese colonialism in Taiwan. It is not simply that Japan, its language, culture and educational traditions continue to exert a considerable historic influence in its former colony. Besides this, as Iwabuchi notes, given their negative feelings towards the authoritarian post-war regime of the Kuomintang Government in Taiwan, many older people, in particular, have come to regard their former Japanese rulers in a positive light. Moreover, given Taiwan's recent economic progress, many Taiwanese now feel a sense of co-evalness or shared temporality, with Japan. As one of Iwabuchi's respondents puts it, 'Taiwan used to follow Japan, [and] always be a "Japan" of 10 years ago. But now we are living in the same age. There is no time lag between Taiwan and Japan'.[110]

To take this perspective is not simply to break away from the conventional equation of the West with America and simplistically 'replace' the figure of the latter with that of Japan as the new centre of modernity – or perhaps Singapore, as the world's first 'fully wired city' (now complete with its new digital animation studios set up there by George Lucas in collaboration with the Singaporean government). More radically, it is to understand that all such configurations are, necessarily, temporally and context bound. It is also to grasp both that, as Braudel argued, modernity always has a moving centre, which is transposed from one geographical locus to another, over time, and that, at any one time, what appears as 'the centre' depends on which periphery you start from. From this point of view, as Rem Koolhaas has put it, 'Who owns the "West" is no longer something "We" can control, but rather a fast developing set of stories that others will now write – and amplify'.[111]

## De-Westernisation and the problem of Occidentalism

The problems raised by these considerations are of particular pertinence for media theory. Here we return to the difficulties noted earlier about the deficiencies of the over-confident abstract generalisations of much globalisation theory, in which, as James Curran and Myung-Jin Park put it 'theorists survey the universe while never straying far from the international airport'.[112] The difficulties with such abstracted theoretical models are several. In the first place, these simplified accounts of globalisation tend to ignore the crucial significance of the local context of globalising processes. Second, interpretive paradigms derived from one situation often tend to be imported wholesale and applied elsewhere, without being appropriately tailored to the local situation. Third, as Curran and Park observe, most Western media theory is both self-absorbed and parochial, with the result that universalistic theories about the media are advanced on the basis of evidence derived usually from the same few Euro-American settings, so that our (supposedly universal) models of the world's media are in fact 'unduly influenced by the experience of a few, untypical countries'. Clearly, as John Downing argues, it is quite absurd to universalise the particular experience of places such as the USA and Britain, as if these affluent, stable democracies, with their Protestant histories and imperial entanglements, could possibly be seen as representative of the world at large.[113]

It is for these reasons that writers such as John Downing and Paul Willemen have argued for the need to develop a more internationally comparative perspective within both media and film studies,[114] and it is this impetus that also drives Curran and Park's commendable project to 'de-Westernise' media studies. However, this is complicated territory. Once of the problems with comparative studies is, of course, the question of where one starts the comparisons from – and if the benchmark is that of a Western perspective, from which all other instances are treated as deviations from that 'norm', then one risks replicating all the conceptual problems of Hegelianism, as argued by Cheah.[115] The analytical process certainly cannot simply be a cumulative or 'supplementary' one, in which a series of 'other' experiences are added in as complications, or interesting deviations from a Western norm. However, cultural imperialism is often precisely a matter of the export of norms, standards and formats, from the West to the Rest, within historically specific relations of power. Thus, notwithstanding the arguments made above about the sense in which, in some places in contemporary East Asia, the 'benchmark' of modernity (from which people take their bearings), might better be seen as located in Tokyo or Taiwan than in New York, it will not help to substitute a philosophically more sophisticated (or perhaps more 'politically correct') model of a potentially multicentred modernity for a careful empirical analysis of where, in fact, the imperial centres of the West do still largely hold sway, in the world of the media and elsewhere. To that extent, we cannot 'de-Westernise' our understandings of these matters simply by paying less attention to the West and more to other places. Rather, a thorough decentring of our analytical framework will still require us to also continue to pay careful attention to the West and its imperial powers, but now from a different perspective, in which the West is seen simply as one, if still particularly powerful, set of cultural forms and norms, among others.

There is now a well-developed literature on the question of Orientalism, concerning Western images of the Other. However, as James Carrier points out, the question of Orientalism's silent partner, 'Occidentalism' – the issue of the derivation of images of the West, both within and without that territory – has been much less explored. This, Carrier argues, is important not simply in terms of the need to turn the conceptual telescope around and consider the question of how others see us, as much as how we see them. More fundamentally, his argument is that Westerners' images of alterity are, of course, fundamentally premised on a certain – and in his view, quite misleading – image of themselves, as the norm against which the 'difference' of others is understood. His interest is in the process of Orientalism in anthropological representation, and he is concerned with the process of self-definition through which people define themselves in opposition to what they see as alien to them, intensifying their own sense of self by dramatising their differences from others. Starting from Kenneth Burke's observation that 'to tell what a thing is, you place it in terms of something else', he argues that the 'Orient' could only ever have been constructed by reference to its (largely) imagined difference from the West's own self image, in the form of the Occident.

Adam Kuper makes a similar point when he claims that while anthropologists have long taken 'primitive society' as their special object of study, in practice, this object often turned out to be, not so much these societies themselves, but rather a negative image of their own society, seen through a distorting mirror, which they then projected onto those who they studied.[116] The West thus produces a badly over-simplified and artificially homogenised image of itself, as an imagined entity, which suppresses its internal differences and obfuscates the many areas of Western life that simply do not conform with this essentialised and idealised vision of its nature. Furthermore, it is on the basis of this misleading vision of itself that the West, in turn, then produces an equally essentialised vision of the Rest of the World, defined by its differences not with what the West is in reality, but in relation to the West's own self-image. Thus, if the primitive world is seen as a simple, static, but irrational sphere, largely governed by magic, ritual, obscure forms of *juju* and gift exchange, this is precisely because these attributes are logically derived, by opposition, from the West's own self conception – as a complex and fast-changing world of consumer choice, governed by science, empirical enquiry and the clarity of rational-choice economics, all founded on the hard-headed practicalities of utilitarian philosophy. The concept of the traditional primitive society is thus generated as the negative and inverted image of the Western conception of what it is to be modern.

The problem here is not hard to spot. The conventional model of East and West, Orient and Occident, gives rise to all kinds of anomalies, in which all kinds of people seem to be in the wrong place at the wrong time ('simple villagers' in Europe, 'fully wired cities' in South-East Asia, fundamentalist sects in the American Midwest). Our alternatives are stark – one would be to engage in a wholesale 'conceptual cleansing' operation, which would somehow account, on a case-by-case basis, for all these myriad anomalies in theoretical terms. However, it might be preferable to recognise that this kind of artificial conceptual binarisation of the world must be abandoned (for all its appealing neatness) in favour of a conceptual schema of a quite different kind. I shall return to these themes later, in my concluding chapter, in an attempt to offer a different approach to the question of how we might better conceptualise the relations between East and West and between modernity and tradition.

# Notes

1  Tayeb Salih (2000) *Season of Migration to the North*. First published 1966. Harmondsworth: Penguin, pp. 49–50, 60.
2  Naoki Sakai (2001) Introduction to *Traces*, p. vii.
3  See Eric Wolf (1982) *Europe and the People without History*. Berkeley, Calif.: University of California Press. Nitin Sawhney, interviewed by Simon Hattenstone in 'I'm a Bit of a Geek', *The Guardian* (Review), 17 March 2003, p. 6.
4  Sakai, ibid., p. viii; see also, H.D. Harootunian (2002) 'Postcoloniality's Unconscious/Area Studies' Desire'. In M. Miyoshi and H. D. Harootunian (eds) *Learning Places*. Durham, NC: Duke University Press, p. 164.
5  From Marx's 'Preface to the First Edition', *Capital*, Vol. I; quoted in D. Chakrabarty (2001) 'Europe as a Problem of Indian History', in *Traces*, p. 163; see also Johannes Fabian (2001) 'Africa's Belgium' in his *Anthropology with an Attitude*. Stanford, Calif.: Stanford University Press.
6  Chakrabarty, ibid., pp. 163–4; Sakai, ibid., p. viii.
7  Sakai, ibid., p. x.
8  Goran Therborn (2002) 'Asia and Europe in the World', *Inter-Asia Cultural Studies*, 3 (2): 292; Kapel and Weigel, both quoted in Samuel Huntingdon (1993) 'The Clash of Civilisation', *Foreign Affairs*, 72 (3, summer): 26.
9  See Talal Assad (1993) *Genealogies of Religion*. Baltimore, Md.: Johns Hopkins Press.
10  Timothy Garton Ash (2005) 'The First World Leader', *The Guardian*, 4 April.
11  John Gray (2004) 'A Second Coming of Belief', *Independent on Sunday*, 26 November. See also Alister McGrath (2005) *The Twilight of Atheism*. London: Rider Books.
12  Ziauddin Sardar (2005) *Desperately Seeking Paradise: Journeys of a Sceptical Muslim*. London: Granta Books; Iftikar Malik and Al Ghazali, quoted in Sardar, ibid., pp. 25–7, 25–6 and passim.
13  Ranajit Guha (1983) *Elementary Aspects of Peasant Insurgency in Colonial India*. Delhi: Oxford University Press; Dipesh Chakrabarty, ibid., p. 167. See Chakrabarty, ibid., for a discussion of the limitations of Hobsbawm's approach to Indian peasant rebellions.
14  Chakrabarty, ibid., p. 168; Guha, ibid., p. 168.
15  Chakrabarty, ibid., pp. 170–1. In this connection, see the recent rise of religious parties, such as the BJP, to dominate Indian politics up until the Congress Party's victory in the elections of spring 2004; see also Arvind Rajagopal (2001) *Politics after Television in India*. Cambridge: Cambridge University Press.
16  John Gray (2003) *Al-Qaeda and What it Means to be Modern*. London: Faber, p. 23.
17  Todd Gitlin (2003) 'Europe? Frankly, America Doesn't Give a Damn', *The Guardian* 3 February. Luc Sante (2003) 'God's Country', *Granta*, p. 207.
18  Luc Sante (2003) 'God's Country', *Granta*, 84: 207–8.

19  Simon Schama (2004) 'Onward Christian Soldiers', *The Guardian* (G2) 5 November. Harold Bloom has recently noted that he finds himself 'wondering if the South has belatedly won the Civil War, more than a century after its supposed defeat. The leaders of the Republic party are all southern; even the Bushes, despite their Yale and Connecticut connections, were careful to become Texans and Floridians'. Harold Bloom (2005) 'Reflections in the Evening Land' *The Guardian* (Review) 17 December.

20  Sante, ibid., p. 207; Suzanne Goldenburg (2003) 'US Defends Role for Evangelical Christian', *The Guardian*, 17 October.

21  Sidney Blumenthal (2002) 'A Moral Dilemma', *The Guardian*, 4 November, and also his (2004) 'The Lowest Ignorance Takes Charge', *The Guardian*, 11 November.

22  Gray, ibid., p. 95.

23  Benjamin Barber (1995) *Jihad vs McWorld*. New York: Ballantine Books, pp. 210–14.

24  In Charles Glass (2003) 'Over There', *Granta*, 84: 32.

25  Salman Rushdie (2005) 'In Bad Faith', *The Guardian*, 14 March; George Monbiot (2004) 'Puritanism of the Rich', *The Guardian*, 9 November.

26  Barber, ibid., pp. 212–13.

27  See Ziauddin Sardar (2002) 'Mecca', *Granta*, 77: 245–6. For a further parallel, concerning how much Islamic fundamentalists have modelled their ideology on Western traditions of Romantic anti-industrialism, see Ian Buruma and Avishai Margalit (2004) *Occidentalism: A Short History of Anti-Westernism*. London: Atlantic Books.

28  Gray, ibid.

29  Keesing quoted in James Carrier (ed.) (1995) *Occidentalism*, Oxford: Oxford University Press, pp. 6–7.

30  Malise Ruthven (2004) *Fundamentalism: The Search for Meaning*, Oxford: Oxford University Press, quoted in Madeleine Bunting (2004) 'Back to Basics', review of Ruthven, *The Guardian*, Saturday Review, 29 April, p. 12. See also Jason Burke's (2004) review of Ruthven's book in his 'The Appeal of Zeal', *The Observer*, Review, 20 June.

31  Ian Jack (2003) 'Introduction', *Granta*, 84: 7; Michael Ignatieff (2002) 'What We Think of America', *Granta*, 77: 49.

32  Gray, ibid., p. 50. I shall return to a further discussion of these issues of religion, tradition and modernity in my concluding chapter.

33  Fernand Braudel (1985) *La Dinamica del capitalismo*. Madrid: Alianza Editorial, pp. 102–3; quoted in José Joaquim Bruner (1993) 'Notes on Modernity and Postmodernity in Latin America', *Boundary 2*, 20 (3, fall): 57.

34  B. Santos (1991) 'Una cartografica simbolica de las representaciones sociales', *Nueva Sociedad*, (Caracas) 116 (November–December): 23, quoted in Nelly Richard (1996) 'The Cultural and Postmodern Decentring', in J. Welchman (ed.) *Reshaping Borders*, Minneapolis, Minn.: University of Minnesota, p. 71; ibid., p. 82.

35  Enrique Dussell (1993) 'Eurocentrism and Modernity', *Boundary* 2, 20 (3, fall): 65.

36  See Sakai, ibid., and Sakai (1988) 'Modernity and its Critique', *South Atlantic Quarterly* 87 (3), on the intertwining of these conceptual planes.

37  Richard, ibid., pp. 72, 79.

38  Francis Fukuyama (1992) *The End of History*. Harmondsworth: Penguin. See the discussion of Fukuyama's work in 'The End of What?', Chapter 10 of D. Morley and K. Robins (eds) (1996) *Spaces of Identity*. London: Routledge.

39  Fukuyama, ibid., p. xv.

40  For a succinct statement of Friedman's economic theory, see the book based on the television series which brought his ideas to popular attention: Milton Friedman and Rose Friedman (1980) *Free to Choose*. London: Secker & Warburg.

41  Samuel Huntingdon (1996a) *The Clash of Civilisations*. New York: Simon & Schuster. See also the original version of Huntingdon's article, on which his book was based in *Foreign Affairs* (summer 1993); and his (1996b) 'The West, Unique, not Universal', *Foreign Affairs* (November/December) and also (1996c) 'The Clash of Civilisations Debate', *Foreign Affairs*.

42  Huntingdon, ibid., 1996a, p. 91.

43  Valéry, quoted in Jo-Anne Pemberton (2001) *Global Metaphors*. London: Pluto Press, p. 65.

44  Huntingdon, ibid., 1996a, pp. 20, 310.

45  Ibid., p. 20.

46  Huntingdon, ibid., 1996c, 'If Not Civilisation, What?', in the *Foreign Affairs/Norton Books* special issue of 'The Clash of Civilisations Debate', pp. 63–4. From the opposite end of the political spectrum, Martin Jacques endorses much of Huntingdon's prognosis, arguing that 'the future is unlikely to be dominated by the Western world . . . Now, without question, the most important region in the world is East Asia' and he observes that from this point of view 'the "American Century" in retrospect, seems to have been 'more like a half-century'. Martin Jacques (2005) 'China well on its way to being the other Superpower' *The Guardian* 8 December.

47  Quoted in Huntingdon, ibid., 1996a, p. 55; Huntingdon, ibid., 1996c, p. 64.

48  See my earlier comments on *Kastom* movements as self-conscious responses to the erosion of tradition.

49  Huntingdon, ibid., 1996a, p. 78.

50  Immanuel Wallerstein (2003) *The Decline of American Power*. New York: The New Press, p. 213.

51  John Ralston Saul (2005) *The Collapse of Globalism*. London: Atlantic Books. See also Martin Jacques' review of Saul's book (2005) 'The End of the World as We Know It?', *The Guardian* (Saturday Review), 23 July.

52  Barrington Moore Jr. (1967) *The Social Origins of Dictatorship and Democracy*, London: Allen Lane; Therborn, ibid., pp. 290, 292. Of course, one could argue that India (or at least some regions of it) is about to disprove this hypothesis.

53 Therborn, ibid., pp. 288, 290, 302–4.

54 Therborn, ibid., pp. 294–6, 305.

55 Bruce Cummings (2002) 'Boundary Displacement', in Masao Miyoshi and H.D. Harootunian (eds) *Learning Places*, Durham, NC: Duke University Press, pp. 286, 293.

56 See Daniel Lerner (1964) *The Passing of Traditional Society*, Glencoe, Ill.: Free Press.

57 H.D. Harootunian (2002) 'Postcoloniality's Unconscious Area Studies' Desire', in Miyoshi and Harootunian (eds), ibid., p. 158; American SSRC 1996 report, quoted in Bruce Cummings, ibid., pp. 288–9.

58 Paul Bové (2002) 'Can American Studies Be Area Studies?' in Masao Miyoshi and H.D. Harootunian (eds) *Learning Places*, Durham, NC: Duke University Press, pp. 207, 222.

59 Rey Chow (2002) 'Theory, Area Studies, Cultural Studies', in Masao Miyoshi and H. D. Harootunian (eds) *Learning Places*, Durham, NC: Duke University Press, p. 108; Bové, ibid., p. 211.

60 Chow, ibid., p. 113.

61 Cummings, ibid., p. 291; Harootunian, ibid., p. 166. The most instructive contrast here is perhaps that between the views of scholars such as George Ritzer (2000) *The McDonaldisation of Society*, London: Sage, for whom processes of glocalisation are no more than a capitalist sop to disguise the essential sameness of McWorld and those such as James Watson (1998) *Golden Arches East: McDonalds in East Asia*, Stanford, Calif.: Stanford University Press and James Lull (2001) 'Global Politics and Asian Civilisations' in B Moeran (ed.) *Asian Media Productions*, Richmond: Curzon Press, who would argue that East Asian consumers of 'Maharaja Macs' and 'Teriyaki Burgers' have now so indigenised these glocalised cultural forms that they are neither victimised nor exploited by them, as this 'accommodation' has taken place as much on Eastern terms as Western ones. For my own views on this, see my (2005) 'Globalisation and Cultural Imperialism Reconsidered', in J. Curran and D. Morley (eds) *Media and Cultural Theory*. London: Routledge.

62 Anne McClintock, quoted in Benita Parry (2002) 'Signs of Our Times' in Masao Miyoshi and H.D. Harootunian (eds) *Learning Places*, Durham, NC: Duke University Press, p. 122.

63 H.D. Harootunian (2002) 'Postcoloniality's Unconscious'/Area Studies' Desire', in Masao Miyoshi and H.D. Harootunian (eds) *Learning Places*, Durham, NC: Duke University Press, p. 152.

64 Harootunian, ibid., pp. 168–9.

65 Haroontunian, ibid., p. 172.

66 His argument is that the work of some of the other founding scholars of post-coloniality, such as Cesaire, Senghor and Memmi has suffered relative neglect largely because they were written in French, which is not a 'world language' in the same sense that English is. However, the counter-example of Fanon, who also wrote in French, but whose theories have achieved global recognition, seems to belie his point.

67  Harootunian, ibid., p. 168; James Fujii (2002) 'From Politics to Culture' in Masao Miyoshi and H.D. Harootunian (eds) *Learning Places*, Durham, NC: Duke University Press, p. 362.

68  See also my comments on this in the interview with Johannes Van Moltke in Chapter 2.

69  Arjun Appadurai (2000) 'Grassroot Globalisation and the Research Imagination', *Public Culture*, 12 (1): 7; see also James Clifford (1992) 'Travelling Cultures' in Larry Grossberg et al. (eds) *Cultural Studies*. London: Routledge.

70  Appadurai, ibid., p. 5.

71  I. Wallerstein (1987) 'Periphery', in J. Eatman (ed.) *The New Palgrave Dictionary of Economic Theory and Doctrine*, Basingstoke: Macmillan.

72  Pheng Cheah (2001) 'Universal Areas', *Traces* 1: 45.

73  See G.W.F. Hegel (1953) *Reason in History: A General Introduction to the Philosophy of History*. First published 1837. New York: Macmillan. See also my comments later in this chapter on the German invocation of their Greek 'ancestry' in the nineteenth century.

74  Cheah, ibid., pp. 47, 49–52.

75  M. Miyoshi and H.D. Harootunian (2002) 'Introduction: The "Afterlife" of Area Studies', in Masao Miyoshi and H.D. Harootunian (eds) *Learning Places*, Durham, NC: Duke University Press, p. 7.

76  Harootunian, 'Postcoloniality's Unconscious', ibid., pp. 151, 161–2.

77  See Johannes Fabian (1983) *Time and the Other*. New York: Columbia University Press. I will return to these issues about co-evalness in my concluding chapter.

78  Appadurai, 'Grassroots, Globalisation and the Research Imaginary', ibid., p. 4.

79  Appadurai, ibid., p. 8; Cheah, ibid., pp. 38, 43.

80  Cheah, ibid., p. 39. For a less theoretical, but more tuneful, version of the same point about relations between the USA and Europe, see Randy Newman's prescient song 'Political Science' (1972) where the singer ironically suggests that the USA should 'drop the Big One' on Europe, precisely on the grounds that it is (even then) 'too old'.

81  Naoki Sakai (2001) 'The Dislocation of the West and the Status of the Humanities', *Traces* 1: 82.

82  Sakai, ibid., p. 80; Antonio Gramsci (1971) *Prison Notebooks*. New York: International Publishers, p. 447, quoted in Sakai, ibid., p. 93.

83  Sakai, ibid., pp. 85, 86.

84  Simon Goldhill (2005) *Love, Sex and Tragedy: Why Classics Matters*. London: Hodder Headline.

85  Robert A. McCaughey (1984) *International Studies and Academic Enterprise*, New York: Columbia University Press, p. xii, quoted in Cheah, ibid., p. 64.

86  See M. Herzfeld (1995) 'Hellenism and Occidentalism', in James Carrier (ed.) *Occidentalism: Images of the West*, Oxford: Oxford University Press, p. 219. On this, see also my earlier discussion of Martin Bernal's (1996) *Black Athena* in D. Morley and K. Robins (eds) *Spaces of Identity*. London: Routledge.

87   Christian Meier (2005) *From Athens to Auschwitz*. Cambridge, Mass.: Harvard University Press.

88   Mark Lilla (2005) Review of Meier, ibid., *New York Review of Books*, 23 June.

89   Meier, quoted in Lilla, ibid.

90   Goldhill, ibid., pp. 282–3.

91   Goldhill, ibid., pp. 25–8.

92   Goldhill, ibid., p. 295; see also Lilla, ibid., on this point.

93   Stuart Hall (2003) 'In, but not of Europe . . .', *Soundings*. London: Lawrence & Wishart.

94   Dipesh Chakrabarty, ibid., pp. 160, 171–2. In this connection Gayatri Spivak reports on how she revised her teaching at Hong Kong University of Science and Technology, when she realised how little her students knew of western literary traditions: 'I scrapped my course immediately and started teaching from Aristotle on down . . . So, with my miserable classical Greek, I'm pushing Aristotle in Greek; with my miserable Italian, I'm pushing Dante in Italian. I kept telling them – you read the West not because everything Western is good, so that you can theoretically apply it to your raw material. Do not read the West because everything Western is bad, so that you can show how Chinese was better. Both are the same thing. Read it because it's there and in certain respects, it won. Then you'll see that it's interesting', Jenny Sharpe (2002) 'A Conversation with Gayatri Chakravorty Spivak' *Signs: Journal of Women in Culture and Society* 28 (2).

95   Chow, ibid., pp. 110, 112.

96   Appadurai, ibid., pp. 7–8.

97   Robert Thornton 'The Colonial, the Imperial and the Creation of the European in South Africa', summarised by James Carrier (1995) in his 'Introduction' to his edited volume *Occidentalism*, ibid., pp. 21–2.

98   Dean MacCanell (1994) 'Cannibal Tours', in L. Taylor (ed.) *Visualising Theory*, London: Routledge, p. 104, drawing on Jill Sweet (1989) 'Burlesquing the Other', *Annals of Tourist Research*, 16.

99   See Yuiko Fujita (2006) 'Cultural Migrants: Young Japanese in Tokyo, London and New York', Ph.D. thesis, Department of Media and Communications, Goldsmiths, University of London.

100  Francesco Bonami (1997) 'The Electronic Bottle: Dreaming of Global Art and Geographic Innocence', in Okuwi Enwezor (ed.) *Trade Routes: History and Geography*, Johannesburg: Greater Johannesburg Metropolitan Council. For a fascinating discussion of how the West has historically been seen from other vantage points, see Alastair Bonnett (2004) *The Idea of the West*. Basingstoke: Palgrave. See also Ariuf Dirlik's important article (2005) 'Asia Pacific Studies in an Age of Global Modernity', *Inter-Asia Cultural Studies*, 6 (2, June).

101  Richard Dyer (1994) *Whiteness*. London: Routledge; Stuart Hall (1996) 'New Ethnicities', in D. Morley and K.H. Chen (eds) *Stuart Hall: Critical Dialogues in Cultural Studies*. London and New York: Routledge.

102  Sakai, ibid., pp. 73, 83; see Fabian, ibid., on the Western denial of 'co-evalness' to other forms of human life.

103 In Nancy N. Chen and Trinh T. Minh-ha (1994) 'Speaking Nearby', in L. Taylor (ed.) *Visualising Theory*, London: Routledge, p. 443.

104 Etienne Balibar, quoted in Sakai, ibid., p. 89; Sakai, ibid., pp. 82, 86, 90–1. On Latour, see Chapter 11.

105 See Koichi Iwabuchi (2000) 'Discrepant Transnational and Cosmopolitan Imaginaries in East Asian Popular Cultural Traffic', paper for Crossroads in Cultural Studies conference, Birmingham, 2000. See also Iwabuchi's subsequent (2002) *Recentring Globalisation*, Durham, NC: Duke University Press.

106 James Carrier (1995) *Occidentalism: Images of the West*, Oxford: Oxford University Press, p. 25. On this point, see Jonathan Spencer (1995) 'Occidentalism in the East', in Carrier, ibid., on Sri Lankan concerns about other South-East Asian, rather than American, cultural influences in their country. See also my essay (1994) 'Postmodernism: The Highest Stage of Cultural Imperialism', in M. Perryman (ed.) *Altered States*, London: Lawrence & Wishart.

107 Mandy Thomas (2000) 'Proscribing Desire: The Vietnamese State and East Asian Popular Culture', paper to Crossroads in Cultural Studies conference, Birmingham, 2000; Thomas, ibid., pp. 3–4. On the ambivalences of 'foreignness' see Dick Hebdige (1988) 'Towards a Cartography of Taste', in his *Hiding in the Light*, London: Routledge, and Ken Worpole (1983) *Dockers and Detectives*, London: Verso.

108 Iwabuchi (2000), ibid., pp. 4–5.

109 This is the inverse of C. Hoskins and R. Mirus's argument about the relative success or failure of cultural imports in a given setting: see their (1988) 'Reasons for the US Dominance of the International Trade in Television Programmes', *Media, Culture and Society*, 10 (4).

110 Iwabuchi (2000), ibid., p. 5.

111 Rem Koolhaas, quoted by Jane Jacobs (2003) 'The Global Domestic', lecture at Goldsmiths, University of London, May.

112 James Curran and Myung-Jin Park (1997) *De-Westernising Media Studies*. London: Routledge, p. 12.

113 Curran and Park, ibid., p. 15. John Downing (1996) *Internationalising Media Theory*, London: Sage, paraphrased in Curran and Park, ibid., p. 3.

114 Downing, ibid.; Valentina Vitali and Paul Willemen (eds) (2006) *Theorising National Cinema*. London: British Film Institute.

115 For a striking demonstration of the conceptual power of an approach that turns the tables in matters of comparison, see Manthia Diawara's film *Rouch in Reverse*, discussed in Chapter 4, in which Diawara turns the French ethnographer Jean Rouch into the subject of an ethnographic film made in his own 'natural habitat', in the anthropological institutes of Paris.

116 Burke quoted in Carrier, ibid., p. 2: Adam Kuper (1988) *The Invention of Primitive Society*. London: Routledge.

**Part IV**

# Domesticity, mediation and the technologies of 'newness'

*Figure 14*  Advertisement for Siemens refrigerator with built-in television. Reproduced by permission of Siemens plc and BSH Home Appliances Ltd.

# 7  Public issues and intimate histories

## Mediation, domestication and dislocation

Having thus far explored a number of general theoretical perspectives on 'new' forms of modernity and their geography at a macro-level, I now turn to a micro-perspective on another form of 'newness' – concerning the new technologies of our age, how they have been 'domesticated' and how we live with them in our quotidien existence. My specific concern in this chapter is to address questions of identity from the point of view of how we are to understand the idea of the mediated home – and also to address questions of technology from the point of view of how we can understand both the historical process of its domestication and the contemporary phenomenon of its dislocation.

In this context I also want to try to develop a perspective which tries to articulate the symbolic with the material dimensions of analysis. Lynn Spigel puts this point another way, when she argues that the 'simultaneous rise of the mass produced suburb and a ubiquitous place called "Televisionland" raises a set of questions that scholars have only recently begun to ask'.[1] In pursuing these questions, I return, following Spigel, to Raymond Williams's formulation of 'mobile privatisation' to describe the lifestyles of mediated suburbia. For Williams, 'mobile privatisation' offers the dual satisfactions of allowing people to simultaneously 'stay home', safe within the realm of their familiar ontological security and to travel (imaginatively or 'virtually') to 'places that previous generations could never imagine visiting'.[2]

Spigel argues that, in the North American context at least, we can usefully understand the genealogy of ideas about domesticity in a media-saturated world as developing through three main phases in the post-war period. As she notes, in the immediate post-war setting, television was widely figured as a bonding agent, capable of bringing together again the lives of families which had been splintered by war, and the technology itself was understood as an agent of desirable forms of 'family togetherness'.[3] The first phase of television's post-war development involved the model of the 'home theatre' (based on ideas of accessibility – bringing 'an imaginary night out on the town' into the sedentary domestic culture of the passive viewers, safe at home in the 'family circle' in their living rooms; allowing imaginary visits to the delights of the city, and an ersatz sense of participation in public life, for family members who, in fact, remained safe in the suburbs. It is this first phase, in Spigel's view, that Williams's model of 'mobile privatisation' really encapsulated. With the advent of portable television sets in the USA in the 1960s, designed to symbolise the aspirations of what the industry now figured as a more active and mobile audience of 'people on the go', this model was superceded by the (still-dominant) model of the 'mobile home', characterised not so much by mobile privatisation as by what she calls 'privatised mobility'.[4]

In the latest stage of these developments, Spigel argues, we see the model of the digitalised 'smart house' (of which more later) which offers not so much an image of mobility but of a 'sentient space' which, we are often told, so thoroughly transcends the divisions of inside/outside and work/home as to make it unnecessary to actually go anywhere any more. In its digitalised form, the home itself can then be seen as having become, in Virilio's terms, the 'last vehicle', where comfort, safety and stability can happily coexist with the possibility of instantaneous digitalised 'flight' to elsewhere – and the instantaneous importation of desired elements of the 'elsewhere' into the home.[5] However, as we shall see, all this 'high-tech' discourse is often carefully framed and domesticated by a rather nostalgic vision of 'family values'.

Clearly enough, in the present context, we have to move beyond media studies' historically rather exclusive focus on television so as to also address the contemporary significance of a broader range of communication technologies. However, I shall also argue that we need to 'decentre' the media, in our analytical framework, so as to better understand the ways in which media processes and everyday life are interwoven with each other. The problems we face will not be solved by contemporary proposals to 'modernise' media studies by reconceptualising it as 'web studies' or the like, for this would simply be to put the Internet at the centre of the equation, where television used to stand. Such a move would merely replicate a very old technologically determinist problematic in a new guise. The key issue here, to put it paradoxically, is how we can generate a non-mediacentric form of media studies, how to understand the variety of ways in which new and old media accommodate to each other and coexist in symbiotic forms and also how to better grasp how we live with them as parts of our personal or household 'media ensemble'.[6]

# The (much-advertised) 'death' of geography

Among other things, these new communications technologies have been trumpeted as heralding the ultimate 'death' of geography. From a UK perspective, one striking contemporary example that would seem to point in this direction is the growth of the telephone 'call centres' based in India which, because of their combination of a low-wage economy and a high level of indigenous English-language skills, now handle a lot of the 'customer services' calls for a variety of British businesses. The workers in these call centres are given crash courses on contemporary British culture and are carefully trained to present to their callers a highly developed form of 'virtual Britishness', entirely disguising their actual geographical location. They are encouraged to use 'English-sounding' first names to identify themselves when answering the phone and, so far as possible, to disguise their Indian accents. Indeed, in some of these centres, the workers are now deliberately taught to speak in regional English accents, the better to establish the authenticity of their 'Englishness' and the veracity of the impression they are taught to create, of responding to their callers from somewhere 'close to home'.[7] These Indian call-centre operatives' computer screens continually show both the current temperature in the UK, and Greenwich Mean Time, on which they are required to operate for the convenience of their British callers. They also have to keep up with British daily news and soap operas and consult local British weather reports, the better to engage their callers in sympathetic conversation.

However, while these call centres no longer need to be on the geographical territory of the UK, in order to deal effectively with British customers, they are not (*pace* the advocates of postmodern nomadology), just anywhere – nor indeed, are they in any significant sense 'deterritorialised'. They are located precisely where they are because India can offer investors the attractive combination of a high level of indigenous English-language skills with a low-wage economy, as a result of the long history of Britain's imperial presence on Indian soil. It is for reasons of exactly the same kind that French and Spanish call centres tend to be located in North Africa. The supposedly 'deterritorialised' geography of our postmodern era is thus much more legible if one reads it as a set of 'secondary' or 'shadow' geographies created through the complex history of imperialism.

Moreover, despite widespread dissimulations of the kind practised in these call centres, cyberspace still has a very real geography. As research at the Centre for Advanced Spatial Analysis in London has shown, the relative density of internet connections per square kilometre in different geographical locations varies enormously and access to these technologies (and to the 'connectivity' which they offer) depends very much on where you are located, in both geographical and social space.[8] The distribution of these new technologies frequently mirrors established structures of power, and flows of internet traffic tend to follow the routes laid down by previous forms of communication. As Matthew Zook demonstrates, the economy of the information age is far from being 'placeless' and the production of knowledge is actually rooted in very particular places, which constitute specific geographical 'milieux of innovation'. As Castells observes in his introduction to Zook's work, the location of internet domains is one of the most spatially concentrated patterns – not only by country, but also by region, and even by specific locations within metropolitan areas.[9] Moreover, as Zook shows, a vastly disproportionate amount of the production, dispersal and consumption of data on the Internet actually takes place within the geographical territory of the USA: not only are one-third of the world's total domain names registered in the USA but almost all the world's internet traffic passes through thirteen 'root servers' in America which hold the master directories of the domain suffixes (.com, .net, .uk, .fr, etc.). Zook notes that the great paradox is that despite the Internet's ability to transcend space, the great majority of the world's dot.com companies are still clustered in a very small number of urban conglomerations: New York, Los Angeles, London and San Francisco.[10]

Besides, as research in the 'Globalised Society' project, based in Copenhagen, has shown, despite all the claims about how the Internet heralds the death of geography, 'where are you?' is (still) one of the most insistent questions in internet 'chat rooms', and questions such as 'where do you live?' (or, more technically) 'where are you posting from?' are posed frequently in internet chat rooms. All of this seems to suggest a continuing desire to reterritorialise the uncertainty of location inherent in online worlds. In her study of multi-user internet spaces, Jenny Sunden observes that the premise of an abstract, free-floating space is constantly challenged by participants who 'spend a considerable amount of time on the creation of geographical anchorage for texts whose earthbound origins are concealed in the [computer] interface'.[11]

To make a parallel with my comments above about the use of 'British time' and British cultural norms in Indian call centres, the Copenhagen researchers also found many examples of what they call the 'taken-for-grantedness of America as place and culture on the net' and of Americanness as the 'silent norm' or default position of internet use.[12] These premises are engrained in attitudes and practices that construct America as the centre of the online universe and all other parts of the world as its periphery and are expressed in give-away phrases such as those in which someone refers to themselves on-line as 'from the South', while assuming that the receiver of the message will understand that they mean the south of the USA – or when people refer to themselves as being on 'East Coast' time, without feeling the need to indicate the east coast of which country.[13] To this extent, in effect, America (and American time) still provides, to a very large extent, the perceptual horizon of what we might call the 'on-line real'.[14]

To take an example from another technological realm, to which I will return later, just like on the Internet, the first question in many mobile-phone conversations is 'Where are you?' Notwithstanding Meyrowitz's arguments that the advent of broadcast television means that 'we' (whoever that is) now live in a 'Generalised Elsewhere', rather than a specifiable place, and despite Wark's claims that we no longer have roots or origins, but only aerials and terminals, it seems that we in fact do still inhabit actual geographical locations, which have very real consequences for our possibilities of knowledge and/or action.[15]

## Mediated histories and the domestication of television

Surrounded as we are by future-oriented debates about the impact of new communications technologies, it may well be that the first thing we need, if we are to avoid the twin dangers of utopianism and nostalgia – and to avoid the historically egocentric error of treating the dilemmas of our own age as if they were unique – is some way of placing these futurological debates in historical perspective. This concern, of course, leads us to one of the central issues in historical work: the question of periodisation and the issue of how to distinguish between the developing forms of media access and provision, as they are transformed by processes of institutional, economic, political, technological and cultural change. We have some guidelines to work with here. John Ellis has rightly pointed to the necessity to distinguish, in the realm of television broadcasting, between what he calls the 'age of scarcity' (when there were few channels), the 'age of availability' (as the number of channels on offer to the viewer gradually increased) and the current 'age of plenty and uncertainty' (as we move into a multi-channel broadcast environment, replete with remote controls, time-shift videos and audience fragmentation).[16]

The key issue is that of what exactly is being transformed here, and how, in response to these changes, we need to adjust our analytical paradigms. Here, alongside Spigel's helpful genealogy of models of domesticity and media consumption we might usefully also consider Robert Allen's work on the transformation of the film industry as a result of both demographic and technological changes, in a context where the increasing centrality of 'family values' in the political sphere is also reflected in the increasing market dominance of the 'family audience/film'. Allen's analysis clarifies not only the way in which, in the USA, domestic video/DVD has now become the main mode of film consumption, but also how film-on-video itself now functions, crucially, not so much as a source of profit in itself (even in 1992, box-office takings were already down to 25 per cent of revenue) but as a form of 'platform marketing' for the sales of the ancillary products (especially toys and games) which today constitute the industry's main source of profit. In relation to my comments above about the need to avoid 'mediacentrism', what both Allen and Spigel's analyses offer us, as exemplars, are ways of tracing the interconnections between political discourses of 'value', demographic changes in household structure, cultural definitions of domesticity, modes of media consumption and their retroactive effects on modes of industrial production.[17]

The development of historical work on the communications media has been one of the key developments of the recent period – notably that of Paddy Scannel in the UK and of Spigel and Jeffrey Sconce in the USA.[18] From a longer term perspective, Siegfried Zielinski's work rightly places the recent history of cinema and television in the broader context of the history of what he calls 'Audiovision', insisting that cinema and television should themselves be seen as no more than *entr'actes* in this history. In a comparable manner, Barbara Maria Stafford and Frances Terpak's edited collection, based on the LA Getty Museum's 2002 exhibition of visual 'devices of wonder' usefully places modern media technologies within the long historical series of 'instruments for the augmentation of perception', from the cabinet of curiosities and the peep show, to the camera obscura, the microscope and the diorama.[19]

However, despite these honourable exceptions, when media history is addressed, it is still too often rather narrowly conceived, either in institutional or technological terms. My own primary concern, in this respect, is with the 'intimate histories' of how we live with a variety of media. One question here is that of how our personal memories – especially of childhood – are formulated around media experiences, such as emblematic programmes and television characters. In this respect we might also usefully draw a parallel with Gaston Bachelard's analysis of how the material structure of the house provides the 'trellis' on which childhood memory is woven – but perhaps we now need to extend the analogy, so as to think of how that 'trellis' now has a mediated, as much as a material, structure.[20]

From this perspective, we also need to pay attention to the complex history of the process of television's domestication, while recognising that, in this respect, the domestic history of television is by no means singular. Just as television has moved, over time, from its fixed place in the sitting room to other household locations, Eliseo Veron and his colleagues in France have detailed the similar pathway traced by the 'journey of the phone' in the household, as it gradually multiplied and moved from the public space of the hallway into the other rooms of the house.[21] Clearly, when we come to the era of the mobile phone (which I shall consider in more detail below), not only is the technology entirely personalised, but it is treated by many of its users as just as much a 'bodypart' as their wristwatch. As one British schoolteacher put it, describing the difficulties experienced in preventing schoolchildren in the UK from taking their mobiles with them into examination rooms where they are forbidden, the problem is that for today's children the phone is just a completely taken-for-granted dimension of their existence: to them, it is 'just like any other item of clothing . . . They put [it] in their pockets in the morning and then don't consciously think about it' – for these children, having their phone with them is simply a normal part of 'being dressed' – and vice versa.[22]

In contrast to Simon Frith's argument that historically, broadcasting technologies enhanced the 'pleasures of the hearth' as a site for domestic leisure activities that had previously taken more public forms, the contemporary issue may be what the emergence of public forms of television and of the new 'personalised' communications technologies now do to correspondingly destabilise the centrality of the domestic home.[23] Today, the mobile phone often becomes, in effect, the person's virtual address, the new embodiment of their sense of home, while their 'land line' becomes a merely secondary communication facility – and one of seeming irrelevance to many of the new generation in the UK, who rarely bother to give out their land-line number (if they have one at all) except as a kind of 'fall-back' or 'last resort', but only their 'mobile' number.

## Mobile households and Palm Pilot parenting

Even if we need to avoid the dangers of any overly generalised 'nomadology' of postmodern life, mobilities, of one sort or another, are clearly central to our analysis. In this context, the extended family has now sometimes to be seen as stretched out across the long-distance phone wires, especially for migrants, who often spend a high proportion of their wages on phone calls home. This, as Roger Rouse puts it, allows them 'not just to "keep in touch", but to contribute to decision-making and participate in familial events from a distance'.[24] All of this points to the ways in which people have adapted to the capacities that these new technologies offer to allow them to literally be in two places at once. What is more, as Kevin Robins and Asu Aksoy argue in their study of Turkish migrants in London, this ability to oscillate between places is now, for many migrants, no more than a banal fact of their everyday lives, as they routinely move back and forward, at different points in the same day, between British and Turkish television channels, local face-to-face conversations and long-distance phone calls to distant relatives or friends, in a rich variety of differentially mediated communicative interactions. To this extent, twisting Raymond Williams's nostrum, Robins and Aksoy insist that, for many migrants, it is now transnational culture which is 'ordinary', at least in its mediated forms.[25]

Evidently, new technologies are increasingly important in the lives of many families, not only those of migrants. The research of Jan English-Lueck, Charles Darrah and James Freeman of San José State University in California, on 'Doing Family in Silicon Valley' is derived from a long-term ethnographic study of families conducted as part of their 'Silicon Valley Cultures Project'. As the centre of the Californian computer industry, Silicon Valley, with its unparalleled concentration of 'techies', offers a natural laboratory for the study of the cutting edge of technological applications in everyday life and, indeed, of the technological saturation of domestic life. To take but one simple indicator, this is a context in which an interviewee in their project apologetically described himself as a little 'old-fashioned' for still actually writing the notes with which he organises his day with pen and paper, rather than using a Palm Pilot.[26]

In researching these issues, English-Lueck and her colleagues have studied a large set of what they describe as 'infomated' households in the area – who commonly possess a critical mass of information devices, including video-cassette recorders, CD players, laser discs, fax machines, answering machines, voice-mail services, pagers, fixed and mobile computers, Palm Pilots and mobile phones. Much as Bausinger argues that, rather than studying the use of media technologies one by one, we should pay attention to how they function in concert, as 'media ensembles', English-Lueck insists that these people should not be seen as simply owning or using individual devices but as operating in particular 'ecosystems of technology'.[27]

Of course, even at the cutting edge of high technology, the same devices can be used in varying ways and can have opposite effects in households of different types, pulling together families that are already close, while allowing others to fly further apart – and thus playing out old patterns and relationships in newly mediated forms.[28] Thus, in some cases, new networks of connectedness are now created by the making and sending of videotapes, through e-mail and now by the electronic distribution of both still and moving images of domestic life via the cameraphone (baby's first steps; what Jack got up to after school today). In other cases, family members report pleasure at being able to be more independent and able to spend more time physically apart, because they feel 'safer' as a result of the virtual forms of contact at a distance enabled by these technologies (indeed, English-Lueck reports that the only time that all the members of one family had been physically co-present in some weeks was when they agreed to all be at home in order to be interviewed by the researcher).

One of the central concerns of English-Lueck et al.'s research is the radical blurring of boundaries between work and home consequent upon the development of the new patterns of home-working enabled by computing technologies. In this context, one focus of interest is the extent to which corporate discourses of identity originating in the business world now increasingly find their way into the home. We find here an environment where families increasingly see themselves and their problems in the terms of management theory. Thus their various activities are scheduled using the principles of business management – as in the case of the family that had its agreed 'Family Mission Statement', derived from Steven Cobey's book *The Seven Habits of Highly Effective People*, printed out and stuck on the door of their fridge.[29]

While such instances of the transfer of computer-based modes of group organisation and scheduling from the world of business to the home are clearly, as yet, particular to the most technologically advanced sections of affluent societies, they are already spreading beyond the confines of Silicon Valley. Throughout the USA, given the increasing spread of mobile-computing devices such as Palm Pilots into the middle-class domestic arena, a variety of web sites now promote internet-based calendars, and programs such as 'WeSync' and 'OrganisedHome.com' now enable dispersed and mobile extended families to continually update and coordinate their schedules of activity at a distance.[30]

As these researchers argue, all this reveals a picture of a situation where the new modes of electronic communication have themselves become the very infrastructure of family life. This, they argue, is especially so among busy, middle-class 'dual-career' parent families, living tightly scheduled lives, where parents have to balance the continually conflicting demands of work and family. Here the scheduling of children's birthday parties is juggled alongside business obligations, and arrangements are negotiated, both between spouses and between parents and children, much as a business might negotiate with its clients. Thus, telecom devices are used to coordinate parents' work obligations and social arrangements in synchronisation with their children's after-school clubs. Rather than seeing any simple opposition between the realms of technology and the family, in this culture, maintaining and upgrading the technical infrastructure that supports and enables the family in its activities is itself now seen as a key form of 'family work'. Moreover, these technologies often themselves now constitute the very modalities of domestic intimacy. As English-Lueck puts it, 'people have told us they'll come home in the evening and sit there side by side with their laptops, accessing their email and talking about it . . . [and] that's what now constitutes their 'couple time'.[31]

For the highly stressed and highly mobile members of these dual-career families, the issue of which parent is to pick up which child from which place at which time from their after-school activity club is negotiated daily by the participants on the move, by mobile phone and by e-mail. When they get home, the children may reel off their activities for the next day, while the parents dutifully enter them in their Palm Pilots, checking problems with the scheduling of their other appointments as they go and promising their children to page them confirmation of their 'pick-up' point/time by mid-afternoon of the next day. This is a world in which virtual parenting now has to carry some part of the burden of childcare and where being in electronic contact with a child (welcoming them home with a text message, hoping that they've 'had a good day' as a way of demonstrating parental concern and responsibility) may come to play an increasing role in patterns of childcare.[32]

## Technological surveillance in the domestic sphere

In the families which are the subject of the Silicon Valley study, mobile communication devices thus carry a substantial part of the burden of parenting – and, predictably enough, particularly that of mothering. Thus, one mother in the study is reported to always carry 'a pager and a cell phone so that she can stay in contact with her teenage children after they come home from school'. In these families there is also an increasingly complex system of family rules that governs the use (and penalises the non-use) of the technical devices through which they communicate, with children being told that they must keep their pagers/phones switched on. At its simplest, one mother says, 'I get stressed when [her child] doesn't have his cellphone on'.[33] Such kinds of technologically mediated 'parenting by proxy' are clearly becoming more widespread. Certainly, in the UK as well, it has now become increasingly common for parents to engage in a variety of forms of teleparenting and for them to equip their young children with a mobile phone precisely in order to then be able to monitor their whereabouts and activities.

This form of technologically enabled parental surveillance is increasingly big business. Thus, in the UK, the summer of 2005 saw the commercial launch, at the start of the school summer holidays, of the 'KidsOK' service, which allows parents to continually track their children's whereabouts via their mobile phones' GPS links.[34] This, of course, is not a one-way street – there are also examples of grown-up children effectively imposing mobile phones on their elderly parents, the better to keep them under surveillance, as part of their 'caring' duties.[35] Nor is it only inter-generational surveillance that is at issue: the UK press has also recently featured a number of articles reporting the newly emerging phenomenon of adult relationships that break up when infidelity is revealed by one partner surreptitiously checking the 'messages received' box on their partner's mobile phone.[36]

In this context, the mobile phone or the pager also becomes itself a concrete symbol representing the permanency of the link between family members. As André Caron and Litizia Caranovia put it, 'regardless of whether it is turned on or off, it is sign of the reciprocal availability of family members and of their being constantly "in touch".' Of course, as they also note, the meanings given to this symbol by different family members may well vary: for a mother, it may be valued as kind of electronic umbilical link to her children, who may themselves nonetheless regard it somewhat resentfully, at times, as a kind of electronic leash.[37]

The extent to which the home transcends the physical space of the household to incorporate 'extensions' such as the car is well established, and these issues of mediated forms of parental supervision at a distance also arise in that context. In the USA, as James Hay and Jeremy Packer observe in their study of the progressive integration of a variety of communication devices into the automobile, it is now possible for parents to install a 'black box' in their car, to monitor the driving behaviour of their teenage children when they borrow the vehicle, which automatically 'warns' the driver that they are speeding or committing some other form of parent-defined vehicular misconduct. As one mother puts it, 'this is something every car should have . . . it's like having a babysitter in the car'.[38]

A note of caution is perhaps necessary here, lest any of these comments should be thought to betoken some kind of irrational nostalgia for a pre-virtual world on my part. While I fully recognise the potential benefits of these technologies in the home, there are, nonetheless, limits to the viability of substituting virtual for real interactions. This is an argument which has been well made by Deirdre Boden, who found in her research with international stockbrokers that e-mail and telephone contact was deemed to be inadequate for the maintenance of the personal trust on which their financial dealings ultimately depended. For these purposes, only face-to-face meetings were deemed to suffice – hence, as she puts it, the 'compulsions of proximity' even in a high-tech world.[39] Whether in the world of high finance or family relations, the issue is how, without such face-to-face meetings, trust can be maintained – and it is hard to achieve this without the degree of communicative 'redundancy' provided by physical proximity in creating and maintaining relationships of trust, especially at times of trouble. However, it is also worth noting that English-Lueck et al. also found evidence of anxiety on this count at an everyday level. Their respondents' anxious awareness of the fragility of all this just-in-time electronic micro-scheduling is graphically indexed by the extent to which they routinely attempt to build in a safeguard of communicative 'redundancy' about their domestic arrangements by e-mailing, paging and phoning each other about the same arrangement, as a form of 'insurance' against the banal, but potentially consequential dangers of a dead battery or technical failure on any particular one of their many communications devices.[40]

## Fragmentation and individualisation

Clearly, family life is changing around us, as people adapt to new technologies and find ways to deal with new structures of work and mobility, and for all its continuing ideological centrality, the nuclear family household is declining rapidly in the West. It may not be possible (or even, ultimately, important) to work out which is the chicken and which is the egg in this respect, but we certainly need to develop a mode of analysis that can articulate these changes in household demographics with the rapid growth of individual 'personalised media-delivery systems' which is going on around us. In this context, it has been claimed that in the UK, the success of a television 'family magazine' programme such as *Nationwide*, which ran so successfully as the bedrock of BBC1's early evening schedule in the UK for many years, could not these days be repeated. In the words of then Channel 4 controller Tim Gardam, who had himself earlier been involved in the *Nationwide* programme, 'it worked because it broadcast to a society and television-watching public that watched together' – a scenario which Gardam declares is now over, as that was 'the last generation of family television'.[41]

Certainly, in the UK, patterns of viewing have changed radically in recent years, with 'family viewing' consistently declining in favour of individualised modes of media consumption. The 'multi-screen' household is now the norm, and this does affect household life in profound ways. More than 50 per cent of children in the UK between the ages of four and nine now have a separate television and frequently also a games console in their bedroom. Many commentators have also pointed towards evidence of the internal fragmentation of the home – such as the trend, in many households, towards the serial 'grazing' of microwave meals by individual family members at separate times. Here we can readily see how the institution of the 'family meal', even if, for many working people, it was always something of a middle-class fantasy, has now been undermined by the combination of 'fast/cook-chill' foods readily available from supermarkets, new cooking technologies and the changed working patterns of the women who, in a previous era, would have prepared the food.

It may be that in order to place these demographic and technological changes in household structures and technological forms in a broader theoretical framework, we need to turn to Ulrich Beck's theories of 'individualisation'.[42] Beck's overall claims about the demise of class structures may be overblown (so far as the UK is concerned, at least), but the central idea of the fragmentation – and indeed the 'individualisation' – of both audiences and the media technologies that service them is evidently pertinent here. To turn directly to the question of the individualisation of media consumption, one might also make an argument that a technology such as the Walkman (or the iPod), routinely used by many young people to create their own autonomous space both within the household and outside, is an intrinsically solipsistic technology or, in Stephen Bayley's striking phrase, a 'sod-you machine' for switching off unwanted interaction with others.[43]

I will return to the particular issue of the Walkman later, but some care is needed here if we are not to foreshorten our historical perspective on these matters. The individualisation of leisure pre-dates the invention of the Walkman by some considerable time and can, in fact, be understood to date at least from the invention of printing. As Witold Rybczynski notes 'the privatisation of reading . . . [was] . . . one of the major cultural developments of the early modern era [and] a milestone in the history of leisure . . . Reflection, contemplation, privacy and solitude are associated with reading books . . . [and] withdrawal . . . from the world around one, from the cares of everyday life'.[44]

However, while the leisure strategy of retreating into the private space supplied by the Walkman may perhaps be analogous in some ways to the practice of solitary reading, many other contemporary forms of individuated media consumption can be argued to have a rather different function. While his argument betrays a somewhat nostalgic tone, the novelist Richard Powers has recently written of the negative aspects of the contemporary decline of reading as a leisure pursuit, in favour of the constant use of individual communication devices that keep us always up to date and 'in touch' with developments in the wider world. For Powers, reading represents the last refuge from the epidemic contagion of 'real time' in which we are 'kept in every loop, current on every development: film of the year, record of the month, personality of the day, scandal of the minute' via our array of technologies offering 'two moments crammed into one. Split screen. Multi-tasking. Mobile wireless voicemail message forwarding. RSS feeds. Picture-in-a-picture' so that we need – and indeed can – miss nothing. This is a world in which

> we are always reachable, always up-to-date, always immersed in the unfolding world image, never alone, never outside the surging current of data intent on moving us ever farther downstream. In real time, we live in two minds, three tenses and four continents at once, and buy back the bits lost in transit with frequent-flyer miles'.[45]

This is a significant, if clearly dystopian, vision of what the technological future holds in store, to which I will return later.

## Domesticating the future

The question of the future and the question of technology are, of course, inextricably intertwined with each other, not least because the future (and, increasingly, the present) is now defined so much in technological terms. If the future represents, for many people, a troublesome realm of constant change, much of this trouble comes to be symbolised by – and in – technological forms. The question then is how this problematic technological realm comes to be naturalised and domesticated, so as to make it less threatening and more manageable for its inhabitants. There is, of course, an alternative 'take' on all this: there are those (defined principally by generation, education and class), for whom the future is a realm of hope rather than of trouble. For them, technology functions as the 'bright and shiny symbol' of those hopes, but in either case, whether positive or negative, these are still issues of the symbolic meaning of technologies.

If, in the affluent West, at least, the everyday is coming to be characterised by what Bausinger once called the 'inconspicuous omnipresence of the technical', one of the most striking findings of research into the domestic uses of ICT[46] is how, in many households, people go to a great deal of trouble to disguise the presence of communications technologies in their homes – often hiding television sets, computers and their wiring in wooden cabinets or behind their soft furnishings. If an increasing array of technologies have now become naturalised, to the point of literal – or psychological – invisibility in the domestic sphere, we need to understand the process of how that has come about.

## Domestication and naturalisation

The other reason why a historical perspective on new media should be central to our approach to these issues is because the dynamic of making technologies consumer-friendly, in practice, often means inserting them into recognisable forms from previous eras. To this extent, technological innovation often goes along with a continuing drive to make the techno-future safe, by incorporating it into familiar formats, icons and symbols. Thus Akiko Busch writes of contemporary 'designer kitchens' that contain 'wood-panelled refrigerators that camouflage themselves as cupboards' and of her own children now watching '*Terminator* movies on a TV set that is housed in a Shaker-style cabinet'.[47]

Sometimes, one can see this nostalgia-driven design strategy as understandably aimed at addressing the techno-fears of an older generation – indicated, for example by the news that, in the UK, a Bristol residential home for the elderly had appealed for a benefactor able to supply them with a 'traditional' red phone box and letter box, so that elderly residents would feel more reassured when making a call or sending letters. In a similar way, one can readily understand the recurring advertisements for CD players that look like old-fashioned record players in UK publications principally addressed to an older demographic, such as the *Radio Times* and *Daily Telegraph*. One of the big successes of the UK consumer-electronics market in 2004 was the retro digital radio – described by Caroline Roux as the 'natural heir to the [1950s] television concealed in the faux cocktail cabinet'. However, it is clearly not only the elderly to whom these things appeal: young people living very high-tech lives also often buy into the same sort of nostalgia. Thus, a leading UK style guide addressed to a young, tech-nologically literate and upwardly mobile audience recently had a feature on 'Seven Magnificent TV Cabinets' variously featuring 'wenge verneer armoire', 'solid oak', 'solid cherry' and 'reclaimed teak', but united in their ostensibly rustic disavowal of the presence of modern high technologies behind their closed wooden doors.[48]

In this connection, David Aaronovitch has written of those in the UK who would perhaps 'really like to live in the centrefold of the "Past Times" catalogue'. In the USA, Aaron Betsky observes that nowadays there seems to be an increasing need for 'the familiar, the known, the old and unthreat-ening – people want to live in the house they imagine their parents grew up in, they want hammers that look old-fashioned even if they have ergonomic grips . . . they want . . . the vernacular' – and the ultimate vernacular would, of course, be naturalised to the point of invisibility.[49] In exactly the same manner, a North American advert for one of the latest multifunctional home-entertainment systems takes the form of an image of family life which shows the new system installed in just the kind of traditional wooden cabinet into which, as we have seen, television sets themselves were incorporated when they were first introduced into the household in an earlier period. Moreover, the advert's imagery, in which everyone in the family group is shown smiling, under the benign gaze of the father, could almost be derived directly from a Norman Rockwell portrait of suburban family life in the USA in the 1950s. The potentially problematic nature of the new technology is thus neutralised by being shown as happily incorporated into the reassuring symbolism of this most conventional of homes.[50]

However, the process of the domestication of the media goes further than this. It is not just a question of how people come to feel 'at home' with the technologies in their houses. In the case of the Silicon Valley households discussed earlier, I argued that the technologies they used to coordinate their lives had, in effect, become the infrastructure of their families. With the advent of the electronic 'Dreamhouse' – whether in the earlier versions that Spigel describes in the 1950s/1960s, or nowadays, in Bill Gates's own 'fully wired' domestic paradise, well analysed by Fiona Allon (see below), we arrive at a new situation.[51] Here, rather than electronic technologies being domesticated, in the case of the 'smart house', the domestic realm itself is mediated and made fully electronic. In this vision of the household, the technologies are no longer merely supplementary to, but constitutive of, what the home itself now is.

Thus, another striking advert, produced in the USA by Applied Materials in their 'Information for Everyone' television campaign shows a large group of trendily dressed middle-class children, whose particular nationality is unmarked, dismounting rowdily from a school bus at the end of the day and jostling their way, in a relaxed and friendly manner, into an empty house which is replete with technology. In the course of the advert, we are shown that while the house seemingly has no adult occupants (though it features a classically friendly and welcoming pet Labrador dog) it does contain an electronic burglar alarm, a television, a video, an array of remote controls, desk, laptop and hand-held computers, a PlayStation, land-line and mobile telephones, a hi-fi set, electronic guitar and keyboards.[52] As they enter the house, the first child (who looks about nine years old) nonchalantly punches in the code to disable the burglar alarm in the hallway, while chatting to his pals and without paying any visible attention to the quite complex technical task that he is performing. As the children spread themselves throughout the house, they variously kick off their shoes, switch on their computers and throw themselves onto the sofa, grabbing snacks with one hand while dialing on their mobiles or fighting for the television remote control with the other. In the end we do not know where these children's home is, geographically, but the one thing we do know, metaphorically, is that they are all completely at home with a highly sophisticated range of technologies. Indeed, their pleasure in returning home at the end of the school day seems largely to be in 'coming home' to technology.

Moreover, it is not only the home which is being transformed in this way – the same is now true of the automobile. As James Hay and Jeremy Packer observe, the installation of telephones, personal computers, navigation and tracking systems in cars is increasingly a central, rather than a merely supplementary aspect of car design. To this extent, the 'intelligence' of the media-enhanced automobile is 'inseparable from the whole communications infrastructure, of which the vehicle is only one relay-point'.[53]

All this leads us towards the need to reconceptualise a new version of Raymond Williams's vision of mobile privatisation, in so far as the technologies that can be used to engage in the new, virtual forms of in-home 'travel' are now far more powerful than Williams ever imagined. However, it is well to remember that the houses that were built in 'Levittown' in the post-war period in the USA also had, as one of the key defining characteristics of their desirability, televisions built into their sitting-room walls. The electronic home itself has a history, which we would do well to remember, as we puzzle over its future.[54] Moreover, to return to the issue of the domestication of 'futuristic' forms of technology, as Allon points out, even Bill Gates represents the form of family life which he envisages conducting in his fully wired 'dream house' in the most conventional, suburban terms possible, which just goes to show the extent to which futurology is almost always as much 'backward' as it is 'forward-looking'.[55]

## Technology and nostalgia in the smart house

Gates's vision of the 'smart house' is based on of the production of a particular kind of networked, but thoroughly domesticated, spatiality – a mode of living compatible with the 'space of flows' of seemingly unrestrained mobility. It also involves the production of an implicit rhetoric of the way to inhabit that space, and the smart/networked house is presented as the way to 'find a place' within the 'great global multinational and decentred communicational network'.[56] Above all, this vision of the technological utopia provided by the 'instrumented house' offers a rhetoric of how to live in comfort and security in an unsafe world. The smart house is presented as a wired, sensitive, security compound, offering a heightened sense of privacy in a world of crime-ridden cities, terrorism and suburban alienation. In this context, the house functions to balance instant technological access to the world outside with inviolable personal safety and quietude. As Margaret Morse puts it, this is a discourse of the 'autonomy of protected selfhood' offering a form of connectedness to the world which is also a defence against it.[57]

This is also a vision in which the home is a space in which the new technology is framed, enculturated and made safe in the context of socially conservative images of the past – of rural harmony and familial stability. Thus, we see the most modern high-tech forms of 'integrated consumption, computing and communications facilities' converging around a thoroughly traditional image of 1950s Hollywood-style nuclear family bliss.[58] Similarly, in relation to the marketing of the Macintosh 'Performa' computer in the late 1990s, Alexander Chancellor noted that, despite the demographic decline of the nuclear-family household, the computer arrived with a brochure showing a photograph of the perfect four-member 'traditional family' grouped around it. Moreover, its software design assumed that the man of the house would determine, via an application called 'At Ease', which family members would have access to which levels of information and control – rather in the (presumably) reassuring, if authoritarian, manner of the classic Victorian *pater familias*.[59]

Gates stresses the homely virtues and family values of comfort, privacy and relaxation, tying his technological utopianism back into a long history of dreams of tranquil domesticity so that, as Allon argues, the virtual world to which Gates aspires is 'pacified and domesticated, void of the disruptive and the unfamiliar . . . a place experienced as a generalised and globalised homeliness, familiarity and intimacy.[60] As we saw earlier, in relation to the domestication of other technologies, the result is, again, a complex hybrid of the high-tech and the traditional, 'a world where "frontages" are often flagrantly at odds with the[ir] interiors; the apparently hand-tooled façade camouflaging hi-tech appointment within'. Here, the internal 'country-style' furniture and natural pine connotes a rustic, if not bucolic, nostalgia for an older, safer world, as if the 'increasingly sophisticated hi-tech appointments of houses . . . need to be balanced . . . by the authenticating seal of past times'.[61]

## And now? Dis-locating the media?

Thus far in my narrative I have traced the long story of the gradual domestication of a range of media, most particularly television, and have taken the 'smart house' as the culmination or 'end point' of this story, where the home itself becomes a fully technologised/wired place and comes to be defined by the technologies which constitute it.[62] However, it could be argued that we now face the beginning of a quite different story, where the narrative drive runs in the opposite direction, towards the de-domestication of the media and the radical dislocation of domesticity itself.

In many countries, television began as a public medium, watched collectively in public places and only gradually moved into the home and then into its further interstices. To take but two examples, in the immediate postwar period in the USA, television was mainly exhibited in public places, such as bars and department stores or on public transport. Similarly, in Japan in the early 1950s, television functioned as a kind of open-air theatre for the public viewing of sporting events such as wrestling matches on sets on street corners and in public squares and parks, where large crowds of viewers gathered together.[63] However, it is evident that having thoroughly colonised the home in the subsequent period, television has now re-escaped from its confines. Nowadays, we find it everywhere, in the public spaces of waiting rooms, train stations and airports and in commercial settings such as shops, bars, restaurants and launderettes. The difference is that this is now a supplement, rather than, as it originally was, an alternative to its place in the home, as Anna McCarthy in the USA and Goran Bolin in Sweden have documented in their studies of the newly 'ambient' forms of public television'.[64]

One important commercial motivation for this development has been the realisation within the advertising industry of the extent to which the home is an environment where television advertisements can, at best, expect only distracted forms of viewer attention. Another is their growing anxieties about the 'virtual mobility' created for the viewers at home by the remote control, which allows them to channel-surf, time-shift and fast-forward through the ads. Yet another is the realisation that some particularly desirable demographic groups (such as highly paid men and young people with high disposable income) are hard to reach on television at home and are better addressed in other places. For all these reasons, there has been a strong commercial imperative to develop public forms of television-based advertising that will reach these potential consumers wherever they may be gathered – as, in effect, more readily 'captured' audiences – whether while out socialising in bars and restaurants or while waiting for their plane at the airport. Having colonised the home, only to find that some of the key consumers it wishes to reach are absent from its confines, commercial-mediated advertising has now decided to follow them outdoors into the public arena.

From the point of view of its sponsors, public forms of television have a number of key advantages: crucially, they are 'zap-free', as it is the programmer, not the viewer who has exclusive control over the contents of the screen; further, the raised placing of the (usually large) set above eye level often gives it an air of authority which the small-scale domestic screen lacks. Moreover, not only are the audiences in many of these 'waiting places' (of one sort or another) often bored and thus on the lookout for some form of visual distraction, but specific demographic groups can also more readily be targeted by showing ads in the 'right' places – where the desired group has, as it were, already self-selected its presence and thus its availability to the advertiser. As an advertising-agency director quoted by McCarthy explains, 'the demographics of the [audience] are controlled by the location in which the message is delivered'.[65]

Naturally enough, if these advertisers can thus be seen as attempting to make 'dwelling in and passing through particular places a . . . "sponsored" . . . experience', the better to reach consumers on the move, they justify the screen's often unwanted intrusion into public life as a 'free attraction, another dimension of a site's publicness'.[66] Nonetheless, many people have come to feel that these kind of place-based forms of commercial television are, in effect, an offence against individual privacy. The apogee of this tendency in the UK was the scandal in 2004 about the installation of commercial television sets at the bedsides of hospital patients by the egregiously named company 'Patientline'. Clearly this form of television addresses an audience which is, by definition, captive. Moreover, the sets were designed so as to come on automatically at 6 a.m. and play without interruption until 10 p.m. In this particular case, literally no one could escape – those who did not want to watch the broadcasts were unable to turn their sets off and were instead subjected to a continuous loop of trailers for the unwanted service and repetitive 'patient-care' messages from the hospital authorities. When pressed on the irritation and distress this was causing to many seriously ill patients, the company spokesman somewhat unconvincingly claimed that their failure to provide the sets with an 'Off' button had been 'an accident'.[67]

These developments must to be understood in the broader theoretical context of debates about the ongoing transformation of the relationships between the public and private spheres. In this connection, Armand Mattelart has rightly argued that for many years now, public space has been gradually transformed by the increasing presence of advertising. Public space is now replete with commercial messages, whether visually – on large scale billboards in the street or the back of bus tickets – or aurally, as in the message on the UK telephone service that tells you that time itself is now 'sponsored by Accurist'. Thus, Abercrombie and Longhurst argue, given the ubiquity of media of all forms in the contemporary world, the old distinction between those who are part of the media audience and those who are not, is now quite outmoded, for the simple reason that we are all now, in effect, audiences to some kind of media almost everywhere, all the time.[68]

## Privatising the public: the car, the Walkman and the mobile phone

If we are almost continuously subject to the address of one or another form of media, one crucial issue concerns the degree and modes of control that we can have over this process. Critically, here we have to consider the ways in which people are enabled by a variety of technologies to construct their spaces of reception as forms of 'mobile home'. Here we need to consider three technologies in particular, as part of a 'conceptual series' which all have a potential role in fulfilling this function: the car, the Walkman and the mobile phone. As Patrice Flichy argues, 'in the 1950's in the US . . . teenagers took their dates to the drive-in movie in their . . . car. Without leaving . . . [it] they passed from the sound-bubble of the car radio to the visual bubble of the cinema. Today, the users of Walkmans [or now, iPods] and cellular phones . . . [also] transport their . . . [own] private sphere with them'.[69]

If we take the car, which, as I indicated earlier with reference to the work of Hay and Packer, has nowadays to be understood as an increasingly 'mediated' environment, we can readily see how the integration of sound technologies makes it more pleasurably 'habitable'. Centrally, this technology enables it to be more effectively used as part of a strategy for managing the personal environment, by maintaining a sense of privacy and control while traversing public space, as Michael Bull argues. He quotes one driver who reports that 'when I get in my car and turn on the radio, I'm at home. I haven't got to a journey to make before I get home . . . I shut my door, turn on the radio and I'm already home'; another says that 'being inside my car is like . . . this is my little world . . . I'm in my own little bubble . . . and I'm in complete control'. To this extent, the 'mobile and contingent space of the journey is experienced precisely as its opposite . . . [because] the driver controls . . . the inner environment of the automobile through sound'.[70] In a similar manner, 'in-flight' personal-entertainment systems on aeroplanes can be seen as functioning to create protective 'experiential bubbles', even if in this case, what they are protecting the user from is not the challenging over-stimulation of the environment of the road, but rather the 'terrible Kafka-like monotony of flying' as the in-flight screen 'organises and narrates the anonymity of suspended time'.[71]

If we shift our attention from the mediatised car to the Walkman, we see a comparable process in play, in which people are able to domesticate public space, though not by retreating into the private physical apace of the car-with-sound but into the virtual space of the acoustic bubble created by the personally chosen soundtrack with which they accompany their journeys. Following on from the work of Iain Chambers, Rey Chow and Paul du Gay et al. on the Walkman, Bull thus explores how a variety of users of the device understand its function.[72] One of them simply reports that 'when you've got a Walkman . . . you've got your own soundtrack'; another says that, with the machine on 'you can be in a crowd . . . it doesn't really matter . . . it's like a wall'; yet another, that it enables him to drift into his own perfect dream world, where everything is as he wants 'because I have familiar sounds with my own music that I know and [I can] sort of cut people out'. One major consequence of this, as Bull notes, is that Walkman-users thus seem to achieve a subjective sense of public invisibility, withdrawing from social interaction and effectively 'disappearing' or subtracting themselves from the public realm, if still physically present within it.[73] To return to my earlier comments on the way in which the history of the individualisation of leisure long pre-dates the invention of technologies such as the Walkman, it is also worth considering here the role of newspaper-reading as an earlier form in which commuters in particular were enabled to subjectively withdraw from public space into a more private world. In this connection, the success of the 'redesign' into smaller tabloid form of some of the UK broadsheet newspapers, which in their original form were cumbersome to read on crowded buses and trains, is surely another index of the successful adaptation and continuing importance of print-based media, in fulfilling these same functions in new conditions.

In his exemplary theorisation of the 'protective' function of sound technologies, Bull draws on the work of a range of urban theorists, from Georg Simmel's concerns with the problematic effects on the individual of sensory overload in the crowded city, to Richard Sennett's comments on the ways in which the contemporary tendency for people to 'retreat' into the sanctuary of 'aural solipsistic ghettos' undermines the capacity to sustain the potentially productive encounters with alterity that constitute the very basis of the public sphere. In doing so, he also introduces the further complexities added to our contemporary difficulties by the development and widespread adoption of the third of the technologies in the 'series' mentioned above: the mobile phone.[74]

In relation to the question of the dynamics of the increasingly privatised public sphere, Bull argues that while we might still all demand our own space, we 'increasingly discount the space of others', in a situation where urban space is now inhabited both by people walking along 'in aural solipsistic dreams, using their personal stereos' and by those, equally indifferent to others, who are busily 'exposing their private lives in public through their mobile phones'. If, as Shin Dong Kim puts it, 'not so long ago it was normally considered shameful to talk about private business in public . . . these manners have evaporated in this era of perpetual contact'. This attitude is well evidenced in the comments of one of Bull's respondents, who simply says that 'when I'm on the phone . . . what's going on around me is of secondary . . . [importance] I'm in my own little world. I work on the assumption that these people don't know me . . . [and] I don't know them'.

It seems that rather than the public sphere running on a basis of the 'civil inattention' which, as Simmel observed, was due between all citizens, for many people, it has now disintegrated into such a complex mesh of different and contradictory public sphericules co-present in the same geographical space that it is felt to belong to nobody rather than to all. Thus, one need not adapt one's behaviour to others' presence, as it doesn't matter if they eavesdrop on your conversation – as not to know others personally may now mean that they literally don't count for anything.[75]

## Mobile communications: the story of the mobile phone

If the Walkman is one 'privatising' technology, then the mobile phone is now perhaps the privatising technology of our age, par excellence. Evidently, one of the things that the mobile phone does is to dislocate the idea of home, enabling its user, in the words of the Orange advertising campaign in the UK, to 'take your network with you, wherever you go'. In a striking example of this, an overseas student at Goldsmiths University recently wrote of his joy when, while travelling on the train to college one afternoon, on the day of Chinese New Year, he received a 'New Year Wishes' phone call from his parents in Beijing at the symbolic moment of midnight Beijing time, saying simply that 'hearing those familiar voices through my little mobile phone, all of a sudden, I had the feeling of being at home'.[76]

The further issue, however, is that like the Walkman, if by a different means, the mobile phone also insulates its users from the geographical place that they are actually in and enables them to fill the empty spaces of the city with their own reassuring soundtrack. Often the user is paying no attention to those who are physically close to them, while speaking to others who are far away, and to that extent, the momentary community of those in the same place or situation is shattered by these external forms of connectivity. To that extent, it might also be argued not only that the mobile phone often functions as a psychic cocoon for its user, but even as a kind of mobile 'gated community'. As one user puts it, 'when I'm surrounded by people I don't know, I can easily connect with a familiar voice . . . speaking on my mobile enables me to distance myself from an[y] uncomfortable situation and brings . . . [me] a feeling of ease'. In her research into the uses of the mobile in business circles, Sadie Plant reports businessmen saying that if they arrive at a meeting where they feel uneasy, because don't know anyone, they 'play for time' by doing things with their mobiles, thus also indicating to the unknown others present that they are indeed, busy and well-connected people of importance, whose time cannot be wasted.[77]

It is usually taken for granted that the mobile phone is principally a device for transcending spatial distance. But just as we know that a large percentage of the world's e-mail is sent between people working in the same building, the mobile phone seems also to often be used in counter-intuitive ways. It is often used not so much to transcend distance as to establish parallel communications networks in the same space, which escape the conventional modes of place-based 'territorial control' (whether the use of text-messaging by pupils in UK schools or their use to make otherwise forbidden contact between teenage boys and girls in Iran). Indeed, this supposedly 'individualised' communications device also turns out to be often used collectively, especially among groups of young people when they are together – with one person's mobile being passed round the group, so that a particularly witty text message can be admired, or the size of a person's list of mobile numbers (an index of their popularity) can be demonstrated – on the principle 'I'm well liked: I must be: see, my Sim card's full'.[78]

As we know, the mobile-phone call disrupts the physical space of the public sphere in a variety of ways: annoying others with its insistent demand for attention or imposing 'private' conversation on those near its user by means of high-volume conversation in the form of what, in the USA, has been described as the 'cell yell'. It is also interesting to see the ways in which these developments have also given rise to a whole new set of debates about the etiquette of communications, focused on this technology. The use of the mobile phone in public places is certainly still an unresolved site of conflict in the UK. In his account of an incident at the Middlesex County Cricket Club's (MCCC) ground at Lord's in London, a very conservative institution which operates a total ban on mobiles, Jason Bennetto reports one MCCC member confronting another with a knife when he spotted him using his mobile during a match.[79]

During his research into contemporary uses of cemeteries, Ken Worpole reports 'coming across a young woman in a fur coat speaking into a mobile phone, for me a final breaching of that tradition which Steven Kern, in his classic account of early modernist consciousness, thought was inviolable: that one would never find a telephone in a cemetery'.[80] This is not to suggest that crises about the forms of public talk are an entirely new phenomenon. By the late nineteenth century, observers were already noting that strange things were happening to conversation as result of the invention of telephony. The 'joke' of Mark Twain's ironically titled 1880 story 'A Telephonic Conversation' is that one can only ever hear one half of these new forms of conversation:

> Then followed that queerest of all the queer things in this world – a conversation with only one end to it. You hear questions asked; you don't hear the answer. You hear invitations given; you hear no thanks in return. You have listening pauses of dead silence, followed by irrelevant or unjustifiable exclamations of glad surprise or sorrow or dismay. You can't make head nor tail of the talk, because you never hear anything that the person at the other end of the wire says.[81]

The mobile phone has now returned questions of contemporary etiquette to the public agenda in a noteworthy way, and in the UK it has been fascinating to see the speed at which new modes of regulation of the device have been developing – such as 'quiet carriages' on trains and notices in restaurants and cinemas banning their use.[82] Recently, in response to these burgeoning forms of pubic disquiet about their use, even the commercial companies which profit from them have felt it wise to change their publicity. Thus, British Telecom, whose advertising slogan for all forms of phone use was for many years 'It's good to talk', has now changed the standpoint of its advertising discourse to acknowledge the limitations of their previous approach, in the face of public disquiet about mobile talk. Its new publicity thus avers that 'There are certain conversations which should never include the phrase "Hang on, I'm just going through a tunnel"' and also poses the question 'Do you really want an intimate chat with your boyfriend, twenty-seven commuters and the ticket collector?' In a similar change of tack, the Orange mobile network's new advertising campaign reminds its UK customers that they should remember that 'Good things also happen when your mobile is off . . . a switched-off phone can say a lot. It can say to the person next to us "I think you deserve my full attention"'.

As we have seen, the mobile phone is often understood (and promoted) as a device for connecting us to those who are far away and thus overcoming distance – and perhaps geography itself. It has been described as enabling the emergence of an even more mobile descendant of the *flâneur* – the *phoneur*.[83] However, just like in internet chat rooms, as we all know, the first question in many mobile-phone conversations is often 'Where are you?' (just as the answer, so often is 'I'm on the train/stuck in traffic, I'll be bit late'). In this respect, the protocol for mobile conversations is quite different from that in traditional land-line talk – where the caller, by definition, knows where the phone is located but does not know who may answer their call. As land lines are structured to fit stable, but collective social systems such as homes or institutions, personal identification is necessary. On the mobile, however, identification is replaced by geography, as it is not a question of who will answer, but of where that person is – and the receiver will customarily begin by informing the caller about their current geographical and situational circumstances, as these may well dictate what can (and cannot) be discussed.[84]

It seems that geography is not, in fact, dead at all and that what the mobile phone allows is, in fact, endless anxious commentary on our geographical locations and trajectories. Perhaps one might even say that the mobile phone is, among other things, a device for dealing with our anxieties about the problems of distance created by our newly mobile lifestyles and with the emotional 'disconnectedness' which that geographical distance symbolises for us.[85]

## Mobile talk: from conversation to chatter?

To pose matters a little more theoretically, the geographer Yi-Fu Tuan distinguishes between 'conversation' (substantive talk about events and issues – a discourse of the public realm) and 'chatter' (the exchange of gossip, principally designed to maintain solidarity between those involved in the exchange – what Tuan calls a 'discourse of the hearth'). Drawing on Tuan's distinction, John Tomlinson has argued that the discourse of most mobile-phone use can be characterised as a form of phatic or gestural communication, which principally functions to maintain social ties of belonging and dependency, rather than to exchange substantive information or debate 'serious' topics. It is in this context that we might perhaps best understand phenomena such as the habit of young people in some of the poorer countries of eastern Europe who regularly 'flash-phone' their friends, throughout the day, without leaving any message because this is simply the cheapest way of confirming to their friends (via the 'call number record facility') that they are still thinking about them.[86]

In these terms, what the mobile phone does is to fill the space of the public sphere with the chatter of the hearth, allowing us to take our homes with us, just as a tortoise stays in its shell, wherever it travels. To this extent, Tomlinson argues, we would be mistaken to see these new technologies simply as 'tools for the extending of cultural horizons or exit portals from the narrow ties of locality . . . or . . . facilitators of a cosmopolitan disposition'. Rather, he claims, we should see them as 'technologies of the hearth: imperfect instruments, by which people try . . . to maintain something of the security of cultural location' amidst a culture of flow and deterritorialisation.[87] This is to place these technologies, along with the car and the technical achievements of automobility, as part of the series of tele-technologies such as television, telegraphy and the telephone, as 'instruments of distance management' crucial to the management of contemporary distribution of people and resources.[88] In a similar vein, Plant argues that the mobile phone both adds and answers to the sense of constant mobility which now characterises our lives: the 'restless, noncommittal feeling that all plans are contingent and may change at any time; an awareness that life is unpredictable and insecure; and the slightly schizophrenic tone of a world in which people have become adept at doing their banking while jogging in the park'. In Bauman's terms, this is a period of what he calls 'Liquid Modernity', featuring the transformation of social systems from the 'solid' state of rigid scheduling to the 'liquid' state of an ongoing stream of renegotiations, reconfigurations involving the constant rescheduling of all obligations and commitments.[89] In this context, Gary Cooper writes that the mobile phone is 'a technology which connects the global . . . with the most local of social interactions . . . [forming] a juncture . . . between [these] different domains'. Adding a historical dimension, Roos argues that what the mobile phone enables is the transposition of a form of *pre*-modern locality, where everybody in the village knows pretty much where everyone else is at a given moment, into a new virtual, deterritorialised form in which this same ongoing form of quotidien intimacy is now dispersed over much wider geographical spaces.[90]

However, to return to Tuan's distinction between discourses of the hearth and of the cosmos, there are conceptual difficulties with the implicitly value-laden nature of his terminology. To some extent, it betrays a problematic parallelism with Basil Bernstein's distinction between what he termed 'restricted' and 'elaborated' linguistic codes – felt by Bernstein to respectively characterise the strengths of middle-class 'educated' speech and the weaknesses of working-class communication. The difficulties with Bernstein's position, especially in so far as it downplays the importance of the community-building aspects of the so-called 'restricted' code, were identified many years ago by his principal critic Harold Rosen.[91] In mobilising Tuan's distinction, despite his insightfulness, Tomlinson also perhaps falls too far into a rather conventionally Habermassian model of the public sphere and what it should be used for – as manifested in the conventional left-wing political-economy critique of 'talk shows' on television, as an index of the lamentable corruption of the proper purposes and functions of the public sphere, as a place for the rational discussion of public issues. The difficulty here is that this position is based on an unproblematised conception not only of rationality, but also of the class, gender and ethnic composition of the public – and of its 'proper' concerns.[92]

In relation to how these points specifically apply in a discussion of the mobile phone, it should be remembered that there was a comparable social panic about the uses of the land-line phone when, having been introduced for business purposes (which were, of course, themselves defined in masculinist terms), it was realised that it was being largely taken over by the 'gossip' of women. It was only when the industry came to understand that the phone was, in fact, principally being used by women, for social and familial purposes, that the marketing emphasis was changed from presenting the telephone as a 'practical' device for business use to one which sold it as 'a medium for comfort and convenience'.[93]

We should also recall here Roman Jakobson's emphasis on the crucial importance of the 'phatic' function in all communications: the role of establishing and maintaining the communicative 'channel' through which the content of communications flows – and without which it cannot function at all. It is also important to note here the work of feminist scholars such as Ann Moyal who have detailed the various ways in which what men tend to regard as women's 'pointless chatter' on the phone (mobile or land-based) can, from another point of view, be seen as a crucial part of the ongoing labour that is needed to sustain familial and social networks.[94] The whole point of many mobile-phone calls (and more especially of many text messages) is that, while their content may well be viewed as trivial, unimportant or even silly, it is their phatic function – the gesture of 'getting in touch', reassuring the other that they are in your mind – which is the critical one. As for the presumed 'redundancy' of the phatic dimensions of communication, it is instructive to note the ways in which, even in business circles, where the (profitable) efficiency of communications is the ultimate prize, it is now increasingly recognised that, as a result of the use of high-speed e-mail communications in many organisations, in which the 'phatic' relationship-building dimension of communication has been too much subordinated to its content, social relations have often broken down – with thoroughly unprofitable consequences. In many cases, this is because correspondents have, too readily, and especially in moments of difficulty, got 'straight to the point' in a seemingly rational and efficient manner and, thus, inadvertently caused offence by neglecting to observe the social and communicative 'niceties' that are necessary to sustain relationships of civility between communicative partners.

## Innovations: the mobile phone as a 'micro-casting' technology

Just in case it might seem that my own overall argument is too negative about the potential uses of the mobile phone, I will end by considering one very different – and radically innovative – example of how it can be used. The example comes from the work of an MA student at Goldsmiths, Gareth Jones, during the making of a radio documentary on the mobile phone in contemporary British culture.[95]

In the UK, as elsewhere, many young people now 'customise' their mobile phones not only with physical accessories such as fascias, but also with electronic ones, such as 'personalised' ringtones (or, for the British Asian consumer market, 'raagtones') in a process whereby they select and record their own electronic tune, to replace the manufacturers' standardised ringing signal whether in the form of the latest popular hit or one of Boosey & Hawkes' new selection of signature tunes from the world of classical music. This process, described by one manufacturer as 'like fashion in clothes . . . another way of expressing your individuality to anyone within earshot', is now a hugely profitable – and fast-growing – dimension of the overall music market, which threatens to soon overtake the economic importance of the CD single. (Indeed, in mid-2005, the 'Crazy Frog' ringtone became the first to also make it to the top of the UK's CD single charts.)[96]

When Gareth Jones interviewed a number of young people in London about what 'ringtones' they had on their phones, he found that the results were, in many ways, deeply depressing. Thus, when asked why they had the particular 'ringtones' that they did, the majority of his interviewees were almost completely inarticulate – beyond expressing their compulsion to have one of the 'latest' ringtones. Their main concern was simply to have installed their own personal choice – because they feared that, otherwise, they would be seen by their friends to be terminally 'uncool', if they just had one of the standard ringtones installed on the phone by its manufacturer. To this extent, his respondents' answers sounded rather as if one was listening to the worst of Adorno and Horkheimer's predictions about the development of the culture industry coming true in a story of how capitalism had now come to provide forms of customised 'pseudo-individuality' for everyone, of all tastes, in a process in which no one need feel excluded, but also one in which no one could escape.[97]

However, in one case, instead of a tune, a young man had recorded on his phone a little piece of social drama in which he and his friends were involved – and every time his phone rang, anyone within hearing distance was made party to a traumatic incident of racial abuse to which he and his friends had been subjected by a shopkeeper, an incident that he had recorded at the time and then installed as his 'ringtone'. In this case, we confront an exceptionally imaginative innovation in mobile-phone usage in which the technology is recruited to play an unforseen role in transforming the relations between the public and private spheres of experience. Here, the mobile phone is used as a kind of mini-broadcasting system, which forces everyone within hearing distance to share the drama of this incident in this young man's life, whenever his phone rings. Here we see the relations of public and private discourse – on matters of considerable consequence – being transformed by a radically innovative and thoughtful redeployment of the mobile phone for purposes quite other than those for which it was first designed.[98]

## Conclusion

If one of the key historical roles of broadcasting technologies has been their transformation of the relations of the public and private spheres, then the questions that face us now concern what these new technologies are doing to those relations, and how they, in turn, may be regulated and domesticated. We find ourselves in a world where we are all audiences to one or another medium, almost all of the time, and where, after its long process of domestication, television (and other media) have now escaped the home – to (re)colonise the public sphere. While the domestic home itself might now be said to have become a fully technological artefact, it also seems that domesticity itself has now been dislocated. As we wander the public realm, protected by the carapaces of our Walkmans and mobile phones, it may be a good moment to re-pose Heidegger's question about what it means to live in a culture of 'distancelessness' where things are neither near nor far but, as it were 'without distance'. But as soon as we make this connection to these earlier debates, we have to recognise that the questions we face today, while undoubtedly urgent, are not in themselves new. Moreover, we have to recognise with Lynn Spigel that if we are ever to get any critical perspective on the discourses of futurology which now surround us, we shall certainly need to put them in a fuller historical perspective than that which they recognise for themselves.[99]

## Notes

1 Lynn Spigel (2001a) *Welcome to the Dreamhouse*. Durham, NC: Duke University Press, p. 15.
2 Raymond Williams (1974) *Television: Technology and Cultural Form*. London: Fontana, p. 26.
3 Lynn Spigel (1992) *Make Room For Television*. Chicago, Ill.: University of Chicago Press, p. 39.
4 Lynn Spigel (2001b) 'Media Homes: Then and Now', *International Journal of Cultural Studies*, 4 (4): 391.
5 Spigel, ibid., 2001, pp. 386, 398; Paul Virilio (1991) *Lost Dimension*. New York: Semiotext(e); quoted in Spigel, ibid., p. 400.
6 On 'media ensembles', see Hermann Bausinger (1986) 'Media, Technology and Everyday Life', *Media, Culture and Society*, 6 (4). For an interesting attempt to develop a non-mediacentric theory of media studies, see Shaun Moore's recent (2005) *Media/Theory*. London: Routledge.
7 Sue Peters (2004) 'Information Mobility', paper for Alternative Mobilities Conference, Lancaster University, January.
8 Martin Dodge and Rob Kitchin (2001) *Mapping Cyberspace*. London: Routledge.
9 Manuel Castells (2005) 'Introduction', to Matthew A. Zook *The Geography of the Internet*. Oxford: Blackwell.
10 See Thomas Jones's commentary on Zook's work, in his (2005) 'Short Cuts', *London Review of Books*, 4 August, p. 22.
11 See Jenny Sunden (2001) 'The Virtually Global: Or, the Flipside of Being Digital' University of Copenhagen: Global Media Cultures Working Paper, No. 8.
12 Sunden, ibid., 18.
13 See Sakai in Chapter 11 on the essential relativity of the terms 'East' and 'West'.
14 Sunden, ibid., pp. 15–18.
15 Joshua Meyrowitz (1985) *No Sense of Place*. Oxford: Oxford University Press; McKenzie Wark (1994) *Virtual Geography*. Bloomington, Ind.: Indiana University Press; see Torsten Haagerstrand (1986) 'Decentralisation and Radio Broadcasting: On the 'Possibility Space' of a Communications Technology', *European Journal of Communications Studies*, 1 (1).
16 John Ellis (2000) *Seeing Things: Television in an Age of Uncertainty*. London: I.B. Tauris.
17 Allen, Robert (1999) 'Home Alone Together: Hollywood and the Family Film', in M. Stokes and R. Maltby (eds) *Identifying Hollywood's Audiences*. London: British Film Institute.
18 Paddy Scannell (1996) *Radio, Television and Modern Life*. Oxford: Blackwell; Jeffrey Sconce (2000) *Haunted Media*. Durham, Md.: Duke University Press.
19 Barbara Maria Stafford and Frances Terpak (2001) *Devices of Wonder: From the World in a Box to Images on a Screen*, Los Angeles, Calif.: Getty Research Institute. Siegfried Zielinski (1999) *AudioVisions: Cinema and Television as entr'actes in History*. Amsterdam: University of Amsterdam Press.
20 Gaston Bachelard (1994) *The Poetics of Space*. Boston, Mass.: Beacon Press 1994.

In this connection we might also consider the burgeoning genre of writing about childhood as a thoroughly mediated experience, see Stuart Jeffries (2001) *Mrs Slocum's Pussy: Growing Up in Front of the Telly*. London: Flamingo; Curtis White (1998) *Memories of my Father Watching Television*. Normal, Ill.: Dalkey Archive Press. More generally, one might point to the whole slew of 'Generation X' autobiographical fiction in the USA, produced by writers such as Douglas Coupland, which would be largely incomprehensible to anyone who did not share that particular litany of American popular television situation comedy, soap opera and its stars. See also Ch. 9 on this point.

21 Eliseo Veron (1991) *Analyses pour Centre d'Études des Telecommunications*, Paris: Causa Rerum.

22 Richard Gardner (2005) 'More Pupils Cheat at School Exams' *The Independent*, 16 April; see McLuhan's comments on technology as a form of dress, quoted in Chapter 8.

23 Simon Firth (1983) 'The Pleasures of the Hearth', in J. Donald (ed.) *Formations of Pleasure*. London: Routledge.

24 Roger Rouse (1995) 'Questions of Identity', *Critique of Anthropology*, 15 (4). A high-street call centre in East London, where I live, advertises its cheap-rate calls to Ghana with an endearing photo of a middle-aged African woman, under which runs the slogan 'Call Mama'. To take another example of migrant uses of technologies originally designed for other purposes, some years ago now, Eliut Flores reported the use, by Puerto Rican migrant families living in New York, of cheap-rate 'downtime' on business video-conferencing facilities in the city as a 'virtual' alternative to actually flying the whole family 'back home' for a visit; Eliut Flores (1988) 'Mass Media and the Cultural Identity of the Puerto Rican People', Paper to IAMCR conference, Barcelona, July.

25 Kevin Robins and Asu Aksoy (2001) 'From Spaces of Identity to Mental Spaces: Lessons from Turkish-Cypriot Cultural Experiences in Britain', *Journal of Ethnic and Migration Studies*, 27 (4).

26 Jan English-Lueck (2002) *Cultures@Siliconvalley*, Stanford, Calif.: Stanford University Press, p. 4 . For further details of this project, see their web site at <http://www2.sjsu/ depts/anthropology/svcp>.

27 Jan English-Lueck (1998) 'Technology and Social Change: The Effects on the Family', paper to COSSA Congressional Seminar, June p. 9; Bausinger, ibid., 1986.

28 English-Lueck, ibid., pp. 6–9.

29 Stephen R. Cobey (1999) *The Seven Habits of Highly Effective People*, London: Simon & Schuster. See Chapter 8 on the importance of the fridge as a domestic communications centre; see English-Lueck et al. (2002) 'Creating Culture in Dual Career Families', unpublished paper, Department of Anthropology, San José State University; see also Costariadis, quoted later, on the penetration of management 'fantasies of control' into the domestic sphere.

30 Peter Meyers (2002) 'Handhelds Juggle Family Agendas', *International Herald Tribune*, 15 July 2002.

31 English-Lueck, quoted in Emma Brockes (2000) 'Doing Family in Silicon Valley', *The Guardian* (G2), 17 May, pp. 8–9.

32 Brockes, ibid.

33 English-Lueck 1998, ibid., p. 4.

34 These parental surveillance technologies are developing fast – there have recently been reports of products for children such as armbands, soft toys and even pyjamas which incorporate electronic tracking devices, so that the child's whereabouts can be continually monitored by their parents. See Lucy Atkins (2005) 'Tagged, and ready for bed' *The Guardian* (Family) 3 December.

35 See my later example in Chapter 11 of two daughters 'imposing' an unwanted mobile phone on their mother, so as to monitor her well-being on her solo trips to their isolated summer house in the countryside.

36 See Andrew Johnson (2005)'The Liddle Effect: Why 3 out of 4 Women Spy on their Men', *Independent on Sunday*, 8 April.

37 André Caron and Litizia Caranovia (2001) 'Active Uses and Active Objects: The Mutual Construction of Families and Communications Technologies', unpublished paper, Department of Communications, Université de Montreal/Dipartimento di Scienza dell' Educazione, Universite di Bologna.

38 James Hay and Jeremy Packer (2004) 'Crossing the Media(n): Auto-mobility, the Transported Self and Technologies of Freedom', in N. Couldry and A. McCarthy (eds) *MediaSpace*. London: Routledge.

39 See Deirdre Boden and Harvey Molotch (1994) 'The Compulsion of Proximity', in Roger Friedland and Deirdre Boden (eds) *NowHere: Space, Time and Modernity*. Berkeley, Calif.: University of California Press. See also my discussion in Chapter 1 of *Home Territories* of Mary Douglas's argument about the fundamental communicative importance of co-presence at family meals.

40 See also my discussion of the importance of 'phatic' forms of mobile communication, later in this chapter.

41 Gardam quoted in John Mair (2002) 'They Made their Name with Skateboarding Ducks – Now They Rule British television', *Media Guardian*, 4 February.

42 See Ulrich Beck and Elizabeth Beck-Gernsheim (2002) *Individualisation*. London: Sage.

43 Stephen Bayley (1990) *Design Classics: The Sony Walkman*. London: BBC Video.

44 Witold Rybczynski (1991) *Waiting for the Weekend*. New York: Viking, p. 190.

45 Richard Powers (2004) 'Introduction', *The Paris Review Book for Planes, Trains, Elevators and Waiting Rooms*. New York: Picador; extracted in R. Powers (2004) 'Real Time Bandits', *The Guardian Review*, 14 August.

46 See Roger Silverstone and Eric Hirsch (eds) (1992) *Consuming Technologies*. London: Routledge.

47 Akiko Busch (1999) *The Geography of Home*. Princeton, NJ: Princeton Architectural Press.

48 (2003) 'Red Alert', *Bristol Evening Post*, 15 January; (2004) 'Magnificent Seven television Cabinets', *The Guardian Style Guide*, 14 August; Caroline Roux (2004) 'To Die For: Retro Technology', *The Guardian 'Weekend'*, 6 November.

49 David Aaronovitch (2002) 'Why Do We Persist with this Morbid Attachment to Heritage and Tradition?' *The Independent*, 27 December; Aaron Betsky (2003) 'The Strangeness of the Familiar in Design', in Andrew Blauvelt (ed.) *Strangely*

*Familiar: Design and Everyday Life*. Minneapolis, Minn.: Walker Art Centre, pp. 45–6. See also Chapter 10 for my discussion of 'retro-fashion' in relation to the mobile phone among trendy young New Yorkers.

50  My thanks to James Lull for this example. See also Rivka Ribak (2002) 'Like Immigrants: Negotiating Power in the Face of the Computer', *New Media and Society* 3 (2), on the transformations of inter-generational modes of power in a world of rapidly changing technologies.

51  Spigel, 2001a, ibid.

52  I am grateful to Dana Polan for his acute observation about the significance of the dog's presence in a discussion of this material at the University of Southern California.

53  James Hay and Jeremy Packer, ibid., p. 217; Couldry and McCarthy, ibid., 'Editorial Introduction', p. 14.

54  See Dolores Hayden (2002) *Redesigning the American Dream: Gender, Housing and Family Life*. New York: Norton.

55  Fiona Allon (1999) 'Altitude Anxiety: Being-at-Home in a Globalised World', Ph.D. thesis, University of Technology, Sydney.

56  Fredric Jameson, quoted in Allon, ibid., 1999: 92, 98; Fiona Allon (2004) 'An Ontology of Everyday Control', in N. Couldry and A. McCarthy (eds) *MediaSpace*. London: Routledge, pp. 255 and 261.

57  Allon, 2004, ibid., pp. 266–7; Morse quoted in Allon, 2004, ibid., p. 267.

58  As Fiona Allon observes, for Microsoft, familialism is not simply an ideology – just as Robert Allen shows in his analysis of the increasing dominance of the 'family film' in the US film/video market, Gates is well aware that families represent his biggest and fastest growing market. Microsoft's founding slogan is, after all, not only 'a computer on every desk' but also 'in every home' (Allon, 1999, ibid., pp. 91, 93–4).

59  Alexander Chancellor (1997) 'Apple's Unoriginal Sin', *The Guardian* (Weekend), 8 February.

60  Allon, 1999, ibid., p. 90.

61  Samuel quoted in Allon, 1999, ibid., p. 110.

62  This is also increasingly true at a literal level: in 'real estate' terms (especially in South-East Asia) in so far as the value of the electrical wiring/capacity of a building is now a substantial part of what the buyer is paying for.

63  Spigel, 1992, ibid., p. 32; Shunya Yoshimi (2003) 'Television and Nationalism: Historical Change in the National Domestic television Formation of Post-War Japan', *European Journal of Cultural Studies*, 6 (4), p. 463.

64  Anna McCarthy (2001) *Ambient Television*, Durham, NC: Duke University Press and Goran Bolin (2004) 'Spaces of Television' in N. Couldry and A. McCarthy (eds) *MediaSpace*. London: Routledge. For a spectacular set of instances of the public life of television, see the mass viewings of the World Cup in many cities across the world, in the summer of 2002. See also Kim Soyoung (forthcoming) 'To Live as a Blade Runner in South Korea', in L. Spigel et al. (eds) *Electronic Elsewheres*. Minneapolis, Minn.: University of Minnesota Press.

65  McCarthy, 2001, ibid., p. 100.

66  McCarthy, 2001, ibid., pp. 103, 111.

67 John Carvel (2004) 'Hospital Patients Forced to Watch television They Can't Turn Off' *The Guardian*, 8 April.
68 Armand Mattelart (1996) *The Invention of Communication*. Minneapolis, Minn.: University of Minnesota Press; Nicholas Abercrombie and Brian Longhurst (1999) *Audiences: Sociological Theory and Audience Research*, London: Sage.
69 P. Flichy (1995) *Dynamics of Modern Communication*, London: Sage, p. 168; quoted in Michael Bull (2004) 'To Each Their Own Bubble: Mobile Spaces of Sound in the City' in N. Couldry and A. McCarthy (eds) *MediaSpace*. London: Routledge, p. 275; see also Bull's later (2005) *Sounding Out the City*. Oxford: Berg.
70 Bull, 2004, ibid., pp. 281, 282.
71 S.L. Kolm and Patricia Mellencamp, quoted in Nitin Govil (2004) 'Something Spatial in the Air', in N. Couldry and A. McCarthy (eds) *MediaSpace*. London: Routledge, p. 239.
72 Iain Chambers (1990) 'A Miniature History of the Walkman', *New Formations* 11; Paul du Gay et al. (1997) *Doing Cultural Studies: The Story of the Sony Walkman*. London: Sage; Rey Chow (1993) 'Listening Otherwise', in S During (ed.) *The Cultural Studies Reader*. London: Routledge.
73 Bull, ibid., pp. 283–5. Headphones can, of course, be used strategically, to deceive others. Thus 'headphoning' has recently been described as 'the act or art of seemingly being in the private, aural world of an iPod, Walkman . . . or cellphone . . . [thus] wearing headphones to deflect conversation', in (2005) 'What's the Word?', *The Observer Magazine*, 11 September.
74 George Simmel (1997) 'The Metropolis and Mental Life', in D. Frisby and M. Featherstone (eds) *Simmel on Culture*. London: Sage; Richard Sennett (1996) *The Uses of Disorder*. London: Faber.
75 Bull, ibid., pp. 278, 286–7; Shin Dong Kim (2002) 'Korea: Personal Meanings', in J. Katz and M. Aakhus (eds) *Perpetual Contact: Mobile Communication, Private Talk, Public Performance*. Cambridge: Cambridge University Press, p. 65; quoted in Bull, ibid. See also the account given to me by a friend of how, on remonstrating with a fellow bus passenger for talking loudly on their mobile, another passenger criticised my friend, on the grounds that, as the bus was a public space, the mobile-phone user was surely at liberty to use it as he saw fit.
76 This point was made in an essay by a Goldsmiths MA student in 2005, Da Wei Guo, who I thank for his permission to quote him here.
77 Robert Luke (2003) 'The *Phoneur*', in P. Trifonas (ed.) *Pedagogies of Difference* London, Routledge; Bull, ibid., p. 286; Sadie Plant (2000) *On the Mobile* www.motorola. com/mot/documents.
78 Alexandra Weilenmann and Catrine Larsson (2002) 'Local Use and Sharing of Mobile Phones', in Barry Brown et al. (eds) *Wireless World*. London: Springer-Verlag.
79 Jason Benetto (2004) 'Police Hunt MCC Member over Knife Incident at Test Match', *The Independent*, 7 August.
80 Ken Worpole, private communication; Steven Kern (1983) *The Culture of Time and Space 1880–1918*. Cambridge, Mass.: Harvard University Press.
81 Mark Twain (1917) 'A Telephonic Conversation', in *The $30,000 Bequest and Other Stories*. New York: Harper's, pp. 204–8. First published 1880. For more

on early debates about 'telephone talk', see Tom Gunning (2004) 'Fritz Lang Calling: The Telephone and the Circuits of Modernity' and Jan Olsson (2004) 'Framing Silent Calls: Coming to Cinematic Terms with Telephony', both in John Fullerton and Jan Olson (eds) *Allegories of Communication*. Eastleigh: John Libbey Books.

82  See Kevin Harris (2003) 'Keep Your Distance: Remote Communications, Face-to-Face and the Nature of Community', *Journal of Community Work and Development*, 4.

83  See Luke, ibid.

84  E. Laurier (2001) 'Why People Say Where They Are during Mobile Phone Calls', *Environment and Planning: Society and Space*, 19: 485–504; J. Mey (2001) *Pragmatics: An Introduction*. Oxford: Blackwell. In Japan, a new etiquette has developed among some young mobile phone users in which, in recognition of these difficulties, it is now considered impolite to ring a friend without first sending a text message to ask whether they are in a situation where they can take your call.

85  John Tomlinson (2001), 'Instant Access: Some Cultural Implications of "Globalising" Technologies', University of Copenhagen: Global Media Cultures Working Paper No.13.

86  Tuan, Yi-Fu (1996) *Cosmos and Hearth*, Minneapolis, Minn.: University of Minnesota Press; Tomlinson, ibid.

87  Tomlinson, ibid., p. 17.

88  See Hay and Packer, ibid., pp. 229–230.

89  Sadie Plant (2002) 'How the Mobile Changed the World', *Sunday Times*, 5 May; Z. Bauman (2000) *Liquid Modernity*, Cambridge: Polity Press.

90  G. Cooper 'The mutable mobile' in Barry Brown, Richard Harper and Nicola Green (eds) (2001) *Wireless World*. London: Springer; J.P. Roos (2001) 'Postmodernity and Mobile Communications', paper to ESA conference, Helsinki, August.

91  Harold Rosen (1972) *Language and Class*. Bristol: Falling Wall Press.

92  See my earlier remarks on the 'gender of the real' in Chapter 1. For a more detailed discussion of this point see my *Home Territories*, pp. 111 onwards.

93  Fischer, quoted in Elizabeth Van Zoonen (2002) 'Gendering the Internet', *European Journal of Communications Studies*, 17 (1): 7.

94  R. Jakobson (1972) 'Linguistics and Poetics', in R. de George and F. de George (eds) *The Structuralists*. New York: Anchor; A. Moyal (1995) 'The Gendered Use of the Telephone', in S. Jackson and S. Moores (eds) *The Politics of Domestic Consumption*. Hemel Hempstead: Harvester Press.

95  Gareth Jones (2003) 'Setting the Tone', MA Radio Dissertation, Goldsmiths College, University of London.

96  See Simon Broughton (2004) 'Editorial', *Songlines*, 27 (October/November); Oliver Burkeman (2003) 'Fellowship of the Rings', *The Guardian* (G2), 13 August; Dan Milmo (2004) '*La donna e mobile*? Key in classic ringtone', *The Guardian*, 23 November; Oliver Burkeman (2003) 'The Tune that Changed the World', *The Guardian*, 13 August; Gerard Seenan (2005) 'Crazy Frog Outsells Coldplay', *The Guardian*, 25 May.

97 Theodor Adorno and Max Horkheimer (1977) 'The Culture Industry', in J. Curran et al. (eds) *Mass Communications and Society*. London: Arnold.

98 There are, of course, at least two substantial methodological problems with this example. In the first case, it is not at all clear that asking people to explicitly articulate their reasons for choosing a particular piece of music as their ringtone is an adequate way of addressing matters of taste and choice, where decisions are often made at a sub-conscious level. The banality of what respondents can say to an interviewer about their choices cannot be taken as any simple index of their supposed lack of sophistication or self-reflexivity in this (or any other) respect. Moreover, in this example, we also confront one of the intractable problems with ethnography. One should not mistake the vividness of this single example of an innovative use of the technology as indicating anything about its generalisability: it could equally well be seen simply as the exception that proves the rule.

99 Martin Heidegger (1971) 'The Thing', in *Poetry, Language, Thought*. New York: Harper & Row; Spigel 2001a, ibid.

# 8    Rhetorics of the technological sublime
## The paradoxes of technical rationality

The terminology in my title derives from Leo Marx, who introduces the phrase 'The rhetoric of the technological sublime' in his book *The Machine in the Garden* written in 1964.[1] This is not simply a discourse about technology per se, but more specifically, in origin, at least, also a discourse about America as the society which, by virtue of its newly powerful technologies, has long been seen as the harbinger of the future of the whole human race – and, thus, as representing the destiny of the world.[2] As we have seen earlier, conceptions of technology and visions of the future are often intertwined, just as our assumptions about the techno-future are often inscribed in particular geographical locations – usually in the West, as the presumed source and site of progress.

Such discourses have, of course, been used in relation to a whole series of technologies besides the digital ones with which we are today so much obsessed. At a previous moment in North American history it was steam-driven technologies which were invested with the metaphysical properties of being able to 'subdue prejudice and . . . unite every part of . . . [America] in rapid and friendly communication'. Later, of course, when disappointment with these particular technologies set in, the coming of the Golden Age was postponed, and the key role in the constitution of Utopia was reascribed to the new technology of electricity, which was, in turn, then seen to have 'the power to redeem all the dreams betrayed by the machine'.[3] The semi-religious dimension of these discourses is still apparent today, as noted by Jeffrey Alexander, in his commentary on how

> The advertising of computer companies resurrects the oldest image of the literate man and weds him to the new computational devices: the priesthood of all believers, everyman a priest with his own Bible, becomes, in the new rendition, the priesthood of all computers, everyman a prophet, with his own machine to keep him in control.

All of which perhaps also takes us back to Marshall McLuhan's character-isation of electricity as a divine force and, in particular, of the computer as a force which 'promises, by technology, a Pentecostal condition of universal understanding and unity'.[4]

Today, we find ourselves surrounded by new rhetorics of how these new technologies will transform our lives. Central here are discourses of the post-industrial/'information' society, in which the new ICTs are seen to be (variously) isolating the family, internally fragmenting the home and transforming patterns of both work and consumption as well as the relations between the public and the private. Here, we might also recall the discourses espoused not so long ago both by 'digitrepreneurs' such as Bill Gates and Nicholas Negroponte and by politicians such as Al Gore and Tony Blair announcing the imminent arrival of the benefits of the information super-highways of the new virtual world of cyberspace. To take but one example, Gore thus spoke, in positively McLuhanesque terms, of how the new 'Global Information Infrastructure' (GII) would 'spread . . . a new Athenian age of [participatory] democracy'.[5]

## Historicising the future

The problem here, as noted earlier, is that the more we speak of the future, the more we have need of historical perspective. We have, of course, (always) been here before, given long history of visions of how 'new' technologies were going to transform the world. As early as 1893, *Answers* magazine enthused about how the electrical home of the future would be 'fitted throughout with . . . electric stoves in every room [which] can be lighted by pressing a button at the bed-side . . . [its] doors and windows fitted with electronic fastenings'.[6] In the context of contemporary excitements about cyber-shopping, one can readily see the transformative potential in a situation where:

> the inhabitant of London could now order . . . sipping his morning tea in bed, the various products of the whole earth and reasonably expect their delivery upon his doorstep; he could, at the same moment, and by the same means, adventure his wealth in the natural resources and new enterprises of any quarter of the world, and share, without exertion or even trouble, in their prospective fruits and advantages.

However, this is in fact John Maynard Keynes writing in 1900, describing the potential significance of the introduction of the landline telephone as a tool for home shopping and virtual commerce.[7]

As long ago as 1909, the Futurist Marinetti was convinced that 'we stand on the last promontory of the centuries! Time and space died yesterday. We already live in the absolute, because we have created eternal, omnipresent speed'. Ten years later, in 1919, Le Corbusier announced that 'the problem of our epoch is the problem of the electronically mediated home', and by 1928 Paul Valéry was speculating on the possibilities of 'a company engaged in the home delivery of sensory reality'.[8] In 1959, the designers of the 'Miracle Kitchen' which went on show at the American National Exhibition in Moscow promised that 'household chores in the future will be gone for the American housewife at the touch of a button or the wave of a hand'.[9]

There is also a long history of visions of how it has been imagined that technical advances in communications – from the telegraph to the telephone to the Internet – will somehow lead to 'better understanding'. The telegraph – or the 'Victorian Internet', as it has been redescribed by Tom Standage – was heralded as ushering in an era of world peace, for this very reason. In fact, the hysteria, or 'telegraph fever', that surrounded the laying of the first transatlantic cable in 1858 surpassed even that surrounding the coming of the Internet today: it was the occasion for 100-gun salutes, celebratory flags were flown from public buildings, bells were rung, and there were fireworks, parades and church services. The whole event took on a religious aura and there were claims that the fact that, as the new invention now allowed people to 'see and hear everyone else in the world', it would somehow lead to a uniting of the human race. Even the august *Scientific American* referred glowingly to the new invention as an 'instantaneous highway of thought between the Old and New Worlds', and there were bold claims that it was now 'impossible that old prejudices and hostilities should . . . exist, while such an instrument has been created for the exchange of thought between all the nations of the earth'.[10]

Armand Mattelart, among others, has already critiqued this ideological vision, which mistakes technical improvements in modes of communication for the growth of understanding in human affairs.[11] In fact, the effect of improved communications can just as easily be to sharpen as to reduce conflict. Moreover, while the contemporary vision of virtual space is usually presented as one of openness and exploration, one can also readily see that virtual space often, in practice, actually functions as a space of withdrawal into closed communities of the 'like-minded' – of those who subscribe to the same e-mail list or bulletin board or chat room. We might also think of the personalised computer news services, about which there has been so much excitement in some quarters, as providing the same 'cocooning' effect. More broadly, it has recently been argued that, in the face of the barrage of spam and computer viruses that trouble so many of its users, the Internet itself is now showing signs of 'Balkanisation' as defensive communities of trust are formed. In this 'new net', traffic is only accepted from known and accredited senders – with the prospect, according to one commentator, that eventually 'there may be two nets – a clean one, where security is part of the infrastructure and a "dirty internet" for all those with old, insecure technologies'.[12]

Just as Freud argued that it is only by paying due attention to the unconscious that we can ever hope to rescue ourselves from its overweening determinations, so Jeffrey Alexander argues that 'only by understanding the omnipresent shaping of technological consciousness by discourse can we hope to gain control over technology in its material form. To do so, we must gain some distance from the visions of salvation and apocalypse in which technology is so deeply embedded'.[13] If improvements in the speed and reach of technologies of communication have often been mistaken for the advent of an Eldorado of greater understanding in human affairs, as Benjamin famously noted, 'it is only by remembrance that we can strip the future of its magic, to which all those succumb, who turn to soothsayers for enlightenment'.[14]

## Technological divisions

It is also worth considering what all these utopian visions actually mean in practice. Not so long ago, while I was at home reading Thomas Friedman's latest account of the inexorable triumph of the wired world of globalisation, it took three whole days of engineers coming and going, huffing and puffing in their frustration, before they got the dedicated computer phone line in my house to work more than intermittently.[15] Perhaps that was just a particular experience of British inefficiency, but the journalist Mary Dejevsky has also written of the hair-tearing frustrations she experienced in trying to achieve the seemingly straightforward objective of transferring an e-mail account across national borders. Her basic point is to show *un*globalised the world remains in the actual practice of everyday living and the extent to which the old-fashioned national boundaries which constitute the limits of a variety of commercial operations negate the putative globality of the electronic marketplace.[16]

As Dejevsky points out, no credit-card issuer likes its customers to live in one country and be billed in another; and if you move countries, not only will you find it difficult to get a credit card at all (because you won't have a 'credit history' in the right country), but you will find it difficult to use the Internet to buy something in one country using a credit card issued by a bank in another. The same goes for booking air travel on-line – you may be able to see a wide array of cheap fares on offer on the Internet, but you can't necessarily book them, unless you happen to have the right credit card registered in the right country. Some airlines insist that you can only book with a credit card from the country where you are starting your trip. Some US sites won't let you book tickets from a non-US billed address; some only recognise US zip codes and not other geographical signifiers such as UK postcodes. The fundamental point is that, for all their potential wonders, these technologies are only as good as the material, social and institutional structures in which they are embedded, from the reliability of the local phone lines or electricity supply to the flexibility of the financial system or the efficiency of the relevant bureaucracy.[17]

The new technologies of our age do not only help to transcend boundaries in any simple sense, but also continually recreate them. This quickly becomes apparent to anyone who, for example, buys a DVD player and then attempts to play on it a DVD from the 'wrong' region. The problem here is that DVDs are divided by their manufacturers into 'areas', each with different technical standards, so as to ensure maximum profits and control over the release dates of films in the various regional markets. Incompatible technical standards and boundary-controlling devices are deliberately built in to many technologies, which is also why a standard European mobile phone will not work in the USA, unless it has been adapted to the USA's tri-band system. Far from areas or regions being a thing of the past, they are now continually reinvented and reinscribed in technical forms. Boddy makes the same point notes in relation to 'broadcasting's bifurcated history of a tradition of technophiliac and utopian internationalism, founded upon the technical indifference of broadcast signals to national boundaries' and its actual existence, as it has come to be shaped 'by regulatory and legal regimes resolutely national in design'.[18]

As for the happy vision of a world of readily integrated technologies, the reason why it is so difficult to hook up a television, a video-cassette recorder (VCR) and a DVD player in that order, is because a copy protection inside the VCR, called Macrovision and designed to deter people from taping DVDs, deliberately degrades the signal from the DVD player. In a similar vein, it now seems that the current prospects of 'ultra-wideband' (UWB) wireless technology are bedevilled by an ongoing stuggle over which format to adopt, comparable to the earlier struggle between the VHS and Betamax video formats. Thus the 'great untangler' – the wireless technology that was supposed to do away with the rats' nest of cables that currently clutter up so many of our homes, is itself now tangled up in an unresolved standards war.[19]

Furthermore, in actuality, far from being 'inclusive', these new technologies often principally work to intensify patterns of communication between those already in contact and to further reinforce the exclusion of the already marginalised. Thus, Robert Putnam's vision of the 'wired world' displacing the world of actual social life and undermining the fundamental processes of community, in his much-discussed *Bowling Alone*, is quite undermined by Barry Wellman et al.'s study of a wired suburban community in Boston, which shows that, in actual fact, those who participate most in the world of virtual communications are often also those who are most socially active in the physical neighbourhood.[20] To make the point more experientially, when, as part of my research for this book, I attended a computer class in my local public library, designed to enhance the skills (and thus the employability) of the socially excluded, my fellow students were all, in fact, middle-class people like me, looking to upgrade their existing skills – the excluded, for whom the event was intended, were nowhere in sight.

Moreover, these difficulties cannot readily be dismissed as mere 'hangovers' from a previous era, which will naturally disappear as the process of globalisation progresses. On the contrary, it was only in 2005 that automatic pumps at petrol stations in France began to display signs saying that payment could be made with 'French Credit Cards Only'. It was also only in that year that credit-card companies in the UK, such as Barclaycard, began to warn their customers that they might find it 'more convenient' to get 'preauthorisation' for use of their credit cards abroad when travelling. Precisely as a response to the rise in the rate of credit fraud to which globalisation has given rise, many credit-card companies' computer systems now have a default setting in which use of your card in a country different from that of your residence is presumed to be fraudulent, unless such pre-authorisation for foreign use has been established for each trip. At that point, the seemingly dystopian vision of a future in which any form of travel requires specific authorisation, combining 'one-time use only' insurance and travel permits, as presented, for instance, in Michael Winterbottom's futuristic thriller film *Code 406* (UK 2003) begins to look eerily prescient.

## Born-again techno-determinism

In recent years, the advent of the 'new media' seems to have occasioned the rebirth of a strand of technological determinism in media and cultural studies which had been dormant, if not discredited, for a considerable time, at least since Raymond Williams's powerful (and indeed, long canonical) critique of such approaches, in his *Television: Technology and Cultural Form*. It is as if, once again, the 'newness' of a particular set of technologies has served to convince many commentators that all previous forms of knowledge are now, *ipso facto*, bankrupt and that we must begin our theoretical work all over again, from scratch, paying attention only to the wonders of these technologies themselves.[21] Among other symptoms of this problem, one might point to the advent of currently widespread forms of 'digitalisation fever' and to the 'resanctification' of Marshall McLuhan as the patron saint of the digital era and the resurgence – not only in popular magazines such as the influential *Wired*, but also in academic work of 'medium theory'. This is a discourse which claims that McLuhan was simply 'ahead of his time' and that his erstwhile critics, such as Williams and Miller, were simply misguided because digital technology has (if belatedly) 'proved him right'.[22]

Despite the claims made by these writers about the historically unprecedented specificity of the technologies with which we must deal today – and thus the need for 'new approaches' – in my own view, we might still do better to bear in mind Raymond Williams's more historically nuanced approach to the relationship between technologies and the cultural forms in which they are institutionalised in any given period. To recap, Williams's argument, in which he distinguished carefully between technique, technical invention and the social processes through which inventions become available and institutionalised as technologies, is that such development follows no natural or preordained course in which the 'intrinsic' capacity of a technology is revealed according to some inner logic, but is always the contingent result of social struggles over the application of technologies, between differentially powerful interests. As Des Freedman notes in his commentary on these issues, whether we take the example of cable television or of the Internet, in both cases we see a process in which a technology that could have developed in a variety of ways has been fundamentally shaped by the distribution of economic and political power. Thus, the Internet has been transformed, over a relatively short space of time, by means of 'decisive interventions by corporations and governments following neo-liberal ideas about the supposed benefits of consumerism and competition' from being a mainly 'non-commercial instrument of information exchange into a highly commercialised tool of mainly private and business transactions' – a process in which technological developments themselves have played only a minor role.[23] Williams himself always stressed that the development of any new technology is a 'moment of choice' and that technological history is not to be understood as a relay race in which the baton of 'progess' is passed between successive innovations. As William Boddy notes, our goal here must still be to 'replace the traditional historiographic trope of "autonomous technology" with an attempt to specify the historical and cultural determinations of technological change'.[24]

Nonetheless, I would agree that the recent attempt made by Martin Lister and his colleagues to readdress Williams's critique of McLuhan and to pose the question of whether Wiliams did, in fact, entirely succeed in demolishing McLuhan's arguments is an important one. The issues they raise about the adequacy – or otherwise – of Williams's humanism for dealing with a world, which, as Latour argues, also contains important non-human *actants*, are certainly of some considerable consequence.[25] They also raise a very important issue when they ask whether there can properly be any satisfactory 'general' argument about technological determinism or whether different technologies may, rather, need to be understood as exercising different modalities of determination.

I am happy to concede that the argument that Lister et al. derive from Ellul concerning the idea that 'while societies have not always been technologically determined they (may) become so at specific historical conjunctures' recasts the question we need to pose in a potentially useful way. Following Ellul, Lister et al. thus argue that 'technological determinism is not a historical constant, but . . . arises at a certain stage of . . . development, where technology saturates the environment'. However, the first problem here is that all ages think that their technological problems are 'exceptional' – as readily demonstrated by Wolfgang Schivelbusch's account of the extraordinary panic caused by the experience of the (then) unprecedented speed of railway travel in the nineteenth century. The second problem is that Ellul was writing in the 1950s and so the 'exceptional' age of 'technological saturation' of which he speaks, as the point at which new and more powerful forms of technological determinism come into play, predates the current bout of digitalisation fever by half a century. To this extent, Ellul is in fact a poor support for Lister et al.'s arguments, and they seem to mistake the peculiarities of our own age for the true 'New Age' or even the 'End of History'.[26]

Nor does it follow from any of this that there is any reason to simply return, as Lister and many other contemporary 'medium theorists' now do, to a revamped version of Norbert Wiener's 'cybernetic' model of communications, in which it is argued that 'the governing technology of an age will shape the society that uses it accordingly'. To return to this kind of technical model of communications would minimally require some form of address to the serious critiques of Wiener et al. offered thirty years ago now by writers such as Stuart Hall, concerning the oversimplifications of cybernetics in abstracting technical processes of communication from their embedding in wider cultural processes. Moreover, the concept of the specificity of the forms of non-linear causality, which are supposedly the particular characteristic of the new media, which is invoked by Lister et al. as a trump card in their argument, avails little if one still argues, as they do (following McLuhan again) that in the end 'it is the physical properties of a given technology that cause it to be used in certain ways'.[27]

There are plenty of curiosities and complexities here. Thus we find Gilles Deleuze arguing at one point, in seeming parallel with Williams's concerns with the cultural and institutional shaping of technology, that 'the machine is always social before it is technical. There is always a social machine which selects or assigns the technical elements used'. Nonetheless, when we then turn to Deleuze's much-quoted work on the cinema, he falls back on the long-discredited model of hypodermic media 'effects' and a corresponding model of a passive audience who are simply there, ready and available to be helplessly manipulated by the media machine.[28]

Technologies certainly do have a whole variety of consequences, both positive and negative – not least in creating previously unthinkable communicative 'opportunities' for good and ill. The problem is how to produce a viable model of how such technological effects can be understood to occur, in all their complexity. An approach that insists that it is simply the physical or technical properties of a medium which are ultimately determinant is unlikely to help us. To follow that path is simply to fall into what Hall memorably described as a 'low-flying form of behaviourism'. The central issue here is that of the cultural contextualisation of technologies. As Hall argued in relation to the supposed direct effects of media messages, before messages – or, in this case, technologies – can have an 'effect' they must first interpellate people as relevant to them, in their particular circumstances; then they must be interpreted, so as to have meaning – and therefore desirability – for their potential consumers; only then can they be used, and thus be in a position to have an effect of any kind.[29]

## Digitalisation and the 'newness' of new media: beyond the binaries . . .

As Carolyn Marvin has noted, 'new media' is always and by definition a 'historically relative term', so the idea that we currently stand at a particularly definitive and absolute moment of 'newness' is evidently one that we should treat with some care.[30] One issue here concerns the widespread tendency to the overestimation of the 'newness' of the digital era, which, after all, is probably best understood as having begun with the telegraph itself in the 1840s. The further problem lies both in the characterisation of these as 'interactive' technologies and in the precise nature of the contrast that is implicitly drawn between them and the older media, such as television broadcasting. Talking recently to a young 'interactive media' professional, she referred unblinkingly, to that 'old' world and, thus, implicitly to the audiences who inhabit it, as that of the 'slouchback' media. This was clearly an updated formulation of the conventional image of the television audience as a mass of 'couch potatoes'. In this phrase, the virtue (and the importance) of the 'new' media are characterised precisely by the idea that its participants are assumed to be sitting forward, actively doing things, *not* 'slouching' back. The problems here are various: in the first place, we know that television audiences were never simply passive. In the second place, the forms of activity that most viewers of the interactive media are engaged in are often relatively trivial, such as clicking a remote control or a mouse to select one item (a camera angle, for example) from a predetermined menu of choices. Nonetheless, it remains the case that these new technologies have been widely credited with producing a range of transformative effects on the way we live, and these are claims that we must now examine.

Again, Spigel's work is exemplary in opening up the issues at stake here. As she notes, if we consider the section on 'adult participation in selected leisure activities' in the 'Statistical Abstract' complied by the US Census Bureau, we discover that while surfing the Internet and playing electronic games are deemed to constitute 'activities', neither watching television nor films (even at the cinema) are counted as such, although watching a play at the theatre or listening to a musical performance do, for some reason, count as 'active leisure pursuits'. The definition of a particular leisure pursuit as active or passive is a critical mode of implicit evaluation of its status, and the association of new technologies with 'interactivity' seems to provide a way in which the approved values of active participation in forms of 'high culture' somehow rub off on anyone using a computer mouse rather than a television remote control.[31]

In a similar vein, in her study of television and new-media audiences, Ellen Seiter remarks on the ubiquity in contemporary techno-discourse of the Manichean division between the Bad screen of television and the Good screen of the computer.[32] Following Andreas Huyssen's arguments about mass culture being coded as feminine, William Boddy helpfully places all this in a longer historical perspective. He notes that in the case of radio, its early (masculine) users were lauded precisely for engaging not in 'passive enjoyment' but in much 'ingenious manipulation' of the medium. He then goes on to show how each new media technology in turn, from radio onwards, has begun its life by being understood as being the exciting preserve of adventurous masculine innovators and ended up, through the process of domestication, in which the technology is made consumer-friendly, being understood as part of the low status – and implicitly feminised – realm of popular culture.[33] As he notes,

> in this regard 100 years of historical experience of electronic communications in the home repeatedly rehearse a series of gendered and normative oppositions between the active and passive audience, from the male wireless amateur versus the distracted housewife in the 1920s, to the degraded 'couch potato' versus the heroic internet surfer of the 1990s.

Television viewing in the post-war period has persistently been figured as a pacifying, emasculating and feminising activity – whereas now, in the moment of what has been described as 'TV's Second Chance', when the world of virtual reality comes to television's 'rescue', we see the rhetorical attempt to 'remasculinise' the television apparatus by associating its technologies of interactivity with fantasies of power and control, so as to 'transform the scorned and degraded domestic TV set into a Good cultural object'.[34]

One curious thing here is that, if we look at the ethnographic evidence, we find that the experiences of watching television and using the Internet are not, in fact, necessarily felt to be so very different. Thus, internet ethnographer Lori Kendall reports that

> when 'MUDDING' for long periods of time, I frequently leave the computer to get food, go to the bathroom or respond to someone in the physical room in which I'm sitting. If the text on my screen slows to a crawl, or if the conversation ceases to interest me, I may cast about for something else off-line to engage me, picking up the day's mail or flipping through a magazine.[35]

As Sean Moores notes in his commentary, this perspective 'places net-use in the context of ordinary, day to day life' and the description of the mundanity of computer use 'could easily be an account of routine, distracted TV-viewing in the home'. It would thus seem that the distinctions between the participants' experiences of analogue and digital media should not be so sharply drawn as they are by the neophiliac discourses that dominate so much current debate.

One difficulty here concerns the increasingly taken-for-granted notion that authors such as Deleuze and Guattari and the other theorists of 'mediology' have produced a theoretical language with some natural 'fit' with the technical apparatus of the digital media – where the unexamined premise is these media's complete difference from all that has gone before. In relation to the invidious tendency to pose overly dramatised binary splits in our theoretical models, Boddy again offers a helpful historical perspective. As he says, quite apart from anything else, 'there is little doubt that the public's first experience of wireless communication 100 years ago represented a period of far more traumatic uncertainty and improvisation' than does our own transition from analogue to digital media.[36]

## The magic of convergence

In this connection, it is also perhaps worth querying the empirical status of a further supposed technical breakthrough of our times – the advent of digital media convergence. While this technical event has been talked up heavily, in practice, it has not, at least as yet, happened on anything like the scale proclaimed. These kinds of 'techno-dreams' in which the world is presumed to follow the logic inscribed in technology are always with us. Not so long ago, there was much excitement about the potential consequences in the sphere of audio-visual production and marketing of the supposed synergetic convergence of North American software and Japanese hardware. This technicist logic was the driving force behind Sony and Matsushita's respective 'buy-outs' of Columbia and MCA. In the event, the cultural clashes between American and Japanese management styles proved far more significant than any technical synergy. In a similar manner, even within the US itself, AOL and Time Warner's much-hyped merger of 'old' and 'new' media companies has been fraught with difficulties which have vitiated many of the potential technical advantages of their new arrangements.

The further issue concerns not only the extent to which these processes are in fact primarily determined by technology, but also the question of how the process of digital convergence is itself being driven. In actuality, the 'driver' here, rather than consumer demand, is often a combination of industry-led 'supply-side' desires to maximise the potential profit of technical developments in combination with misguided governmental and political initiatives of 'modernisation'. If the effects of technologies depend on the regulatory frameworks that discourage or permit particular technical combinations, the issue then is to what extent the emerging forms of digitalised media convergence are less an effect of technological development per se and more a by-product of the political deregulation that has produced the relaxation of rules on cross-media ownership.[37]

Certainly, in the sphere of consumption, we know that, often, digital convergence just doesn't work like it says in the adverts. Most users of digital cable television actually use only about ten channels at maximum, just as many web-site users go repeatedly to the same few web sites, installed on their 'favourites' list on their computer. It seems that beyond a certain level, the fetishisation of 'choice maximisation' is counter-productive, as many consumers find too much choice disabling rather than enabling.[38] Despite the dreams of the digital marketeers, there is very little evidence of people taking up the opportunities offered by convergence for more complex forms of media usage. At least in the UK, most people still show little sign of wanting to watch television on the computer, or vice versa, and few yet use the television for ordering their shopping or checking their bank accounts.[39]

Thus, my local paper has reported research by the district's trading-standards authority, showing that many people are simply bemused by digital interactive services. They find the sites difficult to navigate; they are baffled by the language codes and technical assumptions of tele-ordering lines; when they can penetrate them, they find them to be not only slow, cumbersome and inefficient, but to offer only a very limited range of the goods they actually wanted; and when they encounter problems with using these facilities, the 'customer services' designed to support them are often either unobtainable or unhelpful. Clearly, in this context, as the report says, 'it would be foolish to assume that the evolution of this new complicated medium is going to be anything but slow'. The point here is that consumers rapidly discover that digital technologies are by no means 'plug in and play' objects, but often require hours of complex technical labour to set them up, which not everyone (especially among older generations) is capable of, and it is, in part, for mundane reasons of this sort that the household penetration of the Internet in the UK has stalled in recent years.[40]

It is considerations of this kind that can perhaps best explain developments such as the commercial failure of ITV's 'OnDigital' initiative in the UK, which based its marketing strategy on the supposed appeal of its 'interactive' capacities. Sadly for the company concerned, it turned out that no one much wanted them, and it went into receivership in 2001 following huge financial losses. The subsequent relative success of the Freeview digibox system is, by contrast, instructive. Freeview also uses a digital signal, but markets itself simply as a cheap way of getting 'more TV', rather than as a provider of interactive services.[41]

## The paradoxes of technical rationality

By 1988 Christine Hardyment was observing that 'today washing machines are automated far beyond most households' requirements. Few families can take advantage of the dozen or more programmes that their machines offer'.[42] Nowadays many of the manufacturers themselves are worried by increasing evidence that many people simply cannot understand – and are in fact often put off by – the increasing array of extra functions which are endlessly added to domestic technologies, for their supposed convenience.

This may of course be, at least, in part a generational problem, in so far as older people find it hard to operate the new technologies with which they are now confronted. To put the point simplistically, many people may now have so many different remote controls in their sitting room that they can't, at times, actually work the television – because they have lost track of which particular remote controls which machine – even if their children do know which is which.[43] However, generational status is in itself no guarantee of technical competence – while sales of iPods have been remarkable in the relatively short period since their introduction, there is mounting evidence in the UK that even many their young consumers, who could be assumed to be among the most techno-literate, often lack the necessary skills to use them successfully. Indeed when Carl Barat, former 'frontman' of the fashionable UK band The Libertines, was asked in a newspaper interview what music he was currently listening to, he replied 'My iPod is incomprehensible because I accidentally selected Japanese on the language option and I can't get it back . . . I must get it fixed'. Neither does everyone necessarily find it easy to operate the thirty functions crammed onto four tiny buttons on their digital camera, when what function you get depends on remembering which other buttons you have pressed previously.[44]

At the heart of all this we find a paradox – the irrationality of maximised forms of technical rationality. Commercial (and also governmental) policy is often driven by a supply-side technical logic of 'product optimisation', combined with profit maximisation, according to which, that which is technically possible and commercially profitable is therefore deemed to be (or at least, presented as) a socially and politically desirable form of 'modernisation' and progress.[45] This paradox can appear in many forms, one of which is the interactive voice-response automated telephone answering services (IVR) now installed in the switchboards of most organisations. Once these systems had been invented, they were sold as services which would cut costs and 'wasted time' in customer service departments, by 'pre-sorting' calls by type, to ensure that they would go straight to the appropriate destination.

Unfortunately, one of their main effects is to waste a great deal more time for the caller – who characteristically has to listen to an endless hierarchical menu of choices, none of which seem quite appropriate for their particular query, before finally getting to the option which, if they are lucky, lets them speak to a person to whom they can explain their problem and who probably understands, much better than they do, which of the company's categories their problem is likely to be deemed to belong to. These systems create so much consumer frustration and dissatisfaction that they are now increasingly recognised as major source of lost business and client alienation. Thus, this technically rational system in fact produces a very irrational – and indeed inefficient – result, because not only does it try to use computer technology to do the thing it is least good at (sorting variety) but the price of the problem it solves (cutting employee costs) often proves to be lower than the cost it produces in lost sales and/or client dissatisfaction. The same applies to attempts by airlines to encourage customers to book travel tickets online – supposedly for their convenience. The problem is that, when customers want a question answered or a transaction resolved, automated systems often fail them – especially with any complex issue, such as wanting to book a non-standard itinerary or to cancel a ticket – all of which may well deter them from doing business with that company again.[46]

As anyone who has had cause to consult a technical adviser or 'help-line' can attest, the greatest difficulty for the user is that the adviser often finds it difficult to make the conceptual leap to see the problem from the point of view of someone less well technically versed than themselves – because they naturally tend to operate from within the terms of the particular system in play. The ensuing difficulty is that, without this leap outside the technical discourse being made, it is impossible for them to give comprehensible (and thus genuinely helpful) advice to their client. Often, in these situations, the strictly technical dimension of problem is prioritised, rather than it being realised that what is actually required is a better 'translation' between technical and everyday discourse.

The same point applies in the context of domestic consumption. In a world where much furniture is bought in 'flat-pack' form for subsequent home assembly, the critical factor, beyond the cheapness of the goods, is the notoriously inadequate nature of the assembly instructions. In a classic attempt to invent a technical solution to by-pass this communicative difficulty (which would require the difficult task of writing clear instructions comprehensible to the non-expert) some furniture stores are now experimenting with a system of microchips inserted in their furniture, which will chirp happily when the units are combined in the right way and beep a warning when parts are mis-assembled. The problem, here again is that the matter cannot be resolved either within the simple terms of a Taylorite system of efficient and rational task breakdown, nor can a more advanced technology necessarily itself solve what is, in fact, a complex problem of communication.

Similar paradoxes, whereby processes of seemingly impeccable technical rationality have led to disastrous results, can be found in many domains. If we shift our attention to the realms of architecture, we find that the result of decades of mass public housing in the UK, built using the latest forms of scientifically designed component-part construction processes, leave many people puzzled by the simple question posed by Katherine Shonfield: 'Why does your flat leak?'. The answer, according to Shonfield, is that traditional building methods were more successful in stopping leaks, because they used a variety of overlaps and overhangs to keep out water. However, post-war architects in the UK eschewed such 'messy' approaches, in favour of the seemingly more technologically advanced straight lines and clear, hard edges of the scientifically designed components of which most post war public housing was built. Unfortunately, in so doing, the architects only succeeded in creating many more exposed joins in the buildings, which therefore tend to leak more readily.[47]

Inside contemporary UK homes, we see irrationalities of another sort. Recent research suggests that Britain's homes are now a haven for a whole host of technical gadgets that lie unused, gathering dust in their cupboards. This mountain of fallow gadgetry, estimated at a value of £3.2 billion in 2004, is the result of consumers yielding to the temptations offered to them to purchase a growing array of 'labour-saving' devices invented by manufacturers selling the dream of a technically assisted perfection of domesticity.[48]

The key principle driving the development and implementation of many schemes of technological progress has thus been to subordinate the whole of social life – including now, increasingly, the domestic sphere – to the Taylorist principles of scientific management: efficiency and control. The consequent technological domination and colonisation of life (including the 'electronic home' – which, of course, also delivers enormous powers of continual surveillance, as the price of the consumer conveniences which it offers) derives, for a theorist such as Cornelius Castoriadis from 'a fantasy of total control, of our will or desire mastering all objects and all circumstances'. As Spigel argues, this Taylorist principle involves the drive to continually increase the 'efficiency' of home life – to the extent that the fully interactive smart home becomes a 24/7 work station in which we are encouraged to be continually 'active' . The principle of 'productivity' is enshrined in their very design. Thus domestic spaces like hallways – in which time might otherwise be 'wasted' – are now themselves to be filled with continually updated, information displays of all varieties.[49]

## Alternative approaches: the study of technology in context

In the light of the kind of criticisms of technologically deterministic approaches outlined above, recent years have seen a major shift in research in this field towards the ethnographic study of technology and its uses in particular contexts. The premise of this approach is that the context of consumption and use of technologies – and especially the domestic context, which has been the focus of a number of these studies – itself exercises important determinations on how technologies are perceived, taken up and used in different ways by people in different contexts.[50]

All of these approaches to the subjective geography of technology and to its place in our lives begin their analysis not by looking directly at a technology and its presumed effects, but by looking at the interactional system in play in a particular context and then looking at how particular technologies 'fit' or are fitted into it. In the case of studies of domestic consumption, this is to pose household structure and culture as a determinant of technological 'take-up' and use.[51] If design is to be understood as a strategy, in de Certeau's terms, whereby institutions and corporations attempt to impose a set of ideas about how we should live with manufactured objects, consumption is a set of tactics that operate within the field of the design system to effect a reappropriation of design by its users.[52] From this point of view, the question is what different technologies actually mean to people, how they are perceived, interpreted and used and how they are, differentially, seen (or ignored) by their potential consumers as relevant (or not) to them. Clearly, underlying these approaches is a particular theory of the nature of consumption as an active process of ingestion, incorporation and indigenisation of a variety of materials from the outside world. As Bourdieu and Miller have argued, this is a matter of how we distinguish ourselves from others and create our identities through a particular form of labour. This depends on the work through which commodities are transformed, in the process of consumption, into 'personalised' forms of ownership – making the object 'mine' – a process emblematically expressed in small ways, most obviously through things such as personalised keyrings and mobile phone fascias, etc. In this connection, Anna McCarthy has recently analysed the ways in which computer workers 'personalise' their machines in the workplace by decorating their monitors with trinkets, toys, photographic images and other ephemera.[53]

Within the field of media audience and reception studies, the work of the German ethnologist Hermann Bausinger on how the domestic relations of the familial home determine the process of television viewing has been particularly influential in these respects and has provided a model for studies of other technologies. However, in making this move into the detailed study of technology in context, we must also heed the methodological issues at stake and, in particular, the very real dangers of ethnography. Context may be a crucial research issue, but too much of it can be a dangerous thing if a project is not to collapse under the weight of its own unanalysed data. In following Bausinger's approach to these issues, we must also heed his own warning: that, by themselves, micro-studies – the study of the life of objects in use – do not mean anything at all and may be, in fact, 'complete rubbish'.[54] For him, everything depends on their integration with macro-perspectives and larger contexts even if, conversely, schematic macro-analyses, which are not grounded in the study of everyday life, are clearly no less 'rubbish', for the opposite reason. Thus, as Bausinger himself argues, we need to set ethnographic stories of domestic consumption in the wider context of the discourses of production, design, advertising and marketing and then see how people work with these technologies in and against these existing, powerful discourses which work to construct 'preferred readings' of their desirability and uses. In light of this, I now turn to recent work on these issues in the field of design studies.

## Design studies: strategies of de-familiarisation

Given the way in which we tend to naturalise our own mythologies while decrying those of others, the central issue here, as Paul Rabinow puts it, is to 'anthropologise the West: to show how exotic its constitution of reality has been; to emphasise those domains most taken for granted as universal and to make them seem as historically peculiar as possible'.[55] This is to invoke the idea of the positive role that can be played in understanding our social world by 'de-familiarisation', much in the spirit that it was invoked, at an earlier time, by literary theorists. Here we can usefully turn to recent work in design studies on ways of 'defamiliarising' the dominant forms and uses of contemporary technology. One example here is Kenji Kawakami's experimental work with what he calls 'unuseless' (*chindogu*) objects. These objects are designed to encourage us to think laterally about the presumptions and unquestioned premises which are built into established forms of design, architecture and urban planning and, thus, to consider other possible, but previously unthinkable scenarios.[56]

Kawakami's designs include a 'portable zebra crossing' and a 'portable stop light', both of which challenge the automobile's dominance of the city and are thus described as 'the pedestrian's best friends'. Other examples include a 'fresh-air mask' (a breathing tube attached to a plant in a sealed airbag) described as 'the natural remedy for bad city air'. For domestic use, Kawakami offers the 'telephone dumbbell' which, by making the act of lifting up the phone more arduous, ensures that even the act of making a phone call also provides valuable exercise, as does the 'velcro home jogger' which forces the person exercising to run up and down on an adhesive pad. Many of Kawakami's examples are similarly playful, such as the 'lawn-mowing sandals' with scythes attached to the heel for the lazy gardener, or those with artificial grass on the insoles, which allow their wearer the sensation of always walking on grass. Some address the busy commuter's fantasies, such as the umbrella which doubles as a golf club, allowing them to 'save time' by practising their golf swing while waiting for the bus. Others highlight, in playful mode, the very real problems of urban commuting, such as the 'commuter's helmet for secure subway snoozing', which not only secures the sleeping commuter's neck in an upright position, but also comes with a reusable whiteboard on the front on which he or she can write their destination and sleep more soundly, in the hope that fellow passengers will wake them when they reach it.

The informing principle of these imaginatively designed objects is perhaps most evident in the case of the 'portable lampost', which solves one problem (in this case, the absence of light in a particular place) only by creating another: the need to drag a lampost on wheels around with you. This tendency to solve one problem only at the expense of creating another, we thus come to realise, is a basic characteristic of all design practices. By this means, these *chindogu* objects are designed to reveal the hidden 'opportunity costs' of the particular, but now naturalised technological 'solutions' which we take for granted in our daily lives. To take obvious technologies, the invention of both the motor car and of antibiotics solved some important problems for many people, but they have both also now created new problems of their own. To take a more recent case, and one to which I will return in more detail later, if the kitchen freezer solved certain problems about long-term food storage, it also created its own demands in relation to the time and forethought required for the housewife to deal with the new processes of freezing, thawing and defrosting that it introduced into the domestic economy. A certain degree of suspicion is always appropriate when someone presents us with a new technological solution to an old problem, involving questions such as whose problem is it; who will benefit and who will lose from it and, of course, what new problems might this 'solution' create and for whom?[57]

In a manner that parallels Kawakami's imaginative strategies of product redesign, Anthony Dunne and Fiona Rabey's *Placebo Project* involved the construction of a series of electronically augmented furnishings, constructed to investigate people's attitudes, experiences and relationships to electronic consumer goods. As James Hunt explains in his commentary on their work, these objects were built to explore the 'murky, charged realm of failure, imagination, fear and hope' that lies between 'our appliances incontinent leakages' of radiation and electronic charges and our own 'paranoid, superstitious disposition towards machines'.[58] The 'furnishings' included a compass table on which twenty-five compasses spin when any electronic product is placed on it; a (GPS) table which constantly displays its position in the world on a light-emitting diode (LED) display, or flashes 'Lost' whenever it cannot make contact with a satellite; a 'phone table' which stores a mobile phone and glows when a call is received; an 'electro-draught excluder' which, as a true placebo, supplies only a false sense of protection from 'electronic interference'; and an 'electricity drain'. In their project, in which a variety of people were recruited to live for a time with these electronically animated domestic objects, Dunne and Rabey aimed to explore the 'pathology of material culture' by investigating how interaction with everyday electronic technologies can generate rich narratives of the now technologically saturated realm of the 'infra-ordinary', which lies between the user and the object.[59] Clearly, the radically unfamiliar nature of the objects was bound to provoke a certain short-circuiting of convention, but the degree of this was clearly surprising even to the volunteer participants in the project. Thus, one of the 'adopters' of the GPS table reported that:

> It's silly really, but because the lights flash . . . [as] . . . it moves between its 3 satellite positions and 'Lost', it gives a sense of being alive. There's no other word for it . . . You get the sense that you have to say 'Is it alright?'. It's silly to talk about treating it as a sort of person, but it is [as if you think] 'I'd better go and see if the table's there.[60]

Michael Anastassiades' *Social/Anti-Social Light* project functions in a similar way, to explore the complexities of our relationship to technologies – in his case by deliberately inverting their standard forms of the design of domestic lighting.[61] Although ordinarily a light evidently has the function of providing illumination on demand for the user, his 'anti-social light' performs this task only in the presence of silence. Speech causes it to dim and then switch off. Conversely, his 'social light' will only switch itself on in response to conversation. The former thus dictates an activity such as silent private reading, while the latter demands audible interaction, if it is to function at all. The unconventional relationship between people and things built into these designs intentionally complicates the normally servile role of products to dramatise the very idea of technological determinism. These projects deliberately create a world in which users cannot simply command that objects perform actions, but where the objects themselves to some extent determine both their own functions and what activities are permissible by their owners. In so doing, these designs also reveal, if in less dramatic ways, the part that technologies ordinarily play in constituting the domestic ecology of our lives.

Such projects can perhaps also be seen as a 'literalisation' (or materialisation) of some of the precepts of actor network theory's conceptualisation of objects themselves as non-human *actants*, but here the theoretical capacity of objects to have effects is dramatised in an exaggerated form. They are designed to demonstrate the various ways in which, as Dunne and Rabey put it, 'electronic objects [and] . . . appliances are not brute, dumb . . . machines [but, rather] they "leak" their dreams and thoughts into the places and objects around them'. By dramatising this process, these designers have constructed rhetorical machines for the production not only of technical effects, but also of understanding of our relationships to these technologies.[62]

## Designing inefficiencies and irrationalities

In this context, we might also usefully consider the work of the American designer/architects Elizabeth Diller and Ricardo Scofidio. Here we return to my earlier comments, drawing on Castoriadis, about the ways in which the technological colonisation of contemporary life often involves a fantasy of 'total control'. Diller and Scofidio militantly reject the conventional Taylorist injunction to 'eliminate inefficiency . . . in all our daily acts' and to thus 'achieve expediency by eliminating all repetition and redundancy'. Rather, they are interested in exploring deliberately 'inefficient technologies', or 'technologies which produce nothing' – except, most importantly, a strategically reframed and heightened sense of the everyday conventions we take for granted. Their interest is in exploring what they call 'designed irrationalities' in relation to the technological and architectural forms with which we are most deeply familiar.[63]

Thus, at a micro-scale, in relation to the domestic context, their 'ironing' piece *Bad Press* (from their *Dissident Housework* series, 1993–8) explores in origami style a number of alternative ways of 'mis-ironing' a man's shirt. It thus works to reveal the complex domestic conventions (sleeves first, etc.) of labour and folding which characterise the 'classic' style of ironing such a garment – and to expose that as only one possible style among many alternatives. Similarly, much in the manner of Vito Acconci's *Instant House* and *Bad Dream House* pieces, which deliberately create *unheimlich* spaces by slightly subverting the norms of architectural home design, Diller and Scofidio's upside-down *Withdrawing Room* makes us think harder about the exact contribution of domestic furniture to our sense of conviviality in the home.[64] The 'withdrawing room' uses the recognisable props of everyday life, but now subverted so as to no longer be usable for the purposes for which they were originally designed (beds sawn in half; tables hanging from the ceiling). The piece thus problematises the notion of architectural forms as always involving a normative rhetoric or 'programme of the proper' of 'how to live' in any built space – in this case involving notions of property, propriety and etiquette.[65]

Diller herself has described their interests as consisting, centrally, of 'interrogating the spatial conventions of the everyday', and their anti-heroic architectural work seeks to reveal the normally unquestioned presumptions built into architectural forms (if the pun can be forgiven). Their work is always autocritical, distrusting its own results even as it institutes them, so as to produce what Hays calls an 'inventory of suspicion', which captures the salient aspects of any supposed design 'solution' and slows down the processes of its working sufficiently to make its hidden premises visible. Thus they use technological innovation but at a scale and in a way that denies its seemingly inherent logic.[66] In their work, technology is used against itself. Thus, in the entrance to their *Blur Building* (constructed on Lake Neuchâtel in Switzerland in 2002), lips speak to us insistently, but in an unintelligible language, and the building itself was anyway largely invisible, in so far as its structure was designed to be perpetually shrouded in water vapour. Moreover, rather than follow Reyner Banham's classic injunction that the architect should always seek to create a 'well-tempered environment', in the *Blur Building*, they deliberately created an ill-tempered one, to the extent that, because of the surrounding water vapour, visitors to it had to wear raincoats, even on sunny days.[67]

Their unbuilt *Slow House* design for a vacation house on Long Island (1991) treats the conventional architecture of the house itself, featuring as it does in the West, large areas of transparent glass, especially in the form of 'picture windows', as a mechanism of visual arousal and then subverts the convention by feeding that arousal only very slowly. In this, they offer an implicit critique of the valorisation of speed which is one of the central tenets of all forms of techno-modernism. In their later reworking of this project, *The Desiring Eye: Reviewing the Slow House* (1992) they also insist on treating the picture window as being as much of a cultural construct as the television screen, and they insist on situating them both as parts of a superordinate conceptual series of 'optical devices of escape' which would also include the automobile windscreen. In this connection, they observe that, in so far as 'advanced technology constantly strives to dematerialise its hardware, leaving only its effects' the picture window is, in fact, a more advanced technology than the television set.

Underlying the project is a deeply serious critique of the modernist architectural ideal of 'transparency', in which, as Scofidio puts it, glass (as opposed to traditional masonry) was seen as a 'material of truth . . . an instrument of disclosure [which] like emerging electronic technologies today . . . promised to democratise space and information, in a world guaranteed to become transparent'. One difficulty, here, as he goes on to point out, in an implicitly Foucauldian manner, is that glass not only permits those inside to look out, but at the same time exposes those inside to the external view, so that it is also a mechanism of surveillance. These issues are well dramatised in their pieces *Jumpcuts*, *Overexposed* and *Facsimile*, where video cameras seem to project the (partly 'fictionalised') internal activities of buildings onto their windows for public display.[68]

Diller and Scofidio's work seeks to encourage viewers to question all culturally sanctioned understandings of both vision and transparency. Thus, in relation to the media, their *Soft Sell* piece also parodies one of the central acts of our culture – watching the adverts on commercial television – as a pair of lips asks seductively 'Hey you, wanna buy a ticket to paradise? . . . Hey you, wanna buy a lot in Midtown? . . . Hey you, wanna buy your name in lights? Hey you, wanna buy a left kidney?'. Most importantly, they offer a trenchant critique of modernism's rhetoric of efficiency and productivity: the dream of the technological sublime and the steadfast faith in a 'utopia made possible via electricity and machine innovation' that will engender a better and socially enlightened future through the efficiencies it provides.[69]

## In the kitchen: the social and symbolic life of technologies in the home

A great deal of recent debate in this field has, not surprisingly, focused on the cutting edge of digitalisation and computer technologies. However, here

I want to take a slightly different emphasis and look at two older domestic technologies, the washing machine and the fridge, which have thus far escaped much analysis, except in the realms of design studies and (unsurprisingly, given the cultural gendering of these particular technologies) feminist discourse. Clearly, one key issue here concerns the gendered symbolism of these 'white goods' in the home. I will come later to the ways in which the kitchen is now being reconceptualised in high-tech form in the context of debates about the 'smart house'. My starting point is the question of why these technologies, which are now standard equipment in all homes in affluent societies, have come to be particularly 'invisible', both in everyday life and in theoretical debate.

Earlier, I commented on the general nature of the process through which technologies come to be naturalised and on the in-built drive towards invisibility in vernacular design. However, in the case of these particular technologies, it is also necessary to go back to the questions raised by second-wave feminists in the 1970s about the specific invisibility of housework and domestic labour.[70] However high-tech the design of the modern kitchen may now be, these fundamental questions about the discursive and cultural construction of the relative (in)visibility of different forms of labour and of the technologies associated with them remain central. As a recent ethnography of technologies in the home by Mark Blythe and Andrew Monk has demonstrated, 'the notion of housework as invisible is now reflected in the actual look of the kitchen'. As the authors note, 'the most striking characteristic of . . . [many consumers'] aesthetic choices . . . [is] the extent to which they disguise task-based appliances'. Thus, today's fitted kitchens conceal most of their domestic appliances behind pine doors. The fridge, the cooker and the dishwasher are all often disguised as cupboards, so that the whole domestic labour process is concealed. One simple and perfectly understandable reason for the appeal of this design strategy is that, as one of Bryce and Monk's housewife respondents explained to them, she 'didn't want to be reminded that something need doing'.[71] In a similar vein, Christine Hardyment notes that the very presence of the washing machine often functions for the housewife as a continual, if subliminal, demand to process the next tranche of laundry.[72] However, as we shall see, there is rather more to these machines than their practical uses.

## The washing machine: a queen among white goods?

Despite its ubiquity, the washing machine has been relatively 'invisible' in social analysis and discussions of technology, barring the honourable exception of Hardyment's now canonical discussion of the complex history of its development and patterns of usage. It is also relatively invisible in social life. Thus, in the Brunel University research on ICT use referred to earlier, such machines were often omitted from the 'visual maps' that respondents were asked to draw of the technologies in their house, although, of course, the washing machine was rather more 'invisible' to men than to women, for whom it was a crucial technology, which they often used on a daily basis. These questions about the relative invisibility of different technologies to different people and of the gendering of relations to them are ones that I will explore in more detail below.

The central role of the acquisition of a washing machine in the very constitution of an adult household is the subject of a fine ethnographic study by Jean-Claude Kaufmann.[73] Kaufmann demonstrates that the acquisition of a jointly owned washing machine is often a key symbolic moment in the constitution of coupledom – perhaps even to the extent that we might consider the washing machine as at least as important a signifier of the institutionalisation of a domestic partnership as the wedding ring. As he graphically puts it, for an unmarried couple, 'any discussion about the possible purchase of a washing machine is inevitably a discussion about the [future of the] couple itself'. For this reason, couples may well 'take their decision to buy one as seriously as their wedding vows' as its purchase represents a key part of 'the material proof of the existence of the new couple'.[74]

Beyond this aspect of its potential symbolism in relation the constitution of the household, it is also imperative to consider the symbolism of the washing machine in relation to discourses of hygiene, science and magic. As Kristin Ross has argued, discourses of domestic hygiene, for which the housewife, now as 'domestic scientist' was to be responsible, were central to the development of post-war forms of modernity.[75] Evidently, there are also a whole set of dimensions of symbolism in play in the realms of the 'science' of washing, not least the association of washing powders with magical properties 'guaranteed' by those wearing, in the adverts, what we, in our culture, understand to be the appropriate symbolic costumes for this particular form of *juju*: men in white coats with sets of pens in their breast pockets.

For Barthes, the desire, characteristic of the aspirations of modernity, to possess only objects which are always clean, new and shiny is rather more than a functional or rational question of hygiene. For him, the obsession with cleanliness is also the desire to 'remake the virginity of the object over and over again, to give it the immobility of a material on which time has no effect . . . a practice of immobilising time'. In her commentary on these remarks, Ross rightly indicates that to remake something 'virgin' in this context is less a moral activity than one which involves 'making something absolutely [and eternally] new: the object outside history, untouched by time' and thus to 'retreat inside a controlled, rationally created environment superior to one engendered historically'. Such are the magical dreams of modernity.[76]

## The gendering of technologies

In simple marketing terms, washing machines clearly belong to the realm of 'white goods'. However, at the risk of posing a seemingly simple-minded question, one must still ask why they should almost always have to be white? Evidently enough, this is at least in part because, in Western Christian cultures, whiteness traditionally symbolises cleanliness and purity. However, the symbolism is also heavily gendered, for in these cultures, as Mark Blythe and Andrew Monk argue, 'white also denotes purity, innocence and virginity: the qualities associated with Mary, the Christian paragon of idealised motherhood'.[77]

Certainly, technology has, in effect, been defined *de facto* as the kind of object used principally by men, and technologies which have come to be seen as the preserve of women (such as typewriters and domestic telephones) have tended to correspondingly lose their status as objects of consequence. As Blythe and Monk argue, it is perhaps only when washing machines and fridges are made in black, more in the mode of the aesthetically masculinised entertainment technologies designed for the classic 'bachelor pad', that will they count as 'technologies'.[78] They also point to the significance, in this respect, of recent ethnographic market research exploring the ways in which technologies derive their meanings from gendered contexts of use. Their research thus points to the possibilities, for example, of designing washing-up brushes and other kitchen technologies in black, more on the model of power tools, in order to make them more appealing to men. As a further example, we might also note here the recent success, in the UK, of the aesthetic regendering of the design of home bread-making machines, so as to appeal to masculine forms of 'gadget addiction' and to give the machines themselves more 'gizmo lure'. The success of this particular mode of redesign in encouraging male uses of this particular kitchen technology has been entirely premised on its new aesthetic, which allows the men who use it to see their kitchen labour as not compromising their masculinity. Similarly, in the spring of 2005, the UK chain retailer Argos successfully introduced a new generation of 'macho irons', designed, in the words of a company representative, to 'help young men overcome the perceived stigma of doing their own ironing'. These irons, predictably, featured extra 'powerknobs' and came in black, rather than the traditional white and pastel shades, complete with ironing board covers featuring military style 'camouflage' patterns.[79]

The same point applies in traditionally feminised spheres outside the home. Thus, the UK business press has recently carried enthusiastic reports about the positive effects on young male shoppers of the new high-tech 'self-checkout' systems now in place in some supermarkets. As one retail commentator put it, 'the technology seems to encourage young males to shop. They like to use it to show off in front of their girlfriends' . The same effects can now apparently also be seen in other traditonally feminine realms; thus, a 'wedding-list' manager at one of the big London department stores commented that, since they had introduced a 'hand-held scanner to help couples make their lists' – which 'the boys love' – such lists had seen considerably more male participation.[80]

Thus, it seems not only that technologies have symbolic as well as practical functions, but that the former often come to dominate the latter. Through these symbolic mediations, as we have seen, they are also often gendered. Here we arrive at a further complication concerning the vexed question of technological competence and how it, too, is inevitably learnt in gendered forms. In both the Brunel home uses of ICT study and in Kaufmann's, there was evidence that many women regard their male partners as incompetent in using the washing machine, except under careful guidance. This is not because the men concerned do not 'theoretically' understand the machine itself or know in principle which buttons to press. Rather, their incompetence runs much deeper than that and consists in their lack of understanding of the qualities and nature of the different fabrics of which the clothes to be washed are made. Evidently, this is a specifically feminine form of cultural knowledge in most Western cultures – the cultural 'software' without which the operation of the technical hardware may well lead to disastrous results in terms of shrinkage, fabric damage and colour spoiling in the wash.[81]

In connection to the fridge, a similar point applies. There has recently been some debate in the British press recently concerning a disease known as 'male refrigerator blindness'. The symptoms consist of an inability to find things in the fridge.[82] The point is that this is no simple perceptual difficulty, which could easily be remedied by 'looking harder', or by better glasses. The issue, just as in the case of the washing machine, concerns gendered forms of cultural knowledge – in this case, to do with understanding certain principles of food storage that would enable someone to deduce where in the fridge a particular type of food item should be stored, and, therefore, where it is most likely to be found. It also, of course, concerns the question of domestic labour and of who takes principal responsibility for food shopping and then for stocking the fridge. The key principle here is probably that she who put the food in the fridge is most likely to know where it is – as indicated, in more theoretical terms, by John Hartley's observations (see below) about the symbiosis between the fridge and the mother in contemporary discourses and practices of domesticity.[83]

## The semiotics of the fridge and the foundations of domesticity

Perhaps the single most important contribution to the understanding of the social significance of the fridge as a technology is Ruth Schwartz Cowan's well-known essay 'How the Refrigerator Got its Hum', which gives a magisterial account of the complex array of social, economic and cultural forces that played a part in shaping the particular form of the technology as we know it today. However, Cowan's approach is largely limited to the sphere of production, and it is to its role in the sphere of consumption that I wish to turn.[84]

John Hartley is surely right to argue that, historically, the fridge is a foundational technology for the contemporary domestic lifestyle of the affluent West.[85] As he notes, without it, we simply would never have had the kind of home-based life-styles that form the basis of consumer culture. The fridge can even be said to have created hitherto non-existent entities, such as the domestic audience for broadcasting technologies. For Hartley, without the fridge,

> TV would be impossible, for there would not be enough homes in which to put TV, to sustain it as a mass medium, not enough families staying at home to watch it, not enough goods to advertise on it and no domestic culture within which its entertainments could appeal to audiences.

Before television could be invented as a domestic medium, its potential consumers had to be in the regular habit of being at home – and many of them simply did not have attractive homes to be in. Thus, the first thing that had to be invented was 'the home' as the site of domestic leisure and without the fridge's capacity for convenient and hygienic bulk food storage, a home-based lifestyle was simply not a possibility. Before the invention of the fridge, as one of the key technologies of the 'new domesticity', the home was not, for many working-class people, a primary site of leisure: children played outdoors and adults took their leisure in public places – for men, principally bars and sports grounds, for women principally the cinema or bingo hall.[86] The humble fridge, from this point of view, must then be recognised as having been a 'pivotal item of capitalisation in the home' which encouraged the creation of the home-based lifestyle in which people then became able, as Simon Frith has put it, to enjoy the 'pleasures of the hearth' in their modern, mediated forms.[87] The fridge is, of course, also a heavily gendered object, principally the domain of the woman of the house, and, by contrast to its 'evil twin' the television set, which has been blamed for so many ills, it is largely seen as a good and beneficient object. To this extent, it is caught up not simply in an ideology of domesticity, but also of motherhood, and it is often symbolically registered as a kind of mechanical, surrogate 'good mother'.[88]

Despite its humdrum status as an object with the rather unexciting function of food storage, the fridge has thus long functioned as one of the key technological symbols of consumer lifestyle, standing white and shiny, on display, in pride of place at the heart of the kitchen.[89] In this context, as Kristin Ross puts it: 'The fridgedair appeared in the kitchen . . . enthroned like *Mont Blanc*'. Indeed, the object itself, with its pressed steel, streamlined, rounded casing on which no dust could settle 'conveyed the image of absolute cleanliness and newfound hygiene: its brilliant white finish was the physical embodiment of health and purity', central to the new ideology of modern domesticity. Thus, she claims, the fridge 'as mass object of desire – and as one of the "mature" consumer durables of the post-war age was indeed the object-fetish for the new "modernised" home'.[90] In subsequent years, once the fridge was established as a normal attribute of the modern kitchen, designers turned their hands to the invention of the freezer which, with its extended form of 'preservational magic', became the new symbol of domestic efficiency, hygiene and order. As Elizabeth Shove and Dale Southerton point out, the 'vocabulary of advantage' mobilised by the freezer's marketers stressed issues of health, freshness and economy. Thus it was effectively sold as a mode of time management for the UK's new generation of busy working women, as a way for them to better schedule and coordinate the conflicting demands of their working and domestic lives.[91]

Lest these comments might perhaps seem to exaggerate the fridge's importance, it is well to recognise that it still stands in pride of place in the kitchen, at the heart of our domestic lives. Nowadays, in the form of the fridge-freezer, it is also growing noticeably in size: the 'must-have' centre-piece of the latest high-fashion British kitchen is the super-sized, energy-guzzling 'larder fridge', modelled on a North American design. Perhaps we might best understand this object as the sports utility vehicle (SUV) of the kitchen which, like its four-wheel-drive motoring counterpart, is construed as desirable precisely in so far as its very size is seen to declare an enviable excess of capacity over need on the part of its owner. Evidently, within the terms of what Martha Rosler has termed the 'semiotics of the kitchen', the aesthetics of miniaturisation, which now dominates many other symbolic and technological realms, is far from being the only game in town. In this respect, Thorstein Veblen's theory of 'conspicuous consumption' (in the case of the 'larder fridge', of both space and energy) still has much to teach us about the role of objects (high-tech or otherwise) in the contemporary domestic symbolism of status.[92]

To pursue the semiotics of the fridge a little further, it is worth noting that it is also, increasingly, a decorated object, now often covered with children's drawings and fridge magnets, invitations to birthday parties and social events. Beyond its food-storage capacities, it seems that, in recognition of its central place in our lives, many of us have also begun to treat it as a kind of informal communications centre, using it as the best place to put stick-on notes, reminding other household members about this or that aspect of domestic life and its obligations. It is perhaps the one place in the house where one can place information in the confident knowledge that one's fellow household members can then have no excuse for saying that they did not see it. The point is of more than anecdotal consequence. It is precisely in recognition of this kind of domestic behaviour, in which consumers have begun to use the fridge for communicative purposes, that manufacturers, having recognised the fridge's '24/7' centrality to our domestic lives, are now reconceptualising its design and potential functions. In the context of the contemporary electronic networking of the kitchen, the fridge, as the one technology that can be relied on to be switched on twenty-four hours a day, is now set to stand not simply as a food-storage device but as the command centre of the next generation of 'smart homes'.

## Kitchen sync: the kitchen computer and the smart home

The symbiosis of the figure of the mother and of kitchen appliances has taken a new turn in recent years. In response to the relative saturation of the business and professional markets, first traditional computer manufacturers and now the manufacturers of mobile ICTs have begun to look to the female and domestic markets as the next, as yet untapped realm of potential profit for them. We now see a new raft of computer products specifically aimed at mothers, such as the 'kitchen computer' designed for women's use in the home. In her account of the marketing of '*Audrey* the kitchen computer' by 3Com in the USA in 2000, Michelle Rodino explains that this 'countertop computer', deliberately simplified so as to be 'easier to use' for busy mothers, was marketed as a 'kitchen aid' that would enable women to better combine a number of old and new domestic tasks. In parallel with my comments above about the gendered aesthetics of colour in gadget design, Audrey was available in five very evidently feminine colours ('sunshine', 'meadow', 'ocean', 'linen' and 'slate'). The machine's deliberately *heimlich* retro-design was described by one commentator as making it look like 'the spawn of a toaster oven and a small television'. It was promoted both as a means for the busy housewife to access 'family friendly' web channels and as a way for her to more efficiently serve her family by using this device, which would function as 'the family's nerve centre . . . handling schedules and phone books . . . [so you can] centralise your family calendar'.[93]

In relation to all this, Rodino makes two telling observations. In the first place, she notes, by contrast to the marketing of mobile ICTs aimed at men, which were touted as freeing them from the chains that bound them to their desks, the whole conception of this technology effectively ties women to the kitchen even more strongly (indeed, Audrey's marketing campaign excitedly espoused the virtues of mother doing a 'kitchen sync' after cleaning the sink itself). Clearly, this very traditional conception of gender roles fitted well with the aspirations of the white middle-class North American women who constituted Audrey's target market. However, as she further argues, the over-all consequences of this development are not simply to 're-assert the mother's role as primary family worker' but also to add to her domestic burden as 'Audrey assigns new tasks like monitoring children's web-browsing, updating the family's schedule and uploading it onto the home PC'. To this extent, as she argues, here we have yet another supposedly labour-saving technology which, in fact creates 'More work for Mother'.[94] Evidently, to whom the extra work burden created by such a technology actually falls depends on the socio-economic and cultural circumstances of its deployment: it could be mother or it could be the maid. Thus, there have also recently been reports that in the Hong Kong market for domestic labour, the best jobs now go to those maids who are computer literate enough to take over tasks such as web-shopping for food, monitoring children's computer use and co-ordinating the household members' time schedules.[95]

These 'kitchen sync' scenarios do not relate to some distant future but are already being installed around us apace. In the summer of 2002, a family of four volunteers spent a week in the window of Harrods department store on London's Brompton Road as a living exhibition of what life in the smart home would be like. The display, the centrepiece of which was a huge multi-media fridge connected to the Internet, was sponsored by the giant South Korean manufacturer LG Electronics Digital Appliance Company, as a way of promoting its new range of 'intelligent' domestic technologies. As the company's promotional literature explains, the fridge is designed to be a com-munications and entertainment centre at the heart of the kitchen and, as such, it houses its own touch-screen PC and is able to act as a central server, communicating with other smart utilities in the home, such as washing machines and microwaves. The fridge is to be the main hub of this 'home network', and all this home networking is advertised as 'bringing the efficiency and dynamism of the digital age from the office into our homes'. It is equipped with an in-built videophone, MP3 player, can receive television signals and video, text and handwritten messages can be left on its monitor – thus producing a technologised version of how people actually already use their fridges as informal nodes of paper-based domestic communication. The 'new fridge' is designed to function as a 'home controller', the central device through which other technologies in the home, such as the air conditioning, can themselves be adjusted.[96]

To all this is now added the capacity of the mobile phone to communicate remotely with the home's command centre from a distance. Thus a range of trade exhibitions, such as the 'Combined Exhibition of Advanced Technologies' in Tokyo and the 'Orange House of the Future Exhibition' in London (both 2002) have demonstrated the extent to which these scenarios have already been developed. In this home of the future, it seems, we shall even be able to control our homes by mobile phone when we are absent – letting the on-line supermarket delivery man into the house, adjusting the heating or running the bath for when we get home, before we leave the office, or keeping a surveillant eye on the nanny's behaviour with our children, while we are out socialising. At which point, we may indeed be in danger of participating in a deranged parody of the fantasies of 'total control' identified earlier by commentators such as Castoriadis.[97]

## Notes

1.  Leo Marx (1964) *The Machine in the Garden*. New York: Open University Press. I take up Marx's terminology as it is deployed by James Carey and John Quirk, in their (1989) essay on 'The Mythos of the Electronic Revolution', in James Carey (ed.) *Communications as Culture*. London: Unwin Hyman.
2.  David Nye (1994) *American Technological Sublime*. Cambridge, Mass: MIT Press, p. 143, quoted in William Boddy (2004) *New Media and the Popular Imagination*. Oxford: Oxford University Press, p. 10.
3.  Carey and Quirk, ibid., pp. 120–1.
4.  Jeffrey Alexander (1998) 'The Computer as Sacred and Profane', in Paul Smith (ed.) *The New American Cultural Sociology*. Cambridge: Cambridge University Press; McLuhan, quoted in Carey and Quirk, ibid., p. 116.
5.  Gore quoted in A. Lear (2000) *Welcome to the Wired World*. Harlow: Pearson Education, pp. 181–2.
6.  Quoted in 'Home is Where the Future is', *The Economist: Technological Quarterly*, 18 September 2004, p. 6.
7.  Keynes, quoted in Madeleine Bunting (2000) 'We've Been Here Before', *The Guardian*, 24 February. Keynes's confident use of the masculine pronoun is perhaps the only truly dated thing here.
8.  Marinetti, quoted in Stephen Kern (1983) *The Culture of Space and Time, 1880–1918*. London: Weidenfeld & Nicolson, p. 98; Valéry, quoted in A. Friedberg (2002) 'CD and DVD' in D. Harries (ed.) *The New Media Book*. London: British Film Institute, p. 28.

9.  'Miracle Kitchen', publicity quoted in *The Economist: Technological Quarterly*, 18 September 2004, p. 6.
10. Tom Standage (1998) *The Victorian Internet*. Weidenfeld & Nicolson, pp. 72, 81.
11. See Armand Mattelart (1996) *The Invention of Communication*. Minneapolis, Minn.: University of Minnesota Press.
12. Net technician Karl Auerbach, quoted in Andrew Orlowski (2004) 'White Noise', *The Independent Science and Technology Review*, 7 April; David McCandless (2004) 'Anatomy of a Virus', *The Guardian Online*, 5 February.
13. Jeffrey Alexander, ibid., p. 44.
14. Walter Benjamin *Illuminations*, quoted in Charlie Gere (2002) *Digital Culture*. London: Reaktion, p. 16.
15. Thomas Friedman (2000) *The Lexus and the Olive Tree*. London: Harper Collins.
16. Mary Dejevsky (2001) 'If Only Globalisation Were as Common as Protestors Fear', *The Independent*, 6 August.
17. Richard Quest (2004) 'Windows on the World', in 'Online Travel', *The Independent*, 17 April.
18. William Boddy (2004) *New Media and Popular Imagination*. Oxford: Oxford University Press, p. 4.
19. Wendy Grossman (2004) 'Remote Control', *The Independent Review* (Science and Technology) 7 August; 'Untangling Ultrawideband', *Economist Technological Quarterly*, ibid., p. 36.
20. Robert Putnam (2002) *Bowling Alone*. New York: Simon & Schuster; Annabel Quan-Haase et al. (2002) 'Capitalizing on the Net', in Barry Wellman and Carolyn Haythornwaite (eds) *The Internet in Everyday Life*. Oxford: Blackwell.
21. Raymond Williams (1974) *Television: Technology and Cultural Form*. London: Fontana. See also Jonathan Miller's critique in his (1971) *McLuhan*. London: Fontana.
22. For one example, see the claims in Paul Levinson's (1999) *Digital McLuhan: A Guide to the Millennium*. London: Routledge. Other versions of the same type of technologically determinist argument are also to be found in the recently influential work of writers such as Lev Manovich (2001) *The Language of New Media* (Cambridge, Mass.: MIT Press) and that of Friedrich Kittler (1999) *Gramophone, Film, Typewriter*. Stanford, Calif.: Stanford University Press.
23. Des Freedman (2002) 'A Technological Idiot? Raymond Williams and Communications Technology', *Information, Communication and Society* 5 (3): 425–42.
24. Boddy, ibid., pp. 9 and 2.
25. Martin Lister et al. (2003) *New Media: A Critical Introduction*. London: Routledge; see Bruno Latour (1987) *Science in Action: How to Follow Scientists and Engineers through Society*, Milton Keynes: Open University Press.
26. See Lister et al., ibid., pp. 312, 313. Jacques Ellul (1964) *The Technological Society*. First published in French 1954. New York: Alfred Knopf Inc; Wolfgang Schivelbusch (1986) *The Railway Journey: The Industrialisation of Time and Speed in the 19th Century*. Berkeley, Calif.: University of California Press; see my discussion of Fukuyama on this point in Chapter 6.

27. See Lister et al., ibid., p. 307; Norbert Wiener (1962) *Cybernetics: Control and Communication in Animal and Machine*. Cambridge, Mass.: MIT Press; see Stuart Hall (1974) 'Encoding/Decoding television Discourse' (original version) *Stencilled Paper No 7* Centre for Contemporary Cultural Studies, University of Birmingham; Lister et al., ibid., pp. 306 and 296–314.

28. Gilles Deleuze and Claire Parnet (1977) *Dialogues*. Paris: Flammarion; quoted in Charlie Gere (2002) *Digital Culture*. London: Reaktion, p. 13. See also, Gilles Deleuze (1986) *Cinema 1* and *Cinema 2*. London: Athlone Press.

29. S. Hall (1980) 'Encoding/Decoding in Television Discourse', in S. Hall, D. Hobson, A. Lowe and P. Willis (eds) *Culture, Media, Language*. London: Hutchinson.

30. Carolyn Marvin (1988) *When Old Technologies Were New*. Oxford: Oxford University Press, p. 3.

31. L. Spigel (2005) 'Introduction', to Lynn Spigel and Jan Olson (eds) *Television after Television*. Durham, NC: Duke University Press.

32. See Ellen Seiter (1999) *Television and New Media Audiences*. Oxford: Oxford University Press.

33. Andreas Huyssen (1986) *After The Great Divide*. Bloomington, Ind.: Indiana University Press; William Boddy (2004) *New Media and the Popular Imagination*. Oxford: Oxford University Press, p. 32.

34. Boddy, ibid., pp. 43, 70; *Newsweek*, April 1992 quoted ibid., p. 71. In a similar vein, Barbara Klinger has recently argued that the DVD has contributed to the remasculinisation of film viewing, because the digital aesthetic redefines a 'Good Film' as one which best exploits the technical possibilities of DVD – and the films which does that best are action movies, themselves featuring lots of masculine techno-gadgetry. Barbara Klinger (2005) 'The DVD and Home Film Culture', paper to 'What is a DVD?' Conference, Department of Film and Television Studies, University of Warwick, 23 April, p. 34.

35. Laurie Kendall (2002) *Hanging Out in the Virtual Pub*. Berkeley, Calif.: University of California Press, quoted in Shaun Moores 'The Doubling of Place', in Couldry and McCarthy, ibid., p. 27.

36. Boddy, ibid., p. 16.

37. See James Curran and Jean Seaton (2003) *Power without Responsibility*, 6th edn (London: Routledge), Part III for a fuller discussion of this issue.

38. See Jostein Gripsrud (2004) 'Broadcast Television and its Chances of Survival in a Digital Age', in L. Spigel and J. Olsson (eds) *Television after Television*. Durham, NC: Duke University Press. In her report on the downside of enhanced technological choice, Emily Bell describes UK consumers as 'about to be hit with a tidal wave of choice that we don't really want and which will . . . require too much mental energy to understand' (Emily Bell (2005) 'Sometimes you can have too much technological choice' *The Guardian* (Media) 12 December).

39. This is a fact which is to do with the ordering of the home – i.e. not what the technical capacities of objects are, but *where* it is felt that the objects should be placed (Should a work-related object such as a computer be placed in a

leisure space like the living room?) and what activities are deemed appropriate in which particular domestic spaces. Innovative work on these issues is being conducted in Finland at the Departments of Sociology and Journalism/Mass Communications, Tampere University. See the unpublished papers by Virve Peteri 'The Spatial Articulations of Media Technologies', Anna Soronen and Olli Sotamaa 'And Our Television is a Monkey: Probes from Households'; Tuula Perenen 'Social Dimensions of Media in Everday Life' and Jari Luomanen 'Media Choices and Preferences', all produced by the University of Tampere.

40. *Interactive Digital Television* published by Warwickshire Trading Standards Service March 2004; Maggie Brown (2005) 'The Great Internet Boom Has Stalled', *Media Guardian*, 25 April.

41. On the history of the 'OnDigital' débâcle, see Boddy, ibid., pp. 95–9.

42. Christine Hardyment (1988) *From Mangle to Microwave*. Cambridge: Polity Press, p. 65.

43. There is also some anecdotal evidence of households in which only the children know how to use the 'parental lock' on the satellite channel control.

44. Carl Barat (2005) 'My London', *Evening Standard*, 12 August; Charles Arthur and Helen Johnstone (2004) 'The iPod Set Are Cool but Clueless', *Independent on Sunday* 4 April.

45. According to Jacques Ellul, 'everything which is technique is necessarily used as soon as it is available, without distinction of good or evil. This is the imperative law of our age'. Ellul offers as one good example of this principle the statement by Charles de Gaulle's Minster of Information, Jacques Soustelle, who remarked of the atomic bomb, in 1960, that 'since it was possible it was necessary.' Jacques Ellul (1964) *The Technological Society*. New York: Vintage.

46. Simon Caulkin (2004) 'To Lose a Customer, Press . . .', *The Observer* (Business) 29 August; 'You're Hired' *Economist Technological Quarterly*, September 2004.

47. Katherine Shonfield, *Walls Have Feelings: Architecture, Film and the City*. London: Routledge 2000, especially Chapter 2, 'Why Does Your Flat Leak?'.

48. Maxine Forth (2003) 'Britain's Homes are Haven to £3.2 Bn of Gizmos that Do Nothing but Gather Dust', *The Independent*, 15 September. However, in the kitchen, at least, this domestic story is even more convoluted than it might appear at first sight. When processed foods were first introduced, they were seen as a means to liberate housewives from unwanted domestic labour. Today, for the middle-class housewife at least, it has become a matter of pride for her to do the work herself, but with the help of a growing array of technical 'aides', such as pasta-makers and vegetable dryers, many of which themselves, after the first flush of enthusiastic usage, soon lie fallow.

49. Castoriadis, quoted in Kevin Robins and James Cornford (1990) 'Bringing It All Back Home', *Futures*; see also Kevin Robins and Frank Webster (1999) *Times of the Technoculture*. London: Routledge; Lynn Spigel (2005) 'Designing the Smart Home: Post-Human Domesticity and Conspicuous Production', *European Journal of Cultural Studies*, 8 (4).

50. Among these studies are Hugh Mackay and Darren Ivey (2004) *Modern Media in the Home*. Rome: John Libbey; Shaun Moore's (2000) *Media and Everyday Life*.

Edinburgh: Edinburgh University Press; Roger Silverstone and Eric Hirsch (eds) (1992) *Consuming Technologies*. London: Routledge; Daniel Miller and Don Slater (2000) *The Internet: An Ethnographic Approach*. Oxford and New York: Berg and Elaine Lally (2002) *At Home with Computers*. Oxford and New York: Berg.

51. In this connection, see my commentary on the work of Irene Goodman and Jennifer Bryce in my (1992) *Television, Audiences and Cultural Studies*. London: Routledge.

52. James Hunt (2003) 'Just Re-Do It: Tactical Formlessness and Everyday Consumption', in Andrew Blauvelt (ed.) *Strangely Familiar*, Minneapolis, Minn.: Walker Art Centre, pp. 62–3; Michel de Certeau (1984) *The Practice of Everyday Life*. Berkeley, Calif.: University of California Press.

53. See the work of Pierre Bourdieu (1984) *Distinction*. London: Routledge and Daniel Miller (1987) *Material Culture and Mass Consumption*. Oxford: Blackwell. Anna McCarthy (2004) 'Geekospheres: Visual Culture and Material Culture at Work', *Journal of Visual Culture*, 3 (2).

54. Bausinger, quoting Wilhelm Riehl (1990) in *Folk Culture in a World of Technology*. Bloomington, Ind.: Indiana University Press, p. 1; see also my earlier comments on this in Chapter 3.

55. Rabinow, quoted in James Clifford and George Marcus (eds) (1986) *Writing Culture*. Berkeley, Calif.: University of California Press, p. 21.

56. K. Kawakami (1995) *99 More Unuseless Japanese Inventions: The Japanese Art of Chindogu*. London: Harper Collins.

57. See Neil Postman (2002) 'Stop!', *The Guardian Editor*, 5 December. In this sense, for every technology that is invented, there is the invention of a corresponding new form of malfunction, mishap or accident. Elizabeth Shove and Dale Southerton (2000) 'Defrosting the Freezer', *Journal of Material Culture* 5 (3).

58. Anthony Dunne and Fiona Rabey (2001) *Design Noir: The Secret Life of Electronic Objects*. London: Birkhauser; quoted in James Hunt 'Just Re-Do It: Tactical Formlessness and Everyday Consumption', in Andrew Blauvelt (ed.) *Strangely Familiar*. Minneapolis, Minn.: Walker Art Centre, p. 57.

59. See Perec on the 'infra-ordinary' in Chapter 4.

60. Quoted in Hunt, ibid., p. 68.

61. See Blauvelt, ibid., p. 107.

62. On 'actor network theory', see Latour, ibid.; Dunne and Rabey, ibid., p. 67; see my earlier discussion of these issues in relation to Wodiczko's *Homeless Vehicle* project in Chapter 4.

63. Frederick Winslow Taylor, quoted in Aaron Betsky et al. (eds) (2003) *Scanning: The Aberrant Architectures of diller + scofidio*. New York: Whitney Museum of American Art, p. 98, note 15.

64. See my *Home Territories*, pp. 83–4 for my earlier discussion of Acconci's work.

65. Betsky et al., ibid., p. 129.

66. Diller quoted in Betsky et al., ibid., p. 67; K. Michael Hays (2003) 'Scanners' in Aaron Betsky et al. (eds) (2003) *Scanning: The Aberrant Architectures of diller*

+ *scofidio*. New York: Whitney Museum of American Art, pp. 130 and 133; A. Betsky (2003) 'Display Engineers', in Aaron Betsky et al. (eds) ibid., p. 28. See Chapter 9 for my discussion of the work of video-installation artists such as Nam June Paik, who deconstruct and subvert the taken-for-granted functions of the television set by treating it as a form of sculpture – as a 'container' into which a variety of other things, besides moving electrical images can be placed (goldfish, plastic Buddhas, etc.).

67.   Ashley Schaffer (2003) 'Designing Inefficiences', in Aaron Betsky et al. (eds) *Scanning: The Aberrant Architectures of diller + scofidio*. New York: Whitney Museum of American Art, p. 94.

68.   Edward Dimendberg (2003) 'Blurring Genres' in Aaron Betsky et al. (eds) *Scanning: The Aberrant Architectures of diller + scofidio*. New York: Whitney Museum of American Art, pp. 72 and 75. On this 'series', see also Margaret Morse's seminal (1990) 'An Ontology of Everyday Distraction', in Patricia Mellencamp (ed.) *The Logics of Television*. Bloomington, Ind.: Indiana University Press, where she includes the television, the automobile/freeway and the shopping mall as among correlative parts of this 'series'. One might also refer here to the signifying 'power play' of one-way-view glass in cars in the contemporary city and to the UK debate about the battle in the post-war 'New Towns' between modernist architects' avowal of the virtues of the picture window and housewives' predilection for 'ruining' the logic of the design by putting up net curtains to preserve their households' privacy; see my *Home Territories*, Chapter 3.

69.   See Dimendberg, ibid., p. 79; Schafer, ibid., p. 94.

70.   For one example, see Anne Oakley (1974) *Housewife*. London: Allen Lane 1974.

71.   Mark Blythe and Andrew Monk (2003) 'Ethnography, HCI and Domestic Technology', unpublished paper, Department of Psychology, University of York, 2003. See also their web site at: <http://portal.acm.org/citation.cfm?id=778750&d1=ACM&coll =GUIDE>.

72.   See Hardyment, ibid.

73.   Jean-Claude Kaufmann (1998) *Dirty Linen: Couples and their Laundry*. London: Middlesex University Press.

74.   Kaufmann, ibid., p. 57.

75.   Kristin Ross (1996) *Fast Cars, Clean Bodies: Decolonisation and the Re-Ordering of French Culture*. Cambridge, Mass.: MIT Press.

76.   Roland Barthes (1963) 'La voiture, projection de l'ego', *Realities*, 213, p. 45; Ross, ibid., pp. 105–6; see also Elisabeth Shove and Dale Southern (2000) 'Defrosting the Freezer: From Novelty to Convenience', *Journal of Material Culture*, 5 (3) on the 'preservational magic' of the freezer, of which more below.

77.   Blythe and Monk, ibid.

78.   To return to my earlier example, it may be that it is only then that washing machines and fridges will become 'visible' to men, the next time someone asks them to draw a map of the technologies in their home.

79. Polly Curtis (2005) 'Women Brushed Aside as Irons Become New Boy's Toy', *The Guardian*, 3 June; see Martin Wainwright (2003) 'Machines Turn Dough Makers into Bread Bakers', *The Guardian*, 5 August.

80. Clayton Hirst (2004) 'Supermarket Shake-up as the Bell Tolls for Tills', *Independent on Sunday* (Business), 8 August; 'The World According to . . . Gail Hulett, John Lewis Wedding List Manager', *Independent Review*, 6 April 2005.

81. See Kaufmann, ibid.

82. I should say here that this is a disease which I sometimes suffer from personally.

83. Even here though, things are changing: upmarket style/living supplements in the UK broadsheet press have recently featured fridges clearly marketed at men, complete with wide-screen televisions on their doors which, in the adverts, are always showing football. See the title page to this section (p. 198) for an example.

84. Ruth Schwartz Cowan (1988) 'How the Refrigerator Got its Hum', in Donald Mackenzie and Judy Wajcman (eds) *The Social Shaping of Technology*. Milton Keynes: Open University Press. For a more contemporary equivalent to the general analysis of product design, but one which, like many others, pays scant attention to the importance of the fridge, see Harvey Molotch (2003) *Where Stuff Comes From: How Toasters, Toilets, Cars Computers and Many Other Things Come to Be as They Are*. London: Routledge.

85. John Hartley (1999) 'Housing Television' in his *The Uses of Television*. London: Routledge.

86. Hartley, ibid., pp. 99–100, 102.

87. S. Frith (1983) 'The Pleasures of the Hearth', in J. Donald (ed.) *Formations of Pleasure*. London: Routledge.

88. Hartley, ibid., pp. 106–7.

89. See my earlier discussion of Yoshimi's analysis of the fridge as one of the 'Three Sacred Things' in post-war Japanese consumer culture.

90. K. Ross, ibid., p. 98, emphasis added. Here Ross draws on Adrian Forty's earlier comments on the fridge, in his (1995) *Objects of Desire*, London: Thames & Hudson, p. 156.

91. Shove and Southerton, ibid.

92. On the 'Larder Fridge' as SUV, see Lucy Siegle (2004) 'Hell's Kitchen', *The Observer Magazine*, 12 September; Martha Rosler *The Semiotics of the Kitchen* (1975, video) in her *Positions in the Life World*, Birmingham Ikon Gallery 1999. For a further discussion of the significance of Rosler's work, in relation to today's 'Martha' (Stewart) of the kitchen, see Charlotte Brunsdon (2005) 'Feminism, Post-Feminism, Martha, Martha and Nigella', *Cinema Journal* 44 (2): 110–16; Thorstein Veblen (1970) *The Theory of The Leisure Class*. London: Unwin.

93. 3Com publicity, quoted in Michelle Rodino (2003) 'Mobilising Mother', *Feminist Media Studies* 3 (3): 375–6; see my commentary in Chapter 7 on the use of Palm Pilot technology by busy middle-class families in Silicon Valley, for similar purposes.

94. Rodino, ibid., pp. 376–7.

95.  Paul Peachey (2003) 'Meet the New Cyber-Maids', *Independent on Sunday*, 14 December.
96.  This is by no means a specifically Korean invention: Microsoft now has plans for an 'intelligent kitchen' networked around the fridge, which will anticipate what recipes will be need by the family at different times of the day and remind mother what ingredients she will need to tele-order for them, and the British manufacturer Dyson has plans for an intelligent washing machine which can order its own washing powder and call the engineer up when it needs servicing.
97.  Tim Dowling (2002) 'We're No Dummies', *The Guardian*, 21 May; Robin McKie (2002) 'Mobiles to Take Control of Hi-Tech Home', *The Observer*, 6 October; Jack Schofield (2002) 'Hot News for Your Fridge', *The Guardian*, 17 October; Tamsin Blanchard (2002) 'Touchtone Homes', *Observer Magazine*, 20 October. See Castoriadis, quoted earlier in this chapter.

# Part V

# Techno-anthropology

Icons, totems and fetishes

*Figure 15*  African statuettes. Photo by Martin Durrant, Goldsmiths College.

# 9   Television: not so much a visual medium, more a visible object

In this part I attempt to develop the terms of reference for a 'techno-anthropology' which addresses the symbolic meanings of some of the symbolic objects of our contemporary world, notably the television, the computer and the mobile phone. I begin, in this chapter, with the television set itself. Against the largely unquestioned orthodoxy which characterises television as a visual medium, I consider a number of aspects of the domestic context of television's usage which lead to the suggestion that television might, in fact, be better understood as a primarily aural medium. I then briefly recount the story of the troubled history of television's introduction to the home, the better both to denaturalise television's now taken-for-granted place within that micro-geography and to understand some of the mutual determinations that television and the home have exercised on one another over the past fifty years. My argument then turns to the 'physics' of television, focusing on the largely unexamined significance of the television set itself (rather than the programmes it shows), both as a material and as a symbolic, or even totemic, object. I end with a detailed consideration of the contributions made to our understanding of these issues by the Korean techno-sculptor, Nam June Paik.

Many years ago, John Ellis usefully pointed to the distinctions between cinema and television, in terms of their different regimes of representation, of vision and of reception. Ellis attempts to sketch out cinema and television as particular social forms of organisation of meaning, designed for particular forms of spectator attention. He argues that broadcast television has developed distinctive aesthetic forms to suit the circumstances within which it is used. The viewer is cast as someone who has the television switched on but is giving it very little attention – a casual viewer relaxing at home in the midst of a family group. In this context, attention has to be solicited and grasped segment by segment, which leads both to the amount of self-promotion that each broadcast television channel does for itself, the prevalence of direct address to the viewer and the centrality given to sound in television broadcasting.

As Ellis puts it, sound draws the attention of the look when it has wandered away.[1] Broadcast television is contextualised by the home, the domestic space of our familiar lives. In this sense, the contrast Ellis draws between cinema and television is parallel to that drawn by Roland Barthes:

> In the darkness of the theatre we find the very source of the fascination exercised by film. Consider, on the other hand, the opposite experience, the experience of television, which also shows films. Nothing, no fascination. The darkness is dissolved, the space is organised, by furniture and familiar objects, tamed. Eroticism is foreclosed; television condemns us to the family, whose household utensil it has become, just as the hearth once was, flanked by its predictable communal stewing pot, in times past.[2]

If television viewing is a normal part of domestic life, an activity that up to half the people in the UK, for example, can be counted on to be engaged in, at some point, on most evenings, then the price of this 'normalisation' is that 'television belongs to the everyday, to the normal backdrop of expectations and mundane pleasures' and the consequence is that the domestic spectator is only fitfully attentive to the solicitations of television discourse.[3]

## Television in and for the home

In the first place, we need to recognise how television and the home have gradually redefined one another. If the current form in which television technology has been institutionalised, as a system of relatively centralised broadcasting to a myriad of individual receivers in private homes, is now so naturalised as to seem inevitable to us, it is worth remarking that not only was television, in its initial conception, a technology capable of many alternative uses, its gradual introduction to the home was only the result of a long process of debate and anxiety within the nascent television industry itself.[4] Given the unquestioned assumption that television would have to take its model from the cinema industry, and, indeed, would be a form of 'mini-cinema', there were profound anxieties as to whether television could ever be integrated into the home. There were concerns about the physical demands of the medium and the possibilities of viewers suffering 'eyestrain' – concerns premised on the assumption of the concentrated form of visual viewer attention which, it was presumed, would be obligatory. As one commentator in the 1950s trade debate in the USA put it, 'TV . . . requires complete and unfaltering attention . . . If the eye wanders . . . programme continuity is lost. . . . The thing moves, it requires complete attention . . . you cannot turn your back . . . and you cannot do anything else except listen while you are looking'.[5]

On the basis of these anxieties, some influential commentators predicted that television, by definition, would never be capable of gaining a more than 25 per cent audience share. Given that the driving force behind the development of the television industry in America was the advertisers, who wished to exploit the new medium to market consumer goods, the particular focus of attention was the housewife, as the controller of the domestic purse. The problem was that, quite apart from the anxieties as to whether women could 'cope' with the demands (tuning the set, etc.) of the new technology, the housewife had her domestic duties to attend to, which meant that she was simply not available to spend her time sitting in front of the set that was showing the advertisements for the goods on sale.[6] The solution that gradually emerged to this problem, which was of the enormous consequence and still pertains today, was the redesign of television programming, not on the model of 'private cinema', requiring close visual attention, but on the model of radio: television as 'radio with pictures', where the narrative is mainly carried by the soundtrack and the visuals play a subordinate, 'illustrative' role. The point, of course, is that, in this form, and with this kind of programming strategy, television no longer required full attention so, among other things, the housewife could 'follow' the programme from the soundtrack, while getting on with the domestic duties around the house and was thus potentially 'available' to the advertisers. Of course, just in case she wasn't listening carefully, American television also developed the convention of increasing the volume when the adverts come on.

However, it was not only a question of the redesign of television's programming strategy, it was also a question of the gradual redesign of domestic architecture. Thus, one further part of the solution to the problem of ensuring that the housewife-viewer was 'available' to the advertisers was the development of the integrated 'through-lounge' as a standard aspect of American domestic architecture, in which the housewife's arena of domestic labour is integrated into the main living space so that, in the words of one commentator, 'the cooking/eating area is not separated off, and the housewife is part of the [viewing] group . . . and can share in the fun, while her work is in progress'.[7] Television and the home thus turns out to be deeply entwined in each other's historical development, throughout the post-1945 period, in a complex pattern of inter-determinations.

## The physics of television

Despite these important historical considerations, the impact of television's physical presence as a ubiquitous object in the home has, thus far, been little remarked on within the field of media studies. As Matthew Geller remarks, 'the box itself has largely been overlooked . . . it's omnipresent, yet completely taken for granted . . . We look through the object, to the programming it feeds into our homes. The actual set is, for the most part, invisible when we watch it.'[8] In this context (following Perec's protocols, discussed in Chapter 4), I want to suggest that there is much to be gained by concentrating on that which is normally unremarked, taking the television set's own 'point of view' and looking at the living room in which it is set and the people watching it. Thus, Maud Lavin argues that

> considering how unambiguous television is in our lives, it is surprising how little attention has been paid to the intimate assimilation of the TV set into our homes in visual and spatial terms . . . There are two . . . histories of television be considered. One is an official narrative, a chronology of changes in the TV set, and the other is unofficial, a collection of personal memories of growing up with television, telling how the TV set was incorporated into home, family and leisure time.

This is, as she goes on to note, also, necessarily 'an intimate history: of how we design our spaces, habits and even emotions, around the television'.[9]

The position of television, considered as an object of consumption, is a complex one, which needs to be considered as operating, simultaneously, along a number of different dimensions. In the first place, the television set (along with all the other technologies in the household) is already a symbolic object, qua item of household furnishing, a choice (of design, style, etc.) that expresses something about its owner's (or renter's) tastes and communicates that choice, as displayed by its position in the household, as itself a 'trophy of consumerism'.[10] In order to address these issues, we need to rethink our perspective on television by considering it not only as a distribution system for the words and images that pass through it, but also by acknowledging its physical presence, as a totemic item of furniture, which is central to our contemporary concept of the home. If it is now a commonplace to note that television has replaced the hearth as the centrepiece of the family's main living space, we should note that this 'replacement' occurs literally at the centre of the symbolic space of the family home: a sacred space, by any definition, within our culture. As noted earlier, the arrival of television in the home, much as we may take it for granted now, was a highly contentious and fractious affair, involving disruptions and dislocations of the family and the home. Not only did the furniture have to be moved around to accommodate television, but domestic time itself had to be reorganised. Thus Serafina Bathrick notes correspondence in American 1950s women's magazines, in which mothers fretted about the difficulties of adapting meal times and children's play activities to the temporal disciplines of the broadcast schedules, as their children's lives (and thus their own) came to be, increasingly, 'programmed' around the television set.[11]

Moreover, the acquisition of television, as symbol of a materialist consumer culture, was something about which its new (initially, middle-class) owners sometimes felt uneasy. Thus, Lynn Spigel notes that, in the 1950s, when television was being introduced into American homes, there was a strong tendency to 'camouflage' (or literally, hide) the television set in 'stow-away' cabinets and thus to render it invisible, so far as possible. Moreover, she notes, 'it wasn't only that the TV set was made inconspicuous within the domestic space, it was also made invisible to the outside world'. The women's magazines of the time contained numerous graphics demonstrating how television could be best incorporated into the home and, interestingly, as Spigel points out, 'the overwhelming majority of graphics showed the television placed in a spot where it could not be seen through the windows of the room . . . (as if) . . . there was something . . . profoundly troubling about being caught in the act of viewing television'.[12]

Television, if desirable, was also a problematic object, one that had to be 'domesticated' into family life. Among the ways in which this was achieved was its integration within the overall furnishing scheme for the living room in which it was placed; another was, more literally, by means of the placing of treasured object, such as family photos and mementos, on top of the set, in the style of a family altarplace. If Spigel's historical research is based on the American experience, it is clearly also quite possible to draw parallels with the same history in Britain. Thus, in 1947, in a feature 'Across the Counter, Some Jottings by a Television Dealer', the magazine *Television Weekly* reported one dealer's account of the lengths to which viewers would go in 'domesticating' their sets.

> One customer asked 'will it be alright if I put my aquarium on top of my set?' Other curious decorations that I have seen poised on top of television cabinets include flora of all species, from miniature palm-trees to cacti; chiming clocks; perspex airplanes and pewter pots, an occasional present from Margate; books; dolls; porcelain animals . . . and, believe it or not, a fair sized Christmas tree complete with tinsel, coloured balls and crackers. It is clear that television sets have other uses besides the obvious ones![13]

Nowadays, the idea of television as simply the (fixed) 'box in the corner' seems quite outmoded. Over the years, our relation to the television set itself has undergone a fundamental transition, as its portability has increasingly freed it from its previously fixed place in the sitting room. As Ehrick Long notes, initially, when the set was always in the sitting room, 'there was some distance between us and it. We would never . . . invite it to a meal in the kitchen, much less allow it into the bedroom . . . [but] our relationship with the technology has grown more intimate . . . [with] portable televisions . . . [and] the set's accessibility to more intimate spaces'. As Long notes, nowadays the television set is no longer even necessarily confined to the home (let alone to one particular part of the home) but can be found in lifts, shops, arcades, vehicles – all around us. 'To that extent', she suggests,

> television is now so much a piece of furniture as a potential body-part, not so much as stranger, invited cautiously into one controlled space in the home, but more an omnipresent 'extension of the self', as the television set now appears in every conceivable environment, and television events come to saturate the texture of everyday experience.[14]

## The symbolism of television

In her analysis of the place of television in the home in Brazil, Ondina Leal is also concerned with 'The TV object . . . [as] a fetish . . . infused with an ethereal, magical meaning . . . even when it is turned off and no-one is watching it'.[15] Leal observes that in most middle-class Brazilian homes, the television set is discreetly positioned away from public view. By contrast, in working-class homes, the set is a treasured possession which is given pride of place, and is deliberately positioned where it can be seen from the street, as a public statement of its owners' status. For these newly urban working-class Brazilians, its possession symbolises a hard-won access to an urban, 'rational', modern 'way of life'.

Most interestingly, Leal argues that, in these working-class homes, the television set often functions as a fetish object, placed at the centre of a symbolic 'entourage' of sacred family possessions: 'The repertoire of [these] objects . . . is located next to the television, as a point of magical contagion. There is a common quality among all of its elements – that of fetish . . . They constitute a matrix of significations . . . [whose] arrangements reveals a symbolic strategy'. In one of the homes observed as part of her ethnographic study, Leal reports that their television 'entourage' included 'plastic flowers, a religious picture, a false gold vase, family photographs, a broken laboratory glass and an old broken radio'.[16] Each of the elements in this particular family's 'entourage' has, of course, a quite individual investment of meaning, the plastic flowers being more magical than real ones to a peasant recently arrived in the city, the broken laboratory glass a trophy of the experience of working in a 'modern' hospital, etc.[17]

Of course, practices of fetishism are not confined to the Third World and, evidently, it is not only the television set that can display the qualities of a fetish. Describing ethnographic work on working-class culture in Britain during the 1930s, Humphrey Spender reports on an interesting experience involving a similar moment of symbolic display – of a (then) highly 'modern' consumer good, the vacuum cleaner:

> on one of the few occasions when we went into a house, we found, on the mantelshelf of the front parlour . . . the component parts, heavily chromium-plated and gleaming, of a hoover. There was no electricity connected to the house, so clearly this new invention, this new-fangled thing had another kind of meaning – as a kind of status symbol.[18]

In his historical work on television in post-war Britain, Tim O'Sullivan neatly captures the sense in which, as he puts it,

> TV ownership in the 1950's symbolised status and modernity as well as a commitment to the values of particular types of programmes. The act of getting a television generally seems to be remembered, above all, as a sign of 'progress', a visible sign of joining, or at least, of not being left out of 'the new'.

As one of O'Sullivan's interviewees puts it, reminiscing of 1950s Britain, 'you could tell, from the aerials, who had and who hadn't got sets . . . if you had a car *and* a TV set, you'd really arrived'.[19] We can draw a useful parallel here with Charlotte Brunsdon's commentary on the symbolic meaning of the satellite television dish in contemporary British culture. In Britain, ever since the demise of the short-lived, upmarket, 'British Satellite Broadcasting' station, with its distinctive 'squarial', satellite television has *meant* Sky television – i.e., popular television designed for a largely working-class audience, supplied by Rupert Murdoch. Brunsdon argues that, in this context, the erection of a satellite dish on a house functions as a publicly visible sign of the 'low' taste of the household and its occupants.[20]

Television viewing is, par excellence, generally understood as a private activity, a question of 'personal taste', involving only the consent of the relevant household members within the privacy of their home. However, as Brunsdon notes, the arrival of satellite television has changed all that, because 'unlike channel selection, or programme-watching, which are activities performed in the privacy of the home, erecting a satellite dish is done outside the home' and effectively makes a public statement of private tastes. Thus, she quotes from newspaper coverage of the launch of Sky TV, which notes that while 'under normal circumstances, if your tastes extend no further than *Neighbours*, Capital Radio and *Dynasty*, at least you can indulge yourself without the whole street knowing about it; the problem with satellite television, given the need to erect an external dish, in order to receive it, is that you can't watch it discreetly'.[21]

Drawing ironically on Thorstein Veblen's theory of 'conspicuous consumption', Brunsdon argues that 'the satellite dish has come to signify the conspicuous consumption of a certain kind of [taste] poverty', and she quotes one press commentator as observing that, in many cities, 'the way to tell the middle-class areas from the . . . [working class areas] is that the council houses all have satellite dishes'.[22] Indeed, subsequently, Murdoch's Sky channel, concerned that its down-market image was putting off potential advertisers, began to claim explicitly that it was *not* just 'council-house television', but also had things to offer to the more 'discerning' consumer. Nonetheless, estate agents continue to use the appearance of satellite dishes in a particular street as a worrying sign that the area is going 'down-market', and that house prices there are about to fall. Such abstract symbols of taste in media consumption can, it seems, also have very material consequences.

Of course, Brunsdon's analysis is specific to the particular cultural context of the UK in the period when she was writing. In other places, satellite dishes have come to symbolise quite different things: not so much 'taste poverty' as cultural sophistication in some parts of the Middle East; suspicious forms of unwanted 'Americanisation' in other contexts. In some parts of Europe, they have come to symbolise forms of 'cultural treason' against their 'host nation', through which migrant groups live out a virtual form of diasporic existence. However, if the specific context of the symbolism is culturally variable, the capacity of communication technologies to function in this symbolic mode is a constant – and important – dimension of their existence. If television is a visual medium, it is also one with a physical materiality all of its own and a wide range of symbolic functions, all of which, I suggest, should be given a more central place in the study of the medium.

## Deconstructing visual technologies in theory, video art and sculpture

I now want to develop this discussion further by returning to themes of Chapter 4, about the potential contribution of imaginative and artistic practices and methodologies to academic media research. Richard Dienst has argued that it is 'theory' which is best placed to dislodge television from its 'cozy nest of familiarity' and make it look strange again.[23] In response to this claim, John Hanhardt argues, on the basis of his own consideration of the conceptual sophistication and complexity of Nam June Paik's seemingly naive and playful techno-sculptures, that the work of video artists such as Paik (as of others such as Bill Viola) is also a crucial resource for the academic study of television. One of Viola's central interests is in video as a physical medium:

as he says, 'sitting . . . hearing sound and watching movement is a very physical experience', but one which most media theory downplays or ignores altogether.[24] As Hanhardt notes, many video artists have seen the possibilities of symbolically deconstructing the authority of television as a medium, by literally deconstructing the sanctity of the television set itself as an icon, broken up and then reconstructed in new ways, out of its own parts. Paik's specific approach has been to remove the television set from its familiar position within the home and to strip it of its traditional meaning as an object, prior to representing it for display in unfamiliar settings, as a 'container' for a range of both banal and exotic objects and as a source of either (deliberately) incomprehensible data or (literal) 'interference'.[25]

### Technology, media ecology and participation

Paik's work can usefully be seen in the context of theories and models of media ecology – not least because he himself claims that 'TV is the environment of today'.[26] In his work, he is concerned, among other things, to historicise the taken-for-granted forms in which we live out our technologically mediated environment. Thus his piece *Moon is the Oldest TV* (1965) makes reference to the period before electric light, when the moon and stars were the only sources of nightime light, whereas now, as he says, 'modern

*Figure 16* Nam June Paik, *Real Plant/Live Plant*. Reproduced by courtesy of the Museum of Contemporary Art, Tokyo.

life in big cities has almost extinguished this memory and the cold light of the domestic television set has replaced [that of] the moon'.[27]

Paik's approach to the understanding of contemporary forms of broadcast television shares much with that of Raymond Williams. In parallel with Williams's concept of 'mobile privatisation', Paik considers television viewers as 'stationary nomads' who routinely experience a paradoxical combination of a poverty of physical movement and an excess of visual stimulation.[28] Like Williams, Paik understands the consolidation of the institutional structures of broadcast television in the contemporary world to have determined the content and form of television technology as we have come to know it, in so far as television has come to be defined not as a creative tool for the use of the individual, but simply as a home-entertainment appliance.[29] To this extent, Paik considers conventional television to be a fundamentally oppressive institution given that 'the malaise of our time is the difficult balance in the relationship of input and output . . . we [in the USA] . . . subject ourselves to 40,000 TV commercials a year, but . . . can only afford to buy the goods extolled in 40 spots'.[30] Paik takes as his starting point the proposition that 'TV has attacked us for a lifetime, now we fight back', and in this context he is concerned to develop a kind of participatory television that turns the viewer into a user of the medium – most literally in his piece *Participation TV*, which invites the spectator to speak into a microphone programmed to create abstract displays of electronic imagery on the television monitor in response to the verbal input which it receives.

### Beyond futurism

Much of Paik's work is marked by a significant prescience concerning subsequent developments in communications technologies. Thus his *Silent TV* (1969), which transmits only 'mood art for highbrows', foreshadows by many years the later development of 'mood' channels on the satellite and cable channels of the 1980s and 1990s. His 1984 project *Good Morning Mr Orwell*, broadcast simultaneously in the USA, Canada, France, Germany and Korea, used Orwell's fable to suggest the inherent dangers of satellite television. Other 1980s works, such as *Tricolour Video* (1982) and *Video Flag* (1985), which used large-scale arrays of multiple monitors, showed remarkable foresight in relation to the subsequent development of commercial forms of visual display. These works 'pre-imagined' phenomena such as the commercial 'videowall', which are nowadays a commonplace of marketing/trade shows, as ways to display information in politicised and aestheticised public contexts, thus providing an ironic commentary on video display as one of the building blocks of the celebratory architecture of commercial culture.

However, Paik's work is not involved in any kind of simplistically futuristic perspective. In line with the approach developed by writers such as Bruno Latour to the hybrid forms of high technology, religion and magical belief systems that characterise so much of the contemporary so-called 'secularised' world, Paik deliberately mixes the high-tech with the icons of religiosity.[31] The connections here run deep, for as Paik himself observes, even the contemporary televisual concept of 'prime time' is itself derived from the originary notation of the Gregorian chant as 'prime service'.[32] Works such as *Television Cross* and the *My Faust* series (1989–91), which transposes the 'stations of the cross' of Christian iconography to the thirteen channels that could be selected on a New York television set at that time without access to cable, feature elements associated with religious traditions alongside those of modern design, so as to make up bizarre hybrids.[33] Thus, *My Faust* incorporates Gothic decorative forms of religious imagery from the design of medieval churches, alongside high-tech electronics in a 'neo-classical pastiche that celebrates culture as a new religion, with TV aerials and radio transmitters broadcasting culture to a new technological world'.[34]

### A subversive aesthetics of meta-communication

If television is too often seen as unexceptional and familiar, Paik aims to unsettle and dislodge our comfortable and uncritical view of the medium by developing a utopian, pastoral vision of the infinite possibilities of television technology, in some works gesturing towards a vision of a techno-ecological Eden. Paik's attitude to technology is a complex one, and in his œuvre he has produced what Schmidt describes as a 'technological anti-technology'.[35] This is best exemplified in his *Family of Robots* series, discussed in detail below, where, rather like an anthropologist of technology coming across a race of cyborgs from the future, he 'humanises' the media of television and radio by using them, literally, as the building blocks or 'body parts' out of which he creates his sculptural creatures and, by the same token, magically animates these (now 'anthropomorphicised') technologies.

Paik's project of turning television 'inside out' is motivated by a desire to create alternative forms of expression out of the technologies that routinely dominate our everyday lives. To this end, Paik continually breaks the 'frame' of television by playfully manipulating and breaking the engineered forms of the standardised moving-image culture. His sculptures often use the wooden cabinets of antique television sets from the 1940s and 1950s, removing their screens and insides and filling them instead with things such as live fishes, drawings, abstract electrical patterns or, in one case, a single candle, thus turning them into ironic, media-critical sculptures.[36] His rhetorical deployment of the television set itself as a sculptural metaphor works towards freeing it from its limiting corporate and technological yokes, treating the medium as a means to establish an expressive language that resists the restricted narrative tropes and image-making strategies of conventional television. In this endeavour, Paik 're-presents' the television set in unfamiliar settings and roles, in combination with a wide range of other media and materials. His fundamental aim is to 'break open the safe and secure representations of ourselves and the technological worlds we inhabit, so that we might understand them differently and transform them into something better'.[37]

Much of the force of Paik's work derives from the way it highlights the contrast between the solidity and longevity traditionally associated with the monumental traditions of sculpture and the transitory nature of the electronic images normally conveyed by the television sets out of which his sculptures are made. Thus, the substitution of real objects by 'Tele-Objects' in his work (from *TV Chair*, in its various guises, to *TV Glasses*) takes the endless flow of television images to its inevitable conclusion, in lack of attention and blindness. Against the single television image, Paik has a number of weapons including 'the axe of plurality, [and] the hammer of the tangible'. His almost megalomaniac piling up of television sets and radios in his sculptures is an

> expression of a sense of humour which is very literal, very down-to-earth and very violent; because the . . . proliferation of sets in Paik's installations re-enacts the . . . process of televisual saturation. In them, however, it is not the spirit or the eyes that are stuffed with images, but space itself that is stuffed with mountains of TV sets'.[38]

Paik's literal/sculptural approach and, in particular, his staging of the television set as an object to be looked at as well as through enacts a form of meta-communcation presaged in his early piece *EgoMachine* (1974), in which, by simply retitling an object – in this case a typewriter – he forces us to reconsider its function, in the style of a Duchampian 'ready-made'.[39] In an interview with Paik, O-Ryong Lee suggests to the artist (who does not demur) that

> most viewers . . . regard the TV set as something non-expressive . . . But from the meta-communication point of view, the television enacts itself by communicating the fact that 'I'm a TV set. I'm not a stereo-player, but a TV set.' Usually we don't acknowledge the presence of the TV set itself; we only do meta-communication with it when it's out of order . . . we don't . . . [ordinarily] bring meta-communication into the picture . . . we are more often than not just 'absorbed' by TV.

Finding ways to counter that 'absorption' is the essence of Paik's art.[40]

Paik can be seen as a 'terrorist of aesthetic expectations', destroying the normal functions of the television set and 're-channelling' its energies (and wiring) in search of more liberating and imaginative possibilities.[41] He has also, significantly, gone against the grain of the dominant techno-logic of the day by deliberately exploring the possibilities of deliberately 'low-fidelity' television in the face of the rarely questioned presumption that a high-fidelity image is, per se, 'better'. In defence of this approach, in his characteristically *faux-naïf* manner, Paik simply refers to the enormous significance in the history of painting of the intervention of impressionism, in matters of visual representation. More than a century after Monet, the prevalent assumption that the high-fidelity exactitude fetishised by the developers of the new visual technologies is necessarily the prime virtue in matters of representational aethetics is thus shown to be, in fact, a curiously retrograde approach.[42]

Paik's characteristic strategy of aesthetic 'interruption' or subversion is well demonstrated in his *Waiting for Commercials* of 1971, in which a performance of classical music is interrupted every few bars, so that advertisements can be shown. Similarly, in *Global Groove* (1973), in a television system where seconds are sold for thousands of pounds, Paik's commentary to the video's luscious imagery recommends viewers not to look at the screen, but to close their eyes and listen to the gentle music, as if they were back in the age of radio.[43] This almost sacrilegious instruction is designed precisely to negate the normal modality of television's visual form of expression.[44] Similarly, in *Rembrandt Automatic* (1963) the television set is switched on, but its screen is placed face-down on the floor, so the 'denial' of the image (leaving only the sound and the flickering light seeping out at the edges of the screen) radically alters the viewer's customary relation to the set.[45] By this method, the act of looking and observing associated with television-viewing is once again foregrounded as a way of exploring the fundamental properties of the medium. In each case, Paik's 'subversions' work as meta-communications, which focus our attention on the taken-for-granted formal and aesthetic premises on which the institution of broadcast television is founded.[46]

### Robot families

*Family of Robots* (reproduced on my cover) is perhaps Paik's most developed sequence of work and the one with the most pertinence for my broader concerns. In that sequence of anthropomorphic techno-sculptures (1986), Paik constructs an extended family group of figures made from television and radio sets of different ages. Each figure is different: the grandfather has a central pot-bellied screen, while the mother has large hips and antennae and the father a large head containing miniature television 'eyes'. The baby who, by contrast, is built from modern aluminium sets, poses playfully on an enormous, defunct old television cabinet.[47] Each robot in the group displays generational characteristics: thus, the 'grandparents' have as heads old-fashioned radio sets, indicating that they 'live in the past', whereas the parents' heads are made from new sets, as they look confidently into the future.[48] Here the design of the antique sets, which were understood in their own times as crucial elements of modernity or 'objects of the future', comes to look, in the context in which Paik inserts them, rather 'dated' and even nostalgic, thus exposing, among other things, the rapid rate of transformation that these technologies undergo.[49] As Hanhardt observes, 'the robots are constructed with the industrial remains of mass media history; the antique televisions and radios . . . embody the expansion and consolidation of the broadcast industry'. As I argued earlier, not only did the radio console serve as the prototype for the design of the television set, but the spread of the radio receiver into the American home became the model for the later consolidation of network television. Thus, in these sculptures, the variety of television and radio receivers of different ages and styles of which the different robots are constructed 'adds a layer of history and nostalgia to the structuring of the objects, to suggest the expressive mannerisms, gender, age and personalities of the figures'.[50]

These are not robots that induce fear, but robots with a loveable, antiquated charm – not least because they are made out of materials, such as domestic television sets, which are thoroughly familiar to us. Many people watch television every day at home; we also record our own family lives on videos which we subsequently replay on these same domestic sets. For all these reasons, the rather quirky members of the *Family of Robots* series hold none of the terrors of the invented monsters of earlier times – and their charm is enhanced by the fact that they seem also to have found their 'own kind' and become a loving extended family of a type which is rather familiar to us – almost as if they were our not-so-distant cyber-relatives.[51] From this perspective, Paik can best be seen as a kind of 'video ethnographer' documenting, in an imaginary and metaphorical style, the changing relations of the contemporary family to its domestic technologies. These issues of technological symbolism are ones to which I now turn in relation to the new technologies of our day.

## Notes

1 John Ellis (1982) *Visible Fictions*. London: Methuen, p. 162.
2 R. Barthes (1977) 'Upon Leaving the Movie Theatre', in his *Image-Music-Text*. London: Fontana, p. 38.
3 Ellis, ibid., p.160.
4 See R. Williams (1974) *Television, Technology and Cultural Form*. London: Methuen.

5   Quoted in William Boddy (1984) 'The Shining Centre of the Home: The Ontology of Television', paper to International Television Studies Conference, London, p. 10.

6   L. Spigel (1986) 'Ambiguity and Hesitation: Television and the Housewife', paper to International Television Studies Conference, London, 1986; L. Spigel (1992) *Make Room for Television*. Chicago, Ill.: University of Chicago Press; see also M. Haralovich (1988) 'Suburban Family Sitcoms and Consumer Product Design', in P. Drummond and R. Paterson (eds) *Television and its Audiences*. London: British Film Institute.

7   Quoted in Boddy, ibid., p. 10.

8   M. Geller (ed.) (1990) *From Receiver to Remote Control: The Television Set*. New York: New Museum of Contemporary Art, p. 7. See also Paik, below, on this.

9   M. Lavin (1990) 'Television Design', in M. Geller (ed.) *From Receiver to Remote Control: The Television Set*. New York: New Museum of Contemporary Art, pp. 85, 89.

10  Conrad, quoted in K. Robins and F. Webster (1986) 'Broadcasting Politics', *Screen* 27 (3–4).

11  S. Bathrick (1990), 'Mother as television Guide', in M. Geller (ed.) *From Receiver to Remote Control: The Television Set*. New York: New Museum of Contemporary Art; Spigel, ibid.

12  Spigel (1990) 'The Domestic Gaze', in M. Geller (ed.) *From Receiver to Remote Control: The Television Set*. New York: New Museum of Contemporary Art, p. 12.

13  Quoted in Jane Root (1985) *Open the Box*. London: Comedia, p. 39.

14  E. Long (1990) 'A Member of the Family', in M. Geller (ed.) *From Receiver to Remote Control: The Television Set*. New York: New Museum of Contemporary Art, p. 53. See also my comments in Chapter 7 on the domestic 'journey' of the phone and in Chapter 8 on Anna McCarthy's work on 'ambient television'.

15  Ondina Leal (1990) 'Popular Taste and Erudite Repertoire: The Place and Space of Television in Brazil', *Cultural Studies* 4.

16  Leal, ibid., pp. 21, 23.

17  James Lull's work on television-viewing in China shows the same patterns of television placement in poor homes: see James Lull (ed.) (1988) *World Families Watch Television*. London: Sage, and James Lull (1995) *China Turned On*. London: Routledge.

18  Humphrey Spender, describing 'Mass Observation' work in Bolton in 1937, in *The Long Summer: Linos and Lightbulbs*, TX Channel 4, May 1993.

19  Tim O'Sullivan (1991) 'Television Memories and Cultures of Viewing 1950–65', in J. Corner (ed.) *Popular Television in Britain*. London: British Film Institute. See also my comments on Shunya Yoshimi's work on television in Japan in Chapters 8 and 9.

20  Charlotte Brunsdon (1991) 'Satellite Dishes and the Landscapes of Taste', *New Formations* 15: 38.

21  *London Evening Standard*, 12 July 1989, quoted in Brunsdon, ibid., p. 26.

22  Leith, quoted in Brunsdon, ibid., p. 33; T. Veblen (1889) *The Theory of the Leisure Class*, New York.

23  Richard Dienst, (1994) *Still Life in Real Time: Theory After Television*, Durham, MC: Duke University Press; quoted in John in Hanhardt, (2001) *The Worlds of Nam June Paik*. New York: Guggenheim Museum, p. 248.

24  Viola quoted in Chris Darke (1993), p. 26.

25  John Handardt (1990) 'The Anti-Television', in M. Geller (ed.) *From Receiver to Remote Control: The Television Set*. New York: New Museum of Contemporary Art, p. 113.

26  John Hanhardt (2000) *The Worlds of Nam June Paik*. New York: Guggenheim Museum p. 107.

27  Paik quoted by Han-Werner Schmidt (1993) 'Anti-thesis and Sandwich', in Toni Stooss and Thomas Kellein (eds) *Nam June Paik: Video Time – Video Space*. New York: Harry Abrams Publishers, p. 91; see also Wolfgang Schivelbusch's historical work on the transformation of the nineteenth-century city by the coming of the electric light in his (1995) *Disenchanted Night: The Industrialisation of Light in the Nineteenth Century*. Berkeley, Calif.: University of California Press.

28  Toni Stooss (1993) 'Notes on an Exhibition', in Toni Stooss and Thomas Kellein (eds) *Nam June Paik: Video Time – Video Space*. New York: Harry Abrams Publishers, p. 12.

29  John Hanhardt (1993) 'Non-Fatal Strategies', in Toni Stooss and Thomas Kellein (eds) *Nam June Paik: Video Time – Video Space*. New York: Harry Abrams Publishers, p. 79; see R. Williams, ibid., 1974.

30  Wolfgang Dreschler (1993) 'Sonatine for Goldfish', in Toni Stooss and Thomas Kellein (eds) *Nam June Paik: Video Time – Video Space*. New York: Harry Abrams Publishers, p. 48.

31  Park quoted in Stooss, ibid., 17. See the concluding chapter for my discussion of Latour's work

32  Paik (1993) 'Sixtina Electronica', in Toni Stooss and Thomas Kellein (eds) *Nam June Paik: Video Time – Video Space*. New York: Harry Abrams Publishers, p. 76.

33  Edith Decker (1993) 'Hardware', in Toni Stooss and Thomas Kellein (eds) *Nam June Paik: Video Time – Video Space*. New York: Harry Abrams Publishers, p. 70.

34  Hanhardt, 2001, ibid., pp. 154, 161, 181.

35  Schmidt, ibid., p. 89

36  Wolfgang Herzogenrath (1988) *Nam June Paik*. London: Hayward Gallery, p. 27.

37  Hanhardt, 2000, ibid., pp. 213, 231.

38  Paul-Emmanuel Odin (1993) 'Stasis and Ecstasy: On Paik the Invincible', in Toni Stooss and Thomas Kellein (eds) *Nam June Paik: Video Time – Video Space*. New York: Harry Abrams Publishers, p. 130.

39  Hanhardt, 2000, ibid., p. 29.

40  O-Ryong Lee (1993) 'The Art of Communication', in Toni Stooss and Thomas Kellein (eds) *Nam June Paik: Video Time – Video Space*. New York: Harry Abrams Publishers, p. 128.

41  Alan Kaprow (1993) 'Nam June Paik', in Toni Stooss and Thomas Kellein (eds) *Nam June Paik: Video Time – Video Space*. New York: Harry Abrams Publishers, p. 114.

42  Douglas Davis (1993) 'Electronic Wallpaper', in Toni Stooss and Thomas Kellein

(eds) *Nam June Paik: Video Time – Video Space*. New York: Harry Abrams Publishers, p. 119.

43 See also Paik's *The Best Television is No Television at All*.
44 Schmidt, ibid., p. 89.
45 Hanhardt, 2001, ibid., p. 35.
46 Herzogenrath, ibid., p. 15.
47 Nicky Hamlyn (1988) 'The Far Side of the Screen', *The Guardian*, 10 October.
48 Herzogenrath, ibid., p. 27.
49 See Sunya Yoshimi, 'The Three Sacred Things', ibid.
50 Hanhardt, 2000, ibid., pp. 175–180.
51 Herzogenrath, ibid., p. 29.

# 10  Magical technologies

## The new, the shiny and the symbolic

As we have seen earlier, conventional approaches to the study of technology often leave much to be desired, not least in their exclusive focus on the supposedly rational functions of technology. That perspective tends to make a simplistic equation of modernity with rational efficiency, science and technology and to neglect all the symbolic dimensions of contemporary technologies. An alternative starting point, in this respect, is offered by the work of Hermann Bausinger in the neglected field of ethnology, which in the UK probably equates most nearly to the equally neglected field of 'folk studies'. Bausinger's *Folk Culture in a World of Technology* was first published in Germany in 1961, but was not translated into English until 1990 and is still little known in the English-speaking academic world. His central argument is that, in fact, folk culture is alive and well in modern technological society, which is why he argues that what we need is a *Volkskunde* of the present, if we are to understand all the important continuities between traditional society and modernity.[1]

Bausinger's further argument is that the first thing we must avoid is the deeply misleading binary division in which much social-scientific work remains trapped to this day, whereby the rational, secular, fast-changing, technological world of 'modernity' is opposed to the ritualistic, static irrational world of 'traditional society'.[2] In the British context, his work has strong parallels both with that of the musicologist A.L. Lloyd, who traced the extent to which traditions of folk song and storytelling, far from having died out with the passing of agrarian society, remain a vital part of industrial culture, and also with the contemporary work on folk cultures of artist/ethnographers such as Jeremy Deller.[3]

The key point here is that traditional societies were never static, not least because a static tradition dies very quickly if it fails to adapt to the changing context around it. This is perhaps best exemplified by the (apocryphal) story of an anthropologist in West Africa in the 1960s, who was asked how he might discriminate between authentic 'living' traditions of tribal dance and those which had been instrumentally reinvented by the local state as tourist attractions. His reply was that it was a relatively easy matter to distinguish these two phenomena, as it all depended on whether the dancer's costumes used modern zip fasteners or 'traditional' ones made of leather bands and animal teeth. In his view, given their greater convenience, only those who used zip fasteners could be understood to be part of a living tradition, whereas the fetishistic use of the supposedly 'traditional' (but less convenient) fastenings made of of leather and teeth, was clearly an indication of inauthenticity. In relation to the incorporation of 'foreign' materials such as PVC piping or disused electric wiring in traditional art forms, Laura Mulvey rightly notes the 'ease with which native peoples [have taken up] and made use of the new materials and technologies' that arrived in their country from elsewhere.[4]

*Figure 17* Woman in hill village in Northern Thailand weavng traditional cloth, while herself wearing a Benetton T-shirt. Photo by Alice Cartner-Morley, 1998.

Contemporary African tourist art often appropriates the signs of modern technology as a form of simulation of the wealth, progress and mastery that it represents. Thus, ritualistic objects are often adorned with the artefacts of Western technology: watches, mirrors, car spare parts and sunglasses. In this connection, Benetta Jules-Rosette observes 'in the case of the "Mama Wati" cult in Nigeria, one may well find, on an altarplace, a carved pole with a string attached, representing the telephone line used by the Spirit Goddess to communicate with her worshippers'.[5] Thus, it is also common to find images of automobiles, aeroplanes, telephones or even computers carved in wood in 'traditional' styles. In this process of cultural translation, although the objects are often tinged with a certain pathos, as Jules-Rosette observes, they nonetheless are designed to convey an aura of progress and change. Indeed, in a certain sense, these fetishistic images promise the 'powers that technology bestows without any of its limitations. Wooden telephones and radios do not need to be repaired'.[6] Conversely, one could argue that the endless process of 'upgrading' in which many users of the latest technologies in the affluent world are engaged is no less magical. They are often unable to fully utilise all the functions on their existing mobile phone or laptop and their desire for the 'upgraded' version is perhaps best understood as a desire to possess the magical qualities associated with 'newness'.

The point that tradition is not be confused with some static realm of 'heritage' which must be defended against all change is well made by the journalist David Aaronovich when he notes how ironic he found it when his computer asked him whether he wanted to 'save' the changes he had made to the piece he was writing on the fluid and ever-changing nature of tradition. As Jimmie Durham puts it, traditions exist and are guided by conventions, the most important of which is dynamism as mode of response to constant change in the environment – thus, 'adaptability and the inclusion of the new ways and new materials *is* a tradition'. The point is also exemplified by the British folk musician Kathryn Ticknell, who explains that on her traditional Northumbrian pipes, their bellows are now connected to the 'chanter' pipes by what she describes as the 'traditional piece of washing machine rubber hose' as that is more convenient and efficient for the purpose than any older material.[7]

## New technologies for old purposes

Even the very latest technologies can always be adapted – or domesticated – to suit very traditional purposes. The most popular web site in the UK is now Friends Reunited, which, as its name implies, allows people to refind old friends from their schooldays – clearly a fundamentally nostalgic project, even if in 'high-tech' form. By 2003, the site already had 8 million members

– rather more than the number of those who belong to trade unions or attend church each week in the UK.[8] The web sites now set up by Turkish migrants across Europe for the purpose of facilitating 'arranged marriages' demonstrate the same capacity of old traditions to recruit new technologies to their purposes. Similarly, many young Muslims in the UK now use the Internet as a virtual, safe (and crucially, so far as their community is concerned, 'respectable') way to get round traditional proscriptions on meeting members of the

*Figure 18* Hassidic Jewish man using mobile phone at the 'Wailing Wall'. Photo by Menahem Kahana, Agence France Press. Courtesy of Getty Images.

other sex in an unsupervised manner, before marriage, via web sites such as muslimmatch.com and muslim-marriages.co.uk. New technologies such as the mobile phone can also serve to sustain the most traditional relationships, as witnessed by evidence that at the New Year celebrations in the UK in 2003, mobile-phone users overloaded the whole system, almost to breaking point, by sending each other 120 million traditional New Year greetings in text-message format.[9]

New technologies such as the mobile phone have also readily incorporated religious uses: Catholics can subscribe to a service that brings them a daily message from the Pope at noon each day, and Muslims can download an Islamic ringtone of 'All Praise to Allah' or programme their phone to provide them with a regular '*salaat* alert', reminding them when it is time to pray.[10] Thomas Friedman's book *The Lexus and the Olive Tree* features a striking photo of a Hassidic Jew pressing his mobile phone up against the stones of the Wailing Wall in Jerusalem, with the caption 'Shimon Biton places his cellular phone up to the Western Wall so a relative in France can say a prayer at the holy site'.[11]

Evidently, it is not only the mobile phone that can be used for traditional religious uses. Thus, Reuters recently reported that in China, while paper models of mobiles were now often burnt along with other symbolic offerings to dead ancestors, citizens there also burned virtual candles, sent digital flowers and engaged in various forms of 'internet mourning' in on-line cemeteries on Qing Ming Tomb-Sweeping Day.[12] Clearly, in this context, any conception of a static realm of tradition, which is then transformed by new technologies, will be unhelpful here; rather, we need a conception of how living traditions incorporate new technologies.

## Anthropological perspectives: fetishism and totemism

In trying to understand how we live and work with technologies, the last thing we should do is to make the mistake of imagining that media and communications technologies are desired, consumed and used simply for their functional purposes, increasingly 'marvellous' as these may appear. As we saw earlier, everything that the anthropology of material consumption tells us indicates that, beyond their practical uses, communications technologies often have symbolic meanings that make them also function as powerful totems and fetishes for their owners. As I argued earlier, this is demonstrated by O'Sullivan's work on the television set as a signifier of modernity in the discourse of the 1950s in the UK; nowadays, the computer often performs a similar function. Material objects such as mobile phones, portable MP3 players, iPods and laptop computers can thus be seen as the totems of today's 'technotribes'. The issues at stake were satirised by the

Dutch artist known as Pii in his exhibition in London in 2005, which featured bronze models of laptop computers filled with genetically modified grain and a surrogate iPod carved out of wood. The artist claimed that his 'PiiPod' not only potentially solved the problem of MP3-related muggings and the risk of deafness by being 'specifically designed to be unable to play music and sound files' but still delivered its user with the required 'style-fix' by producing a visible bulge, the exact size of an iPod in its carrier's pocket.[13]

The point about the power of technological symbolism was also well grasped by the Taliban government in Afghanistan, when they hung television sets from the trees, as a potent symbol of the unwanted 'Westernisation' of their country. However, as the iPod example demonstrates, this is clearly not only a matter of strange cultural practices in 'primitive' places. In their studies of Western owners of video and DVD or laser-disc collections, both Uma Dinsmore and Barabara Klinger have demonstrated how the significance of these collections far exceeds that of the simple opportunities they might be thought to provide for the rewatching of the films and has rather more to do with the construction of the collector's identity (for instance, as person of discerning tastes – evidenced by the presence, within one's collection, of the requisite 'classics') or the making of a statement about their self-image and cultural tastes and aspirations ('these are the films I value, and from my selection of them you can see what kind of person I am').

Drawing both on Benjamin's essay on the 'thrill of acquisition' and the enchantment of the 'magic circle' constituted by any private library or book collection, and on Baudrillard's comments on the 'passion for private property' in the realm of everyday objects, Klinger traces the various dimensions of satisfaction available to the avid collector. This may take the form of seeming to enter the secret, behind-the-scenes world of film-making itself and thus becoming party to the forms of 'insider knowledge' imparted by the 'Special Edition' or 'Director's Cut' of a particular film, or the more technophiliac pleasures of the hardware aesthetic which fetishises questions of film ratio transfers and soundtrack quality. In either case, the pleasures of the film's content or meaning are only part of the story for the members of the growing band of 'serious collectors' whose collections are thus infused with powerful forms of personal magic.[14]

## Technological symbolism: the television, the encyclopaedia and the computer

In their collection on the contemporary uses of technology, Silverstone and Hirsch make the essential point that we need to see the significance of technologies in modern society as 'symbolic as well as material objects . . . crucially embedded in the structures and dynamics of contemporary consumer culture'. If this is true of all objects, nonetheless it may still be the case that at different historical stages, it is particular technologies that carry the symbolic function of being what Barthes once called 'the superlative object' of their time.[15] In this respect, Barthes nominated the car as being the superlative object of the 1950s. As we know, in many countries, domestically it has been the triumvirate of the television set, the fridge and the washing machine that have carried this symbolic burden, and we might perhaps think of the digital technologies of our age as their contemporary equivalents.

In parallel with Spigel's work on the history of television's entry to the North American home and O'Sullivan's work on television in the UK, Shunya Yoshimi has investigated the crucial symbolic role played by the acquisition of television in the development of post-war consumer cultures in Japan.[16] Yoshimi traces the history of the *Seikatu Kaizen* campaign for a 'better standard of living' in Japan in the early twentieth century, which brought together ideas of social transformation derived from the Russian Revolution with Western-influenced notions of technological innovation and rationalisation derived from Fordism. In the post-Second World War period, the emphasis of these campaigns moved from their initial focus on industrial production to the use of electrical appliances in the domestic sphere. In this context, in the 1950s, this movement drew on the traditional symbolism of the *Sanshu no Jingi* (The Three Sacred Treasures) of the Japanese Emperor – sword, jewels and mirror – transposing them, domestically, into the triptych of the black-and-white television, the washing machine and the refrigerator, as the sacred treasures in the symbolic repertoire of Japanese consumer culture in this later period. Of course, such a discourse must be, by definition, historically mobile. More recently, the Japanese trade press has featured articles announcing that the new 'Three Sacred Treasures' of the digital era are now the plasma-screen colour television, the DVD recorder and the digital camera – a phenomenon which clearly is by no means specific only to Japan.[17]

In earlier times, knowledge was often symbolised by encyclopaedias, which were, in the UK at least, often sold door to door, especially in poorer areas, where people with less formal education lived, as a form of knowledge for sale. The domestic possession of an encyclopaedia – especially a prestigious one such as the *Encyclopaedia Britannica* – then functioned as a sign that 'knowledge' had entered a particular house, at least in appearance (or self-image) and that its inhabitants were thus 'saved' from ignorance. This is complex territory, for one of the primary functions of such an encyclopaedia was that of display, sitting proudly in its leather-bound casings on the family's bookshelf in the best room, where it might be admired by visitors. This function was in fact performed quite satisfactorily even if none of the family members ever actually consulted its pages, despite their best intentions in the matter. At that time, print technology still enjoyed privilege as the accepted form of materialisation of knowledge – especially in the form of hard-bound books. Moreover, the *Encyclopaedia Britannica* enjoyed a particular status, based on the historically important role of Britain and its empire in the spreading of scientific knowledge and 'civilisation' throughout the world. Nowadays, neither the status of print nor of Britain are what they were, and the status of bound sets of the *Britannica* has declined accordingly.

As for the way in which Britain's historical decline reflected on the status of the *Encyclopaedia Britannica*, Karim Raslan remembers the day when, as a child, a wooden crate containing its twenty-three volumes was deposited outside his house in Kuala Lumpur. He recalls that 'the fat burgundy-coloured volumes were *America* for me' (emphasis added). Raslan found the name of the encyclopaedia perplexing: 'Britannica . . . but not British', as his mother explained, it was definitely not now British, though it had been once. He also recalls that later he wondered how he could ever have made such a mistake: 'there was no way that something as vast and comprehensive and all-encompassing as the encyclopaedia could have come from England . . . England was just too tired . . . small, quaint and tradition-bound'.[18]

Naturally, the *Britannica*'s producers are also alive to the difficulties of the decline in prestige of print and are working hard to remarket it in computerised form, given that it is those technologies, rather than those of print, which are now felt to be the proper enshrinement of the latest forms of scientific knowledge. Indeed, in recent years, it has been computers that have been sold domestically as the key technology of access to knowledge. In the context of powerful public discourses about the importance of computer literacy in saving children from the wrath of the gods of unemployability, the computer has thus displaced the encyclopaedia as the principal domestic symbol of knowledge – regardless, again, of how and for what purposes, other than playing electronic games, it might actually be used.[19]

Thus I recently received from British Telecom, addressed to my home, an invitation to constitute, in effect, a private school (complete with embossed crest) at my own address, by subscribing to BT's own broadband educational service. Simply by plugging in to this technology, the marketing documentation made clear, I could immediately solve my children's educational problems as 'children are likely to do better when you make learning more enjoyable – and nothing makes learning fun like Broadband from BT'. The leaflet confidently claimed that by this method, my children would have 'instant access to the knowledge they need, when they need it', and the technology apparently has the magical (if to my mind, slightly puzzling) powers to 'make geometry exciting – by downloading films of the pyramids'. Evidently, all this relies on a rather simplistic pedagogical theory, but the symbolic appeal of the modernisation of the dull business of gaining knowledge, by converting it into a series of 'edutainment' games played on the latest technology, has a clear market appeal – perhaps most of all in homes where the parents themselves lack educational capital and feel that an expenditure of this kind is a simple way to remedy that lack for their children. Such attitudes are by no means restricted to the UK: in some parts of China, it seems that it is increasingly desirable for a house to have a special room (or at least place) devoted to the computer, where it can be shown off as a symbol of the household's achievements (or aspirations), even if the parents who bought it for their children themselves know nothing of how it works.

## Mobile symbols and icons of mobility

Of all the technical objects of our era, it is perhaps the mobile phone that currently carries the heaviest symbolic burden. Evidently this is not unrelated to the fact that the device, in its more sophisticated versions, is indeed fast becoming the hub of much of our electronic communications – not just for phone calls and text messages, but for access to e-mail and other computer-enabled activities such as finding your way round a strange city via GPS systems. However, the mobile phone clearly performs many symbolic as well as practical functions. It is not only the most expensive object ever to be routinely carried about the person in modern, affluent societies, but it is also itself an 'icon of the new' as Jon Agar puts it.[20]

In the same way that, as we have seen earlier, the video or DVD collection says things about its owner so, inevitably, do other possessions and technologies that we use. Nowadays, a person's mobile phone may well sport a decorative sticker, and, by means of its particular style (plain, silver, unadorned and business-like, or with customised fascia and pop-star pendant), even when not in use, the mobile phone already communicates the particular cultural identity which its owner has chosen for themselves, by means of which they wish to distinguish themselves from others. As Negroponte recognises, the mobile phone can now be expected to have a 'personality' which makes the device seem not only useful but also 'entertaining, relaxing, user-friendly and less . . . [merely] mechanical'.[21]

This is well illustrated in the work of the photographer Martin Parr who, in his *Phone Book* has documented the particular ways in which the mobile phone is used in a variety of different global contexts (how it is displayed or hidden, the characteristic poses and culturally variable ways of standing or walking adopted while using it, as well as the many possible ways of customising or decorating it). In a similar vein, Larissa Hjorth has made a study of the 'customised' decoration of mobile phones in Japan among young people, who personalise their phones by means of a variety of decorative attachments – from commercial 'character mascots' to natural objects such as feathers and pebbles. Such matters are clearly complex, thus Hjorth explores the way in which, at the time of her study, there was a fashion among young Japanese lesbians of attaching to their phones *kawaii* (cute) symbols, such as 'Hello Kitty', which are conventionally dismissed as the height of conformist *kitsch* culture, but which, in the particular subcultural context she studied, were well understood to represent a rather more complex public message about the sexuality of the phone's owner.[22]

The mobile phone has often functioned in recent times as a powerful symbol of its owner's status: 'a glamorous show-and-tell of power and efficiency'. Thus, the early mobile phones of the period themselves came to symbolise the 1980s ethos of competition, so that 'the brick-like cell phone clasped to the ear became part of the conspicuous consumption exhibited by the City high-flier . . . one of . . . the trappings of the yuppy'.[23] In Ghana, it has been reported that the mobile phone is such an essential symbol of status, especially among poorer groups, that they will make great financial sacrifices in other respects and go to great lengths to have one, even when living on the most meagre of budgets, and when they absolutely cannot get one, they are likely to walk the streets with a dummy phone in their hand, rather than be seen to be without one. Conversely, in an affluent society such as Finland, matters can work out in a different way; thus, after the initial rush of enthusiasm for mobile phones in the mid-1990s, by the late 1990s, it had become an inverse status marker among some fashionable groups in Helsinki to be seen in public without one.[24]

However, as Olalquiaga notes, the mobile phone, like all symbols, is also vulnerable to processes of what she calls cultural cannibalism. Thus, she recounts, during one of the worst telecommunications crises in Venezuela's recent history, in the early 1990s, at a point when no one could affectively make phone calls at all and the mobile was functionally useless, many women (especially of low status) who would not have been able to afford a mobile themselves, took to carrying mobile-phone-shaped handbags as a fashion accessory. As she observes, in this gesture, the mobile phone as the 'state-of-the-art icon of the moment', which in Venezuela at that time was largely the preserve of affluent men, but now 'lacking all meaningful connection to the apparatus of production and exchange and therefore reduced to an electronically impotent carcass' was lampooned by its humorous degradation into 'that object of constant male derision, women's handbags'. At times, such processes of cultural cannibalism can also take on a more explicitly political dimension. Thus, in China, as Rey Chow argues, the Walkman has sometimes functioned as symbol of private withdrawal and dissent from the regulated public space of a totalitarian society.[25]

However, beyond this kind of detailed study of the specific symbolisms in play in particular cultural contexts, there may also be more general statements that we can make about the specific type of technological objects that best symbolise the values of a particular time. Zygmunt Bauman has argued that, in the current period of what he calls 'Liquid Modernity', we see a quite particular symbolic logic in play, in which portable or miniaturised technologies play a crucial role. As he puts it, 'fluidity is [now] the principal source of strength and invincibility . . . it is now the smaller, the lighter, the more portable that signifies improvement and progress'.[26] His point is well exemplified by a British television advert for the latest generation of mobile phones, which also features a phone of the older generation, which can no longer be taken out, precisely because its clumsy appearance now makes it an embarrassment for its owner.

Of course, once one recognises that mobile phones operate not only according to techno-logic but also in the realms of the symbolic, then it comes as no surprise that the primary dynamics of the fashion industry also come into play – by which means, last season's avant-garde may well be trumped by this season's retro-fashion. Thus, in a similar process of symbolic inversion to that of those Finns who marked their avant-garde status by their refusal to carry a mobile phone, some fashionable young New Yorkers have constructed visibly 'retro' mobile phones for themselves which are, by today's standards, both evidently over-sized, clumsy and old-fashioned. These fans of retro-technology thus ironically declare their symbolic 'distinction' by cannibalising bits of 'old' technology (an old-fashioned handset attached to the body a new mobile or, less ambitiously, an old-fashioned ringtone on a new mobile) in a highly visible mode of symbolic display of 'analogue chic' which nicely undercuts the presumptions of technological neophilia.[27]

## The mobile phone: the ultimately desirable object, or the last talisman of order?

In one sense, we might say that the mobile phone is now what, in McLuhan's terms, the car was in an earlier period: 'an article of dress without which we feel uncertain, unclad and incomplete in the urban environment'.[28] George Myerson argues that 'the mobile is the object which most closely embodies the spirit of the changing environment. If you want to assure yourself that you belong to the new century, this is the object to have in your hand'. Timo Kopomaa pushes the point further, arguing that the mobile phone has now acquired a particularly important symbolic role for many of its users to the extent that it should be understood, he argues, as 'a portable magic charm'. To this extent we might even think of the mobile phone as the contemporary equivalent of the St Christopher's medallion which Christian travellers, in earlier times, wore round their necks as a talisman to ward off evil.[29]

The correlative of the mobile phone's contemporary importance is, of course, the consequent 'trauma' that owners sometimes feel when they lose their phone. Many users have all their personal data and contact numbers stored on their phone, so its loss can clearly represent a significant inconvenience. Indeed, this is a feature that the makers' advertising now plays upon in adverts such as that by the Orange network warning against the dangers of phone theft, which shows a distraught woman's face in the moment of realisation that, when her phone was stolen from her car, 'She'd lost 97 friends in the car park'.[30] Just as one of Bull's respondents observes that she feels 'lost if I don't have my phone with me', a Mintel survey of young people in the UK in 2004 reported that many of them 'looked on their phone as kind of security blanket, feeling lost without it'. Another survey reports that 'Britain's teenagers can't bear to be without their mobile phones – without them they feel isolated and unpopular'.[31] In the UK there has even been some concern about the number of teenagers now suffering mild forms of sleep deprivation, as their compulsion not to lose contact with their electronic peers leads them to leave their phones on all night and the beeps of the incoming text messages, which they do in fact receive during the night, disrupt their rest. Even more graphically, a Home Office study of young offenders in prison in the UK found that for them not to have a mobile phone was felt to be one of the most painful forms of social deprivation: 'For the boys, phones were an indispensable crutch. Their loss of phones in custody was said to be one of the worst elements of the deprivation of liberty', because it represented the loss of a technology which, for them was equated directly with 'freedom' itself.[32]

However, it is by no means only young people to whom such anxieties apply. People who have lost their phones often speak a medicalised discourse of trauma, even melodramatically comparing the loss of their phone to the loss of a limb. A report of the incident in France in the autumn of 2004 in which the technical failure of one of its mobile networks deprived people of their calls and text messages for twenty-four hours described the country as being 'plunged into techno-shock'. Such a description might perhaps seem overly exaggerated, but it well captures the degree of distress clearly felt by this thirty-two-year-old banker, quoted in the report: 'At first I thought that I had lost all my friends at once. No calls. No text messages . . . . Then I saw the blank screen on my phone, and I realised that something even more dreadful had happened. I was cut off from the world'.[33]

People's dependency on the facility the mobile phone offers for being in 'perpetual contact' is certainly striking. Thus, it is a common sight, at the end of even short flights, to see airline passengers grabbing for their phones in unison, as soon as a plane lands and the use of mobiles is once again permitted, in a touching ritual of the restoration of their electronic 'connexity', which far transcends the urgency of such messages as they might reasonably have expected to receive during the brief period when their phone was compulsorily switched off. In his report on his 'sabbatical' week of going 'cold turkey' and trying to wean himself from being 'electronically dependent modern man', the writer Howard Jacobson describes the irrational surge of panic he feels as he reaches in his pocket for his normally ever-present mobile phone, only to discover that, for once, it is not there. By the end of the week, unable to invigorate his life with the regular electronic 'boosts' on which he, like so many others, has come to depend, he describes himself as 'feeling existentially alone' and is troubled by the sense that he is experiencing 'a premonition of the silence of death, when all the phones stop altogether'.[34] If Jacobson's account is melodramatic, it nonetheless captures an important part of the everyday experience of the multitude of 'twitchers' and 'crackberries' of our times, who feel compelled to constantly check their electronic devices for messages and who feel quite at a loss without the psychic reassurance with which these devices supply them.

One particularly striking measure of the mobile phone's symbolic significance in contemporary British culture is the fact that it has now replaced the umbrella as the single item most frequently left behind on London Underground trains. This is a particularly interesting phenomenon, as at the time of this research there was no effective network coverage on most of the Underground, so these phones were left behind by people who had felt compelled to have them to hand, even when they could not use them for any practical purpose.[35] The journalist Michael Bywater perhaps best captures the emotional resonance of the mobile when he avers that he has

> tucked away in my mind, an inchoate image of the Ultimately Desirable Object: the size of a cigarette case, made of platinum, satellite communications, two months' battery life, international roaming, full graphics, digital recording, voice-activated, it will close with a Rolls-Royce clunk, slip into my breast pocket, and never leave me. With it by my side, I will be at home anywhere on the planet. What will it do? Don't be silly. What it will do is make everything alright.

However, if Bywater and Myerson and Kopomaa well capture the everyday talismanic function of the mobile phone, in situations of genuine emergency, the mobile phone's function, in this respect, emerges all the more starkly. In the wake of the central London bombings in July 2005, one source reported the sight of everybody . . . talking; sometimes to each other, mostly to their loved ones on their mobiles . . . Even those who weren't speaking on their mobiles were holding them in their hands, expecting them to ring, waiting for a signal, or just a talisman of the idea of order, of the idea that this last electronic totem of technology and civilisation would lead them through [this] rude intrusion of chaos.[36]

## Notes

1 Hermann Bausinger (1990) *Folk Culture in a World of Technology*. Bloomington, Ind.: Indiana University Press.

2 Bausinger's argument, in this respect, anticipates Derrida's rather more widely known critique of binary divisions by some considerable time. I return to a more extended consideration of these theoretical issues in the final chapter.

3 See A.L. Lloyd (1968) *Folk Song in England*. London: Panther Books. See Jeremy Deller and Alan Kane (2005) *Folk Archive: Contemporary Popular Art from the UK*, London: Bookworks (Opus 5); see also Jeremy Deller (2001) *Life is to Blame for Everything: Collected Works and Projects 1992–1999*. London: Salon 3 Books.

4 Laura Mulvey (2002) 'Changing Objects, Preserving Time', in Dirk Snauwert et al. *Jimmie Durham*. London: Phaidon.

5 Benetta Jules Rosette (1994) 'Simulations of Postmodernity: Images of Technology in African Popular and Tourist Art', in L. Taylor (ed.) *Visualising Theory*. London: Routledge, p. 354.

6 Jules-Rosette, 1994, ibid., p. 346. On the theorisation of the relationship between magic and technology, see my discussion of the work of Alfred Gell in the concluding chapter.

7 David Aaronovich (2002) 'Why Do We Persist with this Morbid Attachment to Heritage and Tradition?', *Independent on Sunday*, 27 December; Jimmie Durham quoted in Mulvey, ibid., p. 57, emphasis added; Kathryn Ticknell, interviewed in BBC2's Cambridge Folk Festival coverage, September 2005.

8 Sarfraz Manzoor (2003) 'Friends for Life', *The Guardian*, 3 January. Predictably, in a moral panic similar to that which has accompanied the arrival of previous new technologies, the site has come under some criticism for the role that it is argued to have played in facilitating 'nostalgic' forms of adultery between old sweethearts, which have led to the break-up of a number of marriages among its subscribers . For more on Friends Reunited see www.friendsreunited .com.

9 See Kevin Robins and Asu Aksoy (2001) 'From Spaces of Identity to Mental Spaces: Lessons from Turkish-Cypriot Cultural Experiences in Britain', *Journal of Ethnic and Migration Studies* 27 (4); Aisha Khan (2003) 'How to Net a Husband', *The Guardian*, 19 May. Perhaps most curiously of all, it was reported at one point that young men in the UK used their mobiles to phone their mothers more than any other single person – see (1998) 'News in Brief: Sons and Mothers', *The Guardian*, 15 September, p. 7. See also my earlier comments on the diasporic 'reach' of Chinese New Year mobile-phone messages.

10 In other fields, the secular 'faithful' – such as football supporters – can programme their phones to 'text' them when their team has scored a goal.

11 In Thomas Friedman (2000) *The Lexus and the Olive Tree*. London: Harper Collins, p. 397.

12 (2005) 'China's Tomb-Sweeping Day Goes Virtual', available online at <http://news. com.com/Chinas+Tomb-Sweeping+Day+goes=virtual/2100-1038_3-5655312. html>, accessed 7 April 2005.

13 Pii quoted in Patrick Barkham (2005) 'Artist Takes a Bite out of Apple', *The Guardian*, 29 August.

14 Barbara Klinger (1998) 'The Contemporary Cinephile', unpubished paper; Walter Benjamin (1974) 'On Unpacking My Library', in his *Illuminations*. London: Fontana; Uma Dinsmore (1998) 'The Domestication of Film: Video, Cinephilia and the collecting of Videotapes in the Home', Ph.D. thesis, Department of Media and Communications, Goldsmiths College, University of London.

15 R. Silverstone and E. Hirsch (eds) (1992) *Consuming Technologies*. London: Routledge, p. 20; Barthes, quoted in Nick Couldry (2002) *Inside Culture*. London: Sage, p. 88.

16 Lynn Spigel (1992) *Make Room for Television*. Chicago, Ill.: University of Chicago Press; Tim O'Sullivan (1991) 'Television Memories and Cultures of Viewing', in J. Corner (ed.) *Popular Television in Britain*. London: British Film Institute; Shunya Yoshimi (1999) 'Made in Japan', *Media, Culture and Society*, 21 (2) and (2003) 'Television and Nationalism in Japan', *European Journal of Cultural Studies*, 6 (4).

17 Yoshimi, 1999, ibid., pp. 54–5; on the 'new' sacred treasures of the digital age, see (2004) *Asahi Shimbun Weekly* AERA Tokyo, 26 January.

18 Karim Raslan (2002) 'What Do We Think of America?' *Granta*, 77, p. 70.

19 In the USA, James Carey speaks of how 'anxious middle class parents, eager to purchase a place for their children in the occupational structure, pack them off to Computer Camps', Carey, ibid., p. 117.

20 See Mackenzie Wark (2002) *Dispositions* Applecross, Western Australia: Salt Publishing for an account of contemporary life as conducted by means of a hand-held GPS device; see also my comments in Chapter 8 on the 'GPS Table'; Jon Agar (2003) *Constant Touch: A Global History of the Mobile Phone*. London: Icon Books. See also Mizuko Ito et al. (2005) *Personal, Portable, Pedestrian: Mobile Phones in Japanese Life*. Cambridge, Mass.: MIT Press.

21 Nicholas Negroponte (1996) *Being Digital*. London: Hodder & Stoughton, p. 228.

22 Martin Parr (2002) *The Phone Book 1998–2002*. London: Rocket Books; Larissa Hjorth (2003) 'Pop and 'Ma': The Landscape of Japanese Commodity Characters and Subjectivity', in Chris Berry et al. (eds) *New Media in Queer Asia*. Durham, NC: Duke University Press.

23 Celeste Olalquiaga (1996) 'Vulture Culture', in John C. Welchman (ed.) *Rethinking Borders*, Minneapolis, Minn.: University of Minnesota Press, p. 85; Agar, ibid., p. 81.

24 Amin Alhassan Department of Art History and Communications Studies, McGill University, Montreal, posting to Cultstuds e-mail list, 28 October 2003; see also the case of elites who mark their status by not having a mobile, because they can 'afford' to be hard to get hold of. Conversely, poor people often make purchasing these technologies a high priority because they feel that, lacking so much else in their lives, these technologies are, for them 'must-have' symbols of cultural citizenship.

25 Olalquiaga, ibid., pp. 85–6; see R. Chow (1991) 'Listening Otherwise, Music Miniaturised', in S. During (ed.) *The Cultural Studies Reader*. London: Routledge. Here we might perhaps see a parallel with the way in which Polish audiences sometimes ostentatiously put their television sets in their front windows, with their screens turned outwards into the street, when the heavily censored news was on during the authoritarian era there, as a symbol of their refusal to listen to the televised voice of the Government. I thank Mateusz Halava of Warsaw University for providing me with this last example.

26 Zygmunt Bauman (2000) *Liquid Modernity*. Cambridge: Polity Press, pp. 13–14, quoted in James Lull's review of Bauman, ibid., in *International Journal of Cultural Studies*, 5 (1). In an earlier period, Henri Lefebvre argued that it was the motor car which was 'the epitome of objects, the Leading-Object' in so far as it 'directs behaviour in various spheres, from economics to speech'. Moreover, Lefebvre was clear that 'the practical significance of the motor car as an instrument of road communications and transport, is only part of its social significance – the car is [also] a symbol, it stands for comfort, authority and speed and it is consumed as a sign, in addition to its practical use', Henri Lefebvre (1971) *Everyday Life in the Modern World*. London: Allen Lane.

27 Juliet Chung (2004) 'A Digital Generation: Analogue Chic', *The New York Times* 9 September; <http://www.nytimes.com/2004/09/09/technology/circuits>, accessed 11 September 2004. My thanks to Lynn Spigel for alerting me to this example.

28 Marshall McLuhan, quoted in Tim Luckhurst (2004) 'Phones R Us', *Independent on Sunday*, 14 November; see my earlier comments on how for many British teenagers, having their phone in their pocket is simply a part of 'being dressed'.

29 George Myerson (2001) *Heidegger, Habermas and the Mobile Phone*. London: Icon Books, p. 1; Timo Kopomaa (2001) *The City in your Pocket: The Birth of the Mobile Information Society*. Helsinki. Gaudeamus Books; Agar, ibid., p. 142.

30 Orange network newspaper advertisement from their spring 2005 campaign.

31 Bull cited in Chapter 7, p. 285; Mintel, quoted in Neasa MacErlean (2004) 'Youth of Today', *The Observer*, 12 September; N. Fleming (2004) 'Without my Phone', *The Guardian*, 20 December.

32 See Agar, ibid., p. 134.

33 John Lichfield (2004) 'Mobile Phone Meltdown Leaves France on Hold', *The Independent*, 20 November.

34 Howard Jacobson (2002) 'Leave a Message after the Tone . . .', *The Guardian* (G2) 14 February.

35 Richard Adams and Santham Sangara (1999) 'Londoners Losing Track of Phones', *Financial Times*, 27 September. Of course, some of these passengers may perhaps have been using their phones to play on-screen games. In any case, things are changing fast in this respect – mobiles can already be used on the underground in Newcastle, and London Transport is now negotiating to 'network' all tube trains in London for mobile-phone use. Indeed, it was mobile camera-phone photos taken by passengers which first documented the horrors of the London Underground bombings in July 2005.

36 Michael Bywater (1998) 'But Will You Still Love Me Tomorrow?' *The Independent*, 31 July; James Meek (2005) 'Yesterday', *The Guardian* (G2), 8 July.

# Part VI

# Coda

*Figure 19* Thai women in traditional dress parade outside McDonald's, Bangkok. Photo by Rungthip Chotnapalai, 2003.

# 11 Marvels and wonders

## Modernity, tradition and technology[1]

### Progress, modernity and religious faith

Unlike most forms of economic theory, Max Weber's historical argument that some forms of religion (particularly Protestantism) have been incidentally beneficial for the development of entrepreneurialism and capitalist forms of modernity does recognise that there is a relationship between economics and cultural or religious beliefs.[2] However, beyond that recognition, it is also important to trace the broader historical roots of contemporary ideas of what it is to be modern. If the problem is looked at from this angle, it can be argued that the very idea of modernity, which is customarily understood to be based on a form of secular, scientific rationality derived from the European Enlightenment, is itself profoundly mythological. These matters are complicated, as we saw in the earlier discussion of the way in which the contemporary USA, as an intensely religious society, contradicts any presumption that modernity is necessarily secular.[3]

Here John Gray offers the example of the contemporary economic theories of the free marketeers of the International Monetary Fund (IMF), whose peculiar beliefs in the inevitably beneficial effects of globalisation in the form of economic deregulation are themselves far from scientific. He argues that while the proselytisers of the IMF see themselves as scientific rationalists, they are in fact, unacknowledged disciples of the forgotten nineteenth-century cult of positivism invented by Auguste Comte and Henri Saint-Simon. From this point of view, the so-called secular systems by which we in the West are now ruled are the heirs of an Enlightenment faith in progress which amounts to little more than a revamped, economistic version of the Christian message of redemption, if now emptied of transcendence and mystery. As Ernest Gellner once noted, this vision is no more than a 'secularised, upside-down version of the proceeding religious view . . . [in which] it is not the intrusion of the supernatural into nature which brings [illusory] salvation but the exclusion of superstitious belief from the natural world which brings real salvation' in the form of progress based on science.

However, at root, this 'putative teleology of faith and scientific progress' as William Boddy describes it, is still a simplistic story of how Evil will (finally) come to be driven out of the world by Good.[4]

Saint-Simon, with his unlimited faith in the power of social engineering, believed that his 'positive doctrine' of 'social physics' should form the basis of a new religion, of which scientists would be the officiating clergy. In the classical positivist vision of Comte and Saint-Simon, who were so influential in the foundation of the European social sciences, scientific thought was to be the motor of modernisation, bringing with it new technologies which would transcend previous 'inefficient' modes of production. They saw scientific knowledge as the key force in human progress and believed that its benefits would enable humankind to put an end to material scarcity. At the same time, they presumed that as societies moved ineluctably forward from the religious to the 'positive' (or scientific) stage of development, politics and ethics would themselves become sciences. Thus, as rational modes of behaviour then developed worldwide, social conflict would disappear.[5]

Clearly, put in such crude terms, this technologically determinist thesis of the inevitable progress of humankind through scientific advance may seem little more than laughable at the beginning of the twenty-first century, as we stare into the abyss of man-made ecological disaster in the form of global warming and the descent of many areas of the globe into forms of anarchy only intermittently policed (or neglected) according to the interests of the world's one remaining global superpower. Nonetheless, these are, as Gray demonstrates, the key premises of the belief system which still under-lies Western economic policy, which is driven by an ultimately religious faith in the beneficial powers of science, technology and the 'rational' economics of the free market. All that has changed is the name of the prin-cipal technological deity. If Comte and Saint-Simon worshipped the benefi-cially transformative powers of the new communications systems of their day, in the form of canals and railways, and both early twentieth-century American capitalists and Soviet communists worshipped the benefits of electricity, today it is the Internet which is enshrined as the ultimate source of goodness and progress.[6]

In this technologically determinist vision, it is assumed that the practical application of scientific knowledge will inevitably produce a convergence in forms of social life (and values) around one, rational solution, which, as we saw earlier, is the nub of Fukuyama's hymn to the inevitable worldwide triumph of free-market capitalism. The creed of 'market fundamentalism' is, Gray argues, the offspring of a marriage of positivist economics (based on a belief in 'rational choice theory') and a denuded model of human subjectivity in the form of 'economic man'.[7] Nonetheless, on the basis of these dubious premises, the free market is now widely assumed to be the only form of socio-economic organisation which is both rational and truly modern and therefore destined to gradually spread worldwide, bringing with it universal civilisation.

The problem here is that, as we saw in Chapter 6, there are many ways of being modern, and the belief that there is only one way – that of American-style 'democratic capitalism' and that it is always good, is itself metaphysical. Indeed, the fundamental assumption of free-market rationalism, that economic exchange is only and necessarily motivated by a '*quid pro quo*' mode of exchange (in which work must be remunerated by wages, and goods by money at the point of sale, or investment by profit) is challenged by recent research in the leading technological sectors of the knowledge economy. The work of Steven Weber and Eric von Hippel on 'open source' software-sharing and the democratisation of innovation as a result of 'free-revealing' of their 'trade secrets' by inventors, goes a long way to undermining precisely these presumptions, as they quite fail to account for the dynamics of recent developments in the world of 'Free/Libre/Open Source Software' (FLOSS).[8]

Western societies may well be ruled by the myth that, as everyone else absorbs Western science and technology in the course of becoming modern, the whole world is bound to become as secular, enlightened and peaceful as the West imagines itself to be. However, if modernity is more simply, but with better theoretical foundation, understood as the 'mixture of things' actually produced by accelerating technological change, it becomes clear that, in fact, modern societies may well vary widely in their nature. This is because, in line with the arguments of Paul du Gay et al., we need to understand particular sets of economic arrangements as themselves necessarily enmeshed in cultural frameworks. Only thus can we hope to repair the unfortunate effects of the decoupling of classical economics from its grounding in history and its subsequent reconstruction by positivists as a purely mathematical, rationalist science.[9]

Modernity has to be understood as existing in a variety of forms and always involves more than economic arrangements. As Gray concludes, 'economic activity is not a free-standing form of social life. It is . . . [also] an outgrowth of the religious beliefs, family relationships and national traditions in which it is embedded'. Here we might think of phenomena such as the transnational Islamic banking systems which rely on long-distance traditions of trust specific to those cultures. Thus, 'business enterprises operate differently in Eastern Orthodox societies from the way they do in Catholic societies; Chinese capitalism is quite different from Japanese capitalism, [as is] Hindi from Muslim. There are many hybrids [and] . . . as they modernise, the varieties of capitalism will not become more alike'. Modernity is thus neither a single condition, everywhere the same, and some of its forms, as Gray rightly notes, are themselves monstrous.[10]

## De-mythologising the modern

In *We Have Never Been Modern*, Bruno Latour attempts to conceptualise the terms of reference for an 'anthropology of the modern world'. This involves him in two principal tasks — both clarifying the subject matter and methodology of such an anthropology and also reconceptualising the nature of modernity itself. If the conventional vision of modernity, based on Weber's idea of the 'iron cage' of rationality, is that it has 'dis-enchanted' the world, Latour argues that modernity is no simple matter of 'the invention of humanism . . . the emergence of the sciences . . . the secularisation of society . . . [and] the mechanisation of the world'. This is not least because, as I argued earlier, a strong case can be made that, despite Weber et al.'s presumptions, what we actually see around us is the de-secularisation of the contemporary world.[11]

For Latour, modernity centrally involves both a particular conception of the universe in which nature and culture are divided into a clear binary opposition and also a specific conception of irreversible time, which is itself dramatically divided between the time of the irrational, belief-sodden chaotic past of 'tradition' and the clear-sighted 'scientific' realm of the modern era.[12] From this perspective, if the past was a realm of confusion, modernisation is then seen to consist in exiting from this 'obscure age' which mingled all things up, into an era where everything is classified in an orderly fashion, thus liberating humankind from its pre-scientific past. For Latour, 'the chief oddity of the moderns [is] the[ir] idea of a time that passes irreversibly and annuls the entire past in its wake'. This 'modern' idea of the passage of time is, he claims,

> nothing but a particular form of historicity . . . The moderns have a peculiar propensity for understanding time that passes as if it were really abolishing the past behind it. They all take themselves for Attila, in whose footsteps no grass grows back. They do not feel that they are removed from the Middle Ages by a certain number of centuries, but that they are separated by Copernican revolutions, epistemological breaks, epistemic ruptures so radical that nothing of the past survives in them.[13]

In line with Fabian's critique of the way in which modern societies deny what he calls 'co-evalness' to their contemporaries in the less affluent parts of the world, by means of a political cosmology in which We are 'here and now' and They are 'there and then', Latour argues that modern temporality can only produce its defining impression of continuous acceleration 'by relegating ever-larger masses of humans and non-humans together to the void of the past'. From this point of view, it has all been a question of 'radical revolutions in science, technology, administration, economy and religion, a veritable bulldozer operation behind which the past disappeared for ever, but in front of which, at least, the future opened up. The past was a barbarian medley; the future a civilising distinction'. In this same respect, Goran Therborn argues, modernity has been characterised by a strong sense of a 'cultural orientation towards a new, "this-worldly" future and by a decisive break with past time'.[14]

The key question here concerns the source of the 'very modern impression that we are living in a new time that breaks with the past'. Latour's argument is that 'Century after century, colonial empire after colonial empire, the poor pre-modern collectives were accused of making a horrible mishmash of things and humans, objects and signs, while their accusers finally separated them totally'. Of course, as he notes, 'the price the moderns paid . . . was that they were unable to conceptualise themselves in continuity with the pre-moderns. They had to think of themselves as absolutely different, they had to invent the Great Divide'. As a result of this 'retrospective attitude', the Others 'became' pre-modern, by contrast to the moderns, as 'a succession of radical revolutions created an obscure "yesteryear" that was soon to be dissipated by the luminous dawn of the social sciences'. The result of all these 'revolutions' was an increasingly patronising and arrogant attitude towards these others, who had thus to be helped to emerge from their 'confusion' and backwardness by annihilating their own pasts.[15]

Rather than taking at face value modernity's claim to have made a decisive rupture with the realms of the past, Latour argues that the analytical priority is to focus on the very institution of this 'rupture': 'the Great Divide, the great narrative of the West, set radically apart from all [other] cultures'. The objective here is to analyse 'the unconscious of the moderns' by bringing to light what has been repressed in this absolute separation of past and present. Here Latour's position parallels that of Derrida, when he argues that the spectres of the past are permanent factors in our lives, which will only continue to haunt us if we foolishly attempt to banish them completely. It is for this reason that Derrida rejects, as matter of principle, the very idea of decisive ruptures or unequivocal epistemological breaks in human history because, as he puts it, such breaks are 'always and fatally re-inscribed in an old cloth that must continually, interminably, be undone'.[16]

Because Westerners claim that they are absolutely and irremediably different from all others, 'the Great Divide between Us – Occidentals – and Them – everyone else, from the China seas to the Yucatan, from the Inuit to the Tasmanian aborigines – has not ceased to obsess us'. All this is, for Latour, the essence of 'modern exoticism'. While the West has 'artificially created the scandal of the others', he argues that, despite these grand claims, not only are we 'not exotic but ordinary' but that, correspondingly, 'the others are not exotic either'. The principle danger here is well expressed in Kwame Anthony Appiah's acerbic warning that we should 'not overestimate the distance from London to Lagos'. In the light of these considerations, Latour makes the striking assertion that 'no one has ever been modern. Modernity has never begun. There has never been a modern world . . . there has never been a yesteryear or an Old Regime – we could never have left the old anthropological matrix behind, and . . . it never could have been otherwise'.[17]

## Towards an anthropology of the modern world

As Latour notes, in order for it to be possible to construct an anthropology of the modern world, the definition of modernity itself must be transformed. In the first instance, he argues, it is of the essence of anthropology to be comprehensive in its analyses of the societies that it studies. Thus, the strength of a conventional ethnography of a 'traditional' or 'primitive' society is that it will include within its remit everything from the complexities of the kinship system, law, language, customs and property rights to religious and cosmological ideas governing the relations between humans, animals and the universe that constitute that society.

The difficulty, he argues, is that while 'in the tropics the anthropologist did not settle for studying the margins of other cultures', when anthropology 'comes home', it often proceeds as if it can 'apply its methods only when Westerners mix up signs and things the way savage thought does'. Thus, it often 'studies only the margins and fractures of rationality, or the realms beyond rationality'. It is in the same spirit of 'clarification' that social scientists 'have for long allowed themselves to denounce the belief systems of ordinary people' in so far as they are held to be pre-scientific. For Latour, this is too arrogant an epistemological approach which is, at the same time, too timid in its choice of subject matter. Thus he insists that an anthropology of the modern world cannot limit itself to its periphery – to the study, for instance, of what are deemed to be 'hangovers' or surviving bits of irrational flotsam and jetsam from the traditional world. This is the basis of his criticisms of work such as Marc Augé's anthropological studies of France for looking only at 'marginal' cultural phenomena (in his study of the Paris metro) rather than studying the whole 'socio-technological network' in the same way that, in his earlier study of the lagoon-dwellers of the Ivory Coast, Augé had addressed the 'entire social phenomenon' of their lives.[18]

From Latour's point of view, modernity's own conceptual structure, its epistemologies, methodologies and cosmologies (including those of the scientific world), should be treated with exactly the same degree of engaged scepticism as Lévi-Strauss deployed in studying the Amerindian societies of

Brazil. Following Boltanski and Thevenot's argument that 'the modern denunciation is over', he argues that if the 'sacred task' of the moderns was 'to unmask . . . [things] to reveal the true calculations underlying the false consciousness' of primitive or less well-informed others, all that is left to us now is a sociology of criticism, rather than a critical sociology. Such an approach would have the task of 'calmly comparing all sources of denunciation' without allocating an a-priori validity to any one form of supposedly transcendent knowledge, even that which claims the status of science. Furthermore, as he argues, such an approach must refrain from 'making any a priori declarations as to what might distinguish Westerners from Others'.[19]

In a similarly sceptical spirit, a character in Tayeb Salih's novel *Season of Migration to the North* set during the period of 1960s modernisation in Sudan, observes to a compatriot that in his enthusiasm for the modern, he is only 'now believing in superstitions of a new sort: the superstitions of industrialisation . . . of nationalism and the new, contemporary superstition of statistics'. The key point, as Latour notes, is that if, in constituting themselves, some societies mobilise 'ancestors, lions, fixed stars and the coagulated blood of sacrifice', we correspondingly mobilise what are, ultimately, an equally exotic set of beliefs – in 'genetics, zoology, cosmology and haematology'.[20]

In her commentary on the playfully iconoclastic work of the Cherokee artist Jimmie Durham, which challenges Western perspectives from the point of view of Native American Indian folk knowledge, Laura Mulvey makes the point that any truth that is upheld with total certainty implies an element of irrational belief and tends to support a pathological sense of rectitude that justifies intolerance. For Durham himself, the most puzzling issue is that

> everyone *knows* so much these days. Isn't it odd how sure we all are? The New York city taxi driver who wrings a miserable life of unfulfilled dreams from his student days in Iran is sure that Salman Rushdie's death will fix things up. John Major [was] sure that if we return to English Family Values we'll work it all out.

However, for Durham, it is the certainties of contemporary Western science that are the most problematic. Thus, he avers,

> I actually love Science and the Scientific Method, using capital letters. But I don't think it's European and I don't think that it is practised in the science world. I have a great criticism of science, because it operates on belief, it doesn't question its basic beliefs. But science as an analytical concept of questioning and experimenting and saying 'let's see, how does this work and what happens here' – that's genius. Our project is not to

believe, not to find answers, it's to be analytical and to do experiments
. . . it shouldn't lead is to a cheap answer . . . that's why I love science.
[But] its not European – and it doesn't just belong to white people.[21]

## The division of time and space

Following the line of argument developed by Bausinger and Derrida, for
Latour too, the problem with the simplistic binary divide between the static
world of tradition and the fast-changing world of modernity is that 'the idea
of a stable tradition is an illusion that anthropologists have long set to rights
. . . The "immutable" traditions have all budged – the day before yesterday'.
Indeed, he claims that the ideas of a static past and of the corresponding
possibility of a radical rupture with it are 'two symmetrical results of a single
[and peculiarly modern] idea of time'. Just as Benedict Anderson observes
that the fundamental logic of the concept of 'news' is constituted in the
newspaper by the fact that what links the events reported in it together is
that they occurred on the same day, Latour argues that 'modernising progress
is thinkable only on condition that all the elements that are contemporary
(according to the calendar) belong to the same time'. However, as he notes,
'this beautiful order is disturbed once [its contents] are seen as mixing up
different periods, ontologies or genres. Then a historical period will give the
impression of a great hotchpotch'.[22] The key point here is that it 'is not only
the Bedouins and the !Kung who mix up transistors and traditional
behaviours, plastic buckets and animal skin vessels . . . [When performing
some DIY task] I may use an electric drill, but I also use a hammer; the former
is 35 years old, the latter hundreds of thousands . . . Will you . . . [therefore]
see me as an ethnographic curiousity?'. As Michel Serres says, we are all
'exchangers and brewers of time'. Thus, Latour's perspective is centrally
designed to reveal the fact that 'we are no longer so far removed from the
premoderns', since when we talk about them, we have to 'include a large
part of ourselves'.[23]

If Latour is primarily concerned to demolish the temporal binary that
would neatly sever the traditional from the modern, we must also attend to
the geographical dimension, where these phenomena are often not, in fact,
always so clearly divided spatially as is commonly presumed, as I argued in
Part III. In her study of a voodoo priestess based in Brooklyn, Karen
McCarthy Brown made trips with her to Haiti, but her most unnerving
experience of displacement took place in New York itself. As she describes
it, when she first visited her subject's area of the city:

> Our nostrils filled with the smells of charcoal and roasting meat and our
> ears with overlapping episodes of salsa, reggae and the bouncy monotony

of what Haitians call jazz. Animated conversations could be heard in Haitian French creole, Spanish and more than one dialect of English. The street was a crazy quilt of shops: Chick-Licka, the Ashanti Bazaar, a storefront Christian church . . . and one of the apothecaries of New World African religions, offering 'fast-luck' and 'get rich quick' powders . . . I was no more than a few miles form my home in Lower Manhattan, but I felt as though I had taken a wrong turn, slipped through a crack between worlds and emerged on the main street of a tropical city.[24]

While elements of Haitian culture are readily found in some parts of New York, it is also the case, conversely, that many of the forms of modernity are readily found in places where, according to the classical ordering of things, they might not be expected to fit. Thus, in his study of village modernity in West Africa, Charles Piot observes how things such as imported tin roofs, Western clothes and medicine, cars and radios, a money economy and certain forms of Christianity have been readily absorbed into the vernacular of village life. As he notes, there is plenty of evidence that people who believe in traditional spirits are also able to embrace the spirit of capitalist enterprise. Thus, he finds villagers who are quite acclimatised to the sight of their president flying in by helicopter to attend the traditional summer wrestling matches in which young men are ritually initiated into manhood and which have now become state spectacles, broadcast on both radio and television, for those who cannot themselves travel to the venue for the occasion.[25]

The hybrid nature of historical experience has long been a key issue for Latin American scholars attempting to produce a periodisation of contemporary experience in that particular location, with its complex imperial and post-colonial histories. Many of these scholars have deployed the concept of *mestizaje* as central to their analysis of how Latin American modernities have taken distinctive forms that syncretise a complex mixture of linguistic, cultural, religious, ethnic, political and economic influences. Thus, for Jesus Martin-Barbero, *mestizaje* reflects 'cultural discontinuities of social formations and structures of feeling, of memories, of imaginaries which mix together the indigenous . . . the rural and the urban [with] folklore . . . the popular . . . and with mass culture'.[26]

Debates about the concept of cultural hybridity have been at their sharpest in areas defined as the peripheries of the modern world system, which have long experienced the dramatic intrusion of a variety of forms of alterity into their societies, in the forms of imperialism and colonialism (as a result of what Jimmie Durham calls the 'Hey guys, we've been discovered' moment). Nestor Garcia Canclini, in particular, is concerned with how, in post-conquest Latin America, combinations of pre-Columbian and colonial traditions have emerged in syncretic forms which intertwine heavily sedimented forms of both pagan and Catholic religiosity with the cultural modes of modernity. In this context, he argues the 'traditional v. modern' distinction is certainly no longer pertinent, as people live in a complex system in which different temporalities coexist. In this situation, if traditional and folkloric elements remain strong and 'people live a great deal of time in the midst of rituals', they also engage with a variety of forms of modernity – and simply 'to be a resident in a big city . . . implies being able to relate oneself to varied [cultural] fields' simultaneously. This, however, is not to argue that hybridity only exists in the wake of situations of imperial conquest and colonialism, for culture is everywhere a hybrid amalgamation, even if we need to distinguish its particular forms and varieties.[27]

## Technology, tradition and modernity

Although the world of tradition is usually counterposed to that of modern world of science and technology by reference to the supposed irrationality of traditional societies, many traditional forms of behaviour are deeply rational. As Arjun Appadurai also notes in his critique of the supposed specificity of the economic arrrangements of contemporary societies based on forms of commodity exchange, gift exchanges in traditional societies are also based on deeply rational and calculative modes of behaviour. This is to conceive of gifts as a specific cultural mechanism for creating economic forms of obligation, which, in effect, are simply a different cultural form of what we call economic rationality. All these insights were, of course, first articulated long ago by Marcel Mauss in his classic study *The Gift*, in which he explained that there is no gift without bond, without bind, without obligation or ligature. In that study, Mauss demonstrates that in primitive societies, in the absence of a state, gifts function as way of forging and sustaining the ties of sociality. However, gift-giving also remains a crucial part of social (and especially familial) relations in contemporary affluent societies. In these conditions too, its calculus is precisely calibrated, as anyone who has ever, at a festive occasion, inadvertently given a less expensive present to a sibling than they received from them will know very well. Of course, if the key element in gift-giving is reciprocation, people nonetheless give gifts for all sorts of reasons: 'to show off their wealth . . . to manipulate others, to repair relationships, and relieve guilt'. In all of these activities, (even if perhaps at times unconsciously) we pursue, by economic means, ends which are every bit as rational as any in the Friedmanite universe of contemporary economic theory.[28]

Moreover, not only is gift-giving a routine practice in contemporary Western life (and not at all necessarily reserved to 'special occasions') but the most modern technologies often now provide the very medium of gift exchange — in the form of iPod tunes, personally recorded audio tapes, or CD 'compilations' specially made for a friend, of digital-camera photos and videos 'swapped' among a family or social network, or of jokes and titbits culled from the Internet and circulated by e-mail, as a sign of amity between sender and recipient. Naturally, just as in traditional societies, some gifts are not simply calculative, obligatory or manipulative, but downright unwanted by the recipient — but the fact that they come in the form of the gift makes them very hard to refuse without giving offence. In one striking case, reported in research on technology use in contemporary Finland, two daughters, concerned about their mother's safety on her solo trips to their family's rural summer house, having failed to persuade her that she should get a mobile phone for use on these trips, then resorted to buying her one as a gift, which she was then, of course, obliged to accept.[29]

From the perspective of cultural anthropology, one critical issue, if we are to transcend the unhelpful binary divide between the traditional and the modern, is to restore the cultural dimension to our analyses of contemporary societies, which are all too often thought of simply as 'economies writ large'.[30] This is not to deny the importance of economic factors in social life, but it is to recognise that otherwise advanced industrial economies are themselves also cultural forms and discourses, which not only involve economic calculation but are also replete with symbols. One example here would be the presence of the portrait of the monarch on the English currency, which has provided a major focus of concern for those opposed to the UK 'losing its identity' in joining the European single currency. In this connection, Paul du Gay has rightly insisted on the need to develop a 'cultural economy' perspective capable of dealing with such issues, just as Roger Silverstone has commented on the way in which cultural forms and norms still provide the crucial support to the supposed bedrock of economic life, in so far as they frame and lie 'below the bottom line' of processes of economic calculation. The key thing here, as Gellner argues, is that what really matters in economics 'are those features which [are usually] swept under the carpet of "*ceteris paribus*" clauses or hidden in unquestioned assumptions', whereas contemporary economic theory continues 'to take for granted the institutional, psychological and evaluative frameworks whose very conditions of emergence . . . are *just* what are most problematical'.[31]

To put it another way, and to return to the issue of media and communications, as I argued earlier, technologies such as the television and the computer are not only technical but also symbolic or totemic objects for their users. As Eric Hirsch notes, our contemporary uses of communications technologies are so often riddled with ritual and symbolic practices that we should not kid ourselves that we are 'really so different from (so-called "primitive") Melanesians in the way we sustain relationships through material forms'.[32] We would be fools indeed to proceed in our analysis as if 'belief' is efficacious only in traditional societies, while modern societies are solely governed by rational calculation. Ironically, these factors come most dramatically into play at the very heart of the international system of finance, especially if we consider the various irrationalities of the stock exchange and the notorious sensitivity of international money markets to panics based on very subjective issues such as market 'confidence' in different currencies. As Vincent Tucker puts it, 'we can no more understand the workings of modern capitalist society than we can the . . . societies of the Mbuti pygmies without understanding the power and potency of belief', and it is only because we assume that 'belief is efficacious only in traditional societies, while modern societes are governed by science that we so assiduously delegitimise the myths of other societies while failing to deconstruct our own'.[33]

## Ritual, enchantment and magic in a technological society

Here we also have to address the persistence of ritual in contemporary affluent and otherwise modern societies and, in particular, its continuing inscription in forms of new technology. Bausinger follows Hegel in understanding reading the morning newspaper as having been the particular 'form of prayer' of early modern societies in the era of print technology. Thus, he argues, that for many people, reading the morning newspaper is still a constitutive part of the ritual of breakfast. He then asks what the exact nature of the 'crisis' is that is caused when the paper is absent, beyond the absence of the information contained in the paper (about which few of us can actually do anything much anyway, from our breakfast tables). His argument is that, whatever its worrying content, the very presence of the newspaper shows that the breakfast-time world of the reader is in order, at least at a micro-level, and, conversely, its absence is primarily problematic because it disrupts that everyday ritual of well-being. This example has a very contemporary parallel in the form of irrational panic into which many people (myself included, on occasion) are sometimes thrown if their e-mail is 'down' when they arrive at their desks in the morning. To imagine that the problem is simply that of the absence of the information which might be contained in the temporarily inaccessible e-mail is to miss the point, especially given how much of it is likely to be spam or other unwanted and non-urgent, bureaucratic or commercial circulars. The key issue is that in this moment, the daily ritual of confirmation of one's participation in and belonging to a wider, technologically mediated community is disrupted.[34] As Elaine Lally puts it, our sense of security in a complex world is now increasingly tied to 'our reliance on technologies to function as expected'. Hence, technical mishaps, such as a 'computer crash' can provoke not only feelings of 'frustration and anger . . . but [also] . . . an assault on our ontological security itself'.[35]

For James Carey and John Quirk, the future itself is best understood as 'a participation ritual of technological exoticism'. In the same spirit, in his novel *Cosmopolis*, Don DeLillo captures something of this magical attitude to technology and, particularly, to the contemporary forms of idolatry of information. In his fictionalised description of the electronic data displays on the streets of New York, he speaks of a situation where

> beneath the data strips . . . there were fixed digits marking the time in the major cities of the world. Never mind the speed that makes it hard to follow what passes before the eye. The speed is the point . . . We are not witnessing the flow of information, so much as pure spectacle, or information made sacred [so] . . . the monitors . . . become a . . . [site] of idolatry . . . where crowds . . . gather in astonishment'.[36]

In his analysis of 'technologies of enchantment and the enchantment of technology', Alfred Gell speaks of 'the power that technical processes have of casting a spell over us, so that we see the real world in enchanted form'. He argues that it would be quite misleading to imagine that just because modern societies now rest on a technical base, 'technology is a cut-and-dried affair which everybody understands perfectly'. Indeed, his claim is that we tend to see any technical process which transcends our understanding (which is, of course, for most of us, true of the majority of the technically mediated activities on which our social existence now depends) as, in effect, magical. The difficulties we have in 'mentally encompassing' how the objects they produce come into being means that we have no option to do otherwise. Thus, when Gell speaks of the 'alchemy involved in photography . . . in which packets of film are put into cameras, buttons are pressed and (in due course) pictures of Aunt Edna emerge', his point is that our attitude to our part in, and control over, these technically mediated processes is no more or less 'magical' (or rational) than that of the participants in any Melanesian cargo cult.[37]

In a similar spirit to Gell, Marvin notes the strong connections in nineteenth-century debates about technological innovation between the rhetorics of rationalism and magic and between those of science and the séance. As Boddy points out, the wireless was strongly associated with ideas of telepathy, and the nineteenth-century interest in electricity was part of a more general Romantic obsession with all things that 'flow'. By the beginning of the twentieth century, research into electrical communications had a long-standing association with more general discourses of the uncanny, the occult, spiritualism and 'ether theory'. In this connection, as Jeffrey

Sconce observes, 'the question guiding . . . research, even at the dawn of the computer age, was not *if* electronics could be used to contact the dead, but rather *how* it would be used' to do so. The 'affinity of spirits and electricity' means that electronic media have always been wrapped up with 'fantastic folktales' and occult fantasies whether involving superstitions bound to the historical imagination of 'electronic presencing' in an earlier age or, in these days of *The Matrix*, 'kitted up with the bells and whistles of cybernetic fashion'.[38]

For Gell, magic is not opposed to knowledge, science and technology, but is inherently part of it and is indeed, in many senses, the 'ideal means of technical production'. As he puts it, the notion of 'magic as a means of securing a product without the work cost that it . . . [normally] entails' provides the 'magic-standard' of evaluation against which the efficacy of all techniques is common-sensically measured. The relative efficacy of techniques is thus routinely understood as a function of the extent to which they converge towards this 'magic standard' of zero work for the same product. From this point of view, 'the propagandists, image-makers and ideologues of technological culture are its magicians . . . and if we no longer recognise magic explicitly it is because technology and magic, for us, are one and the same', and we take as second nature a whole technological complex whose functioning is, in fact, largely mysterious to us.[39]

These points, as so often, have both a quotidien and a theoretical application. Earlier, I noted Shove and Southerton's commentary on the crucial forms of 'preservational magic' which the freezer supplies to the contemporary home. We might also recall Barthes's and Ross's observations on the recurrent aspiration of modernity to give objects the immobility of a material on which time has no effect and, by immobilising time, to retreat inside a controlled, rationally created environment which transcends history. However, if we follow Gray, Latour, Bausinger and Gell in rejecting the simplistic binary divide between the modern and the traditional – and between the rational and the magical – then we must recognise the presence of an admixture of rational and symbolic elements in both traditional and modern societies. To return to the arguments made in Part III, it is not only the temporal binary between the traditional and the modern, but also the geographical equation of modernity with the (supposedly) secularised West that is ill founded – as is the corresponding equation of the realms of the traditional and the irrational with the Orient. At which point, we have to begin to entertain the possibilities for a wide variety of (not necessarily secular or Western) modernities, in different parts of the globe, where science and magic, along with technology and tradition, may be mixed together in many new ways.

*Figure 20*  Boatman chatting on mobile phone, Kerala, South India. Photo by
     Alice Cartner-Morley, 2006.

## Notes

1  The reader will, no doubt, by now have already noted my prediliction for
   quoting extensively from the work of other scholars in the fields which this book
   surveys, rather than in offering my own precis of their work – a tendency which
   is particularly pronounced in this concluding chapter. Here I rely heavily on the
   work of a small number of leading scholars in different fields – John Gray in
   political philosophy, Bruno Latour in science studies, Herman Bausinger in
   ethnology and Alfred Gell in anthropology. The only claim to originality I would
   make, in respect of my own contribution here, consists in my editing of these
   voices from disparate disciplines to create (hopefully) some new and as yet
   unheard echoes, reverberations and harmonies, as I weave these materials
   together.

2  Max Weber (2001) *The Protestant Ethic and the Spirit of Capitalism*. London:
   Routledge.

3  Thus, Gray argues that 'Of all modern delusions, the idea that we live in a secular
   age is the furthest from reality . . . liberal humanism itself is very obviously a
   religion – a shoddy replica of Christian faith markedly more irrational than the
   original article and in recent times, more harmful' – Gray, quoted in Andrew
   Brown (2005) 'The Contrarian' in *The Guardian* (Review) 3 December.

4  John Gray (2003) *Al Qaeda and What it Means to be Modern*. London: Faber, pp. 42–3; Auguste Comte (1858) *The Catechism of Positivist Religion*. London: John Chapman; Henri Saint-Simon (1975) *Selected Writings*. London: Croom Helm; John Gray (2004) *Heresies: Against Progress and Other Illusions*. London: Granta; Ernest Gellner (1964) *Thought and Change*. London: Wiedenfeld & Nicolson, pp. 6–7; William Boddy (2004) *New Media and the Popular Imagination*. Oxford: Oxford University Press, p. 22.

5  Gray (2003) ibid., p. 30. See also Gray's comments on the continuing – and here explicit – influence of positivism in some parts of the world, such as Brazil, where Comte's slogan 'Order and Progress' is part of the national flag and where 'temples' of positivism still function today, ibid., p. 34; on Comte and Saint-Simon, see also Armand Mattelart (1996) *The Invention of Communication*. Minneapolis, Minn.: University of Minnesota Press; see also my earlier comments in Chapter 8 on Diller and Scofidio's scepticism about these Taylorist principles.

6  See my earlier comments on the computer as a totemic object. On this, see also, Alf Hornborg (2001a) 'Symbolic Technologies', *Anthropological Theory* 1 (4) and also his (2001b) *The Power of the Machine*. Lanham, Md.: Alta Mira, Rowman & Littlefield. My thanks to Bob Jessop for bringing Hornborg's work to my attention.

7  Gray, 2003, ibid., pp. 2, 7; see Francis Fukuyama (1992) *The End of History*. Harmondsworth: Penguin; see Ernest Gellner on liberalism as itself ultimately a form of fundamentalism in his (1964) *Thought and Change*. London: Wiedenfeld & Nicolson; John Gray (2002) 'Britain', 'What do We Think of America', *Granta*, 77: 38; see my earlier comments on Milton Friedman in Chapter 6. Given the American sense of their nation's universal mission to be the true saviours of the world's future, what Gray calls the 'cult of the free market' is thus perhaps now best seen as the 'one true American faith', Gray, 2003, ibid., pp. 48–9.

8  See Lawrence Lessig (2005) 'Do You Floss', Review of Steven Weber (2004) *The Success of Open Source*. Cambridge, Mass.: Harvard University Press and Eric von Hippel (2005) *Democratising Innovation*. Cambridge, Mass.: MIT Press, in *London Review of Books*, 18 August.

9  Gray, 2003, ibid., pp. 112, 118; see Paul du Gay et al. (2001) *Cultural Economy: Cultural Analysis and Commercial Life*. London: Sage; on du Gay, see also later in this chapter.

10  Gray, 2003, ibid., pp. 1–2, 56; see my earlier comments in Chapter 6 on this.

11  Bruno Latour (1993) *We Have Never Been Modern*. Harlow: Longman, p. 34; Weber, ibid.; Theodor Adorno and Max Horkheimer (1977) *The Dialectic of Enlightenment*. London: Verso. On the 'de-secularisation' of the world, see Chapter 6; see also Kwame Anthony Appiah's incisive comments on these issues in his (1992) *In My Father's House*. London: Methuen.

12  See Barthes, quoted in Chapter 8 on modernity's claims to transcend all previous forms of time and thus escape from history.

13  Latour, ibid., pp. 47, 68, 71, 133.

14 Johannes Fabian (1983) *Time and the Other*. New York: Columbia University Press, p. 39; Goran Therborn (2002) 'Asia and Europe in the World', *Inter-Asia Cultural Studies*, 3 (2), p. 290; Latour, ibid., pp. 130, 135.

15 Latour ibid., pp. 39, 38, 36, 47; see my comments in Chapter 6 on Daniel Lerner and the modernisation theory of the 1960s.

16 Latour, ibid., pp. 112, 37; Jacques Derrida (1994) *Spectres of Marx*. London: Routledge, p. 64; Jacques Derrida (1981) *Positions*. London: Athlone Press, p. 24.

17 Latour, ibid., pp. 97, 104, 122–3, 127, 47; Appiah, ibid., quoted in Chapter 5.

18 Latour, ibid., pp. 7, 100, 51, 106; Marc Augé (2002) *In the Metro*. Minneapolis, Minn.: University of Minnesota Press; Marc Augé (1975) *Theorie des Pouvoirs et Ideologie*. Paris: Hermann. Latour is perhaps rather unfair here on Augé's 'Metro' study, but his general point about the lack of symmetry between anthropological studies in the Third and First Worlds remains important.

19 Latour, ibid., pp. 44, 103; Luc Boltanski and Laurent Thevenot (1991) *De la justification*. Paris: Gallimard, quoted in Latour, ibid., p. 44.

20 Tayeb Salih (2003) *Season of Migration to the North*. First published 1969. Harmondsworth: Penguin; Latour, ibid., p. 106.

21 L. Mulvey (2002) 'Changing Objects, Preserving Time', in L. Mulvey et al. *Jimmie Durham*. London: Phaidon Press, p. 43; Jimmie Durham (2002) in L. Mulvey et al., ibid., pp. 147, 250. See also my comments on Flaubert's attitude to science in Chapter 4.

22 Benedict Anderson (1983) *Imagined Communities*. London: Verso; Latour, ibid., pp. 73–6; see Fernand Braudel (1988) *Civilisation and Capitalism*. London: Collins/Fontana on 'differential' historical times; see also Raymond Willliams's comments *passim* on the co-existence of residual, dominant and emergent elements in any one historical period. Latour, ibid., p. 75.

23 Serres, quoted in Latour, ibid., p. 75.

24 Karen McCarthy Brown (1991) *Mama Lola: a Voudou Priestess in Brooklyn*. Berkeley: Calif.: University of California Press, p. 1; quoted in J. Clifford (1997) *Routes*. Cambridge, Mass.: Harvard University Press, p. 56; for a UK parallel, which addresses these issues of hybridity as they pertain to contemporary London, see Gareth Stanton's exemplary study (2005) 'Peckham Tales' in James Curran and David Morley (eds) *Media and Cultural Theory*. London: Routledge.

25 Charles Piot (1999) *Remotely Global: Village Life in West Africa*. Chicago, Ill.: University of Chicago Press.

26 Martin-Barbero (1987) *De los medios a las mediociones*. Barcelona: Gustavo Gili, p. 165, quoted in Nelly Richard (1996) 'The Cultural Periphery and Postmodern Decentring', in John C. Welchman (ed.) *Rethinking Borders*. Minneapolis, Minn.: University of Minnesota University Press, p. 78.

27 Nestor Garcia Canclini (1993) 'The Hybrid: A Conversation', *Boundary 2* (fall): 80, 81, 90. In this connection, José Joaquim Bruner argues that postmodernity in Latin America is best understood as the specific regional form which modernity takes, given the particular fluidity and destabilisation of the meta-narratives

of modernity there; see José Joaquim Bruner (1993) 'Notes on Modernity and Postmodernity', *Boundary 2*, 20 (3).

28  Marcel Mass (2002) *The Gift*. First published 1954. London: Routledge; Roger Highfield (2004) 'Why You Always Get a Present You Don't Want', *The Daily Telegraph*, 3 November. On these issues, see also Marilyn Strathern (1992) 'Qualified Value: The Perspective of Gift Exchange', in Caroline Humphrey and Stephen Hugh-Jones (eds) *Barter, Exchange and Value*. Cambridge: Cambridge University Press.

29  Tuula Puranen (2003) 'Social Dimensions of Media in Everyday Life', Department of Journalism and Mass Communications, University of Tampere, 2003. However, the mother later demonstrated her reservations about the gift by failing to switch her phone on at the times that her daughters felt were appropriate.

30  A. Appadurai (ed.) *The Social Life of Things: Commodities in Cultural Perspective*. Cambridge: Cambridge University Press, p. 12.

31  Paul du Gay, ibid.; Keith Negus (1999) *Music Genres and Corporate Cultures*. London: Routledge; Roger Silverstone (1992) 'Below the Bottom Line', Economic and Social Research Council Programme on Information and Communication Technology Research Lecture, London; Gellner, ibid., p. 37, original emphasis.

32  Eric Hirsch (1998) 'Domestic Appropriations', in Nigel Rapport and Andrew Dawson (eds) *Migrants of Identity*. Oxford: Berg, p. 176.

33  Vincent Tucker (1997) 'Introduction' to his *Cultural Perspectives on Development*. London: Frank Cass, p. 8. It was not for nothing that Charles Mackay's *Extraordinary Popular Delusions and the Madness of Crowds* became compulsory reading for stockbrokers on the London money markets in the 1990s (1995. First published 1841. Ware: Wordsworth Publishing).

34  Hermann Bausinger (1984) 'Media, Technology and Everyday Life', *Media, Culture and Society*, 6 (4).

35  Elaine Lally (2002) *At Home with Computers*. Oxford: Berg, p. 210.

36  James Carey and John J. Quirk (1989) 'The History of the Future', in James Carey *Communication as Culture*. London: Unwin Hyman, p. 174; Don DeLillo (2003) *Cosmopolis*. London: Picador, p. 80. For a thoroughly dystopian view of the dilemmas posed in a society characterised by 'information', see Scott Lash (2001) *Critique of Information*. London: Routledge. I do not, however, share Lash's view that there is 'no longer' any space left for critique in such a society: to argue that is to prematurely grant the total efficacy of all this 'informational magic': see below on Alfred Gell.

37  Alfred Gell (1992) *The Technology of Enchantment and the Enchantment of Technology*, in Jeremy Cote and Anthony Shelton (eds) *Anthropology Art and Aesthetics*. Oxford: Clarendon Press, pp. 44, 49, 50, 57–8. This is no less true of digital than of the analogue photography of which Gell was speaking, though in the UK we now confront an interesting new form of fetishism, in which processing stores offer to generate what they call 'real' photos from digital cameras.

38  Marvin, quoted in Boddy, ibid., p. 11; Boddy, ibid., pp. 12, 13; Jeffrey Sconce

(2000) *Haunted Media: Electronic Presence from Telegraphy to Television*. Durham, NC: Duke University Press, pp. 84, 209, 170, 190.

39 Alfred Gell (1988) 'Technology and Magic', *Anthropology Today*, 4 (2, April), p. 9. For an interesting parallel to Gell's approach, see Lee Worth Bailey (2005) *The Enchantments of Technology*. Chicago, Ill.: University of Illinois Press.

# Index

# Related titles from Routledge

## Media and Cultural Theory

### Edited by James Curran and David Morley

*Media & Cultural Theory* brings together leading international scholars to address key issues and debates within media and cultural studies including:

Media representations of the new woman in contemporary society
The creation of self in lifestyle media
The nature of cultural globalisation
The rise of digital actors and media

These subjects are analysed through the use of contemporary media and film texts such as *Bridget Jones* and *The Lord of the Rings* trilogy as well as case studies of the US and UK after 9/11.

ISBN10: 0–415–31704–5 (hbk)
ISBN10: 0–415–31705–3 (pbk)

ISBN13: 978–0–415–31704–7 (hbk)
ISBN13: 978–0–415–31705–4 (pbk)

Available at all good bookshops
For ordering and further information please visit:
www.routledge.com

# Related titles from Routledge

## Media/Theory: Thinking About Media and Communications
### Shaun Moores

'A grasp of an enormous body of work is displayed adroitly…overall the book is a genuine contribution to the literature. It should help to shape the future of critical reflections on media institutions and practices.'

David Chaney, Emeritus Professor of Sociology,
University of Durham

'This is an accomplished and elegant set of discussions, where an unusually broad range of theory from the humanities and social sciences, much of it to do with media but much of it not, is examined and organized.'

Graeme Turner, Professor of Cultural Studies,
University of Queensland

*Media/Theory* is an accessible yet challenging guide to ways of thinking about media and communications in modern life.

Shaun Moores connects the analysis of media and communications with key themes in contemporary social theory:

- Time
- Space
- Relationships
- Meanings
- Experiences

He insists that media studies are not simply about studying media. Rather, they require an understanding of how technologically mediated communication is bound up with wider processes in the modern world, from the reproduction of social life on an everyday basis to the reorganization of social relations on a global scale.

Drawing on ideas from a range of disciplines in the humanities and social sciences, *Media/Theory* makes a distinctive contribution towards rethinking the shape and direction of media studies today.

ISBN10: 0–415–24383–1 (hbk)
ISBN10: 0–415–24384–x (pbk)

ISBN13: 978–0–415–24383–4 (hbk)
ISBN13: 978–0–415–24384–1 (pbk)

Available at all good bookshops
For ordering and further information please visit:
www.routledge.com

# Related titles from Routledge

## Media, Technology and Society
### Brian Winston

*Media Technology and Society* offers a comprehensive account of the history of communications technologies, from the printing press to the internet. Winston argues that the development of new media forms, from the telegraph and the telephone to computers, satellite and virtual reality is the product of a constant play-off between social necessity and suppression: the unwritten law by which new technologies are introduced into society only insofar as their disruptive potential is limited.

Winston's fascinating account examines the role played by individuals such as Alexander Graham Bell, Gugliemo Marconi, and John Logie Baird and Boris Rozing, in the development of the telephone, radio and television, and Charles Babbage, whose design for a 'universal analytic engine' was a forerunner of the modern computer. He examines why some prototypes are abandoned, and why many 'inventions' are created simultaneously by innovators unaware of each other's existence, and shows how new industries develop around these inventions, providing media products to a mass audience.

Challenging the popular myth of a present-day 'information revolution' *Media Technology and Society* is essential reading for anyone interested in the social impact of technological change.

ISBN10: 0–415–14229–6 (hbk)
ISBN10: 0–415–14230–x (pbk)

ISBN13: 978–0–415–14229–8 (hbk)
ISBN13: 978–0–415–14230–4 (pbk)